Engaging Students in Ac Literacies

MW01133814

The second edition of this important and practical text provides specific information to guide teachers in planning and carrying out genre writing instruction in English for K–8 students within the content areas. Informed by systemic functional linguistics (SFL)—a framework conducive to instruction that views language as a meaning-making resource—this book guides teachers by presenting concrete ways to teach writing in the language arts, science, and social science curricula. Introducing theory of language that is effective in addressing the writing development of all students, especially multilingual/multicultural groups, the book provides essential scaffolding for teachers to design and implement effective, inclusive curricula while building their own knowledge.

Fully up to date, the second edition features new genres appropriate for middle school, examples of student writing, an expanded focus on genre pedagogy, a new chapter on bilingual learners, guidance for teaching in the middle grades, as well as clear steps to prepare genre units based on two decades of experience working with whole schools. The chapter units cover distinct genres, including memoirs, historical, genres, fictional narratives, arguments, and more. With ready-to-use tools, the new edition prepares elementary and middle school teachers to meet and adapt to the variable demands of their own educational contexts. Easy to navigate, this teacher-friendly text is an essential resource for courses in academic writing, English education, and multilingual education, and for pre-service and practicing English Language Arts (ELA) teachers who want to expand their teaching abilities and knowledge bases.

María Estela Brisk is Professor Emeritus of Language and Literacy at Boston College, USA.

Engaging Students in Academic Literacies

SFL Genre Pedagogy for K–8 Classrooms

Second Edition

María Estela Brisk

Routledge
Taylor & Francis Group

NEW YORK AND LONDON

Cover image: © Getty Images

Second edition published 2023
by Routledge
605 Third Avenue, New York, NY 10158

and by Routledge
4 Park Square, Milton Park, Abingdon, Oxon, OX14 4RN

Routledge is an imprint of the Taylor & Francis Group, an informa business

© 2023 María Estela Brisk

First edition published by Routledge 2014

ISBN: 978-1-032-35905-2 (hbk)
ISBN: 978-1-032-01193-6 (pbk)
ISBN: 978-1-003-32927-5 (ebk)

DOI: 10.4324/9781003329275

Typeset in Goudy
by Apex CoVantage, LLC

Access the Support Material: www.routledge.com/9781032011936

Contents

Preface

Education reforms promoting high levels of literacy in connection to subject matter content have increased the urgency to prepare teachers to deliver instruction that acquiesce to these demands, for example, in the United States, the Common Core State Standards (CCSS) (2010) and the Next Generation Science Standards (2013) and in Australia, the Australian Curriculum: ACARA (2012). Britain launched a series of educational reforms in 1988 with wide implications on language and literacy (Chen, 2007). In addition, language specific standards such as WIDA English Language Development Standards (2020) have added to the focus on literacy proficiency for English language learners (ELLs). This book is designed to meet these demands on school districts and schools by providing explicit ways to approach writing instruction within language arts, science, and social studies curricula.

The purpose of *Engaging Students in Academic Literacies* is to provide teachers with an approach to teaching writing grounded in systemic functional linguistics that will expand students' knowledge of a variety of genres useful in various disciplinary contexts. This approach guides teachers in developing pre-school through middle school (ages 4–13 years old) students' ability to construct texts using structural and linguistic features of the various genres encountered in school.

Approaching writing through the lens of genres appeals to teachers because there is a clear purpose and structure of texts to be taught to students, and genres naturally connect to content areas. For example, reports, explanations, and procedures are frequently encountered in science, while writing in social studies includes biographies, historical recounts, and accounts. Moreover, the curricular frameworks set up by these new reforms organize writing around text types or genres. The essential contribution of SFL genre pedagogy is the development of language resources to make meaning given the topic, audience, and voice, and whether the written text is clearly organized and makes sense to a reader.

Overview

This book consists of nine chapters. Chapter 1 includes brief explanations of the theory and general recommendations for practice. Chapters 2–8 cover various genres. Chapter 9 addresses the particular needs of bilingual/bicultural learners, present in many schools all over the world, and of bilingual schools.

Chapter 1 contains brief sections explaining systemic functional linguistic (SFL) genre pedagogy, SFL theory, genres, register, the Teaching and Learning Cycle, and metalanguage. It also compares SFL genre pedagogy with a widely used writing practice and the CCSS and presents a summary of studies documenting the effectiveness of SFL genre pedagogy. The remainder of the chapter briefly addresses topics related to writing instruction in general and not specific to particular genres. The chapter concludes with recommendations on how to plan a school-wide writing program.

Chapters 2–8 present ways to create units of writing for various genres: Procedure (Chapter 2), Recounts and Memoirs (Chapter 3), Historical Genres (Chapter 4), Fictional Narratives (Chapter 5), Reports (Chapter 6), Explanations (Chapter 7), and Arguments (Chapter 8). Each chapter further breaks down some of the individual genres as follows:

Chapter	Genre	Break down
Chapter 2	Procedures	
Chapter 3	Recounts	Personal
		Procedural
		Factual
	Memoirs	
Chapter 4	Historical Genres	Autobiography
		Biography
		Empathetic Autobiography
		Historical Recount
		Historical Account
Chapter 5	Fictional Narrative	Fables
		Historical Fiction
		Realistic Fiction
		Myths
		And Others
Chapter 6	Reports	Descriptive
		Comparative
		Historical
		Classifying
		Whole-to-Part
Chapter 7	Explanations	Sequential
		Cyclical
		Causal
		Systems
		Factorial
		Consequential
		Conditional
Chapter 8	Argument	One-Sided to Do
		One-Sided About (without or with rebuttal)
		Two-Sided

The genre chapters contain suggestions for unit preparation and teaching of purpose, stages of the genre (text structure), and aspects of language most helpful to develop for students to write in that particular genre. Each aspect is explained and illustrated with examples of students' performance. Examples of lessons are briefly developed to give teachers suggestions but allow for flexibility and adaptation to each classroom context. Lists of valuable resources at the end of each chapter support implementation, such as forms to analyze student work, graphic organizers, suggestions for mentor texts, and articles that illustrate implementation of the particular genre.

The concluding Chapter 9 is divided into two sections. The first presents a concise account of children's writing development, including features of bilingual learners. The second section addresses principles and practices to consider when working with multilingual populations.

Because this work and the resulting book were developed to enhance what was happening in actual schools, it does not cover the response to literature genre or review spelling and mechanics. Most schools cover just those two skills in writing instruction. The recommendations in this book expand that concept of writing to include a greater variety of genres with a strong emphasis on language as meaning-making resource. Language is more than content vocabulary; it is also a resource to give information, reveal point of view, express preciseness in instructions and explanations, describe, show personality and state of mind of characters and people, and so on.

Changes to the Second Edition

Six years of experience using the first edition of this book to prepare teachers resulted in a number of changes to respond better to their needs. Changes include the following:

1. **Inclusion of the middle school grades**. A number of schools do not include only the elementary grades but also grades 6–8 (11–13 years old), necessitating support for teachers of those grades as well.
2. **Complete reorganization and additions to the genre chapters**. Using the experience of guiding scores of teachers to create genre units, I reorganized the content of the genre chapters and added material where needed.
3. **Addition of genres**. Several groups of teachers asked for advice on creating Memoirs. This genre was explicitly included in the recount chapter. With the addition of the middle grades, the types of reports, explanations, and argument genres were further developed to provide for middle school students.
4. **Elimination of chapters 2 (Instructional Practices) and 3 (Language Features)**. Often teachers would just cover the genre chapters depending on the genre that they were teaching, skipping these two chapters from the first edition and the important information contained in them. As a result, instructional practices and explanations of features of language were added to the genre chapters to help teachers prepare to implement genre-specific units.
5. **Embedding lessons on language within lessons on purpose and stages**. In the early work with schools, purpose and stages were the initial focus because teachers felt more confident teaching these topics. Language was introduced later. After a few years, many teachers found that language was always difficult for students and realized that the students greatly benefited when (a) only a few key aspects of language were stressed and (b) emphasis on language started from the very beginning of the unit. This second edition reflects this change in approach by introducing the description of the aspects of language to be taught together with purpose and stages. Lessons on language alternate with lessons on purpose and stages. In addition, it is recommended that each grade level introduces and practices a few aspects of language throughout the unit. By doing vertical alignment, where each grade level takes responsibility for certain aspects of language, schools cover all the students' language needs over the grades.
6. **Chapter with a focus on bilingual learners**. Many of the schools implementing SFL genre pedagogy either have bilingual students or are bilingual schools teaching all their students in two languages. SFL genre pedagogy is particularly helpful for students learning a second language because the theory is context based, considering the specific situation where writing takes place. The approach to teaching explicitly analyzes texts to help students discover the organizational features and how language choices are made to mean in different situations. This chapter was included to add a further lens on children's development and principles of practice with multilingual populations.
7. **Edits to the theory and lessons**. After many years of applying the earlier version, it was evident that a number of theoretical descriptions needed clarification. Many of the lessons were edited or added to reflect the actual experience working with teachers.

8. **Resources at the end of the chapter.** Analysis forms, graphic organizers, mentor texts, and other resources were moved online and are downloadable for easy use (see section "Support Material Online").

Background

The content of the book draws on work in two urban schools carried out over three years in one and ten years in the other. The whole staff participated in professional development, analysis of student work, and implementation of units. Their work is featured throughout the book. Their names have been used with their permission because they are important contributors to the development of this book's content. Both native speakers of English and linguistically and culturally diverse students were enrolled in these schools. Because of the flexibility of the approach, teachers were able to adjust the content to a variety of students' background and levels of development.

The success of one of these schools in a large urban district led to requests for similar professional development (PD) from other district schools. After providing in-person PD in multiple schools for two years, I developed three four-week asynchronous and synchronous online courses on the genres of writing. Over the past six years these courses have supported whole schools to change the way they teach writing. These are project-based courses where participants develop a unit to teach one genre at one grade level. In the past three years an increasing number of bilingual schools in diverse districts sent teachers to the courses. The work with teachers on unit development, guided by the first edition as well as the online asynchronous content, influenced greatly the content and organizational changes in this second edition.

How to Use the Book

This book aims at making teachers experts in SFL genre pedagogy so that they can create units that fit their educational context. It does not provide a fixed curriculum. To develop the expertise and confidence needed to use this pedagogy, I recommend the following:

1. Choose the genre for your unit, and read the chapter that covers that genre as well as chapters 1 and 9.
2. In the genre chapter, read the initial section that guides you with unit preparation to decide within which content area you will teach writing, what is appropriate for the grade level, resources to support teaching, and so on.
3. With the information obtained from analyzing the uncoached writing, decide on which lessons you need to emphasize in the unit.
4. Consult the lessons included in the chapter and adapt them to your instructional content.
5. Read articles reporting application of the genre in other context cited as resources at the end of each chapter.

Planning grade level units is ideally done in the context of a whole school plan, as suggested in Chapter 1. Over the grades, students should be exposed to various genres in connection to language arts, science, social studies, and other content areas, covering a variety of language features.

Support Material Online

Some of the tools referred to in this book are available for download on the Routledge website. You can access these downloads by visiting www.routledge.com/9781032011936. Then click on the tab that says "Support Material" and select the files. They will begin downloading to your computer.

The following resources are available online:

Chapter 2 Procedures

- Analysis of Student Work: Purpose, Stages, and Language
- Graphic Organizer
- Mentor Texts That Illustrate the Genre
- Internet Resources With Mentor Texts to Illustrate the Genre

Chapter 3 Recounts and Memoirs

- Analysis of Student Work: Purpose, Stages, and Language
- Graphic Organizers:

  - Personal Recount (K–2)
  - Personal and Memoir Recount (3–5)
  - Recount and Memoir Graphic Organizer
  - Factual and Procedural Recounts

- Mentor Texts That Illustrate the Genre
- Internet Resources With Mentor Texts to Illustrate the Genre

Chapter 4 Historical Genres

- Analysis of Student Work: Purpose, Stages, and Language
- Graphic Organizers:

  - Autobiography, Empathetic Autobiography, and Biography
  - Historical Recount
  - Historical Account
  - Procedural Recount

- Mentor Texts That Illustrate the Genre
- Internet Resources With Mentor Texts to Illustrate the Genre

Chapter 5 Fictional Narratives

- Analysis of Student Work: Purpose, Character Development, and Stages
- Graphic Organizers:

  - Character Development
  - Orientation
  - Plot

- Mentor Texts That Illustrate the Genre
- Internet Resources With Mentor Texts to Illustrate the Genre

Chapter 6 Reports

- Analysis of Student Work: Purpose, Stages, and Language
- Graphic Organizer
- Mentor Texts That Illustrate the Genre
- Internet Resources With Mentor Texts to Illustrate the Genre

Chapter 7 Explanations

- Analysis of Student Work: Purpose, Stages, and Language
- Graphic Organizers:

  - Sequential/Causal Explanations
  - Cyclical Explanations
  - Systems Explanations
  - Factorial/Consequential Explanations
  - Conditional Explanations

- Mentor Texts That Illustrate the Genre
- Internet Resources With Mentor Texts to Illustrate the Genre
- Videos of Sequential Explanations

Chapter 8 Arguments

- Analysis of Student Work: Purpose, Stages, and Language
- Graphic Organizer
- Mentor Texts That Illustrate the Genre
- Internet Resources

Acknowledgments

This second edition emerged from years of using the first edition to prepare undergraduate and graduate teacher candidates as well as practicing teachers. Their hard work applying the ideas of the first edition taught me what could be improved to prepare them better and guide them through implementation of this novel way to teach writing. I am especially grateful to my colleagues Elizabeth MacDonald and Tracy Hodgson-Drysdale for collaborating in the implementation of the online courses, which have reached so many teachers and gave me clear ideas on how to improve the book. Further gratitude goes to Mariam Gorbea Ramy, my former undergraduate research assistant and current collaborator with the online courses, for applying this work to supporting bilingual schools. Always the second language writer, I appreciate those who review drafts to edit my "interlanguage" and point out where I need to be clearer, including Bill Brisk, Mariam Gorbea Ramy, Cheryl O'Connor, and Alejandra Trumble.

Without courageous and bright teachers ready to learn and try new things, this work would have never come to be. They and their students have taught me much of what I know.

Chapter 1

Principles for Practice

Systemic functional linguistics (SFL) informs the approach to teaching writing, called SFL genre pedagogy, developed in this book. SFL is a theory of language proposed by Michael Halliday (Halliday, 1985; Halliday & Matthiessen, 2004). According to this theory, texts exist in context. Language users' choices impact and are constrained by the social context. SFL was applied to the study of texts and genres by James Martin and by other scholars (Martin & Rose, 2008; Rose & Martin, 2012). From experiences in schools, the Teaching and Learning Cycle (TLC), an instructional approach for literacy development, emerged and was refined over time (Callaghan & Rothery, 1988; Rothery, 1996).

To help educators position the content of this book in past and current contexts of teaching writing, this chapter makes the connection between the pedagogy proposed in this book and process writing, the dominant approach to teaching writing, both in the United States and other parts of the world. The genres developed in this book are compared with the "text types" proposed in the Common Core State Standards (CCSS), standards which have been adopted by 45 states, the District of Columbia, four territories, and the Department of Defense Education Activity. Other countries also adopted literacy and basic disciplinary standards, such as the Australian Curriculum, Assessment and Reporting Authority (ACARA, 2012). The chapter also reports on the impact of SFL genre pedagogy on education, and concludes with general suggestions for classroom instruction as well as for planning a school-wide writing plan.

The theory and practices put forth in this book apply to classrooms with native speakers of English as well as multilingual students. In the United States, where the WIDA English Language Development Standards (2020) are used for English as a second language instruction, this book is particularly useful because these standards draw heavily on SFL.

SFL Genre Pedagogy

SFL genre pedagogy, also known as genre-based pedagogy, emerged from the collaboration of SFL linguistics and educators in Australia under the leadership of J.R. Martin (Martin, 1985). Its development and implementation were driven by the desire to "democratiz[e] the outcomes of education systems" (Rose & Martin, 2012, p. 4) by giving all students a chance to master the genres used in schools to gain control of the language of power. To avoid being a reproductive literacy approach, teachers encourage students to understand how the language of power develops in a society, how they can use it for their benefit, and how they can break norms by bringing different languages, language varieties, and ways of making meaning to school (Gebhard, 2019; Hasan, 1996; Khote, 2018).

This pedagogy is widely used in Australia (Derewianka & Jones, 2016; Humphrey, 2017; Rose & Martin, 2012) and in the United States (see reviews of the literature by Accurso & Gebhard, 2020 and by Santiago Schwarz & Hamman-Ortiz, 2020). This book focuses on the teaching of

DOI: 10.4324/9781003329275-1

writing in English to students of different language backgrounds, including English, from pre-school through middle school (4–13 years old). Teachers have adapted information in the book to both high school students as well as writing instruction in Spanish.

What to teach is based on SFL genre and language analysis, while how to teach stems largely from the Teaching and Learning Cycle (TLC). SFL analysis of texts in distinct genres details the purpose, text structure, and distinct linguistic features of each genre, giving students resources they need to write effectively. The TLC provides an apprenticeship to writing where students learn by analyzing published texts and by writing with teachers before writing on their own or in collaboration with peers. This process builds confidence for students to create independent pieces.

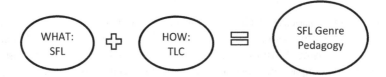

The emphasis on language and the scaffolded approach to teaching have impacted all students' writing but especially bilingual students. As one teacher put it, it "uncovered" the secrets of English by teaching the language and its function in the context of specific genres and situations.

Systemic Functional Linguistics

SFL is rooted in Halliday's (1985) scholarship on social semiotics, emphasizing the relationship between text and context. SFL is "a very useful descriptive and interpretive framework for viewing language as a strategic, meaning-making resource" (Eggins, 2004, p. 2). SFL also helps teachers by giving them concrete information on aspects of the discourse, sentence, and word level features of various genres.

An essential premise of SFL is that language is conceived as whole text rather than isolated words or sentences. These texts exist in the immediate context of the situation, which in turn is nested in the larger context of culture (Butt et al., 2012). The writing practices of a culture are characterized by recurrent forms of texts used for specific purposes, each characterized by specific discourse organization and language features. These are called *genres* (Martin & Rose, 2008). Each genre differs and is achieved through the stages or text structure used. For example, while arguments include a thesis statement, reasons supported by evidence, ending in the reinforcement of the statement, fictional narratives start with an orientation, followed by a series of events that include a crisis and resolution.

In addition to the context of culture, texts exist within the context of situations where language choices vary with respect to three variables: field, tenor, and mode. These variables constitute the *register* and correspond with three metafunctions of language (Eggins, 2004; Halliday & Matthiessen, 2004; Thompson, 2004). Language reflects the *field* or content of the text (experiential function) through clauses formed by processes, participants, and circumstances. When clauses combine in clause complexes, the logical function serves to express relationships, often signaled by conjunctions. The *tenor* of a text reflects the relationship between language users. In writing, language choices depend on the author's awareness of the intended audience as well as the writer's voice or identity. Language resources used to create a cohesive text constitute the *mode*. Language choices will differ depending on whether the text is oral, written, or multimodal.

Meaning is realized through three levels of language, functioning in close interrelationship: *discourse*, at the level of the text; *lexicogrammatical*, at the level of the clause; and *phonology* or *graphology*, at the level of sounds or letters (Rose & Martin, 2012). Language users need all these resources to produce the functions introduced earlier. The role of teachers of all disciplines is to guide students to develop these resources to be able to make meaning effectively. Because these levels work together, they should never be taught in isolation. Students need to know how to spell words that are part of a clause that exists with other clauses in a whole text. The specific goal is, of course, to make meaning (Halliday, 1985).

Genres

The most common writing genres in elementary and middle schools include different types of recounts, fictional narratives, procedures, reports, explanations, and arguments (also known as expositions) (see Table 1.1). Recounts relate a series of events based on personal experience (personal recounts, memoirs), an observed incident (factual recount), or observations of phenomena (procedural recounts). Recounts can also record historical events (autobiography, biography, and historical recounts and accounts; Coffin, 2006). In addition, students may be asked to write in character (empathetic autobiography) as a way to understand a person or time in history (Christie & Derewianka, 2008). By contrast, fictional narratives tell an imaginative story consisting of a problem that leads to a crisis followed by a resolution. Fictional narratives are meant to entertain and to teach cultural values (Martin & Rothery, 1986). Procedures provide instructions for how something is done, whether general or scientific. A report is a factual text used to organize and store information clearly and succinctly (Schleppegrell, 2004). Explanations, like reports, are factual texts that explain how or why things happened. Finally, arguments are designed to persuade readers to a particular point of view, with reasons introduced and supported with evidence (Butt et al., 2012). There are a variety of response to literature genres: personal comment, character analysis, and thematic analysis (Christie & Derewianka, 2008). Often,

Table 1.1 Genres and Their Purpose

Purpose			
Tell Stories	*Give Information*	*Persuade*	*Give Instructions*
Genres			
Personal recounts	Reports:	One-sided argument	Procedure
Procedural recounts	Descriptive	about something	Protocol
Factual recounts	Comparative	One-sided argument to	
Autobiographies	Historical	do something	
Empathetic autobiographies	Classifying	Two-sided argument	
Biographies	Whole-to-part	Challenge	
Historical recounts	Explanations:	Scientific argument	
Historical accounts	Sequential	Historical argument	
Fictional narratives	Cyclical	Response to literature	
	Causal		
	Systems		
	Factorial		
	Consequential		
	Conditional		
	Historical		

students must respond to prompts on reading tests with an argumentative stance, where they need to prove a point through inferencing and supporting a claim with textual evidence.

The purpose of each genre differs and is achieved through the distinct stages and language used. Table 1.1 shows the genres clustered under each broad purpose: tell a story, organize information, persuade, and give instruction. Each genre under these categories has a specific purpose that will be specified in the upcoming genre chapters. The structure and language features of genres in the English-speaking culture have been illustrated by a number of SFL researchers, including Butt et al. (2012), Derewianka and Jones (2016), Humphrey et al. (2012), Knapp and Watkins (2005), Martin and Rose (2008), and Schleppegrell (2004). The genres of specific disciplines have been further analyzed, including history (Coffin, 2006), science (de Oliveira & Dodds, 2010; Fang & Schleppegrell, 2008), mathematics (de Oliveira & Cheng, 2011; Marks & Mousley, 1990; Schleppegrell, 2007), and English language arts (Christie & Derewianka, 2008; Fang & Schleppegrell, 2008).

Traditionally, schools categorized genres in two large generic categories: fiction and non-fiction. More recently the Common Core State Standards (2010) proposed three text types: narratives, informational/explanatory, and arguments. These text types are explained later in the section on the CCSS.

Register

In addition to the context of culture, texts exist within the context of situation where language choices vary with respect to three variables: field, tenor, and mode. These variables constitute the *register* and correspond with the three metafunctions of language (Eggins, 2004; Halliday & Matthiessen, 2004; Thompson, 2004). (The language features introduced in this section will be more thoroughly illustrated throughout the genre chapters.) Language used to express ideas and experience (*experiential function*) reflects the content of the text (*field*) through clauses that convey:

- What is happening: expressed by verb groups (*processes*).
- Who or what is participating: expressed by noun groups (*participants*).
- Where, when, with whom, why, and other additional information: expressed by adverbials (*circumstances*).

For example:

After high school,	Jemison	attended	Stanford University	in California
Adverbial of time Circumstance	Noun group Participant	Verb Process	Noun group Participant	Adverbial of place Circumstance

Clauses combine in clause complexes to express relationships (*logical function*). Clauses are often linked by connecting words (conjunctions and others). For example,

As a child Jemison once told a teacher	that	she wanted to be a scientist.
Clause indicating who is saying	Connecting word	Clause indicating what was said.

The *tenor* of a text reflects the relationship between language users. In writing, language choices depend on the author's awareness of audience and the intended writer's voice or identity.

For example, *Mae Jemison*, a biography from which these examples were drawn, was written for elementary students, thus the language is accessible to that age group. The voice is authoritative and factual by the use of declarative sentences, third person, and no language expressing judgment.

Writing reflects the linguistic and cultural identity of authors through features of topic and voice. For example, a student thought it was humorous to write a story where a donkey was mistreated by its owner, reflecting the attitude of his cultural context toward donkeys. Bilingual writers use linguistic features of one language when writing in the other. For example, Spanish speakers in the U.S. use the word *elevador* in Spanish to mean *elevator*. The Spanish word is *ascensor*. The sentence *He work hard* could stand for either *He works hard* or *He worked hard*, two morphemes (-s and -ed) often dropped by English learners.

Language resources used to create a cohesive text constitute the *mode*. These resources are different depending on whether the text is oral, written, or multimodal. The structure of the Mae Jemison text follows the stages of a biography: orientation, record of events, and conclusion. The individual clauses guide the reader to indicate what the authors are writing about (*Theme*) and what they are saying about it (*New Information*). Consider the following paragraph for example:

> After high school, Jemison attended Stanford University in California. She studied chemical engineering and African-American studies. Chemical engineering is the study of chemicals and their uses. Jemison also participated in theater and dance. She graduated in 1977.

In this paragraph, the authors start the first clause with an adverbial of time to highlight the importance of when this event happened, a salient feature of historical genres. The other clauses mostly start with Jemison as the focus or what she studied, highlighting that the paragraph is about her and her studies at the university. Pronouns help avoid repetition and relate to a referent, allowing the reader to track the participants.

Multimodal texts also include the images that complement the meaning expressed by language. For example, Mae Jemison's biography includes several photographs. Using photographs aligns with the factual voice of the biography.

The structure of the text is also impacted by the *medium*. Students can produce the pieces they write in the different genres in the form of (but not limited to) essays, picture books, letters, poems, brochures, posters, PowerPoints, and blogs. Each one calls for specific organizational structures and language, making it easier or more difficult for students to produce. The traditional English language arts (ELA) literature refers to these structures as genres. Making the distinction between genre and medium is necessary because genres can be produced in any of the various mediums. For example, *A Ballad of Ducks* and *The Mosquito's Song* are both poems, but the first is a fictional narrative while the latter is an argument.

Teaching and Learning Cycle

The choices students make while writing relate to the resources available to them. Teachers build these resources through instruction. The Teaching and Learning Cycle (TLC) is an approach to writing instruction that supports student writing through seven stages: negotiation of field or developing content knowledge, deconstruction of text, joint planning, joint construction of text, group and/or independent construction of text, joint revision, and individual revision (see Figure 1.1). There are two opportunities to publish: after the joint construction and after the individual revisions. These steps represent a modification of the original TLC proposed by educators in Australia (Callaghan & Rothery, 1988; Rothery, 1996), after years of supporting teachers implementing SFL genre pedagogy.

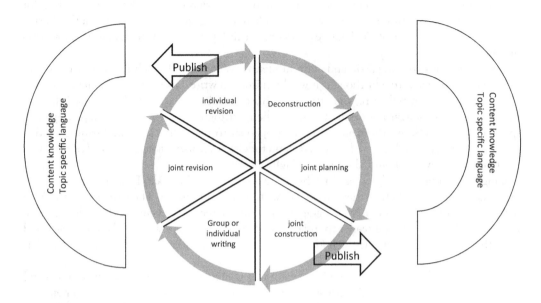

Figure 1.1 Teaching and Learning Cycle.

During the negotiation of field, students develop the content knowledge of the particular topic they will be writing about and the topic-specific language needed to express that knowledge. Topics are embedded in curricular content of the school disciplines. This particular aspect of the TLC actually takes place in anticipation of writing and during the other stages, as well (Rose & Martin, 2012). Teachers guide the students through deconstruction, or close analysis of mentor texts that illustrate the stages and the language features of the focused genre. The focus of the deconstruction is linked to the particular objective of the lesson as determined by the teacher. For example, a kindergarten teacher used the book *Chrysanthemum* to illustrate the stages of fictional narratives by pointing out the orientation, complication, resolution, and ending of the story, encouraging students to recall the name of the stages as she retold the story using finger puppets (Brisk & Zisselsberger, 2011). Teachers and students are familiar with approaching the text as readers to "read for the sake of gaining new information, novel experiences, and interesting viewpoints" (McKeough, 2013, p. 87). When deconstructing a text, teachers and students should read the text as writers to "turn the text inside-out to see how it is made, how it is held together, and what makes it work" (p. 87).

Teachers collaborate with their students to plan to write using graphic organizers and then jointly construct the text. Joint construction is an essential component of learning to write. With all of the knowledge and experience acquired through deconstruction and joint construction of a text, students then create their own independent writing. Although the original TLC suggested going from joint to individual construction, producing writing in a group can be very helpful and a good intermediary step for young students, students working for the first time on a difficult genre, and students who are emergent bilinguals. The group product becomes the publishable piece. Letting students write in a group is particularly useful when students have to conduct research to contribute to the writing because they then share the task of consulting resources. Reading academic texts can be difficult; thus, sharing and discussing what students find in different resources supports comprehension and excites the students. Finally, before groups or individuals publish their writing, they need to revise and edit their pieces. Carrying out joint revision of one or two pieces or sections of student writing helps students learn how to go about revising and helping each other revise. It also becomes a good way to reinforce instruction of aspects of genres, which still presents challenges.

Rothery (1996) represented the TLC as a circle because "there are different points of entry for students according to their development in learning and literacy" (pp. 101–102). She also argued that the TLC is not a linear process but may go back to a previous stage before moving forward to the next. One teacher working on biographies with L2 (second language) learners found it important to repeat the deconstruction, joint construction, and independent construction of each stage (Pavlak, 2013). This greatly facilitated the writing process for the students because they were able to focus on one stage at a time. The TLC has been successfully applied from elementary through college age students (de Oliveira et al., 2020).

Metalanguage

An important aspect of the TLC is its use of metalanguage (to talk about the genre and language features of students' writing). Metalanguage labels with precision the resources the students need to use to carry out their writing. Shared metalanguage allows teachers and students to discuss stages and language features of each genre (Humphrey & Feez, 2016).

Harris (2011) found that her 4th-grade students were able to make better comments on each other's writings when they employed metalanguage to discuss their writing. For example, she reports, "During a peer conference later in the week, Tom agreed that Adam had 'good action verbs'" (p. 109). Similarly, Williams (1999) found that metalanguage is a useful tool for students to understand the grammar of the text, while Moore and Schleppegrell (2014) demonstrate that SFL metalanguage supported understanding literary texts. Gebhard et al. (2014) concluded that

> ELLs benefited from learning how to use SFL metalanguage to read and write disciplinary texts. For example, . . . they learned to identify expected genre moves and register features, classify different types of processes and participants, notice how and why authors shift tenses, catalogue different types of conjunctions, and track theme/rhyme patterns in assigned readings and in their own texts to note how coherence is achieved in extended written discourse.
>
> (p. 123)

The more precise the metalanguage, the more helpful it is for students. Thus, using SFL terms like *orientation, sequence of events,* and *conclusion* (the stages of a personal recount) or *thesis statement, reasons supported by evidence,* and *reinforcement of thesis* (the stages of an argument) is more descriptive of the content in each stage than the commonly used *beginning, middle,* and *end* terminology.

Many teachers tell students to "add details." However, the word *details* can mean different things, including reasons ("OK, but we are not going to come up with more ideas, we want to think of supporting details"), events ("Again, we could leave some of those details of the story for later"), and adjectives ("Include details! This makes your reading interesting!") (Daniello et al., 2014, p. 193). Only by the context can the meaning of the term *detail* be inferred. Therefore, it is better to replace *detail* with more precise terminology. Imprecise metalanguage is not helpful to students. Table 1.2 provides alternative suggestions for some commonly used terms:

Table 1.2 Metalanguage

Precise Metalanguage	Vague Metalanguage
Thesis statement, reasons supported by evidence, reinforcement of statement (argument genre) Goal, materials, method, or steps (Procedure)	Beginning, middle, end
Add information, evidence, adjectives	Add *details*
Pleaded in the sentence: "The king pleaded, "Obey my order!" shows a weak personality. In the sentence: The king said, "Obey my order!" the verb *said* does not show weakness.	*Pleaded* would be called a "strong verb" while *said* would not.
Evidence: information that supports a reason or an assertion made	Evidence: any information found in a text. "Find the evidence of the grammatical person used in a biography."
Adjectives	Juicy words

SFL Genre Pedagogy in Contrast to Process Writing/Writers' Workshop

The approach proposed in this book, SFL genre pedagogy, contrasts in a number of ways with Process Writing, the dominant instructional methodology used to teach writing in many education settings around the world. SFL genre pedagogy introduces a variety of genres and guides teachers through a process that draws on SFL theory and the TLC, described earlier. Using this approach, students are apprenticed to the given genre through exploration of mentor texts and writing collaboratively with the teacher and other students before writing independently. In contrast Process Writing, an iterative approach to teaching writing, focuses on the process: children are encouraged to choose topics, draft pieces, and modify their writing numerous times (Graves, 1983). Students work in a classroom set up as a workshop, where they write under the guidance of an expert teacher (Fletcher & Portalupi, 2001). Thus, this pedagogy is often referred to as Writers' Workshop (WW).

Major differences in the *what* and *how* to teach distinguish these two pedagogical practices. SFL genre pedagogy provides teachers with theory-based specific knowledge of what to teach with respect to the purpose, structure, and language students need to write an effective piece. A shared explicit metalanguage allows students and teachers to explore text in a clear informed way. The theoretical basis for WW focuses on the writing process with no clear focus or metalanguage on the content of writing. SFL genre pedagogy uses an apprentice approach to instruction with intense initial teaching and exploration of the purpose, structure, and language of the genres before students start writing on their own as outlined in the Teaching and Learning Cycle section earlier. WW promotes individual writing, following brief minilessons. After students write, teachers try to mend their products through conferencing (Graves, 1983; Atwell, 1987). Thus, SFL genre pedagogy (top row in Figure 1.2) promotes instruction on writing before and during writing, while WW (bottom row) leaves it to the end of the process.

In a study of a teacher using Calkins' application of the Writers' Workshop (CWW), Westerlund and Besser (2021) documented a series of stark differences between SFL genre pedagogy and CWW, the most popular version of WW used in schools. While SFL uses a shared metalanguage to explicitly name the aspects of the genre and language introduced to students, the teacher applying CWW used metaphors to present the features of a genre, increasing the confusion among students. For example, SFL describes the structure of a report as having a general

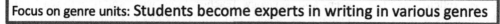

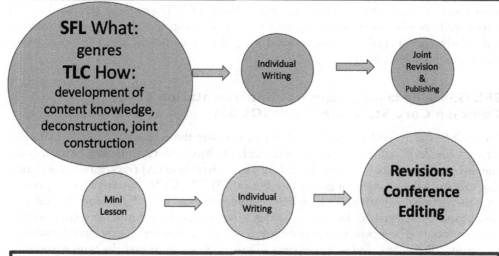

Figure 1.2 SFL genre pedagogy vs. Writers' Workshop.

statement and subtopics, while CWW describes it as a rock formed from pebbles bound together, a very abstract description with little direct relation to reports. Another difference was that CWW-based instruction lacks emphasis on developing language resources, a key aspect of SFL genre pedagogy. The one aspect of language CWW names, transitional words, is actually the least used in most genres. Narratives, historical genres, and sequential explanations use adverbials of time to connect paragraphs and move the narrative or explanation sequence forward. Reports do not use transition words. Procedures tend to use numbers for the steps or nothing at all. Arguments may use transition words when introducing new reasons. A third major difference is the approach to the amount of explicit content of writing. While SFL genre pedagogy provides teachers with explicit knowledge of purpose, structure, and language features of various genres to guide students when deconstructing text, the teacher applying CWW carried out open-ended discussions about text without explicit features in mind to look for.

Research conducted in Australia and the United States have explored the impact of WW on students' writing. Concerned linguists and educators in Australia argued that students' writing resulting from the widely used WW demonstrated that,

> most students had to make use of text types they were familiar with from spoken language outside the school—including short observations and comments on past experience, and recounts of unproblematic sequences of events. This limited experience of writing did very little to prepare students for learning across the curriculum in primary school, for writing on the specialized subject areas of secondary schools, or for dealing with the various community genres they might encounter as the most fluent English speaker of their family.
>
> (Martin, 2009, p. 11)

Teachers working with multilingual classes with different levels of language proficiency felt that SFL genre pedagogy allowed them to have high expectations for all their students because of the explicitness of the content and pedagogy. Teachers knew what and how to teach, and the students were clear as to what they needed to learn (Brisk & Ossa Parra, 2018). On the other hand, the limitations on content and pedagogy of WW promotes successful writing among students who have the background to write well but does not support all students, particularly multilingual students, exacerbating the inequities of the education system (Westerlund & Basser, 2021).

SFL Genre Pedagogy Supports Implementation of the Common Core State Standards (CCSS)

The CCSS, widely used in the United States, consider three broad text types: narratives, informational/explanatory, and arguments. Each of these text types include standards and sample texts (Appendix B). Using the SFL lens to analyze these text types, it becomes evident that each includes a variety of genres (see Figure 1.3). The CCSS narratives cover personal recounts, fictional narratives, and, perhaps, autobiographies. The all-encompassing informational/explanatory category includes procedures, reports, explanations, biographies, and historical recounts. The arguments category covers one-sided arguments (exposition), two-sided arguments (discussion), and some response to literature genres. It uses the term *argument* for the upper grades but the term *opinion* for the lower grades. No research on persuasive writing ever labels such writing as *opinion*, only the term *argument* is used. There is no indication of where procedural recounts and empathetic autobiographies would fit; perhaps in the all-encompassing informational/explanatory category that seems to embrace what traditionally was known as non-fiction.

The problem with the CCSS broad text types (circles in Figure 1.3) is that the genres within, as defined by SFL (rectangles in Figure 1.3), have different features. Therefore, the more precise distinction with respect to purpose, text structure, and language made by SFL is more helpful to teachers and students. Table 1.3 shows how the CCSS addresses the various genres covered in this book.

The CCSS writing standards only include text types. Language is a separate category with generic standards with respect to vocabulary, grammar, and conventions. SFL, on the other hand, shows that specific language features better accomplish the purpose of a genre. For example, a CCSS vocabulary standard for Grade 1 states, "Distinguish shades of meaning among verbs differing in manner (e.g., *look, peek, glance, stare, glare, scowl*) and adjectives differing in intensity (e.g., *large, gigantic*) by defining or choosing them or by acting out the meanings" (CCSS.ELA-Literacy.L.1.5d). SFL considers the choice of these types of words a function of voice. By choosing a particular word, writers show their point of view and try to influence their audience, a critical feature of argument writing (Humphrey et al., 2012). SFL provides information to implement language standards by tying vocabulary and grammar with the genres and register. The SFL-informed approach presented in this book, therefore, provides teachers with much needed direction, clarity, and specificity to implement the CCSS, now demanded in a number of U.S. states (Daniello, 2013). Moreover, even if the CCSS are someday eliminated, teachers can still use the approach in this book because it defines the kind of academic writing expected by schools and provides the tools to teach writing to meet these expectations.

The CCSS also include Research Projects as a separate category. The description of what is required, that is, to answer questions drawing on a number of sources, is not that different from what is described in this book in relation to several genres, such as reports, explanations, arguments, and the historical genres. Students choose a topic, research several resources, organize the information given the genre, and come to some conclusions. Research papers as required in high school and college would be considered a macro genre because the text is a combination of genres, each section with a different purpose (Martin & Rose, 2008).

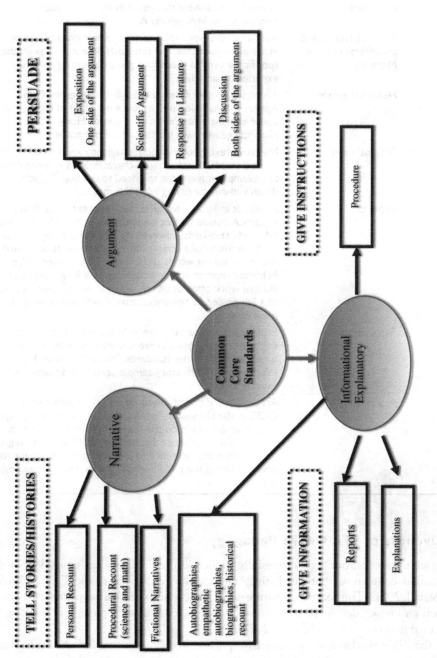

Figure 1.3 SFL and CCSS.

Table 1.3 SFL Genres and the Common Core State Standards

Book Chapter	Genre	CCSS
2	Procedure	No consideration for this genre in the text types. Short mention in Appendix A.
3	Personal, factual, and procedural recount Memoirs	Narrative text types refer to writing narratives of real or imagined experiences. The standards do not distinguish the specific features of these four genres belonging to "real experience narratives."
4	Historical genres	There are no specific standards for these genres. Only Appendix B, sample texts, includes examples of biographies under Informational/Explanatory genres. However, the historical genres have the features of narratives.
5	Fictional narratives	Narrative text types mention "imagined experiences." There are few standards referring to characteristics in more detail. For example, it mentions the need to develop characters in depth without specifying what this means.
6	Reports	Standards in Informational/explanatory text types fit in general reports. A couple of recommendations in the 6th-, 7th-, and 8th-grade standards, however, are not found in reports, such as the inclusion of a conclusion—optional in reports—and the use of linking words and phrases (*also, another, and*, etc.). Published reports do not include these linking words, but student work often does. For example, in a 17-sentence report of a 5th grader, 15 sentences started with *also*, making for poor writing.
7	Explanations	Explanations presumably are included in the Informational/explanatory text types. There is nothing specific pertaining to explanations in the standards. Only in Appendix B do the Informational/explanatory sample texts include sequential explanations.
8	Arguments	Arguments are one of the three text types included in the CCSS. In the elementary grades, they are referred to as *opinion*. Only after 6th grade do the standards refer to *arguments*, without much distinction between types. Other metalanguage that differs is the reference to *facts* and *details* for elementary grades, while in the middle school grades, the word *evidence* is used.

Effectiveness of SFL Genre Pedagogy

SFL literacy instruction has been successfully applied in the English-speaking world as well as other cultural contexts in Europe, Latin America, the Middle East, and China (Brisk & Schleppegrell, 2021). The contextual nature of SFL theory and practice has permitted its implementation for literacy development in non-Western societies as well, preserving the ways language is used in those contexts (Quinn, 2021).

Since the 1980s SFL has been successfully applied for teaching writing and reading in Australia. The greatest gains came from students testing at the lowest literacy levels before they experienced SFL genre pedagogy and Reading to Learn (R2L) instruction (Rose & Martin, 2012). These positive results led to writing the English Language Arts curriculum based on this work (*Australian curriculum: English* www.australiancurriculum.edu.au/f-10-curriculum/english/).

Following the success in Australia, many researchers and educators in the United States implemented SFL informed pedagogy for reading and writing instruction. Most of the work has been done in English, but Aguirre-Muñoz et al. (2015) show successful results when applied to Spanish writing instruction. Two recent reviews of the literature report on the positive impact of SFL-informed instruction on teachers' professional development (Accurso & Gebhard, 2020) and student learning (Santiago Schwarz & Hamman-Ortiz, 2020). This approach to instruction improved students' writing "by strengthening students' ability to write genre-specific texts, promoting their academic language and literacy skills, facilitating content learning, and developing their critical language awareness" (Santiago Schwarz & Hamman-Ortiz, 2020, p. 9).

Principles of Practice

Practices described in this section address curricular issues and perspectives on language. The principles suggested are reflected in the genre chapters.

Teach How to Write Original Texts as Opposed to Writing as Response to Literature (RTL)

In this book all the lessons lead to writing original pieces. Books are used as mentor texts to analyze how a writer produces text in a particular genre or as research resources to get information on content. In RTL, students imitate the style and content of books or do an activity that draws on the book's content. As a result, students mostly imitate the content and copy from the text because they do not learn how to write their own text. For example, Flores (2020) reports a writing activity in a 2nd-grade class where the teacher reads with students the book *Abuela* and then they write a story where the characters use Spanish for a specific purpose. This is not teaching how to write but having students imitate a book without considering the genre and features of the register. Writing an original piece in this context would have used *Abuela* as a mentor text for writing fantasy, a type of fictional narrative where characters do things—like flying over the town—that humans cannot do. Students would learn the purpose, the text structure (stages) of fantasies, and how to use language features to develop character, including using other languages to define the identity of the characters.

This practice is prevalent in middle schools. When made aware of it, teachers expressed their frustration,

> [The] writing that we did [before] was always some sort of prompt at the end of each unit based on the book we read . . . I don't think it was really teaching writing. It was analyzing literature . . . which I think is important as well, but we weren't actually teaching them how to write . . . A lot of teachers didn't like it but couldn't articulate why they didn't like it.

Students who learn how to write original pieces still need practice in RTL for a few weeks before exam time because in high-stakes tests, all the writing prompts are RTL.

Integrate Writing in the Curriculum

Writing should never be addressed as an after-thought to reading units. Writing is a tool that helps students explore, comprehend, deepen, and retain content (Fang et al., 2010; Marzano, 1991). The benefits of writing, therefore, go beyond literacy development. The best approach is to skip the writing part of reading programs and plan genre units of writing that parallel the reading units. In one district, schools using the Expeditionary Learning curriculum with cycles that included two modules on reading and a third on writing eliminated the latter and replaced it with genre units—taught parallel to the reading modules—that related to the reading unit and took advantage of the texts to use as mentor texts or research resources. For example, for a unit on countries, in one 3rd-grade class, students wrote reports on different countries, using the books, written as reports, as mentor texts. Another 3rd-grade class carried out an argument unit, where students wrote brochures, convincing people to visit a country. The same books were used as research resources, while the teacher found other texts that illustrated the argument genre.

Alternatively, writing is embedded in curricular content by integrating writing with specific grade level knowledge development. For example, a 2nd-grade teacher had students write reports on individual insects in a unit on insects. A team of 7th-grade teachers exploring the war in Sudan had the students write a consequential explanation of the effects of this war on the country and its people.

Connect Writing Topics to Students' Lived Experiences

The current emphasis on culturally sustaining pedagogies in educational contexts for multicultural and multilingual students is essential because often school curricula does not address the background of those students (Paris & Alim, 2017). Culturally sustaining pedagogies need to go beyond studying immigration. Teachers should connect topics covered in the curriculum to students' lives by relating them to the students and their families' experiences, to what is happening in their communities, and to current events. For example, the unit on insects could include insects they find in their immediate environment, in their countries of origin (if the students or their families come from other countries), and in the news, such as what is happening to monarch butterflies. In the case of the unit on the war in Sudan, connections could be made with students who have experienced war or have family members involved in a war; students could also discuss wars happening at the moment and how they affect people in their communities with connections to the country at war.

Remote Learning

During the COVID pandemic, teachers adapted to teaching remotely. Some had already been using some virtual platforms that allowed them to create electronic products, and many had become familiar with video conferencing tools through attending online professional development. Teachers carried out the steps of the TLC supported by various applications, either chosen by the schools or by themselves (see suggestions in Figure 1.4).

Include Language Instruction in the Writing Units

Writing instruction tends to focus on the content of the writing with little attention to the language students need to make meaning. Children learn language, about language, and through language (Halliday, 1993). Instruction needs to include not only learning the language but how it functions to help make meaning. Through the TLC teachers and students engage in talk about language in order to make effective choices. Talk about language can also address the larger social context where different varieties (text message language, oral language, Spanish, Black English, and so on) are used as well as the societal attitudes toward these varieties. Because students learn through language, curricular content must be connected with the language needed to express concepts and experiences. Teaching the language of science is an inextricable component of teaching science.

Language instruction within writing needs to address all these aspects of language. It is important, therefore, to teach language from the very beginning of each unit in connection to both content and aspects of the genre and register. In order not to overwhelm students, it is best to focus on a few aspects of language based on (a) students' language maturity and (b) importance for a particular genre. For example, modifiers are particularly important in reports because they carry a lot of information. With very young students, teaching adjectives is sufficient, but with upper elementary and middle school students, a range of modifiers should be introduced. In order

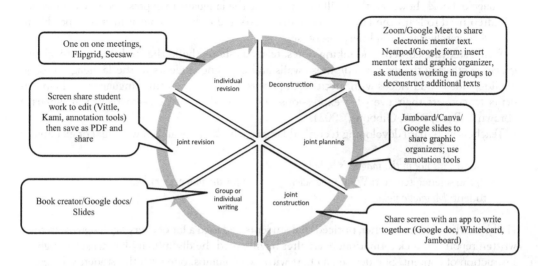

Figure 1.4 Applications to carry out the TLC remotely.

to cover all aspects of language through the school years, schools should plan vertically to ensure they cover a few aspects within each genre. Over time students therefore will be exposed to all the needed aspects of language so that they have the resources they need to make meaning.

Teach Students to Make Language Choices Based on Function and Tenor (Audience and Voice)

Teaching language means more than just identifying parts of speech; it also means understanding the function of language in the context of different genres. For example, verbs are used in procedures to give precise instructions (*slice the onions*), while they reflect the personality or state of mind of a person in a recount or narrative genre (*he yelled at the students*). Modifiers tell precisely the materials or ingredients needed to carry out a procedure (*blue construction paper*), while they give most of the information in reports (*three-foot long reticulated snake*).

Students need to learn how to make language choices given the audience or voice they want to reflect in their writing. For example, when writing a report to show to the school principal how much they knew about a topic, students were encouraged to include technical language to write effectively about the topic. When writing to younger audiences, students can choose less technical language to make what they write comprehensible to their audience. Language choices are also involved in creating voice. Choosing statements and third person helps create an authoritative piece, while use of first and second person, questions, and exclamations make a piece more informal. In order to have these choices, teachers must build students' language resources and make the students aware of the impact their choices have on their writing. As a middle school teacher expressed, "it's not really useful to say 'that's a preposition.' It's way more useful to say why you would use that or why an author used it and why it benefits a reader."

Teach Students to Appropriate Technical Language

A key component to knowing a discipline is to know the language used to express the content of that discipline. Thus, language and content are inextricable from each other. Often, students are told to write in their own words rather than to copy from books. If children do not learn the language of books, however, they will never acquire the language to express technical concepts. Children need to learn the language of written texts and to know what it means to be able to express themselves in disciplinary discourse.

While studying content and taking notes, teachers should build the students' technical language by creating thematic word/phrase walls and exposing students to the language through reading, videos, and videos with subtitles. A powerful way to teach this language is to help students to convert their everyday expressions—either oral or written—to technical language (Brown & Ryoo, 2008; Gibbons, 2002).

Teachers work hard developing technical language both orally and in writing. For example,

> Student: *it's not in the magnet's bubble.*
> Ed, the science teacher: *What's the scientific word for the magnet's bubble?*
> Student: *Magnetic field.*

Holly, another science teacher, noticed that students had used a lot of everyday language in their written reports on rock formation, even after having used the disciplinary language throughout instruction of content. She devised a chart with two columns, one with the students' language and one with the technical expressions:

Everyday Phrasing	Scientific Phrasing
Rocks are made by	Rocks are formed by
Melted rock	Molten rock or magma
Igneous rocks forming outside	Extrusive igneous rocks
Igneous rocks forming inside	Intrusive igneous rocks
Pieces of rocks	Sediment
Animal skeletons	Fossils

She compared them and discussed their meaning with the class. Then, she asked students to review their pieces to see if they could change their language.

It is important to encourage the acquisition of technical language to be precise in making meaning within the discipline and not because it is better than the language students normally used in conversation. Gibbons (2002) documented how, in a science classroom, students used their conversational language when working in small groups solving science problems where the meaning was largely supported by the context. When the students reported to the whole group, however, the teacher encouraged the use of more precise and technical language to more effectively communicate the ideas to the whole class. When writing, they were further encouraged to use technical and more lexically dense language, typical of written language. Khote (2018) guided secondary students to analyze critically their language practices and those promoted in schools and disciplinary texts. Such discussions made his students realize that "they had agency in deciding what register variables to use in realizing their communicative purposes" (p. 165).

Planning for School-Wide Implementation

School-wide implementation of SFL genre pedagogy requires schools to plan (a) genres, (b) language, and, in the case of dual language programs (c) language of instruction. To plan at which grade level to teach which genres and in the context of which discipline, it is best to work with the whole school staff to coordinate (see Table 1.4 as an example). Each grade inserts its own

Table 1.4 Sample Writing Calendar for an English Medium Pre-K Through Grade 8 School

	September	October	November	December	January	February	March	April	May	June
K1	Oral Story-telling ELA		Personal Recount ELA		Reports Science		Procedure ELA/Science		Argument ELA	
K2		Personal Recount ELA	Report and Cyclical Explanation Science: plants and their life cycle			Procedure ELA/Science			Argument ELA	
1		Personal Recount ELA			Report Science			Argument ELA		Explanation Science
2	Personal Recount ELA			Procedure ELA/Science/Math		Biography Social Studies	Report Science		Explanation Science	
3		Autobiography ELA		Report Social Studies	Fictional Narrative ELA		Biography Social Studies		Argument ELA/Social Studies	
4	Report Science			Argument		Biography/PARCC Writing Social Studies			Fictional Narrative ELA	
5	Argument Current Issues			Report Social Studies		Empathetic Autobiography/PARCC Writing		Systems Explanation		Multiple genres newsletter
6		Autobiography ELA		Historical Recount Social Studies	Report Science		Procedure Math	Argument Current Issues		Explanation Science
7	Historical Recount Social Studies			Factorial and/or Consequential Explanation Social Studies		Fictional Narrative ELA		Multiple genres for science fair presentation		
8	Argument Current issues			Historical Account Social Studies	Explanation Science				Fictional Narrative ELA	

Table 1.5 Features of Language to Be Introduced and Practiced K–8

Lessons on Language	K	1	2	3	4	5	6	7	8
2. Teach Formation of Third Person Singular in Present Tense and Past Tense (for L2 Learners in Particular)									
4. Teach to Use 3rd Person									
6. Teach Students to Use Appropriate Academic Language— Noun Groups									
9. Expanding Noun Groups by Using Pre-Nominal Modifiers and Post-Nominal Modifiers (4–8)	√								
12. Participants (Generalized vs. Specific; Beings vs. Institutions) (If needed teach formation of plural in English)						√			
13. Use of Clause Complexes to Make Meaning									

proposal in a school-wide calendar, followed by a review of the resulting calendar to make sure that over the grades different genres are covered and topics are not unnecessarily repeated. For example, there shouldn't be an animal report written at each grade level. One school plan did not include explanations; teachers then identified appropriate explanations to teach with several of the science topics. In addition, the chosen genres should be appropriate for the grade level. For example, one school moved fictional narratives from 2nd to 4th grade and eliminated personal recount in the upper elementary grades.

Dual language schools must decide in which language they will teach which genre. If the same genre is done in both languages, then the topic should be different so the material is not repeated. For example, for the report genre, insects might be taught in the other language and states in English.

Language features need to be planned across the grade level depending on genre and students' maturity. Each genre chapter includes all the aspects of language important for that genre. Teachers need to coordinate which they will introduce in their grade level so that all aspects are covered by the time students reach middle school. Table 1.5 illustrates one plan to teach language in the context of reports throughout the grade levels. Most schools expect students to write reports in all grade levels, so changing the topic and type in each grade is vital. Thus, even if the aspects of the language are the same, the specifics will be related to the topic and discipline.

Conclusion

Implementation of SFL genre pedagogy requires school-wide commitment and teacher expertise on the purpose, text structure, and language of the genres. School-wide commitment impacts on planning across grade levels and disciplines. As writing is developmental, it takes time for students to learn the structure and the language of written text. Plotting the content of writing instruction over the grades supports students' natural language and literacy development and avoids repetition of genres and topics. When all teachers in a school implement this approach to writing, they can support each other.

Because SFL genre pedagogy is not a prescribed curriculum, teachers need to become knowledgeable of the theory and practice in order to make decisions with respect to the topic, genres, and language they will teach given the curriculum of the school and the background of the students. Teachers must become knowledgeable of the theory and good at analyzing both mentor texts and student work. By analyzing texts, teachers can guide students to learn and critique the language and structure of the texts used in school and those produced by themselves.

References

Accurso, K., & Gebhard, M. (2020). SFL praxis in the U.S. teacher education: A critical literature review. *Language and Education*, 35(5), 402–428. https://doi.org/10.1080/09500782.2020.1781880

Aguirre-Muñoz, Z., Chang, R., & Sanders, J. (2015). Functional grammar instruction impact on writing. *Educational Policies and Current Practices*, 1(2), 71–85.

Atwell, N. (1987). *In the middle: Writing, reading, and learning with adolescents*. Portsmouth, NH: Heinemann.

Australian Curriculum Assessment and Reporting Authority (ACARA). (2012). *The Australian curriculum*. Retrieved from www.australiancurriculum.edu.au

Brisk, M. E., & Ossa-Parra, M. (2018). Mainstream classrooms as engaging spaces for emergent bilinguals: SFL theory, catalyst for change. In R. Harman (Ed.), *Bilingual learners and social equity: Critical approaches to systemic functional linguistics* (pp. 127–151). New York: Springer.

Brisk, M. E., & Schleppegrell, M. J. (Eds.). (2021). *Language in action: SFL theory across contexts*. Sheffield: Equinox.

Brisk, M. E., & Zisselsberger, M. (2011). "We've let them in on the secret:" Using SFL theory to improve the teaching of writing to bilingual learners. In T. Lucas (Ed.), *Teacher preparation for linguistically diverse classrooms: A resource for teacher educators* (pp. 111–126). New York: Routledge.

Brown, B., & Ryoo, K. (2008). Teaching science as a language: A "content-first" approach to science teaching. *Journal of Research in Science Teaching*, 45, 529–553.

Butt, D., Fahey, R., Feez, S., & Spinks, S. (2012). *Using functional grammar: An explorer's guide* (3rd ed.). South Yarra, Victoria: Palgrave Macmillan.

Callaghan, M., & Rothery, J. (1988). *Teaching factual writing: A genre-based approach*. Sydney: Metropolitan East Disadvantaged Schools Program.

Christie, F., & Derewianka, B. (2008). *School discourse: Learning to write across the years of schooling*. London: Continuum.

Coffin, C. (2006). *Historical discourse: The language of time, cause and evaluation*. New York: Continuum.

Common Core State Standards Initiative: Preparing America's Students for College and Career. Retrieved on 2/14/22 from www.corestandards.org

Daniello, F. (2013). Language in the Common Core: One cannot live on seeds alone. *Journal of Pedagogy, Pluralism, and Practice*, 5(1), 1–17. Retrieved from www.lesley.edu/journal-pedagogy-pluralism-practice/frank-daniello/language-common-core/

Daniello, F., Turgut, G., & Brisk, M. E. (2014). Applying systemic functional linguistics to build educators' knowledge of academic English for the teaching of writing. In A. Mahboob & L. Barret (Eds.), *Englishes in multilingual contexts* (pp. 183–204). London: Springer.

de Oliveira, L. C., & Cheng, D. (2011). Language and the multisemiotic nature of mathematics. *The Reading Matrix*, 11(3), 255–268.

de Oliveira, L. C., & Dodds, K. N. (2010). Beyond general strategies for English language learners: Language dissection in science. *The Electronic Journal of Literacy Through Science*, 9(1), 1–14. Retrieved from http://ejlts.ucdavis.edu/article/2010/9/1/beyond-general-strategies-english-language-learners-language-dissection-science

de Oliveira, L. C., Jones, L., & Smith, S. L. (2020). Interactional scaffolding in a first-grade classroom through the teaching/learning cycle. *International Journal of Bilingual Education and Bilingualism*. http://doi.org/10.1080/13670050.2020.1798867

Derewianka, B., & Jones, P. (2016). *Teaching language in context* (2nd ed.). Melbourne: Oxford University Press.

Eggins, S. (2004). *An introduction to systemic functional linguistics* (2nd ed.). London: Continuum.

Fang, Z., Lamme, L. L., & Pringle, R. M. (2010). *Language and literacy in inquiry-based science classrooms, grades 3–8*. Newbury Park, CA: Corwin Press.

Fang, Z., & Schleppegrell, M. J. (2008). *Reading in secondary content areas: A language based pedagogy*. Ann Arbor: University of Michigan Press.

Fletcher, R., & Portalupi, J. (2001). *Writing workshop: The essential guide*. Portsmouth, NH: Heinemann.

Flores, N. (2020). From academic language to language architecture: Challenging raciolinguistic ideologies in research and practice. *Theory Into Practice*, 59(1), 22–31. http://doi.org/10.1080/00405841.2019.1665411

Gebhard, M. (2019). *Teaching and researching ELLs' disciplinary literacies: Systemic functional linguistics in action in the context of U. S. school reform*. New York: Routledge.

Gebhard, M., Chen, I., & Britton, B. (2014). "Miss, nominalization is a nominalization": English language learners' use of SFL metalanguage and their literacy practices. *Linguistics and Education, 26,* 106–125.

Gibbons, P. (2002). *Scaffolding language scaffolding learning: Teaching second language learners in the mainstream classroom*. Portsmouth, NH: Heinemann.

Graves, D. H. (1983). *Writing: Teachers and children at work*. Portsmouth, NH: Heinemann.

Halliday, M. A. K. (1985). *An introduction to functional grammar*. London: Edward Arnold.

Halliday, M. A. K. (1993). Towards a language-based theory of learning. *Linguistics and Education, 5,* 93–116.

Halliday, M. A. K., & Matthiessen, C. M. I. M. (2004). *An introduction to functional grammar* (3rd ed.). London: Hodder Arnold.

Harris, E. (2011). *Portraits of writing instruction: Using systemic functional linguistics to inform teaching of bilingual and monolingual elementary students* (Unpublished doctoral dissertation). Boston College, Chestnut Hill, MA.

Hasan, R. (1996). Literacy, everyday talk and society. In R. Hasan & G. Williams (Eds.), *Literacy in society* (pp. 377–424). Harlow: Longman.

Humphrey, S. (2017). *Academic literacies in the middle years: A framework for enhancing teacher knowledge and student achievement*. New York: Routledge.

Humphrey, S., Droga, L., & Feez, S. (2012). *Grammar and meaning*. Newtown, Australia: Primary English Teaching Association Australia.

Humphrey, S., & Feez, S. (2016). Direct instruction fit for purpose: Applying a metalinguistic toolkit to enhance creative writing in the early secondary years. *Australian Journal of Language and Literacy, 39*(3), 207–219.

Khote, N. (2018). Translanguaging in systemic functional linguistics: A culturally sustaining pedagogy for writing in secondary schools. In R. Harman (Ed.), *Critical systemic functional linguistics: Promoting language awareness and social action among K-12 students and teachers* (pp. 153–178). New York: Springer.

Knapp, P., & Watkins, M. (2005). *Genre, text, grammar: Technologies for teaching and assessing writing*. Sydney: University of South Wales Press.

Marks, G., & Mousley, J. (1990). Mathematics education and genre: Dare we make the process writing mistake again? *Language and Education, 4*(2), 117–130.

Martin, J. R. (1985). *Factual writing: Exploring and challenging social reality*. Melbourne: Deakin University Press [republished Oxford University 1989].

Martin, J. R. (2009). Genre and language learning: A social semiotic perspective. *Linguistics and Education, 20,* 10–21.

Martin, J. R., & Rose, D. (2008). *Genre relations: Mapping culture*. London: Equinox.

Martin, J. R., & Rothery, J. (1986). What about functional approach to the writing task can show teachers about "good writing". In B. Coutoure (Ed.), *Functional approaches to writing: Research perspectives* (pp. 241–265). Norwood, NJ: Ablex.

Marzano, R. J. (1991). Fostering thinking across the curriculum through knowledge restructuring. *Journal of Reading, 34*(7), 518–525.

McKeough, A. (2013). A developmental approach to teaching narrative composition. In S. Graham, C. A. MacArthur, & J. Fitzgerald (Eds.), *Best practices in writing instruction* (2nd ed., pp. 73–112). New York: The Guilford Press.

Moore, J., & Schleppegrell, M. (2014). Using a functional linguistics metalanguage to support academic language development in the English Language Arts. *Linguistics and Education, 26,* 92–105.

Paris, D., & Alim, H. S. (2017). *Culturally sustaining pedagogies: Teaching and learning for justice in a changing world*. New York: Teachers College Press.

Pavlak, C. M. (2013). "It is hard fun:" Scaffolded biography writing with English learners. *The Reading Teacher, 66*(5), 405–414.

Quinn, M. (2021). SFL in Solomon Islands: A framework for improving literacy practices in primary schools. *Ikala, Revista de Lenguaje y Cultura, 26*(1), 185–201.

Rose, D., & Martin, J. R. (2012). *Learning to write, reading to learn: Genre, knowledge and pedagogy in the Sydney School*. Sheffield: Equinox.

Rothery, J. (1996). Making changes: Developing an educational linguistics. In R. Hasan & G. Williams (Eds.), *Literacy in society* (pp. 86–123). New York: Longman.

Santiago Schwarz, V., & Hamman-Ortiz, L. (2020). Systemic functional linguistics, teacher education, and writing outcomes for U.S. elementary English learners: A review of the literature. *Journal of Second Language Writing, 49*. https://doi.org/10.1016/j.jslw.2020.100727

Schleppegrell, M. J. (2004). *The language of schooling: A functional perspective*. Mahwah, NJ: Lawrence Erlbaum Associates.

Schleppegrell, M. J. (2007). The linguistic challenges of mathematics teaching and learning: A research review. *Reading & Writing Quarterly, 23*(2), 139–159.

Thompson, G. (2004). *Introducing functional grammar* (2nd ed.). London: Arnold

Westerlund, R., & Besser, S. (2021). *Reconsidering Calkins' process writing pedagogy for multilingual learners: Units of study in a fourth-grade classroom* (WCER Working Paper No. 2021–4). University of Wisconsin-Madison, Wisconsin Center for Education Research.

WIDA ELD Standards. (2020). *Amplification of the English language development standards, kindergarten-grade 12*. Madison, WI: State of Wisconsin.

Williams, G. (1999). Ontogenesis and grammatics: Functions of metalanguage in pedagogical discourse. In C. Ward & W. Renandya (Eds.), *Language teaching new insights for the language teacher* (pp. 243–267). Singapore: Seameo Regional Language Center.

Chapter 2

Procedures

The purpose of procedures is to give instructions or directions to accomplish a goal. This genre is found in many aspects of people's lives, such as in recipes, instructions for arts and crafts, directions to assemble products, and instructions to play games. In school, students encounter procedures when doing lab experiments. Although procedural writing might be accessible for children, it is not a genre that they typically engage in when given a choice in their writing (Fang, 1998). If children are to become proficient in this type of writing, teachers need to more deliberately engage them in this work.

At times procedures are confused with other genres.

Difference Between Procedure, Protocol, Procedural Recount, and Sequential Explanation

---

Procedure: How to make a paper plane
Protocol: Classroom rules
Procedural Recount: How the teacher made a paper plane
Sequential Explanation: How sneakers are made in a factory

Procedures contain directions to do or to make something sequentially, while protocols list instructions "that are designed to stay in place simultaneously" (Butt et al., 2012, p. 267). Protocols are mainly used to control behavior, for example, rules for classroom behavior or bus safety. The language features of protocols are similar to procedures; thus, the suggestions for procedures can be applied to protocols. Procedures should not be confused with procedural recounts, where the writer tells what happened when following a procedure. For example, a procedure describes how to make a paper plane, while a procedural recount tells what happened in the process of making a paper plane. Some sequential explanations present a sequence of steps of how something is done without the purpose of instructing the reader how to do it. Thus, the book *How Crayons Are Made* informs students the process of making a crayon rather than expecting them to make a crayon.

A procedure unit can be carried out in three to four weeks. It is a fun unit to implement because it can be connected with engaging, hands-on activities that help develop vocabulary in a wide variety of topics. It is a good unit to implement at the beginning of the year because the texts can be short and the stages are clear. Moreover, procedures usually do not require a lot of background knowledge. On the contrary, procedures are often used to build background knowledge. For example, in the Explanation unit (Chapter 7) where the mentor text describes making recycled paper, teachers can use a procedure to have students actually make their own recycled paper to better understand the process. Many science texts include procedures for experiments that help students understand the scientific principles of the lessons. For example, the book *Animal Senses: How Animals See, Hear, Taste, Smell, and Feel* includes procedures for experiments

DOI: 10.4324/9781003329275-2

in connection to each of the senses. Similarly, social studies texts include procedures. For example, the book *The American Flag*, about the creation of the flag, includes a procedure to construct a flag at the end.

Development of Units

To develop units, teachers need to consider a number of factors that play a role on what and how to teach and what materials to use. With this in mind, they then plan lessons.

Unit Preparation

To prepare a unit, teachers need to consider the following:

- Grade level
- Connection with content areas
- Mentor texts
- Research resources
- Potential projects, audience, and medium
- Uncoached writing and planning content of the unit

Following the suggestions for preparation of the unit, the remainder of the chapter (a) explains the theory related to purpose, stages, and language; (b) illustrates students' challenges; and (c) suggests lessons.

Grade Level

Procedure is a good genre for the early grades (pre-K–2; ages 4–7) and for beginners to the English language. In the later elementary grades through middle school (3–8; ages 8–13), procedures are used with science and math. Some high-stakes math and science tests require students to set up a procedure for an experiment to prove something. For example, students were asked to design an experiment to test the power of a fertilizer on the growth of tomato plants. They were required to write precise instructions to carry out the experiment.

The language of procedures must be precise and specific in order to produce clear and accurate instructions (see Table 2.1). Some aspects are targeted for lessons. Others are taught through deconstruction of mentor texts and editing, depending on grade level.

Even young students need to include precise imperative verbs, description of materials, and some adverbials to have precise instructions. Teachers could limit the lesson to verbs and do the other through questions while jointly writing and editing. (For detailed coverage and lessons of all aspects of language, see Brisk, 2021.)

Connection With Content Areas

Procedures can be written in connection with various content areas (see Table 2.2). Before delving into procedures in the chosen content, it is a good idea to do a few procedures related to the students' life experiences. For example, have students look for procedures at home in board games, boxes and cans of food products, and instructions to assemble something their family bought. Skills students or family members have, such as sports, games, musical instruments, and others, make good sources for procedures.

Table 2.1 Key Aspects of Language to Teach

Aspect of Language	Grade Level to Teach	Example
Precise imperative verbs without the "you"	All grades	_Cut_ the paper in half
Simple adjectives	All grades	_Colored_ paper.
More complex modifiers	Grades 4 and above	A _thick_ sheet _of 8 1/2 x 11 inch colored paper._ (Prepositional phrase modifying _sheet._ Additionally, it has adjectives modifying _paper._)
Adverbials of manner, place, and time	K–2 edit together; Grade 3 and up teach as lessons	_Cut_ the paper _in half._ (manner) _Rinse and dry_ _completely._ (manner) _Create a one-inch (2.5-centimeter) layer of stones_ _on the bottom of the jar._ (place) _When it gets too heavy, watch it storm._ (time) _Fry them_ _for 3–5 minutes._ (time)
Clause complexes	Grades 3 and up, edit together	A 3rd-grade student wrote: _place the banana in the freezer for 2–3 hours until it is frozen._ This complex clause could be edited to become a simple more direct clause: _Freeze the banana for 2–3 hours._
Reference ties	All grades, edit together	A 6th grader mentions corn seeds in the method but not in the materials. _One anes [ounce] of corn syrup, dish soap, water and_ _two corn seeds._

Table 2.2 Procedures in Various Content Areas

Content Area	Curricular Topic: Elementary Middle School	Example of Procedure
ELA	Connected to specific topics or readings	Crafts: How to make a paper plane, How to make slime
		Recipes: How to make lemonade; how to make a dish from my cultural heritage
Social Studies	U.S. history	How to make an American Flag
Science	Water Cycle	Procedure to carry an experiment to demonstrate evaporation
	Ecosystems	How to make a terrarium
Math	Geometry: shapes, volume	How to calculate the surface of a geometric figure
		General procedure for finding the volume of any rectangular prism
	Various topics	How to translate a real-world problem to an equation

In ELA, procedures can be self-contained lessons. With lower grades, it is best to use crafts because they can be easily carried out in class. Recipes are also appropriate, but they can be more cumbersome to demonstrate in class because they may involve cooking. Historical topics lend themselves to procedures to create objects related to the historical period. For example, how to make a basket, when studying cultures that used them.

Procedure is also a foundational element in the chain of scientific genres. Children need the opportunity to write procedures before they can begin to write scientific reports, explanations, and, finally, arguments (Veel, 2000). Procedures are the starting point for various experiments. The students carry out the experiment following the procedure. Then they make observations, write procedural recounts of what happened, and end up with some form of explanation or argument. In science classes, all of these writing activities constitute the macro genre that is traditionally called a lab report (Hyland, 2007). If the school has a science teacher, the classroom teacher should work in coordination with the science teacher. For example, a 3rd-grade science teacher taught procedure writing when constructing a crayfish habitat with the students, setting up the graphic organizer with the materials and the steps. This teacher taught technical scientific terms and explained the scientific reasons for each step as they jointly filled out the graphic organizer. Then the classroom teacher worked with the students to actually create final products, writing out the steps, checking their language, and adding illustrations.

In mathematics, having students verbalize or write procedures for mathematical drawings, problems, or algorithms "helps clarify the nature of mathematical processes for the students and the logical orders in which these might be carried out" (Marks & Mousley, 1990, p. 128). A middle school teacher had students create procedures on how to translate a word problem into an equation. The teacher remarked that students better understood the process by writing the procedures.

Mentor Texts

Mentor texts are written in the genre of the unit and are used to show students the features of the genre. There are abundant resources for procedures in books and on the Internet. Some books solely consist of procedures, whereas others include procedures in addition to writing from other genres. There are several types of procedures, such as crafts, science experiments, and recipes.

Type	Sample Mentor Text
Crafts	Boursin, D. (2007). *Folding for fun: Origami for ages 4 and up*. Buffalo, NY: Firefly Books.
Science experiments	Ardley, N. (2015). *101 great science experiments*. New York: Penguin Random House
Recipes	Griffin Llanas, S. (2012). *Easy lunches from around the world*. Heshan City, Guangong, China: Leo Paper Group.

Everyday life provides many examples of procedures, such as recipes on canned or boxed products, instructions that accompany products, and instructions to play games. Additional suggestions for mentor texts can be downloaded from the *Support Material* tab in the book's webpage.

For young students it is better to have mentor texts that include images showing the materials or ingredients and for each step. In this way the language of the instructions can be simpler. For older students, procedures tend to have just an image of the final product. Videos are a great source to help students write their own procedures. They provide the content and the language, usually orally, and students have to recreate it in writing. A media teacher had students script their procedures and then create videos as their assignments.

There are books that appear to be procedures by their title (e.g., *How Are Sneakers Made?* by Henry Horenstein). However, this text is an explanation of the process of making sneakers and does not include instructions for the reader to make a sneaker. Other texts are procedures as part of a fictional narrative, such as *How to Wash a Woolly Mammoth*. This is a fun text, but it is not a good model as a procedure because it is not realistic, and the language is a mixture of procedure and narrative. For example, in the same page it says "STEP ONE: Fill the bath tub" followed by

"If your mammoth is feeling thirsty, this may take a while," including a picture of the mammoth drinking all the water in the tub.

Research Resources

Writing starts with what each student knows to facilitate engagement. At the same time, building new knowledge is an essential aspect of preparing students for writing. For example, for a procedure unit, students can create a book of home recipes or games from their culture and then move on to procedures related to science experiments, involving instruction of new content.

The best way to develop knowledge of the content to produce procedures is to actually carry out procedures with the students, show them videos of procedures, or tap into their own experiences. Simultaneously, it is important to build the language the students will need to be precise, especially verbs, modifiers, and adverbials.

Potential Projects, Audience, and Medium

Because procedures are short, students will likely produce a number throughout the course of the unit. In preparation to write each piece, the class should discuss the potential audience(s). Having students write for different audiences enhances their awareness of how audience impacts the choice of language and images in a procedure. Instructions show awareness of the audience if they are clear and precise in order for the audience to carry out the procedure successfully. In writing a procedure, authors show awareness of their audience by the amount of information they provide through language, as opposed to images and the specific choice of language. Procedures written for children include illustrations of the materials or steps, or both. The images accompanying the steps are essential for students to understand the procedure. They allow for the use of less complex language in the instructions.

Table 2.3 shows a few examples of units planned by teachers of various grade levels. The various projects illustrate how teachers help students find an authentic audience and

Table 2.3 Examples of Units

Grade Level	Content Area	Mentor Texts	Projects/Medium/Audience
2	Social Studies	*Folding for Fun: Origami for Ages 4 and Up* by Didier Boursin *Highlights High Five Bilingüe Magazine*	Each student writes their own procedure text of how to make something tied to their country of origin/heritage country from the Cultural Mosaic social studies unit. The procedures will be created in posters to teach 1st graders.
2	Science Erosion	*101 Great Science Experiments* How to build an erosion model. www.fizzicseducation.com.au/150-science-experiments/geology-rocks/build-a-simple-erosion-model/	Procedures for experiments to demonstrate water erosion for students in their class, made as PowerPoints or Google slides.
Middle School	English	How to make a pilgrim hat. www.youtube.com/watch?v=I7MtQxl6uhs How to properly frame a shot in video. www.youtube.com/watch?v=Qj3QIQXYyik How to edit video in Adobe Premier? www.youtube.com/watch?v=YJhJuuPAzvg	Students produce videos. As a whole class: How to properly clean up after your lunch: trash, recycle, compost to be posted in the cafeteria. Create videos in groups with procedures to orient new students to school routines.

produce the writing in a medium appropriate for their audience and their language resources. Regardless of the medium, procedures usually include a title because the goal is often embedded in it.

Uncoached Writing and Planning Content of the Unit

At the beginning of the unit, give students a cold prompt to find out how much the students know about writing procedures.

- Use the uncoached writing as data to inform instruction only.
- The prompt should be a test of the genre and NOT of the content.
- Skip this step with kindergarten and 1st grade.

The prompt should be simple and without guidance. The content of the writing should be familiar to the students and not a test of students" knowledge of the content of the unit. Potential prompts are:

- *Write instructions on how to make a ham and cheese sandwich.* Care should be taken that the product is something familiar to students given their cultural backgrounds.
- Carry out a simple experiment in front of the class and ask the students to write the instructions. For example, the experiment with water, soap, and oil to show how materials layer.

Using as a guide the Analysis of Student Work forms (downloadable from the *Support Material* tab in the book's webpage), teachers determine what students can already do and what their challenges are. The results help the planning of lessons.

Purpose, Stages, and Language: Theory and Practice

With all of the preparation described in the previous section on hand, teachers need to think about the actual lessons they will carry out to teach about purpose, audience, stages, and various aspects of language. They also need to include lessons on medium if using one unfamiliar to the students. Moreover, they will need to teach students how to do research and how to use software applications, if the teaching has to be done online.

The organization of the unit should consider the curricular content, features of the genre, and instructional strategies following the TLC by developing the content, deconstructing of texts to learn a new aspect of the genre, jointly planning and constructing to apply the knowledge, and independent or group writing. *Teaching the curricular content* usually starts before teaching the genre and continues throughout the genre unit. Teaching the features of the genre starts with the purpose followed by the stages. Language instruction should start from the beginning, even when focusing on content, and carried out parallel to everything else. It is best to focus instruction on a couple of key aspects of language, reinforcing them throughout the lessons. Additional aspects of language can be done through joint revision and conferencing. It is also a good idea to discuss early on the projects they will carry out, their audience, and the medium(s) they will use. Table 2.4 gives suggestions on when to introduce language lessons connected to purpose and stages. As always, results of the uncoached pieces help make decisions on what needs to be emphasized.

The rest of the chapter will explain each aspect to be taught, give examples of student work, and offer suggestions for lessons.

Table 2.4 Lessons to Teach Procedure

Lessons on Purpose and Stages	Lessons on Language
1. Exposing Students to Procedures and	Use of the Imperative
2. Deconstruction of Texts to Identify Stages	3. Deconstruction of Text to Find Verbs
	4. Carry Out Procedures and Reinforce Verbs
5. Organizing the Stages and Learning How to Sequence Steps	Reinforce Verbs and Introduce Numbers as Text Connectives/Transition Words)
6. Practice Procedure Writing	With Emphasis on Modifiers (Adjectives)
	7. Deconstructing Text for Adverbials (or Modifiers)
8. Joint Construction of Procedures, Using Precise Language (Pre K–8)	Using Precise Language
9. Group Construction of Text (Grades 2–8)	Continue to practice precise language
10. Individual Construction of Procedures (Grades 2–8)	Continue to practice precise language
	11. Using a Barrier Activity to Show the Importance of Being Precise
12. End of a Procedure (Grades 2–8)	13. Add Adjectives and Adverbials With the Help of Questions
	14. Text Connectives
	15. Joint and Individual Revision of Clause Complexes (Grades 3–8)
	16. Reference

17. Adding Images to the Procedure

The following resources to support implementation of these lessons are downloadable from the *Support Material* tab in the book's webpage:

- Analysis of Student Work: Purpose, Stages, and Language (forms/rubrics)
- Graphic Organizer
- Mentor Texts That Illustrate the Genre
- Internet Resources With Mentor Texts to Illustrate the Genre

Purpose of Procedures

The purpose of procedures is "to tell how to do something" (Butt et al., 2012, p. 266). Procedures are written in the imperative. The person following the instructions is not named (e.g., Color and decorate . . .). Only rarely are "you" or "one" used, and if this does occur, it is mostly found in oral language.

Features of Students' Writing

Francisco, a 3rd grader in the SEI class, wrote the following procedure after the initial lessons of the unit. Analysis of the following piece illustrates the various aspects of purpose, stages, and language that are helpful to cover in the unit.

How to make a ham and cheese sandwich

First you get the braed and put
the bread in the toster for a kopl
minets in tell it pops. 2 When the
bread pop up you get it and
you get the cheese and put the cheese

in the bread. 3 When you put
the cheese in the bread you put
the Ham in the bread. 4 after
you did your bread you get a
drike and eat it.

	1	2	3	4	Uncoached Writing Comments
Purpose To give directions to accomplish a goal.			√		
Verb Conjugation *Use of Imperative* Person carrying the action is not named. Rarely is referred to by the use of "you" or "one."		√			Uses "you" imperative

Although this student understands the purpose of procedure after a few lessons, it is still written like a narrative rather than being laid out as a procedure. The class uncoached pieces at the beginning of the unit included chunks of story elements with the instructions. The prevalence of narrative writing may be attributable to the types of texts that children are accustomed to reading. In the elementary grades, children are overexposed to texts from recount and narrative genres. Procedures are about generalized participants, in contrast to stories, which are about specific characters or people (Fang, 1998). This underscores the need to provide children with examples and mentor texts that are clear examples of procedures and not told as narratives.

Avoiding personal pronouns to keep the detached voice of instructions is a challenge for students. Francisco used "you" in front of the imperative form of the verb throughout his piece. In addition, to using *you* with the imperative, other students used a variety of persons. For example, one 3rd grader changed from second, to first and finally to third person, *you pour flour, next we pour 1/2 cup salt, Next Ms R put the Playdoug in microway.*

Middle school students' uncoached pieces showed understanding of the purpose of procedures and rarely used *you* with the imperative verb. Their uncoached pieces, however, written after the teacher carried out the experiment, needed much more precise information in order for the reader to carry out the procedure. For example, Brendan wrote:

Title how are the earth's layers studied?
Materials
water
dish soup
corn syrup
mechering cup
cup

procedure
Pore 1 onc of water and corn syrup into the cup, corn syrup, dish soup, and take 2 pop corn curnals

Lesson 1. Exposing Students to Procedures and Use of the Imperative

Goal: To discover the purpose of procedure writing and learn the imperative form through exposure to different procedures, including those in the students' everyday experiences.

Materials: A procedure written on chart paper or projected and the materials to carry it out. Procedures in books, Internet examples, games, and household goods, such as boxes or labels from cans for cooking instructions and directions on assembling furniture. Cards to write words. Projector.

Activities

- *For 2nd grade and up*: Read the examples of procedures aloud, or have students in groups read them, or do both. Discuss the purpose of giving instructions for somebody to follow in sequence in order to get something done.
- *For all grades*: Show the procedure on chart paper or projected. As you read, carry out the instructions, demonstrating how to do the procedure. Then discuss the purpose of procedures and where they have seen procedures in their lives.

To teach the imperative:

- If you carried out a procedure, go back to it. If not, project a procedure.
- Help students find the imperative verbs.
- Clarify the meaning if needed, and point out that the verb is usually by itself and not preceded by "you."
- Give groups of students one procedure each. Have them find the imperative verbs and write them on cards or post-it notes to start creating a verb anchor chart that will support their writing later in the unit. With younger students, do this activity as a whole class.
- Remind students of the purpose of procedures and the use of the imperative as needed.

Additional Suggestions: There are a number of games that also help young children practice the imperative, such as Simon Says, or make a crown for students to put on and give an order, which the students then follow.

Stages of Procedures

The stages of a procedure include the title, goals or aims (sometimes included in the title), materials or ingredients (in the case of recipes), method presented in sequential steps, and an optional evaluation (Butt et al., 2012). Procedures are not written in traditional paragraphs. Instead, each stage is set up differently. The title is chosen considering the context of situation and medium. For example, if the product is a recipe by itself, it may be titled *How to Make Spring Rolls*. But if it were to be included in a cookbook, *Spring Rolls* would be enough. If not part of the title, the goal or aim is included right after the title. In recipes, instead of materials, it is called ingredients, and for children often utensils are included. Some instructions do not require materials (e.g., what to do when first coming to the classroom in the morning; how to operate a machine; and math procedures). If the procedure has materials or ingredients, they are listed under the title or goal. The method or steps follow sequentially, each starting on a separate line and sometimes numbered.

Stages	Example of a Published Procedure (www.ehow.com/how_4855654_make-cheap-maracas.html)
Goal or Aim	Included in title: *How to Make a Maraca*
Materials	• Dried Beans • 2 plastic cups • Duct tape • Stickers

Method or Steps	1. Take one cup and fill it a quarter of the way with dried beans.
	2. Place the other cup on top upside down so that the top of the two cups are touching.
	3. Close the two cups together using duct tape to seal them.
	4. Decorate with stickers.
	5. Hold the maraca around the middle and shake.

Frequently, procedures conclude with the last step, as in the *How to Make a Maraca* mentor text. Recipes frequently end with such instructions as "Serve cold, garnished with mint leaves," or "Serve right away" (*Around the World Cookbook*). They may also simply end with how many the recipe serves, such as "Serves 4." Occasionally, a procedure ends with a suggestion for how the success of the procedure can be evaluated. Occasionally, the last sentence may be of a different type. Games often finish with a statement describing how players win or lose the game. Crafts may include comments referring to the end product, such as, "You now have a beautiful Kokeshi doll," or "You now have a great butterfly decoration" (www.enchantedlearning.com/crafts). In very rare occasions procedures for children include an encouraging note. For example, in a book of craft activities, only one craft ended with an exclamation, "Prepare to sail off!" (*Folding for fun: Origami for ages 4 and up*, Boursin, p. 45).

Features of Students' Writing. Following is the analysis of the stages from Francisco's piece presented earlier.

Goal or Aim	NA		Embedded in the title but given by the teacher
Materials	√		Missing list of materials
Method presented in a series of sequential steps		√	Includes instructions to get the ingredients and concludes with a command to eat the sandwich. Both are unnecessary.
Layout	√		Written as a narrative

The main problem that students have with the stages is providing a vague list of materials or no list at all, as Francisco did. In the science procedure written by the 6th grader shown earlier, the student listed *water, dish soap, corn syrup*, with no specific quantities. In addition, it was missing the materials for the last step: *popcorn kernels*. With respect to the steps, there are two challenges: (1) steps can be vague or missing, and (2) the first steps tend to be related to getting the materials (*First you get the braed, Get the ornaments in a Christmas tree store, take the milk from the refrigerator*). The steps are related to doing something with the materials. Obtaining the materials is up to the person carrying out the procedure, and it does not have to be indicated in the steps. Some middle school students made the first step to get the materials: *first you get the materials* with the list of materials

- *3 pieces of bread*
- *turkey or ham*
- *mayo*

The list of materials would suffice without making it into a step.

Francisco's steps are very repetitious, and the conclusion is an unnecessary command to eat the sandwich. In the middle school example shown earlier, the steps are so limited that it would be impossible to carry out the procedure.

Almost all of the students in a 3rd-grade class changed their voice at the end of the procedure to address the audience with an encouraging exclamation. For example, Yarissa finished her recipe with *Tada! The ensalada mixta is done! Enjoy!*

Language Features of Procedures

Verb Groups

In procedures, the verbs used in the instructions are usually action verbs written in the imperative, describing the action precisely (*take, fill, place, close, decorate*). This is a key aspect of the language of procedures, and all students should learn it.

Modifiers

The main function of modifiers (adjectives, prepositional phrases, or embedded clauses with finite or non-finite verbs) is to describe the materials or ingredients with precision, for example, **dried** *beans*, **duct** *tape*. Without them the reader could choose canned cooked beans or a thin adhesive tape, neither of which would work well. Children rarely use modifiers; consequently, it is best to start with simple adjectives and later on include the other more complex ones.

Adverbials

Adverbials enhance the steps by giving additional information on how, where, and when/for how long/how often the actions take place. For example, adverbials of manner indicate *how* the action needs to be done (*a quarter of the way; with dried beans; upside down; so that the top of the two cups are touching; together; using duct tape to seal them; with stickers*). Adverbials of place indicate where the action takes place (*on top; around the middle*). These are the most common types of adverbials found in procedures. Recipes and science experiments have adverbials of time, answering the questions: *when, how long, how often*. For example, Bake the slices in the oven *for about 20 minutes. While the roots are still moist,* place plants in the holes. *When it gets too heavy,* watch it storm. The last two examples are clauses indicating time.

Text Connectives

Procedures do not use text connectives (also called transition words), except sometimes, especially in procedures for children, numbers precede each step. The function of these numbers is to facilitate distinguishing and following the steps in order. Often, teachers encourage children to use connectives such as *first, next,* and *last*. However, these connectives are never used in published procedures. Therefore, students should not be taught to write them. It is important to check published texts because they often illustrate what the culture expects.

Clause Complexes

Procedures for older students or adults sometimes include clause complexes with either finite or non-finite (non-conjugated verb) clauses. For example, a procedure for older students on how to make maracas combines three clauses in one sentence: *When the mixture is smooth, dip newspaper strips into the paper mache and cover the balloon and toilet tissue tube.* However, procedures for elementary age children tend to be predominantly written with simple clauses or occasional dependent clauses with non-finite verbs (underlined): *Using the black paint, paint a jack o'lantern face on your jar. Cut the cheesecloth into squares large enough to drape over your bottle.*

A science teacher required students to include not only the steps for a procedure, but also the scientific reason for that step, thus demanding a complex sentence. For example, when writing the procedure to create a crayfish habitat in a 3rd-grade class, a student wrote, *Step 3 cut pieces of black paper and glue it on the tank. You need black paper because crayfishes lives under a rock and under a rock is dark.*

Reference Ties

A material or ingredient mentioned in the instructions must appear in the list at the beginning of the text. Otherwise, the person following the instructions will not know the kind or quantity. When materials are named in the steps, they don't require the quantity any longer unless portions are used in different steps.

All these aspects of language are illustrated later in the mentor text *How to Make Maracas*.

Aspect of Language	Examples From the Procedure How to Make Maracas
Action Verbs in the Imperative	Take, place, close, decorate, hold, shake
Modifiers (to give specificity to the materials)	Dried, 2 plastic, duct
Adverbials (to further describe the actions)	Manner (How?): a quarter of the way, upside down so that the top of the two cups are touching, together, using duct tape to seal them, with stickers Place (where?): on top, around the middle
Text Connectives	1, 2, 3, 4, 5
Clause Complexes	... so that the top of the two cups are touching. ... using duct tape (non-conjugated verb) ... to seal them (non-conjugated verb, inside the previous one) ... and shake
Reference Ties	*one cup* (needs the number because material list had *2 cups*) Repeats *dried* and *duct* in the steps although it is not needed.

Features of Students' Writing

Francisco had a number of challenges with language similar to many other students when they first write procedures.

VERBS

As Francisco does, children tend to use generic verbs such as "put" and "get." For example, he wrote, *First you must get all the things*, rather than *assemble all of the materials*.

	1	2	3	4	Mid-way Writing Comments
Verb Types Uses precise action verbs to indicate what needs to be done		√			Uses frequently generic verbs like *get* and *put* (*put the bread in the toaster* rather than "toast the bread")

Another student wrote: *put the pastelitos in the frying pan*, rather than *fry the pastelitos*. A 4th grader wrote in her uncoached recipe for making a ham and cheese sandwich: *Put a ham on top of the mayonesa. Put some onions on top of the ham. Put some pickels on top of the onions.* She could have simply written, *Layer the ham, onions, pickles, yellow cheese, and tomatoes on top of the bread*, using the more descriptive verb "to layer."

One middle school student used *put* for each step, while others like Brendan used more precise verbs, such as *pour*. Several students, however, did not use a verb at all. For example, the first sentence in this method section does not have a verb *1 ouser of corn syrup 1 ouser of dish soap 1 ouser of water and 2 corn seeds. It make layers.*

MODIFIERS

Francisco used no adjectives to help make the ingredients more specific.

	I	2	3	4	Comments
Noun Groups Various types of adjectives are used to give specificity.		√			No description of ingredients.

Like Francisco, students, even in the middle school, tend to name the participants without including much information about them. For example, a 3rd grader listed the materials for her recipe on *How to Make Hot Coco* as "*ingredient: pot, chocolate bar, canela, milk, sugar, stove, spoon, cups*" without specifying any quantities or classifiers for the ingredients. Brendan included some classifiers, such as *mechering* [measuring] *cup* and *dish soup* but no quantities, which are essential in science.

ADVERBIALS

Francisco used a number of adverbials of time and place. The adverbials of time, rather than help the instructions, made it sound like a story. For example, *When the bread pop up you get it*. In a middle school procedure, a student wrote: *after you grab the bread grab the mayo*. For this reason, it is important to constantly remind students of the purpose.

	I	2	3	4	Comments
Adverbials Adverbs, especially of place and manner, are used to make the instructions specific.			√		Uses adverbials of time and place. There is unnecessary repetition.

Children do not always use adverbials of time, place, manner, and degree to help make the instructions more precise. When they do, they mostly use prepositional phrases and clauses. They rarely use adverbs with *-ly*, such as *slowly* or *carefully*. Brendan, as the other middle school students, had an extremely brief set of steps. Brendan's included only one adverbial of place: *into the cup*. As illustrated in the mentor text *How to Make a Maraca*, adverbials of manner are ubiquitous in procedures, but students rarely use them unless they are taught to do it.

TEXT CONNECTIVES

Francisco learned his lesson about the use of numbers, except for the first instruction that begins with "first." However, he wrote the piece without breaks and with numbers embedded in the text rather than using each number to start a new sentence.

	I	2	3	4	Mid-way Writing Comments
Text Connectives Use of numbers or no text connectives. (Connectives such as *then, next, finally* are more appropriate for procedural recounts.)		√			Uses numbers, but does not start each instruction on a new line.

Brendan, like students in his class, did not have numbers or steps lined up. Other middle school students used bullets to line up the steps but in addition used such words as *first*, *after*, and so on.

CLAUSE COMPLEXES

Francisco's piece on making a ham and cheese sandwich includes a series of clause complexes that could be combined into one simple clause: *First you get the braed and put the bread in the toster for a kopl minets in tell it pops* could be written as "Toast the bread for a couple of minutes." Further, *When the bread pop up you get it and you get the cheese and put the cheese in the bread*, could become "Place the cheese on the toasted bread," eliminating the adverbial clause of time. Middle school student writing showed comparable structures: *after you grab the bread grab the mayo and put some mayo on the bread*. This clause complex could simply be written as: "Spread the mayo on the bread."

	I	2	3	4	Mid-way Writing Comments
Clause Complex with finite and non-finite verbs. Help specify instructions, pack information (in procedures for upper elementary).	√				Simple and coordinated sentences could be combined, or eliminated.

Another common problem among both elementary and middle school students is stringing directions with *and*, *then*, or *after*. These could be simply written as separate clauses, each starting on a new line, to make the directions clearer. For example, a 5th grader wrote: "2. If the fish bowl is dirty you can clean by using a long tube filer *and* press the top hole with your finger *and then* let your finger go *and* it should suck all the nasty stuff in there" [emphasis added] (Zisselsberger, 2011, p. 142).

REFERENCE TIES

Francisco failed to write the list of ingredients, so clauses like *get the bread* and *put the cheese* have no reference.

	I	2	3	4	Mid-way Writing Comments
Reference Materials included in steps have been introduced in materials list.	√				Materials were not initially listed, yet they were named in the instructions with "the," *First you get the bread*.

Another student wrote in the opposite way. Not only did he have all of the measures with the materials, but he repeated the measures during the steps, an unnecessary redundancy: *first put in the plastic continer 1 cup of flour 1/2 cup of salt 4 spoons of oil*. In Brendan's writing, only one material in the steps did not have a reference in the materials list. In most procedures written by the middle school students, the materials in the steps had the appropriate referent in the materials list.

Lessons to Practice the Stages and the Language of Procedures

The following lessons help the students become familiar with the stages and the language that supports each stage. As stages are taught, it is also helpful to teach the format in which they are to be written. Initially, it is best to present good examples of the genre and deconstruct them with the students to see how authors accomplish the goals of the genre. Graphic organizers can help show visually what the various stages of the text are. It is always important to point out both the standard features of the genre and how authors vary within the standard structure. Because procedures are generally short, all of the activities involve working on the three stages simultaneously. Even when working on isolated stages, it is good to first present all of them and then work in detail with individual stages.

Lesson 2. Deconstruction of Texts to Identify Stages

Goal: To learn how a procedure is organized in stages. The pattern and format of stages facilitates reading of a procedure to accomplish the goal of the particular procedure.

Materials: Resources used earlier for teaching Purpose. Materials needed for the sample procedures. Examples brought by students from things they find at home (one teacher gave students a "Scavenger Hunt" worksheet to take home to find three procedures). Graphic organizer (downloadable from the *Support Material* tab in the book's webpage) on chart paper or smartboard.

Activities

- Project a procedure with the image of the finished product.
- Point at the picture of the finished product and talk about this being the goal, point at the title or the sentence that describes the goal.
- Read the list of materials as you show the real materials
- Carry out the steps as you/they read.
- Label the stages on the projected procedure: goal, materials, steps or method.

Follow Up Activities

- Have students in groups look at the procedures they brought from home and additional ones that you brought.
- Have them notice stages and how they are laid out.
- Have them label the stages, either writing or with post it notes.

Lesson 3. Deconstruction of Text to Find Verbs

Goal: To use the language of procedure as a resource and a model for the verbs in order to enrich the vocabulary.

Materials: Procedures, preferably familiar to the students, comparable to what students will be writing in their own procedures, such as crafts, recipes, math games, and so on. Cardboard strips or post-it notes to make word cards. Projector.

Activities

- Project a procedure.
- Ask individual students to come up to the screen and find the imperative verbs. As each student finds an imperative, give him or her a card with the verb written on it or have the student write the verb on it. For young children, you can use the term *command* instead of imperative.
- Clarify the meaning, if needed, and point out that verbs are usually not preceded by *you*.

- Have the students add their card to an anchor chart or word wall with "Crafts verbs," "Recipe verbs," or other relevant type of procedure used in class that students can refer to when writing their own procedures later on.
- Continue working as a whole-class with one or more procedures. If students are old enough (2nd grade and up), distribute the rest of the texts and have students do the same activity in groups.
- As a follow-up activity, put the cards in a hat.
- Have students take turns taking a card out of the hat and forming a clause with the verb.

This lesson can be repeated with different topics in preparation for writing other types of procedures. For example, you may start with crafts and then do science experiments.

Jack, a 2nd-grade teacher, had noticed that in the first set of procedures his students had written, most of the commands were the verbs "put" and "get." To help students revise their writing using more precise action verbs, he divided a piece of chart paper into four squares. On top of the first square he wrote, "Cooking," and asked students for suggestions of commands that would appear in a procedure related to cooking. Students suggested such words as *pour, fry, squeeze, flip,* and *heat.* In the next square, he wrote "Arts & Crafts" and asked for suggestions for that type of procedure. Students called such words as *fold, cut, tape, glue,* and *draw.* Then, he asked for other procedures that they had written. One student said, "How to make a snowman." He asked how many people had written that one, and seeing a few hands go up, he wrote "Snowman" over the third square and asked for suggestions. He did the same thing with the last square.

Then, he asked for volunteers to read aloud their procedures. As a student read her piece on how to decorate a Christmas tree, which included several of the commands starting with "Put," Jack chose one sentence ("Put the jingle bells on the Christmas tree") and asked the class to give the author suggestions for words other than "put." One student said, "hang." After a few more students read their pieces and received excellent suggestions, Jack asked the children to go back to their seats, read their procedures, and change a few of the "put" and "get" verbs to a more precise action. Students could refer to the examples in the chart paper. Most of the students made appropriate changes.

Lesson 4. Carry Out Procedures and Reinforce Verbs

Goal: To reinforce the purpose, stages, and verbs by filling in verbs and implementing procedures.

Materials: Procedure written on chart paper with the first imperative verb blank. For young students, have a set of cards with missing verbs written. Materials or ingredients needed to carry out the procedure.

Activities

- Carry out the procedure with the students.
- Take pictures or have students draw each step.
- In collaboration with students, paste pictures or drawings down the side of chart paper next to each step.

- Discuss with class which verb goes in the blank space. (These would have been used orally while carrying out the procedure.) Write the verb or have students write it on the blank space or on a card to paste on the blank space.

Depending on the age and language ability of students, you may repeat this lesson with different procedures, including science experiments.

Lesson 5. Organizing the Stages and Learning How to Sequence Steps/Reinforce Verbs and Introduce Numbers as Text Connectives/Transition Words

Goals:

- To learn the order of the stages and the order of elements within the stages, in order to make the procedure comprehensible for the reader.
- To learn additional precise verbs.
- To notice numbers as text connectives.

Materials: Large sentence strips with the goal (could be in the form of a title), all the materials, and individual steps numbered for a procedure. Highlight verbs. Chart paper. Materials or ingredients to carry out the procedure.

For a follow-up activity: Envelopes for each group with small sentence strips with the goal (could be in the form of a title). Materials or ingredients and steps written on individual ones. A sheet of blank paper for each group.

Activities

- Remind students of the three stages: goal, materials, and steps.
- Tell students that you will read each sentence strip, and they have to tell you to which stage it belongs.
- Take the goal, reread it, and ask the students where it goes. Place it on the sheet of chart paper.
- Take the strip with the materials, and ask the students where it should go. Place the strip on the chart paper.
- Read each strip in the steps pile, and have the students decide the order. Place them on the chart paper. Have them notice that *each step begins with a number* and starts on a new line.
- Have students point out the verbs, check that they understand the meaning, and have them add it to the word wall if not already there.
- Using the materials you brought, have students direct you in carrying out the procedure.

Follow-up activity:

- Give each group an envelope with sentence strips of the procedure and a sheet of paper.
- Have students work in groups to order the sentence strips following the same process as before.
- When students have agreed on an order, have them glue the strips on their worksheets.
- Have them share with the whole class.
- If it is a simple procedure, give a copy for students to take home and do with their family.

In Kathy's 2nd-grade classroom, students regularly work at literacy centers during the ELA block. Small groups circulate through centers such as listening station, smartboard, and guided reading, spending 20 minutes at each center. During the procedure unit, after procedures had been introduced and the students had jointly constructed a few writing pieces, Kathy set up a sequencing center. She wrote out a procedure that was familiar to the class on strips of paper, putting the title, each material, and each step on separate strips. During her ELA blocks, small groups of students worked together, spreading out the strips on the table in front of them and reorganizing them to put the stages and steps in order. As the unit went on, Kathy added two procedures for students to sequence. Over the course of a month, students had multiple opportunities to reconstruct the procedures, becoming increasingly familiar with the stages of a procedure.

Lesson 6. Practice Procedure Writing With Emphasis on Modifiers (Adjectives)

Goal: To understand that adjectives help the person doing the procedure choose the exact materials or ingredients.

Materials: Procedure written in chart paper or projected without materials included. Assortment of materials that include some that are not needed. For example, if the procedure calls for black construction paper, also have construction paper in other colors. Finished version of the procedure.

Activities

- Read the title/goal. For example, *How to Make a Sea Turtle* (https://iheartcraftythings.com/sea-turtle-craft.html).
- Display the materials so that they are visible to all students. For example, a 20 oz and a 10 oz paper bowl; yellow, red, and green stock paper; brown, green, and blue paint; and other materials.
- Have students look at the final product. Point at the body of the turtle made with the 20 oz bowl, then ask them: Which of the two bowls do they need, the 10 oz or the 20 oz? After the students answer, add it to the list of materials in the displayed written procedure. Do the same for other materials.
- Once you finish listing all the materials, underline the adjectives and discuss with the students why they are so important.
- Finish the lesson by carrying out the procedure. Ideally, have enough materials to give to groups of students, and have each group complete the procedure by following the written instructions.
- Repeat the process with a procedure from a science experiment because being precise is absolutely essential in science. Stress the importance of the language that describes measurements and quantities. When writing procedures, students often forget to include the quantities.

Lesson 7. Deconstructing Text for Adverbials (or Modifiers)

This lesson can also be done with adjectives and other modifiers.

Goal: To help students understand the function of adverbials in making instructions precise.

Materials: A couple of procedures projected or written on chart paper with adverbials blocked by strips of paper. Materials needed to demonstrate the steps of the procedures. (If using the Ice Cube experiment, have two identical bowls [same size] and ice cubes.) Projector.

Activities

- Show or read one of the procedures with the adverbials covered.
- Have a few students come to the front of the class. Give them the materials and have them try to carry out the procedure.
- Uncover the adverbials and have the students try again.
- Discuss the differences.

Repeat the process with the procedure from a science experiment because being precise is absolutely essential in this context. For example, do the following Ice Cube Experiment (adverbials are in italics). When you show the piece without adverbials, be sure to cover the title and goal.

The same type of lesson can be done covering the adjectives (in bold).

Ice Cube Experiment

Goal: To measure melting time relative to the size of the ice.
Materials: 2 **identical** bowls; 2 **ice** cubes.
1. Put the bowls *on the counter.*
2. Take **two ice** cubes *out of the freezer* and place one *in each bowl.*
3. Break one of the **ice** cubes *into smaller pieces that are no larger than 1/4 the size of the whole ice cube.*
4. Time how long it takes for all of the ice to melt.

Lesson 8. Joint Construction of Procedures, Using Precise Language (Pre K–8)

Goal: To write procedures together to gain confidence before writing individual pieces.
Materials: Materials needed to carry out a procedure. Camera or sheets of paper to draw on. Large chart paper or computer with a place to project.

Activities

For kindergarten or 1st grade:

- Carry out a procedure with the students.
- Take pictures of every step.
- Work to produce a class procedure together:
  - Brainstorm with the class what the title should be that would also indicate the goal.
  - Brainstorm what materials or ingredients they used in making the procedure. Ask questions to encourage use of adjectives where necessary to describe the items precisely.

- Have students put the pictures or drawings on chart paper, ordering them in sequence. Have them dictate the instruction for each picture, letting students come up to the chart paper to write the letters or words that they know.
- If the students use generic verbs like *put* and *get*, ask questions and point at the anchor charts with lists of verbs to get them to find more precise ones. If they suggest using *you*, remind them there is no need or point at other procedures around the room and show them they don't have them.

For 2nd grade and up:

- Discuss the *audience* with the class.
- Carry out a procedure or show a wordless video of a procedure, teaching the vocabulary connected with the materials and the actions. Write any new vocabulary on word cards or post-its, and add them to the language anchor charts.
- Jointly construct the stages with the students. As this occurs, point out the layout:
  - Decide on the title. Include a goal if not contained in the title.
  - Ask students to tell you the materials or ingredients that were used and list them. Encourage the use of modifiers describing materials precisely by asking questions.
  - Ask students to suggest every step. Keep reminding them that these are directions to be used by the audience reading the procedure so that they can carry out the steps; the verbs need to be precise.
  - If the instructions need them, ask questions with How? Where? and so on to add adverbial phrases expressing circumstance of manner, place, and so on.

While jointly constructing a procedure with her students, Kelly, a middle school science teacher, had to remind them of several features of the steps and materials she had already taught. This demonstrates that joint construction is an essential step in the learning process because students are guided to write through active engagement in the process.

Kelly jointly wrote a procedure for an experiment to demonstrate density of hot and cold water. She had carried out the procedure in front of the class. As she discussed the materials and steps, she wrote them using a Smartboard. As she interacted with the students and wrote the materials list, she kept reiterating the need to be very specific.

TEACHER: See if you can remember, we were at the back table, we did it in two groups. What did we use?
STUDENT: Food coloring
T: Okay, food coloring, what food coloring did you use?
S: Blue
T: Blue, what did the other group use?
S: Yellow
T: So, if you were in the yellow group, you write 6 drops of yellow food coloring, and if you were in the blue group, you write 6 drops of blue food coloring. So, I'm going to write 6 drops blank and you can fill it in based off of what you had. It's important that you're very specific. What else did we need?
S: Small, clear, plastic cup

T: Okay, a small, clear, plastic cup, because you need to be able to see it. What else did we have?

S: Hot water

T: We had hot water. How much hot water did we have? 237 ml of hot water. Where did we get the water from?

S: The tap

T: The tap, so we can be even more specific: 237 ml hot tap water.

The teacher continued in the same way until they had all of the materials listed. The first thing that she needed to remind students was that the steps did not start by indicating to get the materials, something commonly seen among students' writing of procedures.

T: So after that you have the part of the procedure where you tell the steps, right? What is the first thing that you would tell someone to do?

S: The water

T: What about the water?

S: To get the water

T: Okay, do you mean like just go get the water? Because when you do a lab, this is really important, you never want to have your first step be gather your materials. That's the point of the materials list, to gather your materials together.

S: Cool down the cold tap water

T: Yeah, cool down the cold tap water with ice. Does this have any pronouns? Does this say, You go cool it down? No. It uses the imperative, it tells you right away what to do.

She went on in the same way to include all the instructions in the right order.

Note About Mechanics

This is a good time to teach early childhood students about capitalization and punctuation for the steps, with a capital at the beginning of the step and a period at the end.

Lesson 9. Group Construction of Text (Grades 2–8)

Goal: To start releasing teacher responsibility by having students produce procedures while working in groups.

Materials: Images of the materials and steps for a procedure (for example, Linda used directions to assemble IKEA furniture with her SEI students). Have either one copy of the same procedure per group or use different procedures for each group.

Activities

- Ask students (in groups) to label the materials; remind them to describe them precisely.
- Ask students to write the steps next to the images; remind them to use precise imperative verbs and describe the actions by answering How? Where? etc., where appropriate.
- If students have the same procedure, have the groups compare and discuss any discrepancies.
- If each group has a different procedure, have the groups exchange their procedures and discuss whether the others can understand the directions.

Jeanine adapted group construction to create a published product with her 1st-grade class (see box).

Jeannine's 1st-Grade Class at St. Rose Writes a Procedure

Jeannine had practiced a number of procedures with her class. Her culminating activity for this procedure unit, implemented at the onset of the year, involved students preparing the instructions for how to make play dough to give to their buddy 4th-grade class (at her school, all grades have a buddy grade). She had distributed strips with the title, each material, and each step needed to all of the students. The strips with the steps had numbers on the back to help students with the order. As she brainstormed what needed to go first and the following order with the students, the student with the appropriate strip came up and glued it to the chart paper. At the end, they added numbers to each step. Jeannine then made copies and gave them to the students to share with their buddies.

Lesson 10. Individual Construction of Procedures (Grades 2–8)

Although individual construction is not planned for younger grades, if students want to do it, the teacher should encourage them.

> **Goal:** To demonstrate that students have learned to write procedures by producing their own.
> **Materials:** Copies of the graphic organizer for each student. Alternative, wordless video of a procedure.

Activities

- Have students research things from their own experience to share with others. When there are students from multiple backgrounds and cultures, students can consult with their families for information on family recipes, games, or other activities that require a procedure.
- Have students fill out the graphic organizer with the materials and steps (this can be done in consultation with a family member).
- Bring the graphic organizer to class and share them in groups to determine if all of the stages are complete.
- Have students write their procedures using the information in the revised graphic organizer.

Alternative projects done following the same process:

(a) Have students think of procedures found in school, including math games that they have played in class and science experiments that they have done in science.
(b) Show them a wordless video, stopping after each step to give them a chance to write each step. Then they can add the title/goal and materials.

Lesson 11. Using a Barrier Activity to Show the Importance of Being Precise

> **Goal:** To apply the knowledge of modifiers and adverbials to giving precise directions and to understand the implications of not being precise.
> **Materials:** Several copies of a simple drawing, cardboard screens or folders, paper, and pencils. The drawing needs to be something that the students are familiar with so that they have the vocabulary to describe it. Alternative: Two bags of different color pieces with geometrical shapes.

Activities

- Sit students in pairs across from each other with a screen in between them.
- Give one student a drawing and another student a blank paper. Don't let the student with the blank paper see the drawing. (Alternative: give each student a bag with the same kind of geometrical pieces. Ask one of the students to create a design using no more than 4 or 5 pieces.)
- Students with the drawing tell the other students what to do to create a similar drawing. Then, they compare their drawings. (Alternative: students who created the design describe it to the others who try to recreate it with their own set of pieces.)
- Discuss potential language that would have helped to make the drawing more accurate (for example, color, directions, such as left, right, above, below).
- Working in pairs, have students look at their individual procedures and decide whether they need to add or modify language to make it more precise.

Note: the teacher may demonstrate this activity first and have a few students watching each side.

Lesson 12. End of a Procedure (Grades 2–8)

Goal: To explore how different types of procedures end to include the most suitable ending in students' own writing.

Materials: Examples of different types of procedures for different audiences, such as cookbooks, craft books, instructions in boxes, cans, other products found in a household, math games, and science experiments. Chart paper. Markers.

Activities

- Sort out the procedures by type (crafts, recipes, science experiments, games). Give each group of students one type of procedure, a sheet of chart paper with the type of procedure written on top, and markers.
- Have students look at the end of the procedures and write down the last sentence on the chart paper. Then have students discuss the type of procedure, the type of sentence, the similarities and differences among the various examples, who was the author and the audience, and why the author did or did not use a final exclamation to encourage the audience.
- Have groups share and display the sheets with the different ending sentences around the class.
- Have students look at the last sentence in their own procedure and decide whether the ending is suitable for the kind of procedure.

Lesson 13. Add Adjectives and Adverbials With the Help of Questions

Goal: To revise students' work to give more specificity.

Materials: Samples of students' procedures to project or write on chart paper. Blank sheets of chart paper to add questions. Projector.

Activities

- Using one of the students' procedures, demonstrate how to ask questions to make the students' procedures more precise. You may create an anchor chart with questions to help students when they are writing procedures on their own.

- Ask questions to describe materials more precisely. For example, "sugar" questions: How much sugar? "2 tablespoons." What kind of sugar? "Brown sugar."
- Ask questions about verbs that would help students add adverbials and be more precise. For example, for the instruction, "cut each potato," ask the following questions: Cut how? "In half lengthwise." For the instruction, "spread the potatoes," ask the following questions: Spread where? "Onto the prepared pan." For the instruction, "pour the boiling water," ask the following questions: Where? How? "Carefully, pour the boiling water in the sink."

- As you ask questions, negotiate the suggestions given by the students and add the agreed upon revision.
- Repeat with another piece.
- Have students work in groups or pairs to do this activity with their other procedures.

Ms. B., a 5th-grade teacher, gave students a few suggestions for writing procedures and directed them to fill out a graphic organizer with the information. Before writing their drafts, she wrote a procedure to make a kite on the whiteboard and led the whole class in a text analysis of the modifiers and adverbial phrases followed by a discussion of the function of this language in making the instructions more precise. When writing their procedures from their graphic organizers, the students added the elements of language from the lesson, demonstrating the impact and influence. For example, one student had "put rocks in" in her graphic organizer. In her draft, she wrote, "put in your *small* rocks *in the tank*" [emphasis added] adding an adjective and adverbial phrase. Another student wrote, "cut the banana into eight pieces," in his draft, while his graphic organizer just showed "cut the bananas" (Zisselsberger, 2011, p. 141). To further help students revise their pieces, Ms. B had partners acting out the procedures, as well as filling out a worksheet with comments, to help improve the accuracy of the instructions.

Lesson 14. Text Connectives

Goal: To have students use appropriate connectives, if any.

Materials: Sample mentor texts previously used that have different formats, including numbers, bullets, and a list of instructions with each listed on a new line without numbering or bullets.

Activities

- Give groups of students a set of mentor texts that use different formats, for example, numbers, bullets, or without either.
- Ask students to identify how authors indicate that there is a new step. Ask them to guess who is the audience for the procedure and why the author made the particular choice.
- Show a student sample that requires editing, and correct it with the whole class.
- In their groups, have students edit their work with audience in mind, especially editing out words like *the first step, next, you,* and others unless they are essential.

Lesson 15. Joint and Individual Revision of Clause Complexes (Grades 3–8)

Goal: To teach students how to pack or separate a string of clauses in order to make the instructions clearer.

Materials: Students' work samples that need editing with sentences that could be packed or separated. Blank paper.

Activities

- After checking with the authors, put the complex sentences that could use packing up on a smartboard or the board. Do two or three examples with the whole class.
- Ask for suggestions from students, identifying and underlining the verbs to determine the number of clauses.
- Ask for suggestions from students, underlining conjunctions, especially "and."
- Demonstrate how a sentence could be packed. For example:

  - *Put the pastelitos in the fring Pan and wait 10 minutes and the cheese melts.* could become *Fry pastelitos for 10 minutes until the cheese melts.*
  - *First wrap thumb with bandage. If you don't your hand is going to hurt.* could be written as *To avoid hurting your thumb, wrap it with a bandage.*
  - "Take the ice cream scooper and start scooping the chocolate ice cream into the ice cream cup" (Zisselsberger, 2011, p. 168). This clause complex could be packed either by simply stating, *Scoop the chocolate ice cream into the ice cream cup* or by including a subordinate clause with a non-finite verb, *Using the scooper, scoop the chocolate ice cream into to the ice cream cup.*
  - *Get the pan, put water in it, and put it on the stove. Put the potatoes in the pan to boil until tender.* This string of sentences could be packed and the ubiquitous *put* and *get* verbs eliminated by writing something like, "Boil the potatoes in a pan filled with water until tender."

- Give students the rest of their work with one or two sentences underlined that they need to work on. Have students work in groups, look at their writing, and focus on the sentences underlined in green.
- Have students suggest how they could pack a sentence that you have marked.
- Have students write their agreed-upon alternative on a separate sheet.
- Work with groups to review their proposed revisions or have them share with the whole class.
- Agree upon a final revision, and have the authors make changes to their procedures.

Repeat the activity with strings of sentences that could be separated. First do it with the whole class, and then work in groups. This time, students will focus on the sentences underlined in blue. For example, a 3rd grader wrote, . . . *then put it in the microwave for 1 minute then take it out of the microwave then touch it just a piece then stired it then put it in the microwave for 4½ minuetes then take it out of the microwave then take it out and stire it then get some play do* [dough]. Each "then" could be eliminated, creating new sentences with a command written on a separate line, for example, *Put it in the microwave for a minute. Take it out and stir it . . .* Some of the sentences could be combined by joining the two actions with "and."

Lesson 16. Reference

Goal: To help students see the connection between the materials in the list and those named in the steps.

Materials: Sample student work, a couple where the materials in the steps are included in the list and the detailed description is not repeated unless needed and a couple that need revision.

Activities

- Show a sample student work. Circle the materials in the steps and look for them in the materials list. Are they present in the list? Did they repeat the quantity in the instructions? Is it necessary to state the quantity? For example, in Brendan's procedure shown earlier in the chapter, *pop corn curnals* [kernels] appears in the steps but not in the materials list.
- Repeat with the other pieces of sample student work, showing first the ones that do not need revision.
- Have students work in groups to edit their own work.

Images That Accompany Procedures

Procedures for young learners usually include a number of images to illustrate the final product, each of the materials, ingredients, and/or utensils, and each of the steps. With all these images, then the instructions can be less wordy. Procedures for older students usually just include the final product. In addition, only the objects involved in the production are illustrated in the image. Occasionally, a pair of hands may be shown manipulating the materials. Young children's writing, unless instructed otherwise, will include a girl or boy—depending on their gender—carrying out the procedure. This type of image is more typical of storytelling where there are specific participants carrying out the action. In a procedure, the focus is the action. Therefore, it is important to have students review procedures and identify the types of images typically found in them and discuss the purpose of the image, that is, to further clarify instructions.

Lesson 17. Adding Images to the Procedure

Lesson prepared by Magaly, Elissa and Antonella, a group of 2nd-grade teachers at a bilingual school.

1. With the whole group, teacher guides students in analyzing mentor text "Make Paper Marigolds" and leads discussion on what students notice about images:
   - What do you see in the images?
   - How do they help us understand how to follow the procedure?
2. Students then work in groups to analyze other texts from browsing box and answer the same questions about the images.
3. Teacher and students regroup and create criteria for images:
   - show the objects
   - do not include people or background
   - each one shows one step
   - there is an image for the final product
4. Teacher distributes the students' writing "How to make butter" from the previous lesson; it will have empty boxes added. Students then work in their groups to discuss what the images should be and draw them in following the criteria. Students then share their work with the class.

ANALYSIS OF STUDENT WORK: PURPOSE, STAGES, AND LANGUAGE

Key: 1. Needs substantial support; 2. Needs instruction; 3. Needs Revision; 4. Meets Standard; NA: Not applicable

	1	2	3	4	Comments
Purpose To give directions to accomplish a goal.					
Use of Imperative Person carrying the action is not named. Rarely it is referred to by the use of "you" or "one."					
Goal or Aim (may be same as title)					
Materials					
Method Presented in a Series of Sequential Steps					
Evaluation or Final Comment (optional)					
Lay Out of Stages Materials in a list. Each step starts flush against the left margin.					
Verb Types Uses precise action verbs to indicate what needs to be done.					
Noun Groups—Modifiers Various types of adjectives or other modifiers are used to give specificity, especially to materials or ingredients.					
Adverbials Adverbs, especially of place and manner, are used to make the instructions specific.					
Text Connectives Use of numbers or no text connectives. (Connectives such as *then, next, finally* are appropriate.)					
Clause Complex With Finite and Nonfinite Verbs Help specify instructions (3–8 grades).					
Reference Materials included in steps have been introduced in materials list.					

Criteria

1. Needs substantial support: The student writer needs extensive help developing that aspect of the genre.
2. There are gaps in the writer's understanding of the specific aspect. The writer has insufficient control. S/he needs instruction and practice.
3. The paper needs revision on one or two instances of the feature. A conference would be sufficient to help the writer meet the standard.
4. The paper reflects what the student should be able to accomplish and write independently given the instruction provided for this grade level.

(National Center on Education and the Economy, 2004)

Procedure Graphic Organizer

Goal:

Materials or Ingredients*

_____   _____
_____   _____
_____   _____
_____   _____

Steps

1. _____
2. _____
3. _____
4. _____
5. _____
6. _____
7. etc.

*Not all procedures require Materials or Ingredients

Mentor Texts That Illustrate the Genre

For All Elementary Levels

Ardley, N. (2015). *101 great science experiments*. New York: Penguin Random House.

Bolton, F., & Snowball, D. (1986). *Growing radishes and carrots*. New York: Scholastic.

Boursin, D. (2007). *Folding for fun: Origami for ages 4 and up*. Buffalo: Firefly Books.

Burke, J. (1999). *Look what you can make with paper bags: Over 90 pictured crafts and dozens of other ideas*. Honesdale, PA: Boyds Mill Press.

Coy, J. (2003). *Two old potatoes and me*. New York: Alfred A. Knopf.

Gould, R. (1998). *Making cool crafts & awesome art: A kids' treasure trove of fabulous fun*. Charlotte, VT: Williamson Publishing.

Griffin Llanas, S. (2012). *Easy lunches from around the world*. Heshan City, Guangong, China: Leo Paper Group.

Hickman, P. (1998). *Animal senses: How animals see, hear, taste, smell, and feel*. Buffalo: Kid Can Press.

Irvine, J. (1996). *How to make holiday pop-ups*. Toronto, Canada: Kids Can Press.

Parker, S. (2005). *The science of water: Projects and experiments with water science and power*. Chicago, IL: Heinemann Library.

Wiseman, A. (1973). *Making things: The hand book of creative discovery*. Boston, MA: Little, Brown.

Yanuck, D. L. (2003). *American symbols: The American flag*. Mankato, MN: Capstone Press.

For Grades 3–8

Braman, A. (2000). *Kids around the world cook! The best foods and recipes from many lands.* New York: John Wiley & Sons.

Fletcher, R. (2002). How to make a snow angel. In *Poetry matters: Writing a poem from inside out* (pp. 122–123). New York: HarperTrophy.

Johnson Dodge, A. (2008). *Around the world cookbook.* New York: DK Publishing.

King, D. C., & Moore, B. (1998). *Colonial days: Discover the past with fun projects, games, activities, and recipes.* New York: John Wiley & Sons.

Long, L. (2001). *Measurement mania: Games and activities that make math easy and fun.* New York: John Wiley & Sons.

Mebane, R. C., & Rybolt, T. R. (1995). *Water & other liquids.* New York: Twenty-First Century Books.

Rainis, K. G. (2003). *Microscope science projects and experiments: Magnifying the hidden world.* Berkeley Heights, NJ: Enslow (This book has a number of procedures for experiments, each followed with suggestions for a science fair).

Rau, D. (2004). *Jump rope.* Mankato, MN: Compass Point Books.

Rau, D. (2005). *Card games.* Mankato, MN: Compass Point Books.

Robbins, K. (1992). *Make me a peanut butter sandwich and a glass of milk.* New York: Scholastic.

Wiseman, A. (1973). *Making things: The handbook of creative discovery.* Boston, MA: Little, Brown.

Internet Resources With Mentor Texts to Illustrate the Genre

- https://explorer.compassion.com/type/recipes/ This site has recipes from all over the world. Some quite simple.
- www.enchantedlearning.com/crafts Multiple crafts in a variety of topics. Some access is free.
- Marshall, H. *How to make no-cook play dough easily.* www.ehow.com/how_5271462_make-nocook-play-dough-easily.html
- How to make a sea turtle. https://iheartcraftythings.com/sea-turtle-craft.html
- How to make slime, no words www.youtube.com/watch?v=0jfgl9iYq70&t=27s
- Video on *How to Make a Paper Plane.* www.youtube.com/watch?v=I0a0p8ygfQM
- *Hands-On Science: Over 40 fantastic experiments.* www.pinterest.com/pin/244249979765387305/
- *How to make a snow storm in a jar.* www.youtube.com/watch?v=5i6SkoJAEYA

Videos

- Video on How to Tie a Bow Tie with a live actor. It is not a good model of written procedures, but it could be used for students to create a written procedure. www.youtube.com/watch?v=wxKA9be_3Gk
- How to make a pilgrim hat. This one looks a lot like the written procedures. www.youtube.com/watch?v=17MtQxI6uhs
- How to make a paper airplane. It has no oral or written instructions. It makes for a great final activity to have the students write their own procedure. www.youtube.com/watch?v=v29M7Oa1l-A
- How to make a paper snowflake. www.youtube.com/watch?v=oCuk8E-MhdE (In this video there is too much conversation between the two people doing the procedure, making the instructions very unclear. It would be a good video to use toward the end of the unit to see if the students can extract the important information to create their own instructions.)

Professional Articles That Describe Instruction of the Genre

Paugh, P., & Moran, M. (2013). Growing language awareness in the classroom garden. *Language Arts, 90*(4), 253–267 (Procedure and Personal Recount).

References

Brisk, M. E. (2021). *Language in writing instruction: Enhancing literacy in grades 3–8*. New York: Routledge.

Butt, D., Fahey, R., Feez, S., & Spinks, S. (2012). *Using functional grammar: An explorer's guide* (3rd ed.). South Yarra, Victoria: Palgrave Macmillan.

Fang, Z. (1998). A study of changes and development children's written discourse potential. *Linguistics and Education, 9*, 341–367.

Hyland, K. (2007). Genre pedagogy: Language, literacy and L2 writing instruction. *Journal of Second Language Writing, 16*, 148–164.

Marks, G., & Mousley, J. (1990). Mathematics education and genre: Dare we make the process writing mistake again? *Language and Education, 4*(2), 117–130.

National Center on Education and the Economy. (2004). *Assessment for learning: Using rubrics to improve student writing*. Pittsburg, PA: The University of Pittsburg.

Veel, R. (2000). Learning how to mean—Scientifically speaking: Apprenticeship into scientific discourse in the secondary school. In F. Christie & J. R. Martin (Eds.), *Genre and institutions: Social processes in the workplace and school* (pp. 161–195). London: Cassell.

Zisselsberger, M. (2011). *The writing development of procedural and persuasive genres: A multiple case study of culturally and linguistically diverse students* (Unpublished doctoral dissertation). Boston College. Chestnut Hill, MA.

Chapter 3

Recounts and Memoirs

This chapter will cover two types of non-fiction narrative genres: those that recount author's experiences (personal recounts and memoirs) and those that recount authors' observations of experiences that they witness or experiments/math tasks they carry out (factual and procedural recounts). Each has a different purpose, and most of them have the comparable stages (see Table 3.1).

Personal recounts are often called "personal narratives." The two genres where the authors share their experiences provide a tool to create community, allowing students and teachers to know about each other. Children from other cultures will likely follow the norms of narratives in their cultures when writing personal recounts.

Development of Units

To develop units, teachers need to consider a number of factors that play a role on what and how to teach and what materials to use. With this in mind, they have to plan lessons.

Unit Preparation

To prepare a unit in the chosen recount genre, teachers need to consider the following:

- Grade level
- Connection with content areas

Table 3.1 Recount Genres

Name	Purpose	Stages	Example
Personal Recount	To tell what happened at a particular time based on a personal experience and to evaluate its significance.	Orientation Sequence of Events Conclusion	My experience with the gorilla last Sunday at the zoo.
Memoir	To tell what happened in the past, usually about a topic or collection of topics. It shows the author's feelings about what s/he is writing about.		Summers with my grandmother.
Factual Recount	To tell what the writer observed		A dispute between two students during a break.
Procedural Recount	To tell what happened when the author carried out a procedure (by her/himself or with others).	Aim Sequence of Events Conclusion (optional)	What happened when we carried out a scientific experiment.

DOI: 10.4324/9781003329275-3

- Mentor texts
- Research resources
- Potential projects, audience, and medium
- Uncoached writing and planning content of the unit

Grade Level

The Recount genres are taught from the very early grades, adding progressively more difficult types over the grades (see Table 3.2). Teachers across grade levels should plan together when deciding which genre to teach and what aspects of language to emphasize. In the very early grades, oral recounts and whole class recounts are a good way to start. Procedural recounts can be difficult for children to differentiate from personal recount. For example, the students in a 1st-grade science class mixed telling what they were personally doing, such as sitting around a table next to their friend and describing how they filled a pot with dirt, planted a seed, watered it and so on. In math, procedural recounts are commonly demanded of students to explain how they went about solving a problem. Procedural recounts are different from procedure. Procedures include the instructions for how to do something, whereas procedural recounts tell what happened based on observation.

Of the genres that recount personal experience, personal recounts are easier than memoirs and autobiographies. *Personal recount* is a good starting genre with younger students because they can use their personal experiences as the content for the writing. There is no need to research topics. One of the problems with personal recounts is that students often skip events, making the progression of the story confusing to the reader. *Factual* and *procedural recount* help students understand that they need to describe clearly what happened to create a complete observation. When students skip events in their observation, the teacher can easily point to the omission. The structure and language of *Memoirs* are similar to personal recounts, but they are harder for young learners with respect to choosing a topic because they need to abstract from their short lives. It is easier to think about what happened Sunday while visiting grandmother, than thinking of

Table 3.2 Recount Genres Across Grade Levels

Grade Level	Content Area		
	ELA	Social Studies	Science/Math
Pre-K	Personal Recount: Oral, whole class, individual dictation, individual writing		
K			
I			Procedural Recount: Whole class
2	Personal Recount: Individual writing		Procedural Recount: Whole class and individual
3	Memoir Factual Recounts		Procedural Recount: Individual
4			
5			
6			
7			
8			

Table 3.3 Key Aspects of Language to Teach

Aspect of Language	Grade Level to Teach	Example
Verbs: Formation of simple past tense	All grades	I _looked_
Verbs: Variety of one or two verbs repeated often	1st and 2nd grades	I _went_ outside (tiptoed, stepped, walked, etc.)
Verbs: Variety of verbs and of types	3rd grade up	I forked the meat (instead of "ate") Action: _ran_; sensing: _looked, felt, knew_; saying: _whispered_,
Difference between simple past and past continuous	3rd grade up	I _ran_ from the house. My Momma said, Don't slam the door!" I _wasn't listening_.
Adverbials of time and place	2nd grade and up	On a summer evening (time); behind the stairs (place)
Indirect ways of indicating time and place	4th grade and up	The snow fell softly on the trees. (winter); saw her mother cooking (in the kitchen)
Dialogue	3rd grade and up	Don't let your dinner get cold, said Momma. Please, may I go out? I pleaded.
Modifiers: Adjectives (after verb _to be_ and prenominal)	1st–3rd grade	His eyes were _big_ and _brown_. A _dusty_ jar sat on the piano.
Modifiers: All types	4th grade and up	The deer _with big, brown eyes_. I ran to watch the fireflies _making white patterns in the dark._ The deer _that came to my garden_ ate all the pears.

memorable events that happened while visiting grandmother in the summer. When implementing the genres with students who are just learning to write letters and words, students start by narrating orally. In addition, teachers support the writing by doing joint construction or taking dictation. Later in the year students may start writing individually (see Table 3.2).

The grade level where a genre is listed in this table refers to the grade level when the genre is most appropriate to be introduced. It can be practiced again in subsequent grade levels as long as over time there is opportunity to learn all of them as well as the historical genres discussed in Chapter 4. For example, if middle school students have not had a chance to write memoirs in elementary school, they are a good genre to introduce in 6th grade.

Aspects of language are introduced gradually over the grades (see Table 3.3). More complex language features can be developed when teaching historical genres (Chapter 4) and fictional narratives (Chapter 5).

Connection With Content Areas

Personal and _Factual Recounts_ as well as _memoirs_ are naturally part of ELA writing. Sometimes stories read in language arts remind students of personal experiences. They can also be connected with other content areas. _Procedural recounts_ are best embedded in science and math lessons. Examples of units where students carried out one of these genres in different content areas are provided in Table 3.4.

Mentor Texts

Mentor texts are written in the genre of the unit and are used to show students the features of the genre. It is important to choose mentor texts that clearly reflect the purpose of the genre. For

Table 3.4 Connecting Genre with Content Area

Genre	Content Area: Topic	Example
Personal Recounts, Memoirs, Factual Recounts	ELA/Social Studies: Building Communities	Students wrote recounts of experiences with classmates
	Science: Bodies of water	Personal recount about an experience in a body of water or Memoir of times spent near a body of water
Procedural Recounts	ELA/Social Studies: Food in our cultures	Write observations of cooking a traditional family recipe at home
	Math: Fractions	Describe process of solving a word problem involving fractions
	Science: Rock formation	Observations taken while carrying out the Frozen Rock Experiment

personal recounts, the mentor texts are actually fiction, but they are written as an experience that a child is recounting, fitting the genre. For example, *Alexander and the Terrible Horrible, No Good, Very Bad Day* and *Come On, Rain!* These two books have complementary features that support this genre. *Alexander and the Terrible, Horrible, No Good, Very Bad Day* would appeal to boys, is written in the past (expected of narrative genres), and has language accessible to young students. *Come On, Rain!* illustrates the use of descriptive language. It would appeal to girls because all of the characters in the story are female. It is an excellent example of taking a short event that occurred in a day in the life of a child and turning it into an interesting story, as opposed to children's "bed-to-bed" personal recounts describing their day. Mentor texts commonly read with younger students are helpful to teach writing to older students because these texts are more at the level of what they write. For example, Chloe used *Owl Moon* to work with her 6th graders when she first introduced to them to the personal recount genre (Pavlak & Hodgson-Drysdale, 2017).

Mentor texts for factual recounts are not readily available, except some sample accident reports (see mentor texts list downloadable from the *Support Material* tab in the book's webpage). Teachers can create one with the class by asking students to describe an incident they observed during break.

It is important to distinguish clearly between a Personal Recount, which is about a one-time event, and a Memoir, which is about events from the past with an emotional attachment to the author. For example, *Boy* by Roald Dahl has chapters on his childhood adventures. The chapter "The Great Mouse Plot" is short, entertaining, and has lots of the features of memoirs. In *Zlata's Diary: A Child's Life in Wartime Sarajevo*, Zlata Filipovic relates her evolving experience from everyday concerns of a child during normal times to the trying war experiences.

Some mentor texts tend to mix genres. It is important to be aware and, if using them, to make this clear to students. It is hard to find Procedural Recounts. Those such as *One Bean* and *Two Old Potatoes and Me* are good examples of observations of the process of a seed growing to a bean plant and old potatoes growing to full potato plants, respectively. Both, however, are embedded in a personal recount, *Two Old Potatoes* more than *One Bean*. For example, in a couple of occasions, *One Bean* has language that does not belong in a science procedural recount, but rather in a personal recount. The author, considering that her audience would be young children, tried to add some "fun" language, inserting phrases like, "just like in the story of Jack and the beanstalk— something wonderful happened!" and concluded with "I picked a few pods and ate the beans that grew inside them. And they were very, very good!"

For full references of the mentor texts mentioned in this section and other examples of mentor texts in the genres of this chapter, check the mentor texts and Internet resources files download-able from the *Support Material* tab in the book's webpage.

Research Resources

For *personal* and *factual recounts*, students do not have to do research because they are both based on personal experiences. Instead, students need to search their memories for events, not only of what they have done, but also of events they witnessed. They need to choose a memory worth writing about because it was exciting, funny, or it reveals something about themselves. Although children do not need to do research for personal recounts, it is worth teaching students how to explore what and why they want to write. They should consciously choose a topic that will entertain their audience. When connecting recounts to content areas, the topics would have been researched but the students have to search for experiences that relate to that topic.

It helps to introduce personal recounts and guide students through the structure of the text and language by basing writing on a shared experience. Teachers can help students incorporate all of the events because the teachers know what happened. For example, a kindergarten teacher walked her class to the nearby fire station, took pictures along the way (including pictures of individual children), and helped them construct their first personal recount based on this experience and supported by the photos.

Although *memoirs* are based on the students' lives, they still require some basic research, such as interviewing family members who can help the students recall the events in the chosen topic. Reading other people's memoirs may also help students chose a topic and remember events.

Procedural recounts draw their content from science experiments and math activities. In science lessons, the procedural recounts are based on observations that students make when carrying out an experiment or when they observe the habits of a class pet. The students need to take notes to use as the basis for their writing. In math, students solve a problem and then write their procedural recount on the basis of how they went about solving it.

Potential Projects, Audience, and Medium

As we saw earlier, projects can be closely connected with the content area where these writings are embedded. The different genres lend themselves to different audiences. For example, a pre-K teacher had the students illustrate and label a personal recount written as a book with all the activities that they did during the day to take home and show their parents. The audience for memoirs can be other students in the class as a way to build community. Factual recounts are a form of recording eyewitness accounts of incidents when conflicts emerge among students and the teacher needs to help solve them.

Depending on the genre and age, different writing media can be used. Personal recounts can take the form of picture books, letters, diaries, or journals. Memoirs often are written as picture books that include photographs. Factual recounts include texts and diagrams or images illustrating what happened. Procedural recounts often combine visuals illustrating the steps in the science experiments or solving math problems.

Uncoached Writing and Planning Content of the Unit

Sample Prompts for Uncoached Student Writing:

Personal Recount: Because this genre is recommended for kindergarten and 1st grade, there is no need to do an uncoached piece. If using the genre in later grades, teachers can ask the students to write about something interesting that happened to them in the past week.

Factual Recount: Describe an event that you witnessed on your way to school.

Procedural Recount: Carry out a simple experiment and ask the students to write what happened. Ask students to tell how they went about solving a math problem. Do it immediately after you have taught them how to do it.

Memoirs: Write about a memorable event in your life.

Teachers analyze students' writing using the Analysis of Student Work: Purpose, Stages, and Language form (downloadable from the *Support Material* tab in the book's webpage) to determine what the students can already do and what their challenges are. Teachers can use the Unit Template (Appendix A at the end of the book) to plan the necessary lessons.

Purpose, Stages, and Language: Theory and Practice

The rest of the chapter describes the purpose, stages, and key language of features to be included in lessons. Analysis of student work in relation to each aspect uncovers the challenges students have. Suggestions of lessons on purpose and stages are alternated with lessons on language (see Table 3.5). The table includes lessons for many aspects of language important to the genre. Teachers should select only two or three aspects of language to focus on and introduce it where indicated in the table and then practiced throughout the unit. Teachers should select lessons to teach depending on their students' needs and level of maturity. Eventually through the grades and the various genres, students will learn multiple aspects of language.

Purpose of Recounts

All the genres covered in this chapter have as their purpose to recount the past. *Personal recounts* document a sequence of events in an entertaining way and evaluate their significance. *Factual recounts* retell something that was witnessed by the narrator. *Procedural recounts* retell what happened when carrying out a procedure. *Memoirs* focus on a period of the author's life or specific events that the writer finds memorable (Derewianka & Jones, 2016).

Verb conjugation is one aspect of language that is worth exploring with purpose because specific genres call for specific tenses, with some variation. For example, recounts and historical genres, except in dialogues, are written in past tense because they chronicle events that happened in the past. Reports and explanations show how things are, thus they are written in the timeless present.

Young students and bilingual learners will need coaching on how to form the past tense for both the regular and irregular verbs. Some authors do write in the present tense when books are for young children. Even when using these books as mentor texts, the students tend to write their recounts in the past.

Jeanine Morris, a 1st-grade teacher who used the book *Come On, Rain!*, written in the present tense, wrote, "Most, if not all, of the personal narratives we read were written in the present tense, yet, the children automatically told their stories in past tense. I decided to not even call attention to tense when explicitly teaching unless there was a need, as I didn't want to add any confusion since we hadn't learned tense yet. The children never used any language other than past tense. I did however continually reiterate that a personal recount is an event that had already happened" (E-mail communication, 4/19/13).

Table 3.5 Teaching Language Parallel to Purpose and Stages

Lessons on Purpose and Stages	*Lessons on Language*
1. Purpose of the Genre 2. Purpose Is to Be Entertaining	3. Formation of Past Tense (for L2 Learners in Particular)
4. Deconstruction of Text to Learn About Stages of the Chosen Genre	5. Teach to Vary Verbs (Grades 1, 2, and Other Grades as Needed)
6. Practice Through Oral Retelling of Personal, Factual, or Procedural Recounts (Pre-K–Grade 1)	
7. Joint Construction of Personal, Factual, Procedural Recounts (Pre-K–Grade 1)	8. Teach Language Use Organically to Young Learners
9. Deconstruction of Text—Orientation Information (Grades K–8)	10. Hunt for Adverbial Phrases of Time and Place (Grades 2–8)
11. Deconstruction of Text—Style of Personal Recount Orientation (Grades 3–8)	
12. Jointly Constructed Orientations	Adverbials of Time and Place (Grades 2–8) (see Chapter 5, Lesson 15 "How to Write Indirectly the *Where* and *When*" [Grades 4–8])
13. Group or Individually Constructed Orientations	
14. Orientation of Procedural Recount	
15. Deconstruction of Text: Sequence of Events	16. Teach Variety of Types of Verbs by Deconstructing Text (Grades 3–8)
17. Deconstruction of Text: Development of Individual Events	18. Deconstruction: Adjectives (Grades K–2) and Other Modifiers (Grades 3–8)
19. Jointly Planned Sequence of Events (Grades 1–8)	Variety of Verb Types, Avoid Repetition, and Tense
20. Joint Construction of the Sequence of Events	Adverbials and Modifiers
	Teach Paragraph Formation (Grades 3–8) (see example of a lesson in Chapter 4, Lesson 15) 21. Teach to Insert Dialogue (Grades 3–8)
22. Individual or Group Planning and Construction of Sequence of Events	Practicing Language Features Learned 23. Teach the Difference Between the Use of Simple Past and Past Continuous (Grades 3–8) 24. Reference Ties
25. Joint Revision of Orientation and Sequence of Events	Focus on one or two language features in most need
26. Deconstruction of Text to Learn About Conclusion in Personal Recounts or Memoirs	Reinforce Variety of Types of Verb
27. Deconstruction of Text to Learn About Conclusion in Procedural and Factual Recounts	
28. Joint and Individual Construction of the Conclusion	
29. Students Create a Complete Draft of Their Project and Check Coherence	
30. Joint Revision of the Final Draft	Or Additional Language Lesson
31. Titles	

Lessons on Purpose and Stages	Lessons on Language

The following resources to support implementation of these lessons are downloadable from the *Support Material* tab in the book's webpage:

- Analysis of Student Work: Purpose, Stages, and Language (forms/rubrics)
- Graphic Organizers:
- Personal Recount (K–2)
- Personal Recount (3–5)
- Memoirs
- Factual and Procedural Recounts
- Mentor Texts That Illustrate the Genre
- Internet Resources With Mentor Texts

Features of Students' Writing

Of the two purposes of a personal recount (both describing what happened and being entertaining), the first seems to develop more naturally in students' writing. The latter is much harder to accomplish. A teacher commented that boys sometimes interpret "entertaining" to mean being crude. This can be a good time to have the students think about their audience and whether it is appropriate to be crude. A story becomes entertaining through the development of events and the use of language. For example, in *Salt Hands* the author builds anticipation through events of what the girl is going to find outside her house. *Alexander and the Terrible, Horrible, No Good, Very Bad Day* has many verbs describing actions, such as, *tripped, dropped, scrunched, smushed,* and so on.

Initially, kindergarten and 1st-grade students tend to draw a picture and simply describe it. For example, the first uncoached piece by a 1st grader early in the year had a picture of children eating doughnuts that were hanging from strings, and the writing underneath said, *We wr Eating the donuts.* The rest of her classmates had similar products. Personal recounts retell events rather than describe images of events. However, an author may choose to describe a picture as part of a personal recount. For example, in the book *Family Pictures*, each page includes a memory from the author's childhood in Mexico, accompanied by a picture and its description. By 2nd grade, as the following example shows, students understand that they need to retell what happened on the basis of their experiences, but they often feel a need to begin their writing with waking up and conclude with the end of the day, that is, "bed-to-bed" stories rather than focus on an event that it is worth retelling.

My First Day of School

Hello! My name is [student's name]. This morning My Dad said, Wake up Cinderalla! Sometimes My Dad calls me Smelly Marshmellow. Then I brushed my teeth, and changed my clothes.

Then Me and Helen also Kelvin. And all 3 of us combed our hair. And I had to comb Helen's hair first. Then my hair. Then we got in the car at 5:00 AM and we got to school at 6:30 Am Then we went in our classrooms. and I saw Mrs. W and [student's name].

People: Mrs. [teacher's name], My Dad, and [student's name]

	1	2	3	4	Uncoached Writing Comments
Purpose Varies depending on the specific type		√			Tells what happened, not entertaining
Verb Tense (past, except in direct speech)			√		Uses the present to introduce herself. Unnecessary in a personal recount

The second purpose, to entertain, is absent in the uncoached piece. There is no sense of excitement or anticipation in the writing and no description of anything in particular that happened that first day of school. The student did add images to her writing, such as a heart over the "i" in her name and images of a marshmallow face, her clothes, and of her and her siblings labeled with their names. Sixth graders were not any more imaginative when offering ideas on how to write the orientation of their personal recount. For example, a student proposed, "In 2009 I was 10 years old. Me [sic] and my grandfather went to Six Flags" (Pavlak & Hodgson-Drysdale, 2017, p. 29).

With instruction and natural development, students' writing will eventually focus on one aspect of their experience and become more entertaining. Sometimes, the prompts given to students to encourage writing derail the purpose. For example, a class was directed to write a personal recount of their favorite activities. One of the students wrote what read like a list of everything he likes to do, rather than choosing one thing and telling what happened one time.

Young children and L2 learners sometimes write in the present tense, not necessarily because they are unaware that it should be past tense, but because they do not know how to form the past. For example, a 1st grader wrote the following in his graphic organizer for a personal recount: *We went back home in the car and eat chickin nugets.* He changed the verb to "ate" in the final version after conferring with the teacher. Another common problem is the use of the past continuous, *I was going to New York City,* instead of the simple past, *I went to NYC.* There are two possible explanations. The first is that when children draw first before writing, they often write as if describing the picture. The other is that the continuous is the preferred initial tense of L2 learners. They commonly apply it to the present, past, and future. Even in middle school students had difficulty with tense consistency. For example, a bilingual 8th grader mixed the tenses in a personal recount with most in the past but occasionally inserting a sentence in the present: *As we drive home my sister continually talks about her plans . . .*

Lessons to Teach Purpose

Depending on the specific genre, the lesson content will vary.

Lesson 1. Purpose of the Genre

Goal: To discover the purpose of the chosen genre through exposure to different texts in the genre.

Materials: Short books, Internet examples, good examples written by students in previous years.

Activities

- Read to the students or let students read the examples.
- Discuss the purpose (see description of purpose for each genre earlier in the chapter). This can be done during reading time.

Lesson 2. Purpose Is to Be Entertaining (Personal Recount, Memoirs)

What makes a personal recount or memoir entertaining is well developed events and the specific language used. Students will learn these aspects of the genres in later lessons. At this point, it is just good to make them notice.

Goal: To learn what makes a text entertaining for a given audience.
Materials: Texts in the genre. Chart paper. Markers. Samples of student writing that could be edited to make the writing more entertaining.

Activities

- Read the mentor text and other sample texts in the genre to students.
- After reading each text, ask students the following: Did you like it [the text]? Was it fun? What made it fun?
- Jot down the ideas that described what made the text fun on chart paper. Use the list to help remind students when they are writing or revising their stories to add some of those entertaining features. For example, in *Come On, Rain!*, descriptions of the character's activities using language that makes them sound enjoyable to readers:

"It streams through our hair and down our backs. It freckles our feet, glazes our toes. We turn in circles, glistening in our rain skin. Our mouths wide, we gulp down rain."

- Show the students a student sample from the past that is not entertaining.
- Ask students about their audience. How they can write to make their audience want to continue reading their pieces (see Pavlak & Hodgson-Drysdale, 2017 for strategies used by a 6th-grade teacher working with bilingual learners).

Lesson 3. Formation of Past Tense (for L2 Learners in Particular)

Goal: To learn how to form the past tense, both regular and irregular. This is important for L2 learners who are not familiar with English grammar.
Materials: Projector. A paragraph of the recount, such as an excerpt from the autobiography *Child of the Civil Rights Movement*:

At first, I thought Jim Crow was a big black crow that squawked whenever a black person tried to get a good seat.
"CAWWW, CAWWW, you can't sit there!"
But really, he was a white man who lived long ago. He painted his face black and made fun of African Americans. He didn't sound very nice to me.

Chart to fill out with examples of the different past tense forms (see filled out example).

Activities

These activities are for the sections of the text that are not dialogue. When working with beginner L2 learners, you may simply distinguish between regular and irregular verbs working with a chart with just two columns. With intermediate and advanced and other students in general, use the more detailed approach in the activities that follow.

- Project the paragraph and with the whole class circle or highlight the verb groups that are not part of a dialogue.
- Ask the students to identify the present form for the first verb. Discuss the type and add it to the chart. For example, for *thought* it is *think*. Discuss that these verbs are irregular because

the two forms are different, and they just have to learn each form. Then add *thought* under the Irregular column.

- Ask the students with the help of a partner to look for other verbs where the past does not look like the present. For example, *was* and *made*. As they name them, add them to the chart.
- Point at the next verb type, for example, *squawked*. Discuss how this is the most common way to mark the past. They are called regular verbs because they add *-ed* to the present tense form.
- Ask again to find others in the text. They may suggest *tried, lived, painted*. Point out that they are correct to consider them regular, but *tried* and *lived* have a slight change in spelling when adding *-ed*, i.e. *try* to *tried* and *live* to *lived*.
- Point out *sound*. Ask them: Is this verb in the past? Why did the author not add *-ed*? Discuss the formation of negative past and add it to the chart.
- Leave the final chart up so that students can keep adding examples during other activities.
- When coming across a verb that does not change like *put*, add it to the chart, or you may add the most common from the start since they are a limited number. (For a complete list see www.goodverbs.com/english/unchangingverbs/1.)

Regular		Irregular	Unchanged	Did not + verb
-ed ending	*Change in spelling*			
painted	tried	thought	beat	didn't sound
	lived	was	cut	
		made	fit	
			hit	
			hurt	
			let	
			put	
			quit	
			read	
			set	
			shut	
			split	
			upset	

Follow up lessons to be done at various stages of the unit.

- Remind students when jointly and individually constructing text to use the past tense.
- During joint revision of drafts:
  - With permission from one of the students, project his or her writing.
  - Ask the class to point out the verbs in the student's writing, identifying those verbs that are part of direct speech (dialogue) and adding quotation marks when the dialogue does not include them.
  - Focus on the verbs outside of the dialogue. Ask the students if they are in the past. If the verbs are not in the past, ask students how they would change the verbs to be in the past.
  - Continue to add to the list of irregular past tenses (e.g., *bought, took, thought*).
  - Working in their groups or with a buddy, have students edit verb tenses in the pieces that they wrote.

Stages of Recounts

The stages of the various recounts are similar. However, the beginnings and endings tend to differ. Table 3.6 shows the various stages of these genres.

Personal recounts, memoirs, and factual recounts are quite similar in structure, with the exception that in the factual recount all events need to be precise observed facts, and there is no expression of feelings of the author. Procedural recounts are different, starting with the aim of the experiment or math problem. While feelings are expressed in the conclusion of personal recounts, a procedural concludes with the last event. An option is to recount what was accomplished or learned.

Ed, a 3rd-grade teacher, found that writing the sequence of events in a procedural recount helped students to understand the need to include all of the events that make the sequence clear. In personal and factual recounts and memoirs, it is more difficult to avoid gaps because the events are less tangible.

The stages need to come together in a coherent whole, where each stage is well developed and the content of the stages relates to each other.

Language Features of Recounts and Memoirs

Students' writing improves by working on the elements of the clause: verbs, noun groups, and adverbials. In the upper grades, it is also important to support students in their formation of the clause complex, including the ability to use dialogue. The specific language choices will depend on audience and voice. Development of paragraphs, the use of text connectives, and attention to reference ties further helps improve recount writing. Grades 4 through 8 should attend to all of these aspects of language in order to support students in writing texts that make sense to a reader. At this age, students want to express more complex ideas, and they need the language to do so. In lower grades, teachers may select certain language elements, building language skills as students progress through the grades. When working with 3rd grade and up, teachers should consult language lessons in Chapter 4 that are geared for older students and Chapter 5 where students are taught how to introduce dialogue.

Table 3.6 Stages of Recounts, Memoirs, and Autobiographies

Genre/ Stages	Orientation	Sequence of Events	Conclusion
Personal Recount	Who, Where, When, What (*when* and *where* may be indirectly stated)	Well developed events in the order they occurred	Last event, evaluation, or feelings of author
Factual Recount	Who, Where, When, What (explicitly stated)	Precise events in the order they occurred	Last event
Memoir	Who, Where, When, What: foreshadows what will happen	Events include: what happens and feelings, especially of the narrator; may include dialogue	Last events and feelings of the narrator
Procedural Recount	Aim	Events in the order they occurred	(Optional) What was learned or accomplished

Verbs

Verbs are very important in recounts and memoirs. There are five types of verbs: action, saying, sensing, relational, and existential (Derewianka, 2011). They express what participants do (*loaded, pointed*), say (*explained, answered*), think, feel, and perceive (*remembered, felt, thought, saw, sniffed*). The verbs *to be* and *have* (relational verbs) are used for descriptions. For example, *His eyes were big and brown. He had a chubby, round face.* There are other relating verbs, such as *become, appear, posses, include, represent* that give information about or describe what is named before, for example, *She appeared distressed.*

Existential verbs indicate a state (*there is/are/was/were*). For example, *Papa and Mama had not learned English. There was no need for it in the fields.* Students need to build their verbs resources to better communicate these meanings. In addition, they need to be able to write with a variety of verbs. Often, students repeat the same verb.

Students may need to use the passive voice in procedural recounts when using the third person (e.g., *the plants were watered twice a day*). Passive voice is useful in science when the focus is on the experiment rather than on the person doing the experiment. The switch in person is particularly difficult for children who are more likely to write, *I watered the plants twice a day*. In the early grades, students will likely write in the first person. In later grades, third person should be encouraged to keep the focus on the experiment.

Children also need to learn how to form the past tense in English when writing these genres. If the uncoached piece reveals this need, then it should be addressed early on in the unit. For that reason, lessons on past tense were added earlier with lessons on purpose. Tense will also need to be reviewed when teaching dialogue, which requires a variety of tenses.

Noun Groups

Well-developed noun groups help to describe precisely what the author is talking about, making the reading of their pieces more enjoyable for their audience. Even the simplest personal recount can show the author's knowledge of the subject through the nouns and modifiers used. For example, in *Come On, Rain!* there is substantial vocabulary related to summer weather, such as nouns (*thunder, lightning, heat, heat waves, clouds, sweat, breeze, wind*), adjectives (*broiling, gray, bunched, bulging, purple, crackling-dry, stuffy, hot, sizzling*), and similes (*sizzling like a hot potato, streaks like night lightning*). Through 2nd grade it is sufficient to teach students to use adjectives. In later grades other types of modifiers should be introduced (see Chapter 4).

Adverbials

There are a number of potential adverbials to use in recounts and memoirs, but the most important ones are those that indicate time and place. As recounts unfold, time passes and the action may occur in different places. The *Come On, Rain!* mentor text has a number of adverbials of place (*down the block; over rooftops; inside; in the dim, stuffy cave of her room; against her screen; in the kitchen*) and of time (*while Mamma weeds, as the clouds move off*). Adverbs of manner also help express how things happen (*quietly, purely, hard, tromping through puddles*). Narrative genres often use adverbials of time to connect sections of the narrative, rather than such words as *and* or *then* often used by young students, or sequencing words, such as *next, last, finally*.

Reference

A grammatical feature that helps achieve cohesion in a text is the use of referring words that refer back to something that has already been named. The most common is the use of pronouns.

For example, in the sentences: *Papa piles our suitcases into the trunk of our old car.* **He** *slides in our cooler.* The pronoun *he* refers to *Papa*, named earlier. Another referring word is the determiner *the*, used when the participant has been previously named. For example, the first time the author refers to a car, it reads, *We drove* **an** *old car.* Later, the reference to the car reads, **The** *car broke down half way to our village.*

Features of Student Work

Eric, a third grader, wrote this piece at the beginning of the personal recount unit. He showed a number of the typical language features of students' recounts before instruction.

Lego Land

I woke up in the morning and then I was in my car my DaD was Driving to Lego Land I went with my brother, 2 aunts, 1 uncle, my mom, grandma and grandpa. we Final got there then I walk in and i saw the huge Lego man. my First ride was a Lego rollercoster the rollercoster was made out of Legos. then i went on the volcano Swings then i had to Put some glasses on. Then went to the Lego Park. Last but Least I got a toy and my Family had Fun and they DiD the same thing as me. I went home and ate Food touh a Shower and went bed.

Aspect of Language	1	2	3	4	Uncoached Writing Comments
Verb Groups • Types • Repetition			√		Action verbs: *woke up, was driving, walk, put on, ate, took a shower, repeats, went, got* Sensing verb: *saw* Relating verbs: *Was, had*
Noun Groups **Use of Modifiers**	√				adjectives: *huge, some, Lego, my* (multiple times), *first, same, 2, 1, volcano*
Adverbials	√				place (*in my car, to Lego Land, there, on the Volcano Swings, to the Lego Park, home*) time (*in the morning, last but not least, Final* [Finally]) accompaniment (*with my brother …*).
Reference				√	There are no problems with reference. The students uses *we* with clear referents. The rest of the recount includes only the pronoun *I*.

Besides the use of past tense discussed earlier in the chapter, other challenges in verb use include using a variety of verb types to develop characters, make the story more exciting, and avoid repetition. Eric used mostly action verbs. There are no verbs indicating whether he was enjoying the experience. Children seldom use verbs indicating these feelings or thoughts. When using saying verbs, they tend to repeat *say*. For example, a 2nd grader in her short personal recount repeated *said* five times. Without instruction students tend to use the same verbs multiple times. Eric repeats *got* twice, *was* four times and *went* five times. A 1st-grade teacher commented that *went* was prevalent in his students' personal recounts. He encouraged them to think of other possible verbs, such as *dashed, drove, walked,* or *took the bus.* Even middle school students used *went* and *was* multiple times. *Was* can be eliminated by packing sentences, something to be taught beginning in the latter part of 3rd grade. For example, *First ride was a Lego rollercoster the rollercoster was made out of Legos* could be packed to "We first rode a rollercoster made out of Legos," eliminating both *was*. Word repetition and using *and* to connect sentences signals the need for sentence packing. For example, a 7th grader wrote *After the movie we went to John's Pizza and ordered a large cheese pizza.* It could be packed to "After the movie we ate a large cheese pizza at John's Pizza," eliminating *went* and *and.*

The greatest challenge with noun groups is the lack of modifiers describing the people and places in the recounts. In Eric's piece only *huge* adds interest to the description. If there is a description, it is usually as a relational sentence and not a complex noun group. For example, a 1st grader wrote, *I saw a piranha. It was big . . .*, rather than simply adding the adjective to the noun group, *I saw a big piranha.* As Eric's piece shows, students tend to use mostly numerals and possessives. Without modifiers the writing does not reflect the author's perspective. For example, a 7th grader starts his personal recount about his birthday with *A fun day.* However, the descriptions do not really reflect it was fun. The whole piece is mostly a list of all the activities he did with his friends. There were no modifiers indicating that the activities were fun. For example, *we went to the movie* does not say anything about the movie. He could have added "a movie that I had wanted to see for a long time." *We played soccer* could have been qualified by writing, "my team won a contested game of soccer."

With respect to adverbials, most students use adverbials of place and some of time, but the latter are often rather generic, such as *once* or *after.* As they mature, they use adverbial phrases or clauses, such as *As the car parks* (8th grade) or *At around 9:30* (7th grade). Even in middle school, it is rarer to find students using adverbs of manner with *-ly* endings, such as *carefully* and *sadly.* In Eric's piece, the adverbial of time *Finally*, lacked the ending *-ly.*

Using pronouns with a clear referent is a challenge for young writers. A typical feature of personal recounts in students' writing is the use of *we* early in their recount before naming who the participants are who make up *we.* For example, a 4th-grade student started his personal recount with *"Hurry up, we are going on a trip,"* my dad yelled. For the rest of the orientation, it would appear that the narrator and the father are going somewhere together. In the next paragraph, however, the mother is mentioned and two paragraphs later a sister is mentioned. Thus, *we* stood for all four people. However, there was no way to know that *we* referred to four people in the first paragraph.

Younger children have difficulty tracking the appropriate use of pronouns and names of the participants described in their involved recounts. For example, a 3rd grader wrote a recount about being injured during break. As she describes being taken to the nurse, she refers to *he* and *they* helping them, but it is not clear who *they* are and whether the *he* and *they* represent different participants.

Lessons to Learn About Stages and Language of Recounts

The first lessons present the stages in a general way. Later, each stage (orientation, sequence of events, and conclusion) is presented in more depth, including challenges that students encounter. Another consideration is whether to teach and have students write one stage at a time or complete one class project together and then have individual or groups work on their own projects. The former is easier than the latter because students do their own specific section of the text immediately after it has been deconstructed and jointly constructed as a class. The lessons in this chapter illustrate the first approach, and those in Chapter 4 demonstrate how to work with the whole class, producing together one whole project first and then having the students follow the same process to produce their own pieces.

Teachers are encouraged to review all of the lessons related to the stages and decide what will be appropriate for their own grade level. In early grades, a teacher might create a whole project together for publication, while in later grades the class can publish a text produced together and others produced individually.

Oral recounts can continue throughout the unit, directing the questions to the focus of the lesson. For example, when the focus of a lesson is to teach students to name their participants, if a student says, "I went with my cousin . . .," the teacher should ask for the name of the cousin. Observations of oral recounts provide data for future lessons. For example, if an L2 learner says, "She bringed me a toy," the teacher should note to include the irregular past of this verb when teaching the past tense.

Lesson 4. Deconstruction of Text to Learn About Stages of the Chosen Genre

Goal: To notice in a broad way the stages of the genre in published texts.
Materials: Short mentor texts familiar to the students. Graphic organizer on large chart paper.

Activities

- Re-read some of the books, including the mentor text.
- Discuss the stages in a general way. For example, ask students to notice what kind of information the author includes at the beginning, in the body of the text, and at the end. Point out the stages in the graphic organizer as you discuss them, using their names: orientation, sequence of events, and conclusion.
- With grades 3–8 discuss coherence of the text, i.e., the topic of the text aligns through the stages, making it comprehensible to the reader. For example, in the memoir *The Great Mouse Plot* by Roald Dahl, the orientation introduces the secret place, and all the events relate to what the students planned and carried out to annoy their teacher.

Lesson 5. Teach to Vary Verbs (Grades 1, 2, and other Grades as Needed)

Young students tend to overuse the same verbs, for example *went*, *got*, and *said*, when using dialogue. If students in later grades do it too, then use this lesson.

A. Teach to Vary Verbs

Goal: To have students avoid repeating *went*, *got*, *said*, or any other verb that appears multiple times in their writing.
Materials: Student work.

Activities

- Have students write a personal recount based on what they have already learned.
- Project one of the student's pieces, and ask the author to circle *went*, *got* or *said*. It is best to work with just one verb at a time. For example, a 1st grader started his personal recount,

  *When I was five me and my DaD went to Columdia on a plane. We were at the airport. I **got** foob. I **got** a bonut and milk. I **got** on the plane*

- Have them brainstorm with your help other ways to say *got*. For example, the edited version would read, "My dad **ordered** food. I **chose** a donut and milk. I **boarded** the plane."

- For *went* and *said*, you can brainstorm and make a list of verbs first, such as *run, walked, tiptoed, drove,* or *answer, asked, whispered,* and then have the class suggest where to insert substitutions. Not all need to be changed.
- Working with a partner, have them circle the verbs *went, got,* or *said* in their writing.
- Ask students to propose changes.

Lesson 6. Practice Through Oral Retelling of Personal, Factual, or Procedural Recounts (Pre-K–Grade 1)

Goal: To practice telling a personal recount orally in order to enhance the components of the recount.

Materials: A class list with the days of the week to keep track of which students have shared and when.

Activities for Personal Recount

- Sit in a circle. Tell students that a few will be sharing something that happened to them.
- Tell your own (the teacher's) personal recount the first time to model.
- Choose one or two students each day to tell something that happened to them.
- Probe when more information is needed. For example, when students start telling their recount, have them make it clear when it happened, where it happened, and who (other than the narrator) was there. If students skip events, making the recount unclear, probe them, and encourage other students to do the same. This practice can be done throughout the year.

Activities for Factual Recounts

- Have students observe students playing during break, an animal at the zoo, or some other activity and take a series of pictures.
- Using the pictures, have a few students share observations.
- Support them by asking questions when they leave out important facts.
- Repeat with other activities, choosing different students to share.

Activities for Procedural Recount

- Carry out an experiment and take a picture of each step, or write down the steps of solving a math equation on chart paper.
- Ask a few students to share the steps they took to do the experiment or solve the equation.
- Support them by asking questions when they leave out important steps.
- Repeat with other activities, choosing different students to share.

Lesson 7. Joint Construction of Personal, Factual, or Procedural Recounts (Pre-K–Grade 1)

Goal: To apprentice students to write recounts by doing them together. This activity can be done several times. For young learners, especially when done early in the year, these can be their final products.

Materials: Chart paper or projector.

Activities for Personal Recount

There are two ways to produce the joint construction:

1 Choose one of the recounts that a student told orally that sounded interesting, remind the class about it, and have the whole class participate in writing the recount on chart paper or project it so that all can see. The (student) author should provide the necessary information.
2 Do an activity together, such as a field trip or a walk around the block. Then, have the whole class construct the recount together. The only problem with this activity is that it will be told in the first person plural (using "we" instead of "I"), differing from the students' individual pieces.

After the piece is finished, you may:

- Publish jointly constructed pieces after undergoing revisions.
- Ask students to copy the joint product in their own notebook and illustrate it. In the case of a field trip, they can take their writing (and drawing, if illustrated) home to share with their families.

Activities for Factual and Procedural Recounts

- Using the photos or math activities in chart paper, ask students what to write.
- Ask questions when students leave important steps out.
- Publish jointly constructed pieces after undergoing revisions.

The teacher should then decide whether the students are ready to write independently any of these types of recounts, stimulating ideas for the joint construction.

Jeanine Morris carried out the following sequence of lessons for the personal recount unit with her 1st-grade class:

1 Teacher read aloud and then deconstructed several texts using the graphic organizer.
2 Students orally told personal recounts related to weather (the topic of the mentor text, *Come on, Rain!*) The teacher gave the first recount, and then students told their own personal experiences.
3 Teacher discussed with the students the purpose of a personal recount, comparing and contrasting with procedure, the genre they had written previously.
4 Teacher and students jointly constructed a graphic organizer using a class story.
5 Teacher and students jointly constructed various stages of the personal recount using the information in the graphic organizer. Steps 4 and 5 were repeated with several class stories.
6 Students wrote individual personal recounts.
7 Teacher modified graphic organizer to facilitate listing events (see K–2 organizer downloadable from the *Support Material* tab in the book's webpage).
8 Class played the writing orientation game.

9 Students worked in groups to create their graphic organizers and wrote a group story. Working with one group, the teacher and students jointly constructed the graphic organizer. She then let them work on their writing while she worked with other groups.

10 Students began independently writing their personal recounts.

11 Students inserted the information for the orientation and the list of events in their graphic organizer.

12 Teacher taught students how to enrich each event by writing probing questions next to the events that needed more information.

13 Teacher conferred with the students and added the information they mentioned in response to her questions in the boxes for each event.

14 Students used the information in the graphic organizer to write their individual personal recounts.

Lesson 8. Teach Language Use Organically to Young Learners

With young students it is best to address language improvement in the context of planning their writing.

Goal: To improve aspects of writing reasonable for their age.
Materials: Students' filled out graphic organizers.

Activities

As students plan their writing in their graphic organizers:

- Confer with individuals, pairs, or groups, focusing on a few aspects of language.
  - For verb tense: point at the tense and ask when the actions were happening.
  - To eliminate too much repetition: ask questions such as *how did he go?* (to find an alternative to *went*).
  - To include more feeling, thinking, or verb types other than action: Ask, how did you feel when your friend shared her chocolate? Did you know what that animal ate? And so on.
  - To include adverbials: Ask, when did it happen? Where did it happen? And so on.
- Do the same for other language aspects without overwhelming the students.
- Add what they tell you to their plans, and encourage them to use it when they write their drafts.

By making the revisions in the graphic organizer, you help the student before they produce a full recount, when it is more difficult for students to be willing to make changes.

Orientation of Recounts

The orientation in narrative genres is the introduction, where the author situates what will happen by introducing some of the people involved, where and when the narrative starts, and giving some indication of what will happen. The orientation in personal and factual recounts as well as memoirs is quite similar and includes answers to the questions of *who, where, when,* and *what happened.* For example, *The Great Mouse Plot* starts

> My four friends and I had come across a loose floor board at the back of the classroom, and when we prised it up with the blade of a pocket knife, we discovered a big hollow place underneath.

The *where* is missing, but it is named later with the next event where it really matters.

In procedural recounts, the orientation usually includes the *aim.* For example, *I created a graph to show the favorite art supplies student use.* Occasionally, the aim may be missing in some recounts as is the case in the book *One Bean,* which starts describing what happened.

In personal recounts and memoirs, some of the features are shown indirectly or through images. For example, in *Come On, Rain!,* the author indicates that it is summer by talking about "endless heat" and "parched plants." In picture books information may be embedded in the images. For example, in Salt Hands the *where* is evident from the image of a child sitting in her bed.

Orientations of personal recounts and memoirs can be written in different styles. These styles can include:

- traditional narrative (*Yesterday morning, I drove to New Hampshire with my Uncle Nestor and his family.*)
- action (*I got up early in the morning and rushed to get dressed and have breakfast. Shortly after, my Uncle Nestor came by to pick me up to go to New Hampshire.*)
- dialogue (*"Hurry up and get dressed," my mother ordered, "your Uncle Nestor is coming in 5 minutes to take you to New Hampshire with his family."*)

Features of Students' Writing

The 2nd grader who wrote "My First Day of School" (shown at the beginning of the unit) had mixed success in writing an orientation in her first uncoached personal recount.

	1	2	3	4	Uncoached Writing Comments
Orientation		√			Starts by addressing the reader directly: *Hello!* Includes the main participant and her father and *when.* *Where* is assumed. Doesn't tell the *what,* except in the title. Uses dialogue.

She starts by addressing the reader, a feature often found in children's writing, but rarely found in published recounts. This habit was pervasive among 4th graders' writing analyzed at the beginning of the personal recount unit in preparation for the state test.

Before coaching, orientations may be missing from student writing altogether or be limited. Several of the kindergarten students early in the year drew elaborate pictures and dictated a sentence that mostly included the *what* of the orientation (*I went to target or I went swimming*). Next, *where* usually appears (*I go to sports to swimming at the doorchestr hoese*). A 3rd grader, rather new to English, also included the *when* (*In the furst Day of somr* [summer] *I whit* [went] *two* [to] *waturcochree* [Water Country]). When working with 4th graders to prepare them for high-stakes test that called for a personal recount, teachers noticed that many practice recounts were interesting and well written except that they began with "One day . . .,"—a rather uninteresting start. Teachers introduced a lesson on adverbial phrases of time that would better describe the *when.*

After coaching, the elements begin to emerge in student writing, but there are still some challenges. First graders included the information, but in multiple short sentences (*I went in my car with my Dad and sister. we drove to the aquarium.*). This could have simply said, *I drove to the aquarium with my Dad and sister.*

Even when all of the information was present, the style in personal recounts did not change until students reached the upper grades when actions and dialogue were introduced. When students are first introduced to these features, however, they may overuse them. For example, a 4th grader wrote, *It was march 25th the best day of this whole year Relax day !!! I screamed till the top of my lungs every one came down the stairs like a bullet . . . .* Only is it in later grades and toward the end of the unit that students use indirect ways of indicating elements of the orientation. For example, a 5th grader showed that her recount started on a road in the winter through her descriptions: *In the back seat in my mom's black Honda . . . I saw towering pine trees covered in a sheet of white snow.*

Prompts can make for awkward orientations. For example, a 7th grader writing in response to a prompt that requested "to write about a fun time you had this past year," started, *A fun day that I enjoyed this past year is my birthday.* It is important to tell students that they do not need to restate the prompt but use it as guide for what they have to write.

Lessons to Teach the Orientation

There are two aspects to consider when writing an orientation: the information needed and the style. Identifying the information to be included in the orientation can be done with students of all ages. Styles are best examined and taught with grades 3 and up.

The lessons that follow can be used with any of the genres and grade levels, adjusting for mentor texts and graphic organizers based on the chosen genre. Students usually write multiple personal recounts of individual or class experiences. For the other genres, because there is research or special activities involved, students or groups may focus on producing one or two pieces. The level of elaboration will depend on the age and language proficiency.

Lesson 9. Deconstruction of Text—Orientation Information (Grades K–8)

If teaching Procedural Recount, first review Lesson 14. This genre has a very different orientation from the others in this chapter.

> **Goal:** To learn the information that goes in the orientation to help students write informative orientations.
>
> **Materials:** Several mentor texts in the recount genre of the unit. Orientation graphic organizer on chart paper. Copies of the graphic organizer corresponding to the genre, i.e., with *who, when, where, what*, for all genres, except with *aim* for procedural recount.

Activities

- Read the orientation in the mentor text. The information of the orientation is found in the first couple of paragraphs.
- Discuss which information will go in which column of the graphic organizer. Point out that authors sometimes give the information indirectly through images or descriptions. You may fill out the graphic organizer or use it to point at the elements. For young students, it helps to ask questions *When? Where?* and so on.

- Repeat the activity with a couple of other books.
- Give each group one or more texts and a copy of the graphic organizer in which they can write down the information found in the book. Walk around the room checking their work and noting anything that will require further instruction. (This last activity is appropriate for students who can already read.)

Lesson 10. Hunt for Adverbial Phrases of Time and Place (Grades 2–8)

> **Goal:** To explore how authors use adverbial phrases of time to move the recount forward and of place to indicate location and change of location of events.
>
> **Materials:** Mentor text in the genre. Additional texts that have examples of these phrases or clauses. Projector.

Activities

- Read the mentor text aloud and ask students to signal when they hear information that tells the reader when events happened, i.e., an adverbial of time. If you have L2 learners, project the text so that they can hear and see the text.
- List the adverbials of time in an anchor chart, and keep it up for students' reference when they are writing.
- Give students other books and, working in pairs or groups, have them look for additional examples.
- Ask students to add examples to the class list.
- Go through the list and ask students to suggest variations. For example, for *Before the sun is up*, they could suggest *Before eight o'clock*, *Before the sun rose*, or *Before my father arrived*.

Follow Up During Later Lessons

- During joint construction: Encourage the use of adverbials as you jointly construct the class project.
- During individual construction:
  - Remind students of the adverbials in the anchor charts.
  - Working in groups, ask students to examine their writing and see where they could add an adverbial of time to improve the meaning of their recount. (You may want to demonstrate with one or two students' samples first.)
  - Repeat the activities with adverbials of place that answer to the question *where?* Alternatively, do both at the same time.

Lesson 11. Deconstruction of Text—Style of Personal Recount Orientation (Grades 3–8)

Although this lesson is more appropriate for upper grades, if younger students notice the differences in the mentor text, you may decide to teach the styles.

> **Goal:** To learn to write orientations in different styles to make them more interesting and varied.
>
> **Materials:** Mentor texts familiar to the students with different orientation styles (traditional, action, and dialogue).

Activities

- Distribute the mentor texts among groups in your class.
- Have students describe the style used in the mentor texts.
- Ask groups to read selections aloud and say which style the author used. For example, in *Come On, Rain!*, the orientation is written as a dialogue. In *Owl Moon*, the style is more traditional: "It was late one winter, night, long past my bedtime, when Pa and I went owling." In *Alexander*, the information of the orientation is included in a series of actions. In the *Red Scarf Girl: A Memoir of the Cultural Revolution*, it starts with a person talking to the narrator: " 'Now, you have to choose between two roads.' The man from the Revolutionary Committee looked straight into my eyes."

Lesson 12. Jointly Constructed Orientations

Goal: To practice defining information and translating it to a written orientation with the students.

Materials: Orientation graphic organizer on chart paper, corresponding with the specific genre.

Activities

- Establish the content of the class recount:

  a *Personal or Factual Recount:* Content based on an activity that was done as or witnessed by a whole class, for example, during a field trip or an event in the school or on an individual student recount, especially one who could use extra help.

  b *Procedural Recount:* Content based on a math problem solved as a class, a science experiment done as a class, or a math problem solved by a student who could use extra help.

  c *Memoir:* Choose one student who could use help with his or her writing. Ask him or her to offer the information and get the class involved by asking questions and making additional suggestions. Alternatively, the teacher could model the joint project with her/his memoir.

- Create a large Orientation graphic organizer.
- Using the content from the focus genre, solicit ideas from the students and write the information on the Orientation graphic organizer.
- Take information from each column of the graphic organizer and ask the class for suggestions on how to write it. Propose revisions if needed.
- For personal recount and memoirs, use the style graphic organizer to get suggestions from the class on how to write three different orientations (grades 3–8 only). Ask the class if they want to change anything in the orientation to indicate some of the information indirectly (this does not have to be done every time). Ask the class to vote for the orientation that they like best, and use it as the beginning of the class recount.

Language Practice: Adverbials of Time and Place (Grades 2–8)

- As the class fills out the graphic organizer, point at the anchor charts with adverbials of time and place to inspire students to use informative adverbials. If students propose generic adverbials, such as *once* or *one day*, ask them questions to think of others.
- Remind students to use them when jointly constructing the orientation paragraph.

When teaching any of these genres to students in grades 4 and up, demonstrate how to write the *where* and *when* indirectly (see Lesson 15 in Chapter 5).

Lesson 13. Group or Individually Constructed Orientations

In this lesson students work in groups planning and producing the orientation of their piece, even when producing individual pieces. Adaptations are recommended for different grade levels. For example, after kindergarten students write their personal recount, the teacher uses questions to help them build their orientations. Ed, a 3rd-grade teacher, after deconstructing mentor texts, had students write the orientation first and then check it with the graphic organizer to see if they covered all the elements. He felt the writing was more fluid than filling out the graphic organizer and then writing.

> **Goal:** To start releasing responsibility and encourage the students to plan and write orientations more independently.
> **Materials:** Copies of the orientation graphic organizer corresponding to the genre, paper, or a Google doc to write on.

Activities

* Group or pair the students (even if producing independent work).
* Give each students a copy of the orientation graphic organizer.
* Ask each group to discuss what they will write about either together or individually.
* Ask the groups to say, draw, or make notes of the information in the graphic organizer (depending on age and ability to write).
* Using the information in the graphic organizer, have students dictate or write their group or individual orientations, depending on their ability to write.
* Depending on students' ability and preference, have students draw before or after they write, illustrate the events, or dictate the recount. In the case of procedural recounts, the visuals tend to be diagrams, rather than narrative illustrations.

Lesson 14. Orientation of Procedural Recount

Since in procedural recount students need to just write the aim, the lesson can introduce all three: deconstruction, joint construction, and individual construction of the aim. These can be done in the same way it was done for the other genres but focusing on the one element: the aim.

As we saw earlier, certain mentor texts start directly with the events. Students can be asked to propose what the aim could be. For example, after reading *One Bean*, ask the student, "What was the aim of the experiment these two children carried out?" They would respond, "To observe how a seed turned into a plant."

Sequence of Events in Recounts

Personal, factual, and procedural recounts include a sequence of events in the body of the text that follows the order in which they occurred. For example, the first few events in the personal and procedural recount mentor texts are the following:

Come On, Rain!	One Bean
• Asks to wear a bathing suit	• Has a dry bean
• Observes what is happening in the neighborhood around her house	• Moistens it
• Sees rain clouds	• Plants the bean
• Runs out to look for her friend, Jackie-Joyce	• Waters the bean
• Runs back home and makes some iced tea for her mother	• Bean sprouts

Memoirs bundle the sequence in various episodes in the life of the author. When working with younger students, the class can create one class memoir of a topic or two, for example, visits to my grandmother, moving to the U.S., and so on. Thus, each student writes about one such episode. For example, in using the memoir *Boy* by Roald Dahl, just *The Great Mousse Plot* served as mentor text.

In personal recounts and memoirs, writers make these events entertaining by developing each of them with interesting events and language. The following two examples from mentor texts describe how an event was further developed in a personal recount (left) and a memoir (right):

Come On, Rain!	*Red Scarf Girl: A Memoir of the Cultural Revolution*
Event: Runs out to look for her friend Jackie-Joyce	**Event**: Principal and soldier come to class
• Crosses a path	• Principal and soldier walk into music class
• Goes by Miz Glick's window	• Description of the soldier
• Peers inside and sees a phonograph playing	• Class stands up and soldier walks around looking at everyone
• Smells the tar and garbage	• Another student and I are told to follow the soldier to the gym
• Gets to Jackie-Joyce's house	
• Jackie-Joyce comes out wearing shorts	
• Asks her to put on her bathing suit and come over to her house	
• Runs back home	

Personal recounts sometimes include a reorientation to round up the events before the conclusion. For example, in *Come On, Rain!* before the conclusion, it says: "As the clouds move off, I trace the drips on Mamma's face. Everywhere, everyone, everything is misty limbs, springing back to life." *Alexander* does not include a reorientation, but instead a final unfortunate event before the concluding evaluation.

Features of Students' Writing

In the early writing, the entire recount is one simple event (*My uncle brought in a pigeon*). The richness of this kindergartener's recount is in the elaborate drawings that included several family members watching the pigeon in amazement. With maturity, the number of described events increases, as we saw earlier in the 2nd grader's recount on the first day of school. However, minimal information about each event is included, and additional details would be helpful.

	1	*2*	*3*	*4*	*Uncoached Writing Comments*
Sequence of Events		√			Includes 4 events that span over time giving little information about them, except #2.

Middle school students listed many more events, but few were fully developed. For example, a 7th grader recounting his birthday included eight different activities he did with his friends, but most were just named. For example, *We played Black Apps. We then had cake and watched tv.* Only some of the better writers in upper elementary and above, with much coaching, elaborated on individual events. For example, a 4th grader describes in some detail his experience using the chair lift when going skiing: *I got my gear and went to the chair lift. I waited less 5 seconds, it was coming towards me and the chairlift scooped me up. When I pulled the bar down, I was so scared. But when I looked out, it was so beautiful.*

Often, young writers conclude their recount describing going to sleep at the end of the day. Rather than rounding up a particular well-developed story, they round up the day.

Lessons to Teach Sequence of Events and Language

Students need to learn how to write a sequence of events and make each event interesting by including several related actions and descriptions. When deconstructing text, it is best to outline the major events and then deconstruct one of them in detail. Further practice of deconstructing individual major events can be done with other recounts that students read.

In the case of factual and procedural recounts, it is important to include and detail everything because the information is essential to accomplish the purpose of the genre.

Lesson 15. Deconstruction of Text: Sequence of Events

> **Goal:** To have students identify major events, to learn how this aspect of recounts is written, and realize that personal recounts are not bed-to-bed stories.
> **Materials:** Chart paper or projector. Mentor text previously used.

Activities

* Project a timeline or write it on chart paper.
* Re-read the mentor text in chunks, and ask students to name the major events.
* Circle, highlight, or write what the students suggest, negotiating changes when necessary. Point out specific features of each genre:

  * Personal recounts: do not usually start with waking up and end with going to sleep.
  * Factual and procedural recounts: cannot skip events.
  * Memoirs: like personal recounts need well-described events that make the piece entertaining.
  * With grades 3–8, discuss how the text is clear to the reader because there are no gaps in information or unrelated information.

Lesson 16. Teach Variety of Types of Verbs by Deconstructing Text (Grades 3–8)

> **Goal:** To provide ideas of how authors use different verb types (action, sensing, saying, and so on) in order to present well-rounded people. This is particularly important in personal recount and memoirs. Procedural and factual recounts use mostly action verbs.
> **Materials:** Paragraph from the same mentor texts used in the previous lesson, ready to share with the whole class. Chart paper or projector. Copies of additional paragraphs.

Activities

* Isolate the verbs in the paragraph using chart paper or a projector. For example, in the memoir *The Great Mouse Plot*, the author writes:

*The other four **stared** at me in wonder. Then, as the sheer genius of the plot **began to sink in**, they all **started grinning**. They **slapped** me on the back. They **cheered** me and **danced** around the classroom. "We'll **do** it today!" they **cried**.*

- Describe verbs as words that tell us what is happening, what the participants are doing, saying, and sensing (i.e., feeling, thinking, perceiving) and relating (mainly *be* and *have* but also *become, appear, possess, include, represent,* and others).
- Discuss with students how the variety of verb types the author used gave us a good picture of the excitement of the boys. Action: *started grinning, slapped, cheered, danced, do.* Perceiving: *stared.* Thinking: *began to sink in.* Saying: *cried.*
- Start an anchor chart organized by type of verb. Continue to add examples and leave it displayed throughout the unit for students to consult when writing.
- Working in groups or pairs, distribute copies of additional paragraphs and have students repeat the activity. Invite them to add examples to the anchor chart.

Follow Up

- Encourage use of a variety of verbs when doing joint construction by pointing them out in the anchor chart, and suggest other verbs as needed.
- Encourage use when doing individual construction.
- Review use through conferencing and joint revision.

Lesson 17. Deconstruction of Text: Development of Individual Events

Goal: To show students how each event is well developed to make their writing more interesting or informative depending on the genre.

Materials: Chart paper or projector and mentor text.

Activities

- Choose a major event in the mentor text, and project it or write it on top of the chart paper (see examples shown earlier from *Come on, Rain!* or *Red Scarf Girl: A Memoir of the Cultural Revolution*).
- Re-read the passage and ask students to identify the detailed information that the author gave.
- Circle or highlight on text or write these notes in collaboration with the class on the chart paper. Leave the chart paper up as an example.
- For grades 2 and up, give groups of students a mentor text from the genre of the unit and a worksheet with space to write the major event from the text at the top. Have students look at the text, choose one major event, write it on top of the worksheet, and then write the sub-events below.

For 1st grade, a teacher helped the students expand their events through questions (see the following box).

Jeanine, a 1st-grade teacher, worked to enhance the events in their personal recounts by conferring with the students about their notes in their graphic organizers. Students increased and varied the information in their plans in response to Jeanine's questions. As students made suggestions orally, she wrote them down in their graphic organizers. For example, a student had written in one of the event boxes, *Then we went inside the aquarium*. After answering questions and discussing the material from the graphic organizer, the new sentence read, *We went inside. I saw a piranha. It was big. I felt a shark. It felt soft. It was cool. I wasn't afraid. My sister was a little afraid. A shark almost bit her!* As the student transferred this information to his final piece, he added more things that he saw.

Lesson 18. Deconstruction: Adjectives (Grades K–2) and Other Modifiers (Grades 3–8)

Goal: To impress upon students the power of adjectives or other modifiers when portraying a picture of what they are writing about.

Materials: One or two paragraphs from the mentor texts used in the previous lesson. Chart paper or projector.

Activities

• Display one or two paragraphs from the mentor text, covering the modifiers.

For example, if you are teaching personal recounts, project this example paragraph with adjectives covered (crossed out text):

I dressed the doll in a ~~long full red~~ skirt, ~~tiny black felt~~ boots, and a ~~bright yellow high-necked~~ blouse.

Ask to students to (a) draw the doll or (b) describe what the doll was wearing.

• Uncover the adjectives, read the selection again, and ask the students to draw or describe the doll again.
• Discuss with the students the difference that adjectives make.

For upper grades, find a text that has other modifiers as well as adjectives (in **bold**). For example, this passage from the memoir *Red Scarf Girl*:

I found myself in a **narrow** passageway between the **school** building and the **school-yard** wall. The **gray concrete** walls closed around me, and a **slow** drizzle dampened my cheeks .... I felt like a **small** animal **that had fallen into a trap**.

• As before, ask students to describe the scene first with the modifiers covered and then, with them visible. You can further ask specific questions, such as how was the passageway? What kind of building? What kind of wall? How was the animal?

Lesson 19. Jointly Planned Sequence of Events (Grades 1–8)

Goal: To apprentice the students to planning a sequence of events in order to learn to avoid gaps and be informative.

Materials: A large timeline for 3rd grade and up and a column of boxes for younger grades (see graphic organizers at the end of this chapter). Chart paper or computer and projector.

Activities

- Choose the topic: For personal recount, start with a fresh story, either from an individual student who could use extra help or from an experience that you (the teacher) and the students shared. For the other genres, continue with the topic you started.
- Decide the major events with the class, and write them down either on the timeline or graphic organizer. A kindergarten teacher did a combination of writing and drawing.

WHO	WHEN	WHERE	WHAT
Yasmin	Saturday afternoon	Grandma's house	Family gathering

Events			
			Etc.

- Check for gaps in the events. For autobiographies, discuss with students the identity of the author and check if the major events included relate to that identity. Add any missing events or details.
- Choose one event and write it on top of the chart paper. Ask the class to suggest information that could be included under that subtopic. Work with the class to come up with suggestions and write them on the chart paper.
- Repeat with other events.

Language Practice: Variety of Verb Types, Avoid Repetition, and Tense

As students suggest information to add to the timeline and the development of events, through questions remind them

a) To use feeling and other verb types.
b) To review the plan and suggest alternatives when there is verb repetition.
c) To check that the tense is appropriate and consistent.

Lesson 20. Joint Construction of the Sequence of Events

From 3rd grade and up, students learn how to write paragraphs when writing the sequence of events (see Chapter 4, Lesson 15 for suggestions).

> **Goal:** To write the events based on the notes in the graphic organizer created in the previous lesson.
> **Materials:** Filled out graphic organizer and paper or electronic document to write on.

Activities

- Read the notes in the first event in the graphic organizer.
- Ask students to suggest sentences. When appropriate, before writing them down, ask questions or other opinions to enhance proposed sentences. For example, if a student says, "Once

our whole class went to the fire station," ask, "What day did we go?" Then write "Last Friday our whole class . . ."

- Repeat with all the other events. With upper elementary and middle school, you can write a couple of paragraphs with the whole class and then assign to groups one paragraph each.
- Then read the whole thing and ask questions to propose edits.

For pre-K and kindergarten, this piece becomes the final product.

Language Practice: Adverbials and Modifiers

Depending on the grade level and which one of these aspects you already taught, remind students to use these aspects of language. Refer them to the anchor charts created during lessons for ideas. It is very helpful to ask questions to elicit ideas, such as the following:

Questions for Modifiers	Questions for Adverbials
• Which ones?/Whose? (those shoes/my shoes) • How many? (4 pairs of shoes) • What like? (qualities: facts) (brown shoes) • What like? (qualities: opinion) (pretty shoes) • What kind? (canvas shoes)	• When? He came yesterday. • Where? Yesterday he came home.

You can do this as you write or when you revise the finished product as a class. For example, a 2nd grader dictated her experience:

Student: One day my family and I went to the park.
Teacher (before writing it down): One day? When? Do you remember?
Student author: On my birthday.
Teacher writes: *On my birthday, my family and I went to the park.*
Another student asks: Which park?
Student author: Franklin park.
The teacher inserts *Franklin*.

Lesson 21. Teach to Insert Dialogue (Grades 3–8)

Goals: To teach students how to create dialogue to provide insights into the characters in their recounts and to learn the proper amount of dialogue to include. Also, to teach students how to punctuate dialogue to distinguish it from narrative text.

Materials: Mentor texts with dialogue. Student text with no dialogue that could be enhanced by including dialogue. Projector.

Activities

- Project a couple of pages of the mentor text that has dialogue and narrative. For example:

"I am sizzling like a hot potato. I ask Mamma, 'May I put on my bathing suit?' 'Absolutely not,' Mamma says, frowning under her straw hat. 'You'll burn all day out in this sun.' " (*Come On, Rain!*)

- Discuss the following questions with students:
  - How much dialogue is there in comparison to the narrative?

- What does the dialogue show?
- How does the author distinguish the dialogue from the narrative, for example, by punctuation?

- Show a student text without dialogue. For example:

I got my gear and went to the chairlift. I waited less 5 seconds, it was coming towards me and the chairlift scooped me up. **When I pulled the bar down, I was so scared. But when I looked out, it was so beautiful.** The towering trees covered in a sheet of white snow, the animals in the trees and the other snowboarders below.

- Ask the author to pretend that she was going on the chairlift with her brother. Choose a student to act as her brother and have them act out the sentences in bold (these sentences express feelings from the narrator).
- Jointly construct a dialogue with the class to replace those sentences.
- Repeat the activity.
- Working in groups or pairs, have students look at their writing to see if there is a place where dialogue would enhance the writing. Make sure that students do not overdo it. For example, a 7th grader once wrote a whole recount with dialogue and no punctuation. You may want to show other texts that do not use dialogue and discuss the differences between the two and why the authors did or did not decide to use dialogue.
- As you teach to introduce dialogue, teach and practice the basic punctuation rules:

  - Use a comma after the tag, if quotation follows: *Mama says,* "Home is here."
  - Use a comma after the quotation, if the tag follows (unless the quotation ends in a question): *As we entered the building,* "Do you like music?" *he asked.* "Yes, I like jazz," *I answered.*
  - Use a comma before and after the tag, if it is in the middle of the quotation: *"Then why," I asked, "did you and Mama leave?"*
  - All final punctuation goes inside the quotation marks.
  - Always begin a quotation with a capital, even if in the middle of a sentence:

Please notice that in different languages the rules and even the symbols are different. For example, Spanish uses angular quotation marks (« ») and hyphens instead of commas to separate the quoted language. For literate newcomer students, you will need to point out the difference.

Lesson 22. Individual or Group Planning and Construction of Sequence of Events

Goal: To apply what students have learned about writing a sequence of events to their own recounts, using language features they have already learned.

Materials: Graphic organizers with the orientation information already completed. Paper in which they can write and draw (for young writers) or electronic file. Anchor charts produced during language lessons.

Activities

- Remind students of the aspects of language learned to enhance their writing. Point at the anchor charts to get ideas.

Give students the graphic organizer appropriate for their age (see graphic organizers download-able from the *Support Material* tab in the book's webpage) and have individual students or groups fill in the events.

Liz, a 4th-grade teacher, devised a way to have students elaborate on their events. After they created the timeline, she had them write each event at the top of the page on the right side of the notebook. On the left side, she had them create a timeline of just that event. Using the information, they wrote the developed event underneath that named event. With a whole page to write and all the notes, students produced well-developed events. The following example is a page of the notebook opened to one event noted on the right side with details of the event listed on the left side and the fully developed event on the right side:

• Waited for chairlift • I was scared • Views were beautiful • trees, animals, snowboarders • Got to the end • Jumped off on the top • Went down the mountain	Going up the chairlift *I got my gear and went to the chairlift. I waited less 5 seconds, it was coming towards me and the chairlift scooped me up. When I pulled the bar down, I was so scared. But when I looked out, it was so beautiful. The towering trees covered in a sheet of white snow, the animals in the trees and the other snowboarders below. I was seconds away from the mountain top so I pushed the bar up and got ready to jump on top of the mountain. The chairlift was on top of the mountain, I closed my eyes and jumped, when I opened my eyes, I was on the surface of the mountain. I took 3 deep breaths and I went down the mountain.*

- As students create their graphic organizers, confer with them, asking questions to enhance the information for each individual event. Write down what they say in their graphic organizer.
- When they have information for all the events, have them write following the orientation they had written earlier. Younger students use one page to write and draw each event. Students in later grades do not need to draw events in their personal recounts, memoirs, or autobiographies, but they are still better off writing each event on a separate page so that they do not feel restricted and can add more information if they want. (Some teachers asked students to use photographs to stimulate recall and then let them add them to their final product.) Factual recounts can be complemented with a diagram sketching the events, for example, a collision on the way to school. For procedural recounts, students may include images, graphs, or a math formula.

Practicing Language Features Learned

Point at the different anchor charts with verbs, adverbials, and modifiers to encourage them to use them. As the students write, conference with individual students, asking them questions to encourage them to use different language features. For example, one 7th-grade student had writ-ten: *We then had cake and watched T.V.* Ask the student if s/he could express more precisely *then*?

Student could say, "At the end of the party." Ask, how was the cake? What kind of cake? Possible answer: "delicious chocolate cake," and so on.

Lesson 23. Teach the Difference Between the Use of Simple Past and Past Continuous (Grades 3–8)

This lesson should be included if teachers observe students using the past continuous instead of the simple past. For example, a 3rd-grade student wrote, *I woke up in the morning and then I was in my car my DaD **was Driving** to Lego Land*. This sentence needs to be packed and the tense changed: "Last Saturday morning, my Dad **drove** me to Lego Land."

> **Goal**: To have students use the past continuous only when the action is taking place at the same time as another.
>
> **Materials**: Paragraphs in mentor; examples of student work using the past continuous when the simple past is needed.

Activities

- Show students a few examples from mentor texts with both tenses used, for example,

  I ran to the park to watch the fireflies; some kids were coming behind.
  Ask them, Did the kids come behind before I ran? After I ran? Or at the same time I ran?

- Repeat with other sentences and discuss the use of the continuous form.
- Show examples of one or two students' drafts that need editing.
- Ask students to edit their own drafts.

Lesson 24. Reference Ties

When very young students use pronouns without referents, simply ask, "Who is *we*? Or *they*?" and edit as they respond. With older students carry out the lesson so that they learn to name participants as referents to pronouns on their own.

> **Goal:** To teach students that pronouns need a referent to be able to track participants and understand who or what the author is talking about.
>
> **Materials:** Mentor text that includes pronouns with referents. Student sample work, some of which are good examples of referents' use and some that need referents.

Activities

- Take a mentor text and highlight the pronouns. For example:

  "I run back home and slip up the steps past Mamma. **She** is nearly senseless . . ." or "Jackie-Joyce chases Rosemary who chases Liz who chases **me**. Wet slicking our arms and legs, **we** splash up the block . . ." (*Come On, Rain!*)

- Ask the students who the pronouns stand for, writing the proper name above, and asking them how they know (evidence for their answer). Point out that when there is the possibility of ambiguity, authors use a noun instead of a pronoun.
- Show a chunk of student writing where the referents are missing or the referent is unclear. For example, *I screamed till the top of my lungs **every one** came down the stairs like a bullet, eating breakfast like a pig. Then **we** planned what we're going to do*. (*We* stands for *everyone*. Since this is the beginning of the recount, it is unclear who is *everyone*.)

- Ask the class to suggest modifications.
- Do the same activity with other students' writing.
- Ask students to do the same activity with their drafts and make necessary modifications.

Lesson 25. Joint Revision of Orientation and Sequence of Events

When working with young writers where the final product is the co-constructed piece, the whole class helps revise together, encouraged by the teacher's questions. For grades where students do their own writing, it is recommended to do this joint revision before they write the conclusion.

Goal: to learn how to collaborate revising each other's pieces.
Materials: Draft of the individual or group pieces written so far.

Activities

- Choose one or two students to share their pieces with the whole class. It is best to choose students who can use the extra help.
- Read it aloud or have the author read it aloud in chunks.
- Focus on specific aspects of the stages and language that were taught during the unit, especially those that are a challenge for a number of students (individual problems are best addressed during conferences). Using questions, have students suggest alternatives. Have anchor charts used during lessons for reference. For example, Chloe, a 6th-grade teacher, showed her class how to revise their personal recounts.

Chloe reads aloud one student's piece: " 'Get me out of here!! I'm thousands of feet above ground. Help me!' I said." Said? [asked Chloe].
Student: I shouted.
Student: I pleaded.

The author chooses one of the suggestions (Pavlak & Hodgson-Drysdale, 2017, p. 29).

- Choose the writing of another student, focusing on another general challenge, and repeat the process.
- Have pairs or groups review their pieces for the challenges that were raised when working together. Conference with individuals and address specific additional issues.

Conclusion

Personal recounts may conclude with a feeling, an evaluation of the events, a thought, or one last event.

Feeling: " 'We sure did get a soaking, Mamma,' I say, and we head home purely soothed, fresh as dew, turning toward the first sweet rays of the sun" (*Come On, Rain!*). Notice that the feeling is expressed indirectly through the actions and descriptions.

Evaluation: "It has been a terrible, horrible, no good, very bad day. My mom says some days are like that. Even in Australia" (*Alexander and the Terrible, Horrible, No Good, Very Bad Day*).

One last event that gives closure: "When he was finished, he raised his head and turned away slowly and walked off into the night" (*Salt Hands*).

Final event and thought of the narrator: "I picture them back here, dancing in the streets of La Perla, and I lie there, watching the moon shine on the Christmas star till I fall asleep" (*Going Home*).

Memoirs tend to end with a feeling or thought of the narrator. For example, "I felt like a hero. I *was* a hero. It was marvelous to be so popular" (Dahl, R. 2009. *Boy*). Factual recounts conclude with a last event, while for procedural recounts, the conclusion is optional. It may include what was learned or accomplished.

Features of Students' Writing

Conclusions do not come easy for children. In their first attempt at writing, they are often either omitted or *the end* is used to close all types of recounts. In the 2nd grade example, the student has a last event, but it is not entertaining. Even after coaching, 1st graders concluded their writing with *it was fun*.

	1	2	3	4	Uncoached Writing Comments
Conclusion		√			Final event, not entertaining.

The conclusions of middle school uncoached personal recounts tended to be similar to the elementary students' ones; some conclude with a last event, but none have feelings or thoughts outside having fun. For example,

> 6th grader and 8th grader: *The End.*
> 6th grader: *When we finished the cake, we played cards.*
> 7th grader: *It was a real fun day.*
> 8th grader: *I got to see my teammates that are now like my family.*

Lessons to Teach Conclusions

As illustrated earlier, personal recounts and memoirs have a variety of styles of conclusions while the other genres follow a specific pattern. Thus, included is a lesson focusing just on personal recount or memoirs and another that can be adapted for procedural or factual recounts.

Lesson 26. Deconstruction of Text to Learn About Conclusion in Personal Recounts or Memoirs, and Reinforce Variety of Types of Verbs

> **Goal:** To learn the features of different types of conclusions.
> **Materials:** Sets of mentor texts with different types of endings. Examples of each type of ending written on separate sheets of chart paper.

Activities

- Find mentor texts with different endings. Group them by type.
- On chart paper, show one example of each of the different types of conclusions as presented earlier, using the mentor texts and other books familiar to the students.
- Read aloud the examples of different endings, and discuss what type of conclusion they are. Leave the examples visible so that students can refer to it when writing their own endings.
- Read other endings and discuss which kind they are.
- Identify the different types of verbs used in the various endings. For example, feeling verbs ("I felt like a hero.") and relational verbs with modifiers describing feelings ("It was marvelous.") or evaluation of events ("It has been a terrible, horrible, no good, very bad day.").

Action verbs display the narrator's state of mind ("I lie there, watching the moon shine on the Christmas star till I fall asleep").

Lesson 27. Deconstruction of Text to Learn About Conclusion in Procedural and Factual Recounts

Goal: To learn the features of the endings in the genre in which students are writing.

Materials: Mentor texts. Examples of endings. Chart paper or projector. Handout with examples of conclusions.

Activities

- Project the endings (or post on chart paper) and distribute a handout including them to help students refer to them when they are trying to compose their own conclusions.
- Discuss the type of conclusion common to this genre with the class.
- Give each group of students one text and have them read and discuss its conclusion.

Lesson 28. Joint and Individual Construction of the Conclusion

Goal: To learn to write the conclusion on the basis of what students have learned in the previous lessons.

Materials: Chart paper. Student notebooks.

Activities

- Given what students have learned about conclusions, ask the students to provide a good conclusion for the recount they worked on as a whole class.
- Negotiate the conclusion with the class as you write.
- In a group or with a partner, have students write the conclusion for their own work.

  - If working on personal recounts or memoirs, have students look at the conclusion of one of their previous personal recounts and decide whether it has the appropriate features or if it could use revision.
  - If working on procedural or factual recounts, have students compose an appropriate conclusion with the features previously discussed.

Lesson 29. Students Create a Complete Draft of their Project and Check Coherence

Goals: To have students create a whole text of their individual sections by piecing together all the stages produced in the previous lessons. Also, to learn to create a piece of writing in which all of the stages come together and relate well to each other.

Materials: Student work. Jointly constructed version. Paper or google document.

Activities

- Have students transfer to a clean sheet of paper or electronic file the sections of each stage they created during their lessons. Make sure that they use what they wrote rather than starting new sections.

- Project one good example of a coherent piece. Go over the three stages of recounts and discuss with the class if the student example has all of the elements that they have learned about and whether these elements go well together.
- Encourage students to suggest what was done well and why.
- Repeat the activity with an example that needs some work.
- Ask students to suggest improvements.
- Have them work in groups sharing their own pieces to decide if they want to make any changes.
- Conference with individuals or groups to check on what they are doing and support any revisions they want to make.

Lesson 30. Joint Revision of the Final Draft or Additional Language Lesson

When students give you their final products, decide whether you need to model another joint revision of the whole draft, following the steps used in Lesson 24, or whether you need to present an additional lesson on some aspect of language that continues to challenge a great number of the students.

Lesson 31. Titles

Titles: Titles in recounts either name the topic (*One Bean*, *The Great Mouse Plot*) or are more elaborate and include descriptions (*Alexander and the Terrible, Horrible, No Good, Very Bad Day*) or employ action verbs (*Come On, Rain!*). Memoirs often includes the word memoir in the secondary title (*Red Scarf Girl: A Memoir of the Cultural Revolution*).

> **Goal:** To learn how to write a title that is informative, interesting, and reflective for the genre.
> **Materials:** Mentor texts with different types of titles.

Activities

- Read titles of several texts from the genre.
- Discuss the words that authors use to communicate the topic and reflect the genre. For example, personal recounts hint at what happened.
- Have the class decide on a title for their jointly constructed piece.
- Have two or three students share their recounts.
- Have the author (student) discuss possible titles with the class.
- Have students work in pairs or groups on titles for their group or individual pieces.

Professional Articles That Describe Instruction of the Genre

de Oliveira, L. C., & Lan, S. W. (2014). Writing science in an upper elementary classroom: A genre-based approach to teaching English language learners. *Journal of Second Language Writing, 25*, 23–39 (procedural recounts).

Gebhard, M., Willett, J., Jimenez, J., & Piedra, A. (2011). Systemic functional linguistics, teachers' professional development, and ELLs' academic literacy practices. In T. Lucas (Ed.), *Teacher preparation for linguistically diverse classrooms: A resource for teacher educators* (pp. 91–110). Mahwah, NJ: Erlbaum/Taylor & Francis (authors called them narratives but they are written as personal recounts).

Paugh, P., & Moran, M. (2013). Growing language awareness in the classroom garden. *Language Arts Journal of Michigan, 90*(4), 253–267 (procedural recounts).

Pavlak, C. M., & Hodgson-Drysdale, T. (2017). A writing apprenticeship for sixth-grade English learners: An application of the theory of systemic functional linguistics. *Journal of Education, 197*(2), 25–35 (personal recounts).

References

Dahl, R. (2009). *Boy*. New York: Puffin.

Derewianka, B. (2011). *A new grammar companion for teachers*. Marickville, NSW: Primary English Teaching Association.

Derewianka, B., & Jones, P. (2016). *Teaching language in context* (2nd ed.). Melbourne: Oxford University Press.

Pavlak, C. M., & Hodgson-Drysdale, T. (2017). A writing apprenticeship for sixth-grade English learners: An application of the theory of systemic functional linguistics. *Journal of Education, 197*(2), 25–35.

Chapter 4

Historical Genres

This chapter covers historical genres appropriate for elementary and middle school, including biography, autobiography, empathetic autobiography, historical recount, and historical account. Each has a different purpose, and although most of them have the same stages, each is slightly different as shown later in the chapter (see Table 4.1).

Writing these genres builds on many features learned in Recount genre units. For example, autobiographies and empathetic autobiographies as personal recounts and memoirs are written in the first person. Empathetic autobiographies, however, require students to write from another person's perspective, an essential but difficult literacy skill (Scollon & Scollon, 1981).

One big difference is that the events in the historical genres are *episodic* rather than *serial* as in personal recounts, where all the events in a short span of time are included. Episodic means that only certain events are chosen to be included, guided by the significance of people's lives or events. This is very hard to achieve for young writers as Ed Ballard illustrates in his description

Table 4.1 Historical Genres

Name	Purpose	Stages	Examples
Biography	To tell "the life story of a significant historical figure" (Coffin, 2006, p. 53)	Orientation Record of Events Conclusion	*Mae Jemison*
Autobiography	To retell the events in the author's life to inform and entertain	Orientation Record of Events Conclusion	*Reaching for the Moon* *Rosa Parks: My Story*
Empathetic Autobiography	To tell about the life of a historical figure, writing empathetically as if the author was the person, i.e., writing in character	Orientation Record of Events Reorientation (optional) Conclusion	March on Selma told as if the author were Martin Luther King, Jr., or as if the author were a student organizer
Historical Recount	"To chronicle past events regarded as historically significant, and designed to inform rather than entertain" (Coffin, 2006, p. 56)	Background Record of Events Deduction	Allies landing in France during WWII
Historical Account	To account for why things happened in a particular sequence; to explain why events happen rather than simply record them	Background Account of Events Deduction	Allies landing in France during WWII with reasons for the various strategies

DOI: 10.4324/9781003329275-4

of teaching to write autobiographies to 3rd graders (Brisk et al., 2021). Biographies are more challenging because they need to be written in third person. Children and beginner English writers tend to prefer first person. Historical recounts and accounts are even more challenging because the focus is an event rather than a person.

Development of Units

To develop units, teachers need to consider a number of factors that play a role on what and how to teach and what materials to use. With this in mind, they have to plan lessons.

Unit Preparation

To prepare a unit in the chosen Recount genre, teachers need to consider the following:

- Grade level: Vertical planning of genres and language
- Connection with content areas
- Mentor texts
- Research resources
- Potential projects, audience, and medium
- Uncoached writing and planning content of the unit

Grade Level: Vertical Planning of Genres and Language

The historical genres are most naturally incorporated in social studies lessons to reinforce concepts of the particular historical time being covered. Sometimes science units include biographies of the person associated with the particular science concept or discovery. These genres build on the Recount genres and are best gradually introduced in upper elementary grades. Each of the historical genres is increasingly more difficult. Although *empathetic autobiography* is a genre only found in school contexts, its purpose is to immerse students in a period of history to understand it better, while having fun imagining life during that period. The features of text structure and language are comparable to autobiographies. Further, students' historical and socio-cultural knowledge of the time period must be accurate to make their writing authentic. Therefore, it should be implemented in the upper elementary grades. For younger grades, the same skill of writing from another person's perspective can be practiced without the challenge of historical research by learning to write as if they were a character in a text. This skill is often required of 3rd-grade students on standardized tests.

Biographies present the challenge of having to write in the *third person*. However, they are probably the most accessible of the historical genres. All the recounts and historical genres learned in elementary school focus on a person. In middle school the introduction of *historical recounts* and *accounts* challenge the students to write about historical events, for example, the Boston Tea Party, the French Revolution, or the Opium Wars.

To help build on students' skills acquired through each of these genres, it is important for teachers in a school to plan their writing calendar together and understand what is required at each grade level to support the more difficult genres and language structures encountered as the students move up in grades. Table 4.2 suggests how these genres can be distributed across the grade levels. The table suggests at which grade to introduce the genre, but they can also be practiced or introduced at later grade levels.

Middle school is a good age to do autobiography if the students have not had a chance to do it before. For example, Jen, an ESL middle school teacher, carried out a unit on autobiography

Table 4.2 Historical Genres Across Grade Levels

Grade Level	Content Area		
	ELA	Social Studies	Science/ Math
3	Biography	Biography	Biography
4	Autobiography		
5		Empathetic Autobiography	
6	Autobiography (if not done before)	Historical Recount	
7	Biography	Historical Account	
8			

with her students new to the country. She carefully scaffolded the process by deconstructing in detail a mentor text and orally discussing their own lives as they read. She modeled each stage with her own autobiography and encouraged students to use either or both their native language and English.

Connection With Content Areas

Autobiographies naturally belong in language arts, while *biographies, empathetic autobiographies, historical recounts,* and *historical accounts* are best embedded in social studies topics. For example, a 3rd-grade class wrote biographies during Black History month. Students conducted research and wrote biographies on various African American historical figures. A 5th-grade class wrote empathetic autobiographies in the context of their unit on Plymouth plantation and the Wampanoags. They visited the current museum site, interacted with interpreters of both the colonists and the tribe, and wrote a piece "A day in the life" from the point of view of a Wampanoag or of a colonist. Another 5th-grade class wrote a historical recount about the crossing of the Bering Strait while studying the Ice Age. The historic genres can also be connected to science when writing about the people or historical time period related to particular scientific discoveries.

Mentor Texts

Mentor texts are written in the genre of the unit and are used to show students the features of the genre. It is best to choose short mentor texts that are somewhat connected to the content of the unit where the genre is embedded and that will also be appealing to the students. For example, Lorin, a 5th-grade teacher, taught biography writing in connection to a unit on 16th-century explorers. She used Mae Jemison as the mentor text because it was short and illustrated all the features of the structure and language of biographies. Moreover, it was about a living female astronaut, a person of great interest to the students in her class. Mentor texts listed in Table 4.3 are used to illustrate instruction of this genre. For other suggestions, check the downloadable lists from the *Support Material* tab in the book's webpage.

Biography

Mae C. Jemison 1956–, chapter 6 of the book *African-American Astronauts*, is a short biography that is both accessible and current. There are also many biographies written by David Adler that can be used as mentor texts. The stages in his books are straightforward, making it easy for

Table 4.3 Sample Mentor Texts

Genre	Mentor Texts
Biography	Mae C. Jemison 1956—(chapter 6 in *African-American Astronauts*)
Autobiography	*My First American Friend; I Am a Promise*
Empathetic Autobiography	*Tapenum's Day: A Wampanoag Indian Boy in Pilgrim Times; I Am Rosa Parks*
Historical Recounts	"A Murder That Rocked the Nation" (a chapter in *The Civil Rights Movement*)
Historical Accounts	*The Compromise of 1850* (section in *History Alive: America's Past*, p. 190)

children to learn the text structure of the genre. *A Picture Book of Helen Keller* tends to be a particular favorite text for many children.

Autobiography

My First American Friend is a good mentor text to use with young writers because it was written by a 3rd grader who moved to Boston from China. The language is very accessible, and the examined life span of the author is short, as it will be for the students. Jen used *I Am a Promise*, the story of an Olympic runner from Jamaica, with her middle school newcomer students because it was written in very accessible English, and she was an interesting person for teenage immigrant students.

Empathetic Autobiography

Tapenum's Day: A Wampanoag Indian Boy in Pilgrim Times is one of several books that Kate Waters has written in this genre. This type of literature is uncommon because writing in this genre is used mostly for social studies activities to help students immerse themselves in a historical topic. Brad Meltzer has written a number of "I am . . ." books in the empathetic autobiography genre, such as *I Am Rosa Parks*, *I Am I.M. Pei*, and so on. They are very accessible and entertaining. The style in the "I books" digresses from a true historical genre because in addition to the narrative, there are images of the characters with dialogue bubbles, more typical of fiction. Teachers have successfully used them without students imitating the style.

Historical Recount

"A Murder That Rocked the Nation" is a chapter in the book *The Civil Rights Movement*, a topic usually covered in the upper elementary grades. Teachers should use additional texts related to the social studies unit that anchor the historical recount unit and serves as an additional source.

Historical Account

The Compromise of 1850 is a section of a history textbook commonly used in schools that clearly shows why the events happened. For example, it explains that California was admitted into the union as a free state to please the North, while New Mexico and Utah could vote whether or not to allow slavery to please the South.

Research Resources

Although *autobiographies* are based on the students' lives, they still require some basic research, such as interviewing family members who can tell the students about their birth and earlier years of their lives. Family members can also help with establishing students' identity by commenting on things they are good at and events in their early childhood that showed their talents and preferences.

All the other historical genres require research because they are about events that the students have not experienced but need to learn from. Currently, there is great interest in exposing students, especially middle school students, to primary sources. Although there is great value to this practice because it helps students act as historians, the language of the documents is challenging. These texts, if they come from a previous century, include language and structures not commonly used any more. For example, a 6th-grade teacher used an excerpt from the 1885 *Proceedings of the One Hundredth Anniversary of the Granting of Warrant 459 to African Lodge* for an argument unit,

> That your Petitioners apprehend that they have, in common with all other Men, a natural & inalienable right to that freedom, which the great Parent of the Universe hath bestowed equally on all Mankind, & which they have never forfeited by any compact or agreement whatever.

It is important not only to choose or help students choose resources to do research, but also to teach them how to collect and use the information. To apprentice students to research, Pat and Beverly, who taught 4th and 5th graders, started their class project by doing research together to show students how to look at sources, draw information, take notes using the graphic organizers for the genre, and decide whether to use the terminology in the texts or look for more accessible language for their age group that helped them express the same ideas. They also encouraged students to learn some of the new technical language to incorporate in their own writing.

A 3rd-grade teacher had students doing research in groups: each member of the group read a different source while contributing notes to common topics. This allowed the teacher to distribute sources of different levels of difficulty to make them accessible to various students. She found that having students read different sources led to rich discussions among the students as to what they should note about the topic.

Scaffolding the process of taking notes and then converting them to full text is essential. Otherwise, students start their drafting without attention to their notes and often copy whole chunks of the source texts. Once students have taken notes, Cheryl has her 5th graders put away the source texts and consult their notes to produce their writing. When writing biographies, Jennifer Wyatt, a 2nd-grade teacher working with emergent bilinguals, carefully scaffolded the whole process.

Jennifer read the mentor text aloud, asking students to suggest which information they should add to their notes. As they pointed at a piece of information, she wrote it succinctly on chart paper in the form of notes. Then, she worked with the students to transform the notes into full sentences. She then wrote the sentences in sentence strips and discussed the order with the students. Using these strips, they put together the text. Finally, they revised the text to suggest possible ways to combine sentences. Students followed the same process for the person they had chosen to research individually. The students' small sentence strips were ordered and then glued in their writing notebook. After students had the whole text completed, the teacher and student teacher conferred with the students to discuss potential places to better combine or connect the text. For example, one student wrote, "JFK graduated from Harvard. JFK enlisted in the navy." The teacher suggested combining them as, "After JFK graduated from Harvard, he enlisted in the navy."

In sum, teachers need to:

- Teach students to use a variety of sources.
- Take notes by choosing information and language to support their message.
- Teach students to transform notes to full text.
- Teach to edit the text to ensure fluidity.

Potential Projects, Audience, and Medium

As shown in the earlier section *Connection With Content Areas*, the historical topics lead to different projects and choice of genre. The different genres lend themselves to different audiences. Adults can be the audience for historical genres as a way for students to show off how much they have learned. For example, a 5th-grade class produced a book about their visit to Plymouth Plantation that included their empathetic autobiographies, as well as photographs from the experience. They used software to publish the book and showed it to visitors to the school.

It is important to make all students aware of their audience from the very beginning of their writing. When conferring with students, refer to the audience as you're making suggestions. For example, it is helpful to say, "You haven't told your audience when the event took place." Using audience as a motivator for improvement avoids blaming students for their ineffective writing.

Audience influences the amount of information and difficulty of vocabulary. For example, in the biography mentor text *Mae C. Jemison*, written for elementary school students, when the author recounts that Jemison wanted to be a scientist, but the teacher told her to be a nurse instead, the author writes, "Jemison did not listen to her teacher." However, in Wikipedia, written for adults, the same information reads, "Jemison would not let anyone dissuade her from pursuing a career in science." It is important to have students not only choose the audience, but also to realize that it influences language choices.

Depending on the genre and age, different mediums of writing can be used. When working with younger students or emergent bilinguals, the historical genres can simply be timelines, posters, PowerPoints, or books with visuals or photographs accompanied by captions. Josefina (Fifi) Pérez, a 3rd-grade teacher, was concerned that her students, who were relatively new to English, would have difficulty writing biographies. She encouraged them to create books with images downloaded from the Internet. Students added a short caption under the image. Hence, they had to write only a short sentence for each event. Ed had his 3rd graders, which included newcomer students, write biographies as posters, with the image of the person, a timeline below, and a paragraph with the significance of the person. Depending on the students' language resources, their timelines and paragraph were more or less elaborated. However, all the posters looked the same, equalizing the status of the students.

The language of full text narratives is more challenging. Older or more advanced students in the language better cope with them. Jen had her middle school newcomer students writing autobiographies as full narratives but gave them choice of language.

The 5th-grade teachers started a unit on empathetic autobiographies connected with different periods in history. Linda Drueding's students wrote about historical characters in the Revolutionary War. Beverly chose the Holocaust. She collected a number of books on the topic and had the students search the Internet for information on the Holocaust. She read aloud *Star of Fear, Star of Hope*, a true story where the author takes the identity of a young French girl who tells how she escaped the Holocaust persecution, but her best friend disappeared. Pat Scialoia's class had a field trip to Plymouth Plantation, where there was staff who impersonated colonials and Wampanoag (a Native American tribe) during the early settlement. The students interviewed the interpreters, noticing their language, dress, and customs. One of the children addressed an elder in passing by removing his hat and saying, "Hello, my good man," already behaving in character. As soon as they returned, they started working on their empathetic autobiographies, choosing one of the characters and one of the customs to feature. They worked intensely on content-specific language, evident in their writing:

My faced [face] burned as I stirred the rabbit stew. I made sure the squash was soft & the garlic was mixing. All the deer skin on my back kept me warm. The smoke from all the wetu fires burned my eyes.

The writing goes on for a couple of pages accompanied with photographs. Students shared their drafts and made suggestions for improvements. Their enthusiasm and knowledge of the content was evident.

A 7th-grade teacher created as a class an empathetic autobiography on Fredrick Douglass. Then her students wrote empathetic autobiographies on Boston abolitionists and read them to 3rd graders in a neighboring school, which includes local abolitionists in their social studies curriculum.

Uncoached Writing and Planning Content of the Unit

There are genres, especially in the upper grades, where it becomes harder to do an uncoached piece because of the need for content knowledge. Therefore, the teacher will need to draw on previously taught content or something very familiar to students.

Sample Prompts for Uncoached Student Writing:

Biography: Students write about a family member's life story on the basis of an interview.

Autobiography: Students write about their previous year in school.

Empathetic Autobiography: Students write about what happened that morning as if they were one of the members of their family.

Historical Recount: Students write about some event that happened in the past few weeks on the basis of a newspaper article.

Historical Account: Students write about some event that happened in the past few weeks on the basis of a newspaper article, explaining what motivated the actions in the events.

Teachers analyze students' writing using the Analysis of Student Work: Purpose, Stages, and Language form (downloadable from the *Support Material* tab in the book's webpage) to determine what the students can already do and what their challenges are. Teachers can use the Unit Plan (Appendix A) to plot the necessary lessons.

Purpose, Stages, and Language: Theory and Practice

This section describes the purpose, stages, and key language of features to be included in the lessons. Analysis of student work in relation to each aspect illustrates the challenges students have. Lessons on purpose and stages are combined with lessons on language with the goal of emphasizing language development from the start of the unit lessons. Table 4.4 lists a series of lessons that cover all the aspects of the language. This table suggests the order of the lessons on purpose and stages and when to introduce the various aspects of language. When planning a unit, teachers will choose just three or four aspects of language to teach based on the background of the students and what the students have already learned when studying other genres included in this chapter and Chapter 3. After introducing the chosen aspects of language as suggested in the table, teachers will have the students practice them throughout the unit.

Table 4.4 Teaching Language Parallel to Purpose and Stages

Lessons Purpose and Stages	*Lessons on Language*
1. Purpose of the Genre	Review of Verbs
2. Deconstruction of Text to Learn About Stages and Establish the Theme	3. Reference Ties Using Different Noun Groups
4. Research to Establish the Theme That Threads the Text	5. Technical Language Found in Historical Text
6. Deconstruction of Text for Orientation	7. Grammatical Person
8. Jointly Constructed Orientations	And Review of Adverbials of Time and Place
9. Deconstruction of Text—Record of Events	10. Noun Groups
	Biographies:
	10.1. Proper Names (L2 Learners, Especially Recent Arrivals)
	10.2. Review of Adjectives (Grade 3)
	10.3. Complex Noun Groups (Grades 4–8)
	Autobiographies and Empathetic Autobiographies:
	10.4. Evaluative Language and Graduation (Grades 3–8)
	• Review of Complex Noun Groups (see Lesson 10.3)
	Historical Recounts and Accounts:
	• Review of Complex Noun Groups (see Lesson 10.3)
	10.5. Class or Organization as Doer (Grades 6–8)
	10.6. Choice of Participant as the Doer of the Action (Grades 6–8)
	10.7. Nominalization (Grades 6–8)
11. Deconstruction of Text—Development of Events	12. Adverbials of Manner, Accompaniment, and Reason (Grades 3–8)
	13. Clause Complexes (Grades 4–8)
	13(a). Formation
	13(b). Expressing Relationships Accurately
	13(c). Finite to Non-Finite Clauses
14. Jointly Planned Record of Events	And Focus on Key Aspects of Language

(Continued)

Table 4.4 (Continued)

Lessons Purpose and Stages	Lessons on Language
15. Jointly Constructed Record of Events in Paragraphs	Paragraph Formation, and Use of Text Connectives
16. Deconstruction of Text to Learn About Conclusion of Historical Genres	Reinforce Evaluative Language and Graduation
Follow Up of Conclusion of the Whole Class Project	17. Teach to Quote From Sources and How to Introduce Quotes (Grades 6–8) Focus on aspects that still show general difficulty
18. Adding Images	
19. Individual, Pair, or Group Construction of a Text in the Genre of the Unit: • Establish theme • Research theme • Create orientation • Plan events • Write events • Write conclusion • Insert images • Decide on title (Chapter 3, Lesson 31)	Remind students of the aspects of language you have reviewed and taught (insert your own plan based on what you taught) For 3rd grade: For 4th and 5th grades: For middle school:
20. Joint Revision of Final Draft	*May need to create new lessons on aspects that continue to be challenging*

The following resources to support implementation of these lessons are downloadable from the *Support Material* tab in the book's webpage:

• Analysis of Student Work: Purpose, Stages, and Language
• Graphic Organizers:
• Autobiography, Empathetic Autobiography, and Biography
• Historical Recount
• Historical Account
• Procedural Recount
• Mentor Texts That Illustrate the Genre
• Internet Resources With Mentor Texts to Illustrate the Genre

Purpose of Historical Genres

All the genres covered in this chapter have as their purpose to record the past from history. *Biographies* tell "the life story of a significant historical figure" (Coffin, 2006, p. 53). *Autobiographies* retell "the events of an author's life in order to both inform and entertain" (Coffin, 2006, p. 49). *Empathetic autobiographies* retell events in the life of the author, but from the point of view of a historical figure, defined or general, for example, Paul Revere or a colonial soldier. Authors use their imagination based on research to create scenes, which can make the genre controversial (Christie & Derewianka, 2008). The purpose of *historical recounts* is "to chronicle past events regarded as historically significant, and designed to inform rather than entertain" (Coffin, 2006, p. 56). *Historical accounts* include why things happened in a particular sequence; to explain rather than simply record the past.

The verbs are in the past tense, except at the end of autobiographies, empathetic autobiographies, and biographies of living persons, when they are recounting present circumstances. Young students and bilingual learners will need coaching on how to form both the regular and irregular form of verbs.

Features of Students' Writing

After practice with the genres described in Chapter 3, it is easy for students to understand that the purpose of historical genres is to record events in their own lives, the life of a historical figure, or a historical event. For example, Timothy, a 5th grader, understood the purpose of biographies when he was asked to write about his parents' immigration experience:

> My mom and dad left Vietnam they came to America they didn't speak english so it was very hard to get job and get food. Once they got money they bought two boat tickets and traveled to Hong Kong by boat. My sister was born in Hong Kong. Then three years later my brother was born. Then they came back to America then another brother was born. They got help from my sister by communicating. Then I was born and that's the story of how my parents got there from Vietnam.
>
> The End.

	1	*2*	*3*	*4*	*Uncoached Writing Comments*
Purpose Varies depending on the specific type (Biographies: Tell "the life story of a significant historical figure.")				√	It is about a person's life, yet the assignment was only to tell about the immigration experience. This piece goes beyond.
Verb Conjugation (past, except in direct speech)				√	All verbs in the past.

Most of the students doing the biographical recount project on their parents' immigration experience went beyond and wrote about their whole life. In general students have a good sense of the purpose of the historical genre. One student mixed personal recount with autobiography, making her autobiography as a list of personal recounts rather than events connected with the theme of her identity.

Lessons to Teach Purpose

Depending on the specific genre, the lesson content will vary. Lessons on language that were covered in Chapter 3 with recounts do not need to be repeated unless there are students new to the school or students have persistent challenges.

Lesson 1. Purpose of the Genre and Review of Verbs

> **Goal:** To discover the purpose of the particular historical genre through exposure to different texts in the genre.
> **Materials:** Mentor texts, Internet examples, and/or good examples written by former students in the specific genre of the unit.

Activities

- Read to students or let students read the examples.
- Discuss the purpose (see description of purpose for each genre earlier in the chapter). Contrast with the other types of recounts or historical genres the students have already studied. This can be done during reading or social studies time.

Table 4.5 Stages of Historical Genres

Genre/Stages	Orientation	Sequence of Events	Conclusion
Biography	Who, where, when, theme/identity	Chosen events that build the identity of the person	Significance of the life of the person
Autobiography Empathetic Autobiography	Who, where, when, significant event in childhood connected with the author's identity		What is happening in the present also in relation to the identity or a reorientation: "rounding off with a comment or an expression of attitude" (Coffin, 2006, p. 50)
Historical Recount	Background: summary of the previous historical events	Record of events in order in which they occurred	Deduction: drawing out the historical significance of the events recorded
Historical Account		Record of events in order in which they occurred, adding causal elements	

Review of Verbs

Using the same mentor texts, review the use and formation of past tense, avoid repetition of verbs, and use a variety of verbs if the uncoached writing shows that students have challenges with these aspects or if their first drafts display any of these challenges (see Chapter 3, Lessons 3, 5, and 16).

Stages of Historical Genres

The stages of the various historical genres are similar (see Table 4.5); however, the beginnings and endings tend to differ. The major difference in the body of the text of historical genres from the genres covered in Chapter 3 is that the events in historical genres are episodic (selected events over time) rather than serial (a series of events in a row). For example, the events chosen to develop in an autobiography are related to the identity of the person. In the book *I Am a Promise* about a Jamaican runner, all the episodes are connected to her life as a runner, even starting with her habit of running everywhere from an early age. The major difference in the body of the text between historical accounts and historical recounts is the expressions of causality between events. Table 4.5 shows the various stages of the historical genres.

Orientation

The orientation is the introduction of the historical genres. Each genre starts in a slightly different way.

*   *Biographies.* The orientation of biographies includes the *who*, *where*, and *when*. In the same paragraph or soon after the hint of the identity appears. For example,

    Barack Obama was the 44th president of the United States and the first African American commander-in-chief. He served two terms, in 2008 and 2012. The son of parents from Kenya and Kansas, Obama was born in 1961 in Hawaii.

    In addition, some historical background may be needed to place the particular historical person in context. For example, in *America's Champion Swimmer: Gertrude Ederle*, the author explains the status of women in sports in the early 20th century to help readers understand what an accomplishment it was for Gertrude, as a woman, to succeed in sports.

- *Autobiography and empathetic autobiographies.* The orientation of these two genres usually start with a significant event in childhood connected with the author's name or identity, for example, *I Am a Promise*, the autobiography of an Olympic runner starts:

When I was a little girl I dreamed of winning great races, but I was a teeny-tiny thing in this wide, wonderous world.
An empathetic autobiography about Rosa Parks begins: *Growing up, I was small for my age. I was sick a lot too, since we didn't have money for a doctor. But that didn't mean I was weak.*

- *Historical recounts and accounts.* These genres usually start with the historical background preceding the event being recorded. For example, a historical recount about immigration to America starts:

Thousands and thousands of years ago, there were no people at all in the Americas. Then, during the last great Ice Age, nomads crossed over a land bridge from Asia to what is now Alaska.
A historical account about the Compromise of 1850 begins: *The fight between the North and the South over western lands started again after the Mexican-American War in the 1840s.*

Record of Events and Conclusion

Following the orientation, the historical genres include the record of events and a conclusion. The events are in the order they occurred and connected by the theme tying the whole text. For example, the first few major events in *Mae C. Jemison* (biography) and *A Murder That Rocked the Nation* (historical recount) are as follows:

Mae C. Jamison	A Murder that Rocked the Nation
Childhood exchange with a teacher	Allegedly flirted with a white woman at a store
Attended Stanford for college	Emmett was kidnapped and killed
Went to medical school	Emmett's funeral
Served in the Peace Corps	Two men tried and freed
Was accepted for astronaut training	Two men sold their story

These and the rest of the events are connected by science in *Mae Jamison* and the murder in *A Murder That Rocked the Nation*. These events are also made interesting by developing them with more detail. For example:

Mae C. Jamison	A Murder That Rocked the Nation
Event: Served in the Peace Corps (PC)	Event: Funeral
• goes after medical school	• public funeral with open casket
• members of the PC help people	• 50,000 people attended and saw the beaten body
• was in PC for more than 2 years	• pictures appeared in the newspapers
• worked in West Africa	• The nation was enraged
• taught people about health care	
• wrote rules for health care and safety	
• left in 1985	

Table 4.6 Conclusions in Historical Genres

Genre	Type	Example From Mentor Text
Biography	Significance or impact of the life	"She became a teacher at Dartmouth College. She encourages African-American students and other minority students to study math and science. Jemison encourages students to do all they can with their imagination, creativity, and curiosity" (*Mae C. Jamison*)
Autobiography	What is happening in the present or a reorientation: "rounding off with a comment or an expression of attitude" (Coffin, 2006, p. 50)	"This year, I am in the third grade, and my English is perfect! I have many friends now, and I'm very happy. But I'll always remember Ali, my first American friend" (*My First American Friend*).
Empathetic Autobiography		"I am tired from hunting and fishing and thinking so much today. The warmth of the fire puts me to sleep. *Wunniook*. Be well" (*Tapenum's Day*).
Historical Recount	Deduction: drawing out the historical significance of the events recorded	"The murder of Emmet Till enraged both blacks and whites, causing many people to join the civil rights movement" (*A Murder that Rocked the Nation*, p. 12).
Historical Account		"The Compromise of 1850 left many people unhappy. Southerners accused the North of wanting to destroy slavery. Northerners accused the South of wanting to spread slavery. Later, Abraham Lincoln would warn that the United States could not go on forever 'half-slave and half-free' "(*History Alive*, p. 190).

The conclusions vary slightly in the various historical genres (see Table 4.6), but they are all related to the theme that tied the events together.

Features of Students' Writing: Stages

Veronica's book about her father's immigration experience illustrates the various aspects of the stages that require attention. Each paragraph was written on a page and accompanied with illustrations.

Dad's Journey

My dad left El Salvdor in 1992 He felt very sad to leave El Salvdor, but he needed to find work to help his parents. On October 5th 1992 he traveled to America. He arrived in Boston. He coold not believe his eyes. Boston was huge! He was so thrilled to be here, but sad too.

Then my dad found a house and a job at the car wash. When the first check came in he got $100.00. He was so happy he mailed his parents $50.00 and he kept $50.00 but he was still was homesick

A few years later he met my mom and my four-year old sister Amber. Theay got married. One year later something amazing I. The date was March 29th 2002. I was born When my eyes first opend, My Dad screamed in excitement. My mom, dad My six year old sister Amber, and My self were all one big happy family!
The End
2013
I know it was very hard for dad to Leave his parents but at least now he is living a better life.

Verónica shows both effective features as well as challenges in the stages of her biographical recount.

	1	2	3	4	
Orientation			√		Very brief explanation of the circumstances that prompted his emigration. There is a hint of the theme that ties this biographical recount, i.e., her father's mixed feelings about leaving his home country.
Record of Events (Historical genres)		√			The biographical recount was supposed to be about the journey, which is not developed at all. The rest of the events are not developed either.
Conclusion (varies depending on the specific genre)		√			The concluding thoughts are after the expression "the end."

Orientation. Very few students have difficulty with the basic information, such as the who, where, and when. The background is what is usually lacking. Veronica gave a hint but did not elaborate. Often the theme that makes the life of the person significant is also missing.

Record of Events. The greatest challenge for students is to develop the events. They tend to transfer what they have in their timelines without much elaboration. The assignment illustrated earlier was particularly challenging. None of the students did a thorough account of their parents' journey but rather of their whole life with little detail about the journey itself.

Autobiographies are a very difficult genre for elementary school students because the theme that ties the events is the person's identity, and often students are still too young to have a sense about what is going to make them special and what they will be known for as they mature. To address this challenge, Ed, a 3rd-grade teacher, had the students think about what they were good at, and how they saw themselves in the future. For example, one student told about cooking with his grandmother since he was very young and he was going to become a famous chef, while another student told about his interest in doing experiments and how he was going to be a famous scientist (Brisk et al., 2021). A 6th-grade teacher working with emergent bilinguals had students do the same, but only the student who had done a unit on careers had a clear sense of her identity and showed it throughout the events of her piece.

Conclusion. Conclusions do not come easy for children. Veronica concludes with *The End* and then as an afterthought hints of the significance of her father's immigration. Students can improve their conclusions through coaching and conferencing. For example, a 3rd grader revised his conclusion on Diego Rivera's biography as follows: *Diego Rivera's murals inspired the North American artist to paint in the walls. Diego created a style of art that was entirely Mexican.* He goes on for three more sentences elaborating on the importance of these murals. Some students insisted that they could only write about people who were dead already.

Language Features of Historical Genres

There are many language features that help make meaning in historical genres. Some, such as verbs and adverbials of time and place, were included in Chapter 3. Other more complex features of narrative writing and particularly of the language of history are included in this chapter. Teachers should teach a few features to cover in a unit given the genre and the grade level (see Table 4.4 for suggestions).

Reference Ties Using Different Noun Groups

In history texts, different noun groups are often used in reference to the same person or group of people. For example, in a historical account set in Australia, the author refers to the same group of people using *English settlers, the British,* and *the Europeans* (Coffin, 2006, pp. 59–60). For students with different cultural backgrounds, the use of this type of reference in historic text can be confusing. For example, an immigrant child questioned her 4th-grade teacher why she referred to two sides in the war of independence (in the United States), when this student had read that there were three: the colonials, the British, and the Red Coats. She was unaware that the British and Red Coats referred to the same people.

Grammatical Persons

There are three grammatical persons: first (I, we), second (you), and third (she, he, it, they). The first and second persons overtly express the presence of the writer and the audience. The third person places the focus on the topic at hand, hiding the writer and gearing the piece toward a generalized audience. Autobiographies and empathetic autobiographies are naturally written in first person, while the other historical genres are done in third person.

Noun Groups

There are a number of aspects of noun groups that need to be taught in upper elementary and middle school. They should be introduced with different genres in consideration to age/grade level (see Table 4.7). They may need to be reviewed in later genres depending on what the uncoached writing of the students reveals. Many of the features recommended for instruction in later grade levels may appear in the texts students are reading at lower grade levels since students usually read more difficult texts than they can produce. For that reason, it is appropriate to use lower grade level texts when teaching students to use those features in their writing.

When introducing biographies in 3rd grade, it is best to review the use of adjectives, learned in genres covered in Chapter 3. There are a number of additional features that need to be taught.

Proper Nouns

Nouns can be proper (George Washington) or common (president). For students from other cultures unfamiliar with historical content covered in the curriculum of the country, it is important to practice proper nouns. Unlike other students, they have not heard these names in their daily lives. In turn, L2 learners' own names (an example of proper nouns) may be difficult for their teachers, resulting in incorrect pronunciation of the names. In the worst cases, teachers resort to changing their names so that they can pronounce them better. Two good children's books that address the topic of name changing are *My Name Is María Isabel* by Alma Flor Ada and *Any Small Goodness* by Tony Johnston (see Lesson 10.1).

Table 4.7 Features of Noun Groups

Genre/Grade Introduced	Language Feature	Example
Biography (3)	Proper names (L2 learners)	Harriet Tubman, Dorchester County, the Underground Railroad
	Review of adjectives	Under the **floor** boards was a **secret** tunnel.
Biography (4–5)	Complex noun troups by including multiple adjectives and adding post-nominal modifiers	Harriet was born in **a small one-room log** hut. Members **of the Peace Corps** help people **in poor countries**. Mae Jemison, **the first African-American woman in space**, was born in 1956. Hans, **who had hidden with a Christian family**, reunited with his mother in Amsterdam.
Autobiography and Empathetic Autobiography (4–6)	Evaluative language	He thought I would be an **easy** target.
	Graduation	I participated in a program run by a **remarkable** family therapist.
	Review of complex noun groups	I have listened to **compelling stories about their lives back home**.
Historical Recounts and Accounts (6–8)	Review of complex noun groups, evaluative language, graduation	The **Indigenous** groups **who lived in the present-day Ohio River Valley and achieved their cultural apex from the first century CE to 400 CE** are collectively known as the Hopewell culture.
	Class, institution, documents, laws as participant	**Portuguese mariners** built an Atlantic empire. **Spain** gained a foothold in present-day Florida. **The Empire** needed more revenue to replenish its dwindling coffers. **The civil rights movement** had many leaders.
	Intentional choice of participant as the doer	**Prime Minister Grenville** introduced the Currency Act of 1764, prohibiting the colonies from printing additional paper money and requiring colonists to pay British merchants in gold and silver instead of the colonial paper money already in circulation (*different option:* **The Currency Act of 1764** prohibited the colonies …)
	Nominalization	The **kidnapping** and **murder** of Emmett Till enraged both blacks and whites.

Complex Noun Groups

Complex noun groups are a major feature of written language, rarely found in oral language and seldom used by young writers (Brisk, 2021). By 4th grade students should start using more modifiers beyond the simple adjective, such as those listed in Table 4.7, to give additional information and pack language. For example,

- Multiple prenominal modifiers (adjectives, present and past participles, adverbs): The **trained, young** astronauts boarded the space ship. **A more violent anti-Semitic** phase began in 1938. The **burning cherished ancestral** home glowed in the distance.
- Prepositional phrases: Members **of the Peace Corps**; a public funeral **with an open casket**.
- Appositions: Mae Jemison, **the first African-American woman astronaut,** orbited the earth in 1992.
- Embedded clauses (relative clauses) with a conjugated (finite) verb: Hans, **who had hidden during the war,** survived the Holocaust.
- Embedded clauses with an unconjugated (non-finite) verb: Hans, **hidden by a Christian family,** . . .; An African American Boy **visiting family members in rural Mississippi.**

Evaluative Language and Graduation

Writers use evaluative vocabulary to (a) express feelings (Affect), (b) make moral judgments of behaviors (Judgment), and (c) assess quality (Appreciation) (see Table 4.8). This type of language shows either the positive or negative feelings, judgment, or appreciation on the part of the writer toward the topics or people in the texts. It can also show how writers judge or appreciate the topic at hand. Writers use graduation to increase or diminish the intensity of meanings (Humphrey et al., 2012). For example, *terrible* instead of *bad*, or *tiny* instead of *small*. (For a complete analysis of graduation see Brisk, 2021.)

In autobiographies and empathetic autobiographies the use of evaluative language and graduation allow the author to express the feelings of the writer. In the other historical genres, the author can show his or her point of view toward the persons or events through the choice of evaluative language and graduation. Authors are careful not to sound too opinionated. For example, . . . *and* **achieved** *their cultural* **apex** *from the first century* CE *to 400 CE* . . . . Evaluative language and graduation are also used to show the attitudes of the people they are writing about. For example, *other colonists showed their* **distaste** *for the new act by* **boycotting** *British goods and* **protesting** *in the streets.* With young students, teachers just talk about "persuasive language." Middle school students could discern more the different meanings as to whether the language is expressing feelings, judgment, or evaluation.

New Types and Intentional Choice of Participants

In historical genres the participants can be a class, institutions, laws, or documents instead of a specific person, especially in recounts and accounts, for example, *colonials, the Senate, the Bill of Rights, the Declaration of Independence,* and so on. Students need to understand that these participants can do, say, sense, and so on as shown in the example in Table 4.7. Young students are more used to people carrying out the actions indicated by the verbs. Although middle school students understand these different types of participants, they do not use them in their writing. For

Table 4.8 Evaluative Vocabulary

	Positive	Negative
Affect	Happy, trusting, engaged	Sadly, fearful, bored
Judgment	Lucky, powerful, brave, good	Unfortunate, weak, cowardly, bad
Appreciation	Lovely, well-written, meaningful	Boring, simplistic, insignificant

Source: Humphrey et al. (2012)

example, a paragraph about the Vietnam War written by a middle school student included as participants *the North Vietnamese, the Vietcong, Vietnamese soldiers, civilians*, and pronouns. *The war* was the only participant not referring to people.

In addition, the writer chooses specific participants for actions to give credit or blame. For example, in the examples in in Table 4.7, in the sentence,**Prime Minister Grenville** *introduced the Currency Act of 1764, prohibiting the colonies*, the prime minister gets the credit or blame for the action. In the alternate example, **The Currency Act of 1764** *prohibited the colonies . . .*, no person is mentioned but just the Act, removing responsibility from the person who did it.

Nominalization

Verbs or adjectives are turned to nouns in order to evaluate actions and pack language (see Brisk, 2021, for complete explanation). For example, *In 1850, Henry Clay proposed a second compromise to keep peace between the North and the South. This **proposal** left many people unhappy.* Nominalizations also help connect paragraphs. For example, a paragraph starts, *Prime Minister Grenville announced the imposition of the Stamp Act in 1765.* The paragraph goes on to explain the Stamp Act and the next paragraph starts, *The **announcement** of the Stamp Act raised numerous concerns among colonists in America.*

Adverbials of Manner, Accompaniment, Reason

Circumstances are typically expressed with adverbials in the form of adverbs (*strongly*), prepositional phrases (*in Europe*), noun groups (*the last day of the war*), and subordinate clauses (*after he was wounded*). The latter is actually a clause complex, but it has the same function as the other adverbial forms. Therefore, it is easier for students if the clause complexes are included with all the adverbials. These various types of adverbials express a number of circumstances (see Table 4.9). In addition to adverbials of time and place covered in Chapter 3, as students mature

Table 4.9 Adverbials

Questions for Adverbials	Examples
Time • When?	**In 1849,** California asked …
Extent • How long? How far? How many times?	The war lasted **three long years**.
Place • Where?	She was born **in Decatur, Alabama**.
Manner • How? What with? What like? (*angry, carefully, with all his might*)	He had been **badly** beaten …
Accompaniment • With whom? (*alone, together, with his friend*)	While at the grocery store **with some friends** …
Cause: Reason • Why? (*consequently, therefore, because he wanted to see you*)	People said the reason I refused to give up my seat was **because I was tired**.
Cause: Purpose • Why? What for?	**In order to avoid such a high casualty rate**, President Truman decided to use the atomic instead.

Sources: Derewianka (2011), Butt et al. (2012)

they need to recognize and use other types of adverbials to indicate other circumstances. Authors include the circumstances first in the sentence if they want to stress their importance. For example, instead of saying "The war lasted three long years," the author may say, "After three long years the war ended." In the first sentence the focus is *the war*, while in the second it is the extent of time. The best way to have students think about adverbials is through questions (for a more extensive list see Brisk, 2021).

Clause Complexes

Once in 4th grade, students often start expressing more complex thoughts in their writing. This requires sentences with more than one clause that are structured in different ways and that express a variety of relationships (see Brisk, 2021, for a full analysis). For students in the upper elementary and middle school grades, it is important to learn about complex clauses with non-conjugated verbs (non-finite), which help pack language. There are three types:

> **To + verb:** Jemison wrote rules *to improve public health.*
> **-ing:** The murder of Emmet Till enraged both blacks and whites, *causing many people to join the civil rights movement.*
> **-ed:** *Helped by abolitionists*, they escaped to the North.

Non-finite clauses of all three types are abundant in recounts, narratives, and historical genres. Students use without difficulty the *to + verb* construction. They seldom use the others.

One type of relationship found in recounts, narratives, and historical genres is *projections*. In projections, one clause indicates what someone said (locution) or thought (idea). The other clauses express what was actually said or thought, either quoted or paraphrased (Eggins, 2004). When paraphrased, the two clauses are often joined by *that*. For example,

> **Quoting**: She immediately started yelling, "I'll have you put in jail!"
> **Reporting**: Some Southerners asserted that their States should be removed from the Union.

Reporting is more common in historical genres unless original sources are available to create dialogues based on what actually was said or written in records. In empathetic autobiographies the authors use their imagination to include dialogue. Some biographies for children also use dialogue to make the writing more realistic to students.

Another important aspect of language to teach upper elementary and middle school students in these types of clause complexes is the quoting or reporting verb. These verbs show the state of mind or personality of the person saying or reporting. In the earlier examples, the verb *yelling* showed the person was angry and *asserted* showed the determination of the people making that claim.

There are many other types of relationships expressed by bringing together clauses, such as:

Reason: Southerners were furious **because** entering as a free state would mean having more free states than slave states in the Union.
Additive: They were put on trial, **and** a jury of 12 white men found them not guilty.
Contrast: Lore did not love her new home, **but** at least she was safe.
Condition: **If** you were black, you had to walk to school.
Cause: **As a result of the war**, the United States gained a huge amount of territory.

The important aspect to work with students is that the connecting words or phrases express the intended meaning.

Paragraphs

Paragraphs in all genres need to center around a topic and be well developed to give sufficient information to the reader. For example, in César Chávez biography, one paragraph tells about finding work for the family in a farm, the next one details more about this work, another describes the family living conditions, and so on. An important feature of paragraphs in the historical genres is the choice of *theme*—or initial part—of the first sentence in the paragraph (for details on the notion of *theme*, see Chapter 6 Reports). Authors choose to start sentences with what they consider important to highlight, usually the people, institutions, or events they are writing about or the time when events occur. The following chart shows examples of paragraph starters from a biography, where the focus is people, and from a historical account where the focus is events, institutions, or laws. In all types of historical genres, adverbials of time often begin sentences to show how the events move forward.

César Chávez Biography	Historical Account on The Compromise of 1850
César Chávez	The fight between the North and the South over western lands
César's father	The Fugitive Slave Law
The Chávez family	The Compromise of 1850
In 1944	In 1849

(More details on the formation of paragraphs are included in Chapter 6 Reports and in Brisk, 2021.)

Text Connectives

In recounts, text connectives (also called transitional words) are mostly adverbials of time. For example, *After Columbus crossed the Atlantic Ocean; On the day that Ellis Island opened; After World War II*. Often, there is no connective and the paragraph starts with the person who is the focus of the recount or a new participant. For example, in *A Murder That Rocked the Nation*, the beginning phrases mostly introduce the central events and participants: "The civil rights movement," "Emmett Till," "Till's mother," "Two local men," "The murder of Emmett Till," and one adverbial of time, "After the trial." Very rarely do recounts use such words as *then* or *next*, which are so often taught to elementary children.

Engagement: Use of Language to Present Writer's Position in Relation to That of Others

When writers introduce the word of others, they reflect their own attitude toward what is said through the introductory language (see Brisk, 2021, for full explanation). For example,

> Churchill said, "The support of the Americans was essential." (neutral position)
> Churchill affirmed, "The support of the Americans was essential." (agreeing with the person quoted)
> Churchill claimed, "The support of the Americans was essential." (distancing from the person quoted)

Writers use language resources to open what they say to the opinion of others or to affirm their own opinion with no room for other opinions (see Brisk, 2021). For example, using modals to allow for other opinions: *the Marshall plan **may** have been the key factor . . .* or rejecting other opinions with negatives: *the Marshall plan **did not** benefit . . .*

Features of Students' Writing: Language

The language features at the word level show that Veronica, the author of the piece shown earlier, reveals effective use of language resources as well as some challenges (see Table 4.9).

Verbs

Veronica's writing shows that students can master the use of tense and the variety of verbs after instruction. She could still improve use of verbs to reflect her dad's emotions. For example, she

Table 4.9 Language in Veronica's Writing

Aspect of Language		1	2	3	4	Comments
Verb Groups (review)					√	No repetition except for *was*. Varied action verbs: left, traveled, found, screamed, etc. Some sensing verbs: felt, believe Verbs are in the past and at the very end appropriately change to the present to describe present times. Emotions of the characters are shown through the construction "to be + modifier:" *was so thrilled, was so happy, was homesick*
Reference Ties Using Different Noun Groups		√				None used
Grammatical Person				√		3rd person, switches to 1st person twice
Adverbials of Place and Time (review)					√	Multiple adverbials of Place: *El Salvador, to America, in Boston, at the car wash*, etc. Time: *in 1992, On October 5th 1992, When the first check came*, etc.
Text Connectives				√		Uses *then* once and the adverbial phrase *A few years later*
Noun Groups	Proper names				√	Family rather than historical figures because of the topic of the writing
	Adjectives (review)		√			Possessive: *his, my* Happy, sad, huge, few, (the majority in the construction *to be + adjective*)
	Post-nominal modifiers	√				No other types of modifiers
	Evaluative language			√		Some evaluative vocabulary reflecting the main character's attitude: *thrilled, happy* and the author's point of view, *amazing*
	graduation			√		*Screamed, very* hard, *so* happy
	Class, organization, etc. doer				√	Because it is a biography all the doers are people
	Intentional choice of participant as doer					NA
	Nominalizations		√			None

Aspect of Language		1	2	3	4	Comments
Adverbials other than time and place		√				Manner: in excitement (excitedly)
Clause Complexes	Non-finite clauses to pack language	√				To+ verb: *to leave El Salvador*
	Reported and quoted clauses			√		None
	Connecting words	√				Multiple clauses with *but*: *he felt sad but needed to find work.* Clauses with *when*: *When my eyes first opened, . . .* And with *and*: *He mailed his parents $50.00 and he kept $50.00.*
Paragraphs			√			Theme of first sentence as expected; Paragraphs underdeveloped
Engagement		√				No quotations or opening/closing doors to other opinions

could write, *he hurried to mail his parents $50.00* to denote excitement about his earnings. Another problem is the overuse of the structure to be + adjective, which is the structure children use when first introducing adjectives. Thus, even when these features are taught with earlier genres, students can still improve. Even in the middle schools, some students showed challenges in the use of verb tenses. For example, 6th graders writing about events in one of the wars kept switching between present and past tense.

Reference Ties Using Different Noun Groups

Veronica does not use this language resource in her biography because she was writing about her father rather than a historical figure. Students need to be taught both to understand them in the articles they read when doing research and in what they write. For example, a teacher suggested to a student that she did not have to repeat Hillary Clinton every time. She could use Hillary or Clinton or presidential candidate.

Grammatical Person

Veronica appropriately used mostly third person in a biography. Writing a biography about her father led her to insert herself in the narrative, using the first person. Keeping a text all in the third person is usually very hard for students of all ages. It is not unusual for students to revert to the first person either at the beginning or end of a narrative written in the third person.

Adverbials

Veronica uses adverbials of time and place effectively, giving a sense of when and where things were happening. Adverbials of place come more natural to students. As was the case with Veronica, she used effectively adverbials of time as a result of instruction. Some of these adverbials are prepositional phrases. The use of prepositions is very difficult for L2 learners. Sometimes, they choose the incorrect one (*And then I got hit in [on] my chest and hit so hard that my Mom called a doctor*). Other times they may omit the preposition (*My family is happy living [in] America and hope to someday visit Vietnam*). This can be a persistent challenge that is never quite overcome.

Text Connectives

Veronica uses both the person she is writing about and adverbial phrases of time to start sentences. Once she uses *then*, which results vague as a transition. Without instruction students tend to overuse *then*, *and*, *and then*, and *so*. For example, in a 248-word recount, a 5th grader used the word *then* 11 times.

Noun Groups

One general challenge with noun groups is the general knowledge of content language related to the topic of the writing. For example, a 3rd grader used the word *thing* throughout his biography of Ben Franklin rather than naming the objects or their category: *Ben invented so many things and had many jobs, and invented things like the stove, and discovered many things, and invented many things* . . .

There are a number of aspects to consider when working with noun groups:

- *Proper Nouns.* For Veronica this was not an issue because she was writing about her father and about places familiar to her. For many students, when researching in order to write historical genres, they encounter names of people and places that are unfamiliar. They often have trouble spelling and retaining the names.
- *Adjectives (review).* Veronica needed some review of adjectives by encouraging her to use more and in structures other than "to be + adjective."
- *Post-nominal modifiers.* Veronica does not use any postnominal modifiers. Lacking descriptions, students writing does not call for modifiers. Including descriptions of places, hardships, feelings, and motivations in the writing would have given more opportunities to use adjectives to make the recount more interesting and engaging for the audience.
- *Sentences that could be packed into a complex noun group.* Another problem comes from the use of multiple short sentences. For example, a student wrote: *Till's mother required a public funeral. She wanted the casket to be open.* These two clauses could become one by adding a prepositional phrase as a modifier: "Till's mother required a public funeral *with an open casket.*"
- *Evaluative language and graduation.* Veronica uses some evaluative language to express her father's feelings, such as *happy, sad,* and *homesick* and intensified those feelings by adding the adverbs *very* and *so*. Students need to be taught how evaluative language and graduation can be used to reflect the authors' perspective with respect to what they are writing. Once they learn, however, they may overuse it.
- *Class, institution, documents, laws as participants.* Veronica's topic and limited writing is not conducive to writing about institutions and classes of participants. Connecting immigration with laws and historical circumstances would have provided more of an opportunity to using these other types of participants. Middle schools in general have difficulty using this type of participants.
- *Intentional choice of participant as a doer.* The same problem as with the earlier item is reflected with respect to this one. Middle schools students can be made aware of how authors manipulate participants to reflect their own position and could be coached to do it when jointly constructing text. It would still be too hard for them to do it on their own.
- *Nominalization.* There are no nominalizations used in her writing. Middle school students begin to become aware of nominalizations and the impact it can make on their writing in 6th grade. It is not until 8th grade that they can use it more independently with practice over time.

Adverbials Other Than Time and Place

Most students use adverbial phrases and clauses of time and place. As students advance in grades, they should be encouraged to use adverbials describing other circumstances, especially adverbs ending in -ly, such as *carefully* and *sadly*. For example, Veronica substituted it with a prepositional phrase: *in excitement* rather than *excitedly*.

Clause Complexes

The clause complexes Veronica used are the most typical students use. She did not use any non-finite clauses with -*ing* or -*ed*. The use of non-finite clauses helps to pack sentences. For example, a 4th-grade student wrote, *I slid down and laughed the whole way*. It could be packed to, "I slid down, laughing the whole way" (Brisk & DeRosa, 2014). The only relationships she expressed are with *when, but,* and. Sometimes students have difficulty expressing these relationships and using the appropriate conjunction. For example, a 3rd grader wrote, "He hate the smell of waxs and hate making candles." What he meant was, "He hated making candles because he hated the smell of wax." In addition, Veronica wrote many short sentences, some of which could have been packed. For example, *My dad left El Salvdor in 1992 . . . . On October 5th 1992 he traveled to America. He arrived in Boston,* could have been packed into one: "On October 5th 1992 my dad left El Salvador for Boston, U.S.A."

Paragraphs

The theme of the initial sentence in Veronica's paragraphs start, like most biographies, with either the person who is the focus of the biography or an adverbial of time. For example, *my dad, then, a few years later*. Only the last sentence tagged after the end starts with I. A bigger issue in her paragraphs is that each contains topics that could have been further developed, breaking each paragraph into more than one. For example, the first paragraph includes leaving from his country, traveling to America, and arriving in Boston. Each could have been expanded, making *leaving* and *traveling* two separate paragraphs. Arriving in Boston could be combined with the next one that addresses settling in Boston. This is a common challenge in all the recount and narrative genres, and as suggested in Chapter 3, it should be practiced in all genres.

Engagement

There are no quotations or reporting on what others say in Veronica's text. Usually by 6th grade students are introduced to the notion of quoting other people's language. Both the function and mechanics of quotations are the initial focus. Most of the times teachers encourage the use of neutral language to introduce the quotations. Through deconstruction and joint construction, students become familiar with using language to reflect their own opinion. By 8th grade they apply these resources in their independent writing.

Mastery of the language to open or close the door to others' opinions does not happen until high school. In middle school teachers start to introduce the notion through deconstruction.

Lessons to Learn About Stages and Language of Historical Genres

Having done the genres described in Chapter 3, the students have a good background to start on the historical genres in 3rd grade. The lessons in this chapter apply to any of the genres; the specific features of the stages of each genre and the difficulty of language features need to be considered given the grade level. It is always best to present all the stages in a general way followed by more detailed lessons on each stage (orientation, record of events, and conclusion), including challenges that students encounter. Teachers are encouraged to review all of the lessons related to the stages and language and decide what will be appropriate for their own grade level. Because of the nature of autobiographies, instead of jointly constructing a class project, teachers either modeled by first writing each stage of their own autobiography with students following with theirs, or they carefully scaffolded students' drafts through questions and ample oral discussion (Brisk et al., 2021).

In Chapter 3, which covers genres usually done with younger learners, the process of teaching, modeling, and student writing was clustered by stage, i.e., orientation, sequence of events, and conclusion. In the historical genres usually taught to students beyond the early grades, the lessons cover the teaching and completion of a jointly produced project, followed by students creating their own individual projects. Teachers can use either approach based on what they think will work best for their students. For example, Jen, a middle school teacher working with newcomer students, deconstructed the whole mentor text but then focused on one stage at a time when modeling and having students write their own autobiography.

The lessons on language included in this chapter will focus on those most typically found in historic texts. Depending on the language development of students, they may need to review aspects of language covered in Chapter 3, such as verbs and adverbials of time and place. The uncoached piece should reveal the students' needs. If needed, use lessons from Chapter 3. Clusters of language features are inserted at various points, and they can be introduced with different genres based on their difficulty (see Table 4.4). Teachers need to select a few appropriate for their students' needs and level of maturity to teach.

Lesson 2. Deconstruction of Text to Learn About Stages and Establish the Theme

Goal: To notice in a broad way the stages of the genre in published texts and the theme that connects the events and the conclusion.

Materials: Short mentor texts that have been read during social studies lessons. Graphic organizer on large chart paper (see downloadable examples in the *Support Material* tab in the book's webpage).

Activities

- Re-read the mentor text in chunks corresponding to the stages and highlight or mark.
- Simultaneously, discuss the stages in a general way. For example, ask students to notice what kind of information the author includes in the orientation, the record of events, and the conclusion. Point out the stages in the graphic organizer as you discuss them.
- Have students notice in the conclusion the identity and significance of the person's life or the significance of the historical event, i.e., the theme that ties together the whole piece.
- Re-read the text, having the students notice how all the events, even those early on in the life of a person, relate to the identity or significance.
- Give groups of students copies of one or two more texts and have them identify the stages and the theme. For example, in the Mae Jemison biography, there is an orientation, several events, and a conclusion. Throughout the piece beginning with an early experience in elementary school, the theme is science.

Lesson 3. Reference Ties Using Different Noun Groups (Grades 4–8)

This lesson is appropriate for upper elementary and middle school. For younger students, just teach them the words authors use to avoid repetition.

> **Goal:** To have students recognize when different nouns refer to the same group of people.
>
> **Materials:** Mentor texts that use these types of constructions, preferably of the historical time they are studying.

Activities

- Read aloud a chunk of text.
- With the help of the students, circle the various historical participants.
- Based on what is happening, have the class identify any participants that seem to be connected with a topic and may be the same participants named with a different name. For example, show the students the following text (appropriate for middle school):

The Stamp Act Congress was a gathering of landowning, educated White men who represented the political elite of the colonies and was the colonial equivalent of the British landed aristocracy. While these gentry were drafting their grievances during the Stamp Act Congress, other colonists showed their distaste for the new act by boycotting British goods and protesting in the streets.

- Ask them, how many groups are there involved in what is happening here? The piece refers to:

  a) *landowning, educated White men,*
  b) *political elite,*
  c) *British landed aristocracy,*
  d) *gentry,*
  e) *other colonists.*

- After the discussion, the class should conclude that a, b, and d are the same people. The *British landed aristocracy* is another group that the first is being compared to but are not involved in the conflict. The second group is the *other colonists.*
- Give groups of students additional chunks of texts and have them identify the noun groups and decide if they are naming the same people. To facilitate the process, you may tell the students how many participants they are looking for.

Lesson 4. Research to Establish the Theme That Threads the Text

> **Goal:** To determine the identity of the person they are writing about or the significance of the historical event.
>
> **Materials:** Mentor texts in the genre. For example, the teachers teaching autobiography, described later, used *Reaching for the Moon* (3rd) and *I am a Promise* (6th grade). Additional sources that cover the topic.

Activities

The following description is based on what two teachers did when teaching autobiography writing to 3rd and 6th grade. (The 6th grade was a hybrid class because of COVID, so everything was done using the Goggle classroom.) The same steps can be done with any of the historical genres.

- The teacher read aloud the ending of the mentor text and discussed the identity of the author and the reason for his/her notoriety. The teacher wrote it down for all the class to see.
- Once the identity was established, the teacher told their students that they were going to start at the beginning to see how this identity was reflected in the rest of the autobiography.
- The teacher read aloud each page and asked the class to identify where the identity was reflected. He/she noted down the students' suggestions. The teacher made the students notice how even in the early life of the author there was a hint to the identity.
- The teacher went through the whole text doing the same.
- The teacher often stopped to have students relate each aspect they were discussing with their own lives. Given that the students are still young, when discussing the conclusion, the teacher suggested that the students should think of what they see themselves in the future based on their current abilities and interests. When discussing early events in their lives, even the young 3rd graders were able to identify events that signaled their future as chefs, scientists, artists, and so on (Brisk et al., 2021).

Lesson 5. Technical Language Found in Historical Text

Technical language in historical text consists of mostly nouns and verbs. The following lesson is based on a combination of what Pat and Beverly did in 4th and 5th grade (Brisk et al., 2018).

> **Goal:** To have students appropriate technical language to incorporate in the class as well as individual projects.
>
> **Materials:** Research resources used to develop the topic, with chunks representing important events earmarked. Graphic organizer with a column for stages and a column for language divided in nouns and verbs (shown later).

Activities

- Project or show on chart paper the first chunk and read aloud.
- In collaboration with the students, underline important technical noun groups and verbs. Discuss with students if they know the meaning. If they do not, have them look it up in the dictionary or thesaurus.
- Suggest synonyms that are more accessible to students. Discuss whether they should use the technical term or the more common term. Decide whether they should know and use the terms, or if by using them, the language in their writing would not sound like the language of somebody their age. For example, working together with the students, the teacher found possible alternatives (in handwriting font) for more technical terms and wrote them above the term.

> The *Fugitive Slave Law* surprised and angered many Northerners. In Illinois, a
> *Becoming known*   *shocked*
> *rising political leader* named Abraham Lincoln was *stunned* by the law.
>
> Some states passed laws forbidding officials to help *slave hunters*. Opponents of
>   *went in by force*
> slavery *broke into* jails to free *captured runaways*.

- List all the terms to be learned and use in the graphic organizer.
- Decide what to write in the notes to identify the major event and note it down.

Notes on Events	LANGUAGE	
	Noun Groups	Verbs
Fugitive Slave Law surprised the Northerners	Fugitive Slave Law Rising political leader AL was stunned Captured runaways	Broke into

- Together with the class, write up the event using the terms noted in the graphic organizer.
- Repeat with the whole class another chunk following the same steps.
- Have students working in groups do the same with additional chunks.

Follow Up

Use the same graphic organizer when planning the class project (Lesson 14) and have students use it when doing their individual or group pieces (Lesson 22).

Lesson 6. Deconstruction of Text for Orientation

Goal: To learn the information that goes in the orientation to help students write informative orientations.

Materials: Several mentor texts in the same historical genre. Orientation graphic organizer on chart paper. Copies of the graphic organizer, one per group.

Activities

- Read the orientation in the mentor text. The length of the orientation will vary. Sometimes, the orientation will be the first paragraph, but more often will be the first couple of paragraphs.
- Discuss which information will go in which column of the graphic organizer. You may fill out the graphic organizer or just have it present to point at the elements.
- Repeat the activity with a couple of other books.
- Give each group one or more texts and a copy of the graphic organizer. Have them write down the information from the book's orientation in their graphic organizer. Walk around the room checking their work and noting anything that will further instruction.

It is helpful to compare authors who do things a little bit differently to show students that there are choices within expected structures. For example, Maria, a 4th-grade teacher, when teaching students about orientations to biographies, showed two different examples and commented, *Now you can see the difference between the first author and the second author . . . The second author started not with when she was born, but decided to start with something fantastic about her . . . So you ask yourself, do I want to begin my book with . . . and either way is OK.* (Classroom observation 3/12/13)

Lesson 7. Grammatical Person

Usually the challenge for students is consistency of choice of person, especially in text written in the third person. Often students tend to switch to the first person, particularly at the end. Although autobiographies and empathetic autobiographies naturally call for first-person voice, occasionally students switch to third person when writing empathetic autobiographies, forgetting they are writing as if they were the person themselves. Some students also use the second person as if addressing the audience in general. For example, a middle school student wrote in a historical recount: *If you don't* [didn't] *like the war, you would join a protest march.* The use of first and second person makes the text less authoritative.

> **Goal:** to learn to write in the person appropriate for the genre and the voice.
> **Materials:** Image from a historical text, mentor texts in the genre they are writing used before and in a genre that uses a different person.

Activities

- Project the image and point at one person.
- Working in pairs, have one of the students narrate as if they were the person in the image. For example, the book *Coming to America* has a picture of a boat full of immigrants. The student can say, "I was in a boat with my parents and grandparents coming to the New World."
- Have a few groups share.
- Have the other student in the pair say the same idea but narrating about the person. The student would say, "She was in a boat with her parents and grandparents coming to the New World."
- Project and read a chunk of the mentor text in the genre they are learning about, and ask the students in which person it is written.
- Project and read a chunk of a mentor text in another genre that uses a different person, preferably a genre they have already studied.
- Choose an image from a mentor text in the genre of the current unit, and direct them to write a couple of sentences practicing the person they will have to use.

Follow up

Joint construction: Before starting a piece with the class, discuss which person they should be using given the genre and the voice. Negotiate the decision with the class and make sure they understand the reasons for the choice.

Individual construction and joint revision: Remind the students of the use of person before they start their individual pieces, and address it during joint revision. For example, if a student writes in the second person as in the earlier example, *If you don't* [didn't] *like the war, you would join a protest march*, discuss what needs to be done to translate it to third person to make it more authoritative. Have the whole class make suggestions. If they agree that the writing needs to be authoritative, then have students circle any use of "I" or "you" in their writing (as long as the genre is not autobiography or empathetic autobiography) and discuss changes.

Lesson 8. Jointly Constructed Orientations and Review of Adverbials of Time and Place

Even if the adverbials of time and place were practiced with recount genres (Chapter 3), students may need a reminder to use adverbials of time that clearly define the time. For example, a 5th grader used *then* 11 times in his piece. Adverbials of time in historical texts function as text connectives at the beginning of paragraphs to move the action forward. Writers do not include them in each paragraph but when indicating the passage of time is necessary. For example, *Before the sun is up, As I start to run, When he asks me to stay* (*Tapenum's Day*).

> **Goal:** To practice planning and writing the orientation with the students and learn how to research the content. Review the use of adverbials of time and place.
>
> **Materials:** Orientation graphic organizer on chart paper, corresponding with the specific genre; research resources with information about the content of what they are writing.

Activities

- Establish the content of the class recount and find two or three sources to consult:

  Biography: Choose one person related to the content of the unit to do as a class project. For example, for a unit on climate change, you can choose a scientist or activist for the biography.
  Empathetic Autobiography: Choose one person related to the historical topic that the students will eventually draw from to write their own independent empathetic autobiography.
  Historical Recount: Choose one aspect of the historical period you are studying. For example, if the mentor text came from a book on the Civil Rights Movement, then choose one event from this movement to make the class recount.
  Historical Account: Choose an event from the historical period you are covering where one event caused another. For example, a recount of the bombing of London by the Germans in WWII and how it caused families to send their children to the countryside to live with others.

- Create a large orientation graphic organizer.
- Project and read aloud the content, and ask suggestions of where in the graphic organizer to write the information.
- Take information from each column of the graphic organizer, and ask the class for suggestions on how to write it. Propose revisions if needed. As students make suggestions, encourage them to be explicit with respect to time and place. Remind them of expressions used in the mentor texts they deconstructed.

Follow Up: Adverbials of Time and Place

Please note the use of the term *adverbials* rather than *adverbs* because these circumstances are not only expressed by an adverb (*tomorrow*) but by noun groups (*last night*), phrases (*at the end of the war*), and clauses (*as he walked toward the bridge*).

Address again the use of these adverbials, especially those of time:

- when jointly constructing the record of events
- when students write individually
- when jointly revising student work

The best way to do it is through questions:

Time
- When? (soon, at 10 o'clock)
- How long? (briefly, overnight, soon)
- How often? (always, never, daily)

Place
- Where? (here, inside the house)

Lesson 9. Deconstruction of Text—Record of Events

> **Goal:** To have students identify major events and understand how they are connected to the conclusion.
>
> **Materials:** Chart paper or projector. Same mentor text as used in lessons 4 and 5. If possible, have copies available for all students or for groups.

Activities

- Project a timeline or put up onto chart paper.
- Remind them of the text used in lesson 4. Ask them to look at the conclusion and suggest what is the content. Include it in the graphic organizer. For example, for the historical recount *A Murder That Shocked the Nation*, the conclusion addresses the consequences of the murder of Emmett Till.
- Identify the first major event after the orientation, and make a note in the timeline. For example

  - Allegedly flirted with a White woman at a store

- Working in groups, have the students identify additional major events and suggest what to write on the timeline, negotiating changes when necessary. For example,

  - Emmett was kidnapped and killed
  - Emmett's funeral
  - Two men tried and freed
  - Two men sold their story

  - Alternatively, you can project a copy of the text and annotate on the text itself.
  - Remind them how the themes of the events connect to the conclusion.

Lesson 10. Noun Groups

To improve their noun groups, students need to be precise in the nouns they use and add modifiers to further describe the nouns. For example, when writing empathetic autobiographies after a visit to Plymouth Plantation, one of Pat's 5th-grade students wrote, *I stirred the soup*. Through questions, Pat guided that student to write *I stirred the rabbit stew* instead.

In this section there are multiple aspects of language to review and teach. Use the information from the uncoached samples to decide what needs review. Depending on the genre and the level of maturity of your students, choose a couple of new aspects of language to work with your students. It is best to coordinate across grade levels to decide when to teach what.

Lesson 10.1. Proper Names (L2 Learners, Especially Recent Arrivals)

Although this lesson is important for recent arrivals, other students may need to learn the pronunciation, spelling, and historical and geographical facts about the people and places.

> **Goals:** To familiarize students with key people or places encountered in mentor texts and research resources. To practice the pronunciation.
>
> **Materials:** Mentor text or research resource they need to use given what aspect of history they are studying. For example, *A Picture Book of Sacagawea*. Short video with comparable content, for example, *Sacagawea for Kids* www.bing.com/search?FORM=U523DF&

PC=U523&q=video+about+Sacagawea+for+kids; worksheet with images of the people and a map of the United States.

Activities

Read the first page of the mentor text, for example, *A Picture Book of Sacagawea*.

Make two columns with headings—People and Places—and write the proper names in that first page:

People	Places
Sacagawea	Rocky Mountains
Shoshone	Etc.
Etc.	

- Read the names aloud.
- Project the images of the people, and display a map of the United States. As you repeat the names, point at the pictures and the map. Explain who the people are and the significance of the geographical location. Have students think of comparable people and places in their own countries.
- Give groups of students a worksheet with images of the people and a map of the United States. Have them write the names where they belong.
- Reread the page and have students point at the image when you read the proper name.
- Repeat with additional pages that introduce key figures and places, e.g., Thomas Jefferson, Meriwether Lewis, William Clark, Missouri River, etc.
- Show students the short video and have them raise their hand when they hear a familiar name. Stop the video and ask them to point at the name they heard and repeat it.
- Have groups write a short paragraph where they use two or three of the proper names introduced.

Lesson 10.2. Review of Adjectives (Grade 3)

Do Lesson 18 in Chapter 3 using text from the genre you are teaching. Then practice again when jointly constructing text, reminding students to use modifiers where appropriate when writing their own pieces and once more when jointly reviewing student work. When taking notes as shown in Lesson 5 in this chapter, noun groups are listed with modifiers as a way to emphasize their use in and their importance in making precise meaning.

Lesson 10.3. Complex Noun Groups (4–8)

This is an important aspect of language to help students develop. You can start in upper elementary, but it is essential in middle school in connection with any historical genre. Thus, regardless of whether it was introduced in earlier genres or grades, it needs to be reviewed in all the other genres and grades. The review can be done in whole class or group lessons or during conferencing, depending on need.

Goal: To teach students to recognize complex noun groups and understand their content.
Materials: Chunks of the mentor text used in Lesson 9, which include complex noun groups; chunks of the mentor text in the original form and with the noun groups converted to simpler structures and language.

Activities

- Identify, with the collaboration of the whole class, complex noun groups in one of the chunks of the mentor text. For example,

Adolf Hitler, a failed student and artist, built up **a small racist, anti-Semitic political party** in Germany after World War I. **Hitler's Beer Hall Putsch** failed. In prison, he wrote *Mein Kampf*— **an account of his movement and his views.**

- Getting the class involved, break up each noun group, creating multiple sentences and even translating the language to everyday language to ensure comprehension (Fang et al., 2006). Do the activity orally first, and then create a chart in writing. For example,

Adolf Hitler, a failed student and artist, built up . . .	Adolf Hitler was a poor student and artist. He built up . . .

- Give groups of students additional chunks of the mentor text to identify complex noun groups and break them up.
- Have a few groups share.
- Give the groups a set of complex noun groups from yet another chunk of the mentor text already broken up for them to create complex noun groups. Encourage them to change any everyday language to technical terms they learned in Lesson 5 if appropriate. Give them a copy of the original to compare with what they did and discuss.

Follow Up

There are three opportunities to reinforce this aspect of language:

1. During joint construction, negotiate with students if they propose language that could be packed into complex noun groups (Lesson 15).
2. Remind students to use complex noun groups when writing their individual pieces. Refer them to the charts you created (Lesson 19).
3. During joint revision, use student work with sentences that can be packed into a complex noun group to model, and then suggest specific instances in their work by underlining the sentences that could be packed (see Lesson 20).

Lesson 10.4. Evaluative Language and Graduation (Grades 3–8)

Goal: To learn how to express point of view through the use of language resources that express attitude (evaluative language) and increase or decrease the intensity of what is expressed (graduation).

Materials: Paragraph from a mentor text in the genre of the unit that includes such language. For example, "One of the *most tragic* events was the murder of a 14-year-old boy named Emmett Till. The *horrifying* event . . .". Sample of student work in the same genre from the past. Projector.

Activities

- Project and read the paragraph from the mentor text *A Murder That Rocked the Nation*.
- Ask the following questions: Is the author's attitude toward the event positive or negative?

What language in the text gave you this feeling? [*horrifying* and *tragic*] Does the author increase or decrease the intensity of any of those words? [*most*] (You may point out that the author does not say "I think . . .," a common tendency among children, but uses adjectives, to describe the event that shows his point of view.)

- Show the sample of student work:

My mom and dad left Vietnam because they wanted to visit America where their parents lived. When my mom and dad arrived in Massachusetts they decided to stay in America.

- Ask students, How did the author feel about his parents staying in America? They will probably say that they are not sure. What language would you add if you wanted to show that you feel glad they stayed? For example, the author could add *fortunately* to the clause, *they decide to stay in America*. What would you add if you wanted to show displeasure? For example, add *unfortunately*.

Follow Up

1. During joint construction first ask students what's their attitude toward what they are writing and if it is appropriate to show it. Then after drafting a few sentences, ask if they could add language to show this attitude (Lesson 15).
2. Remind students to use evaluative language and graduation when writing their individual pieces but not to overdo it. Refer them to the charts you created (Lesson 19).
3. During joint revision, choose one paragraph of a student's work that would be enhanced with this type of language or one where the use of evaluative language and graduation could be revised. For example, a student wrote: *WWII was the most chaotic war in history.* You could suggest that no war is orderly. Thus, the claim that any war is "the most chaotic" would be hard to prove. One could write about WWII that the *intensive* bombing from airplanes, especially the use of the atomic bomb caused *massive* casualties and *heavy* destruction of cities. (see Lesson 20).

Lesson 10.5. Class or Organization as Doer (Grades 6–8)

Goal: To have students recognize and incorporate in their writing, especially of historical recounts and accounts, a class, institutions, laws, and documents instead of person as participants.

Materials: A chunk of text in the genre of the unit that includes these kinds of participants.

Activities

- Show students the chosen paragraph. For example,

In December 1960, the **National Liberation Front** *emerged* to challenge the South Vietnamese government. **A civil war** *erupted* for control of South Vietnam, while **Hanoi** *sought* to unite the country under its own communist leadership. The **Second Indochina War** *began* in earnest with the US commitment to prevent the communists from overrunning South Vietnam. In spring 1961, **the administration of John Kennedy** *expanded* US support for the South Vietnamese government.

- Underline the verbs that do not have specific people as participants. For example, *emerged, erupted, sought, began, expanded.*

- Ask students to name the participant who is doing the action of the verbs underlined. Circle them as they name them (bolded in the example). What does each stand for? Discuss.
- Have them think of similar kinds of participants in their own environment. For example, the post office, the neighborhood, the government, the traffic laws, name of the city or town where they live, and so on. List them. Choose one of the participants and have students suggest a sentence. For example, *The post office delivered a big package.*
- Working in groups, have students think of sentences with the other participants in the list.

Follow Up

As students do research for the class project and their own projects, have them list such participants in their notebooks to use when doing their own writing.

Lesson 10.6. Choice of Participant as the Doer of the Action (Grades 6–8)

This is still a difficult concept even for middle school students. It will be presented through deconstruction to start building background for them to be able to do it later in high school.

> **Goal:** To make students aware that history authors choose specific participants to hide or put blame on those doing the action.
> **Materials:** Mentor text containing examples.

Activities

- Project and read two passages on the same topic but with different participants as the doer. For example,

  - On the morning of August 6, 1945, the B-29 bomber Enola Gay dropped an atomic bomb on the Japanese city of Hiroshima.
  - On August 6, 1945, the United States dropped an atomic bomb on the city of Hiroshima.

- Discuss the two different participants: *the B-29 bomber Enola Gay* and *the United States.* The first one blames an airplane for dropping the bomb and the second, the country. Both hide the actual person who gave the order. The first participant does even more. Those headlines were written by people wanting to avoid blaming President Truman for giving the order. The Japanese most likely would have reported something like: "the president of the United States ordered the pilot of the Enola Gay to drop the bomb on Hiroshima," directly blaming President Truman.

Follow Up

Encourage the students to find and share other examples when doing research.

Lesson 10.7. Nominalization (Grades 6–8)

> **Goal:** To recognize nominalizations and their two key functions: (a) to expand or evaluate an action and (b) keep the flow of the writing connected.
> **Materials:** Chunks of mentor texts in the genre that contain nominalizations. Worksheets with sentences with a verb underlined that could be nominalized.

Activities

- Show students a chunk of text. For example,

  - Top military commanders wanted to **invade** Japan. They advised Truman that such an **invasion** would result in U.S. casualties of up to 1 million. In order to avoid such a high casualty rate, President Truman decided to use the atomic instead.

- Make the students notice the words *invade* and *invasion*. Ask them to discuss with their partner and group how they relate in form and meaning.
- Show them another paragraph that includes a verb followed by the nominalized form of the verb. Explain how using the nominalized form of the verb allows them to talk more about the action, make some judgment of it, and continue the flow of information.
- Put up a sentence. For example,

  - *A high school prohibited the use of cell phones by teachers and students while on campus.*

- Ask them to follow it up with a sentence that nominalizes the verb *prohibited*. For example,

  - *This prohibition angered a number of the students.*

- Give groups the worksheets with the additional sentences for them to propose following sentences with nominalization of the underlined verb.

Follow Up

During joint construction encourage students to use nominalizations if appropriate. In joint revision, propose addition of nominalization if appropriate.

Lesson 11. Deconstruction of Text—Development of Events

Students need to learn how not only to write events that relate to the significance of the life of the person or historical event, but also to make each event interesting by including several related actions and descriptions.

> **Goal:** To teach students to develop each event to make their writing more interesting.
> **Materials:** Chart paper or projector. Mentor text.

Activities

- Take one of the major events in the mentor text, and write it on top of the chart paper.
- Re-read the passage from the major event chosen, and ask students to identify the detailed information that the author gave. For example, taking one event from the mentor text used in Lesson 9:

  Event: funeral
  - Public funeral with open casket
  - 50,000 people attended and saw the beaten body
  - Pictures appeared in the newspapers
  - The nation was enraged

- Write these notes in collaboration with the class on the chart paper. Leave the chart paper up as an example.

- Assign each group of students one of the major events in the mentor text (see Lesson 9). Give them a worksheet with the event written at the top. Have students look at the text, find their assigned major event, and then write the sub-events.
- With the notes of the paragraph you did together, write a whole paragraph with the class, looking only at the notes.
- Have students write a paragraph based on the notes of the paragraph they worked in their groups, making sure that they only base it on the notes and not the mentor text.

Follow Up

Demonstrate this again during joint construction, and encourage students to do the same when planning and writing their events. Review again during joint revision.

Lesson 12. Adverbials of Manner, Accompaniment, and Reason (Grades 3–8)

Goal: Identify adverbials other than those of time and place and what function they play in historical genres.

Materials: Questions (*How? What with? What like? With whom? Why? What for?*) written on chart paper or the board with space to write underneath each question. Mentor text that use these adverbial phrases (for example, *A Picture Book of César Chávez*). Additional texts that have examples of these phrases or clauses. Projector.

Activities

- Put a simple clause on the board and ask the questions. Let the students propose answers. For example: *Yesterday he came home.*

  How? Yesterday he came home *angry.*
  What with? He came home and knocked *with his umbrella.*
  With whom? Yesterday he came home *with his friend.*
  Why? He came *because he wanted to see you.*

- Show the class a chunk of a mentor text that has adverbials.
- Together with the class, identify and discuss what kind of information they give and how it helps the meaning. For example,

  *As a child, César Chávez traveled **with his family** from one farm to the next **to pick beans, broccoli, and lettuce**.*
  The first tells the reader whom he traveled with, and the second gives the reason, adding information to the notion of traveling.
  List adverbials in the anchor chart to keep visible examples for students to refer later when they do joint and individual writing.

- Give students other chunks of texts, and working in pairs or groups, have them look for additional examples.
- Have students add examples to the class list.
- Go through the list and ask students to suggest variations. For example, "President Obama worked with his cabinet." "The Americans dropped the atomic bomb over Hiroshima to stop the war."

Follow Up

Ask questions during joint construction to encourage addition of adverbials. Do the same in joint revision.

Lessons to Improve Clause Complexes
(Grades 4–8)

These lessons are most appropriate for students in 4th through the middle school. Three lessons addressing different aspects of clause complexes are illustrated. Specific lessons should be chosen depending on students' needs and grade level. Some lessons can be done with other genre units or done in group conferences with students who need it most.

Lesson 13.1. Formation

Goal: To identify clause complexes in mentor texts and break them apart to see how an author puts ideas together. To apply to students' own writing.

Materials: Chunks of mentor texts with clause complexes. Samples of students' work with simple clauses that could be combined.

Activities

- Project an example from the mentor texts: "Her family moved to Chicago, Illinois, when she was three years old." (*Mae C. Jemison*) and separate the ideas into simple sentences (e.g., *Her family moved to Chicago, Illinois. She was three years old.*).
- Discuss how the author combined the separate ideas and sentences and why.
- Repeat with other examples.

Lesson 13.2. Expressing Relationships Accurately

Goal: To teach students how to combine sentences with the conjunctions that express the relationship, rather than always resorting to *and*.

Materials: Clause complexes from mentor texts that express relations similar to the ones that students have had trouble expressing themselves. Sample of students' writing that needs revision. Additional students' work with a sentence underlined that requires revision. Projector.

Activities

- Project a clause complex from the mentor text, break it into separate clauses, and discuss the order in which events or steps happened. For example, the clause complex "Soon after I got to America, I started first grade" (*My First American Friend*) has two clauses: (1) Soon after I got to America, and (2) I started first grade. Ask students how the author conveys the time and meaning in the events. Have students point at the words that help give the meaning.
- Repeat with another set of examples.
- Working in groups or pairs, have students do the same with other examples from mentor texts.

Lesson 13.3. Finite to Non-Finite Clauses

Goal: To show students how to pack writing or add information by using non-finite clauses.

Materials: Paragraphs from mentor texts with non-finite constructions. Samples of students' writing that could be packed by changing clauses with conjugated verbs to non-finite clauses. Samples of students' writing to which non-finite clauses could be added to enrich the description. Projector.

Activities

- Project or show on chart paper examples of non-finite clauses from the mentor text. Choose text that illustrates all three types.
- Ask students to convert the clauses into clauses with a conjugated verb (e.g., from *Lifting the glass to her lips, she takes a sip* to *She lifts the glass to her lips, she takes a sip.*). Write the new clauses down next to the original version.
- Have students compare and discuss how much more compact the writing is.
- Give groups of students sentences from mentor texts that you have changed from non-conjugated to conjugated. Ask them to combine them, and then show them the original mentor texts to compare with what they did.

Follow Up When Doing Joint Revision of Students' Drafts

Use students' notebooks with either (a) one or two groups of sentences underlined that could be combined; (b) clause complexes that need a more precise combining word or phrase; and/or (c) sentences that could be packed by the use of a non-finite (non-conjugated) clause. Show one sample of the student's work that requires changing, for example:

(a) From simple to clause complexes: for example, in Veronica's biography the beginning reads, *My dad left El Salvdor in 1992 He felt very sad to leave El Salvdor, but he needed to find work to help his parents.* These three clauses could be combined into two by combining two of the clauses: *My dad felt sad when he left El Salvador in 1992 but he needed to find work to help his parents.*

(b) *We changed into our bathing suits and found a place to sit.*). Have students break it up in clauses and ask them what kind of connection there is between these clauses. In this sentence, there is a connection of *time* that is better shown with *after*: *After we changed into our bathing suits, we found a place to sit.*

(c) Packing clauses by using non-finite ones: *When the first check came in he got $100.00. He was so happy he mailed his parents $50.00 and he kept $50.00*, could be packed to *Sharing his first $100 paycheck with his parents made him feel happy.*

Working in groups or pairs, have students work on one or all of these aspects that you have underlined in their notebooks. Confer with the groups as they are doing this work.

Lesson 14. Jointly Planned Record of Events and Focus on Key Aspects of Language

Goal: To apprentice the students to plan the record of events in order to learn to avoid gaps, be informative, and connect the events to the conclusion. To identify technical language (see Lesson 5) and specific aspects of language that you are focusing on in the unit.

Materials: Chart paper or computer document to list the key events in the timeline. Additional sheets with the events on top and columns for (a) notes about the event, (b) technical language, and (c) column(s) for the key aspect(s) of language covered in the unit. Research resources on the topic of the class project.

Activities

- First establish what is the significance of the person or event in history by having groups of students read concluding sections of texts that write about this person or event. Make notes in the Conclusion anchor chart.
- Demonstrate how to find the first event in a resource that relates to the theme established in the conclusion, and write it in the anchor chart with major events.
- Have students in groups review one resource per group and suggest other events. Add them chronologically to the anchor chart.
- Review to check that they relate/are important to the significance. Discuss if the list sounds complete.
- Take the first item in the list, and write it on top of the chart paper. Read one source with the class, and take notes on the important information about that event.
- Go over the text again, and identify technical terms and examples of the focus language. For example, if adverbials and clause complexes are the focus, when reading this paragraph, the anchor chart would look like the following:

Poor people gain power through voting in elections.

Notes	Technical Language	Adverbials	Clause Complexes (#s indicate individual clauses)
- met Fred Ross - explained importance of voter registration - Chavez sought people to register	Community Service Organization Register voters Speak out	In June 1952 Door-to-door At first Later In about three days okay	(1) Went door-to-door and (2) urged people (3) to register (4) to vote (1) *He was so frightened* (2) *he couldn't talk.*

- Have students working in groups fill the graphic organizer for the other key events and share with the class. Ideally, they should use a google document where charts like the one shown earlier are included for each key event. This way, after the groups have completed their event, the whole class can edit the information and all the students have access to it.

Lesson 15. Jointly Constructed Record of Events in Paragraphs, Paragraph Formation, and Use of Text Connectives (Grades 3–8)

Goal: To teach students to turn the information in their graphic organizers developed in the previous lessons into well-constructed paragraphs.

Materials: Mentor texts. Graphic organizer with the information developed in the previous lesson. Material to write and share. Projector.

Activities

When doing this lesson, you can address the fact that a paragraph is usually indented in manuscripts. In printed books, paragraphs may be indicated by extra space. In picture books, they may be indicated by a different (or new) page. The important thing to remember is that content makes a paragraph and not indentation.

- Project a mentor text.
- Identify the paragraphs. Discuss their content and how the information is distributed in the paragraphs. Important things to point out are:
    - The content of a paragraph or page in a picture book relates to one subtopic of the whole text.
    - Beginning of Paragraphs. Paragraphs usually start with either an adverbial of time indicating the passage of time or participants in the event, especially new ones or the focus one. For example, in César Chavez's biographies, some of the paragraphs begin with
        - *In June 1952*
        - *Ross*
        - *At first* (Cesar Chavez's biography)

        Some paragraphs in a historical recount on WWII start with
        - *By the time of the Trinity test*
        - *General Douglas MacArthur*
        - *Hiroshima, a manufacturing center of some 350,000 people located about 500 miles from Tokyo.*

        Occasionally, there is a text connective. For example, in a 9-paragraph text about bombing of Hiroshima and Nagasaki, there is one such text connective: *In fact.*

    - Start or theme of sentences in a paragraph: The choice of what to put at the beginning of all sentences in the paragraph shows what the author wants to highlight. For example, the sentence *After arriving at the U.S. base on the Pacific island of Tinian, the more than 9,000-pound uranium-235 bomb was loaded aboard a modified B-29 bomber* starts with an adverbial of time, stressing when things were happening. If the author wanted to focus on the bomb, the sentence would have read, "The more than 9,000-pound uranium-235 bomb was loaded after the bomber arrived at the U.S. base."
- Project the graphic organizer of the stages produced in the previous lesson.
- Choose one event with the notes about that event.
- Have the class suggest how to write the paragraph, how to start, what to choose for the beginning of the paragraph, and what to choose for the beginning of sentences.
- Do the other paragraphs the same way, or have groups work on individual paragraphs on chart paper or a google document and share with the whole class when finished to read together and edit.
- Read aloud the whole piece. Ask questions when you feel there is need for editing.

Lesson 16. Deconstruction of Text to Learn About Conclusion of Historical Genres and Reinforcement of Evaluative Language and Graduation

Goal: To learn the features of the endings in the genre in which students are writing. To realize that the conclusion is closely related to the theme of the events.

Materials: Mentor texts. Examples of endings. Chart paper or projector. Handout with examples of conclusions.

Activities

- Project the endings (or post on chart paper) and distribute a handout including them to help students refer to them when they are trying to compose their own conclusions.
- Discuss the type of conclusion common to this genre with the class.
- Give each group of students one text and have them read and discuss the conclusions.

Remind students of what they learned in Lesson 10.4, and point out that this type of language is frequently found in the conclusion of the historical genres.

Show them the endings from mentor texts they used in this lesson and have them find this type of language. Discuss that it is important because it shows attitudes and feelings toward the person or event covered in the text. For example, in the sample conclusions shown earlier in the chapter, all include some instances of evaluative language and/or graduation (in bold).

Biography	"She became a teacher at Dartmouth College. She **encourages** African-American students and other minority students to study math and science. Jemison encourages students to do all the can with their imagination, creativity, and curiosity" (*Mae C. Jamison*).
Autobiography	"This year, I am in the third grade, and my English is **perfect**! I have **many** friends now, and I'm **very happy**. But I'll always remember Ali, my first American friend" (*My First American Friend*).
Empathetic Autobiography	"I am **tired** from hunting and fishing and thinking so much today. The **warmth** of the fire puts me to sleep. *Wunniook*. Be well" (*Tapenum's Day*).
Historical Recount	"The murder of Emmet Till **enraged** both blacks and whites, causing **many** people to join the civil rights movement" (*A Murder That Rocked the Nation*, p. 12).
Historical Account	The Compromise of 1850 left **many** people **unhappy**. Southerners **accused** the North of wanting to **destroy** slavery. Northerners **accused** the South of wanting to **spread** slavery. Later, Abraham Lincoln would **warn** that the United States could not go on forever "half-slave and half-free" (*History Alive*, p. 190).

Follow Up of Conclusion

Practice writing conclusions by jointly constructing a conclusion for the class project and further practice during individual writing. If editing is needed, do it during joint editing.

Follow Up of the Whole Class Project

Read with the whole class the entire text produced and check the following:

- All the stages are included.
- The events are developed.
- The technical language was effectively used.
- The aspects of language taught were applied to this text.

Lesson 17. Teach to Quote From Sources and How to Introduce Quotes (Grades 6–8)

Goals: To teach how to introduce quotes, where to insert quotes, and how to use punctuation, dates, and page numbers.

Materials: Texts that were used to research on the topic. Sentence starters.

Activities

- Read with students a chunk of one of the sources used to do research on the topic.
- Discuss if there is any section of the text that would be a good quote to support the writing. For example, if the class project was the biography of Harriet Tubman, you may choose the following quote: "Harriet Tubman was an icon of courage and freedom" (p. 47).
- Show students the following sentence starters:

Larson (2005) says that [*neutral*]
Larson (2005) demonstrates that [*agrees*]
Larson (2005) claims that [*creates distance*]
Larson (2005) inaccurately states that [*disagrees*]

- Read each starter followed by the quotation and ask them whether the writer agrees, disagrees, is neutral, or creates distance with the author of the quote.
- Ask them which one they choose to introduce their quote.
- Discuss where would they insert this quote. Given this particular quote, it would be best in the final paragraph.
- Repeat with one or two more quotes.
- As they do this activity, teach them how to use punctuation for quotes and how to add page numbers.

Follow Up

As students do research for their own topic, have them underline introductions to quotes that their sources use, discuss how the writer feels about the quote, and add them to the list started. After they have worked on their draft, have them add one or two quotes to their writing following the same process and choosing from the sentence starters listed. By the 8th grade, they should be able to create their own introductions to quotations using verbs that effectively reflect the writer's position toward the quoted idea.

Lesson 18. Adding Images

Goal: To learn the type of image that supports historical text and insert images in their final drafts.

Materials: Mentor texts with different kinds of images. Historical texts include photographs, paintings, engravings, maps, tables with relevant information, maps, and others. When written as picture books, texts have images done by an illustrator that are realistic, unlike those from fictional narrative books. Bookmarked Internet sites where they can download images for their work.

Activities

- Have students look at mentor texts for different age groups. Ask them what types of images they see. Have students notice the number of images. The younger the audience, the more images the text has.

- Using the class project, demonstrate where it would be good to insert images and which kind.

Follow Up

After the students have finished and revised their drafts, have them work in groups to look for images on the Internet and decide which ones they want to insert in their texts. Have a few share their ideas with the class, discuss, and then encourage them to add images.

Lesson 19. Individual, Pair, or Group Construction of a Text in the Genre of the Unit

> **Goal**: To have students create a piece in the genre of the unit, working individually, in pairs, or groups.
>
> **Materials**: Mentor text, research resources bookmarked, graphic organizers, and all materials used when teaching lessons and creating the classroom piece.

Activities

- Have students create their pieces going through the same steps they took to create the classroom piece:
  - Establish theme
  - Research theme
  - Create orientation
  - Plan events
  - Write events
  - Write conclusion
  - Insert images
  - Decide on title (Chapter 3, Lesson 31)
- Do all these steps with attention to the aspects of language focused on during the unit.
- For each one of the steps and aspects of language, remind them what they need to do to get them started.
- As students work, conference with them.

Lesson 20. Joint Revision of Final Draft

This lesson is good to apply to challenges that appear in a lot of students' writing and that were taught during the unit. Individual challenges can be addressed through conferencing.

> **Goal:** To learn how to collaborate revising each other's pieces.
>
> **Materials**: Last draft of the completed individual or group pieces.

Activities

- Choose one or two students to share their pieces with the whole class. It is best to choose students who can use the extra help.
- Project and read it aloud or have the author read it aloud in chunks.
- Focus on specific aspects that were taught during the unit. For example, if paragraphs start with *then* or *and then*, have students circle the adverbials at the beginning of the paragraphs and ask them what they notice. Have them suggest alternative adverbial phrases that better describe what is happening. Have anchor charts used during lessons for reference.

- Have students help each other check on the same feature in their writing.
- Choose the writing of another student, focusing on another general challenge, and repeat the process.

Follow Up

Revision of individual pieces.

- Have students work on their whole piece, while you conference with individuals.
- Have students prepare a final version for publication, adding images appropriate for the genre.

Professional Articles That Describe Instruction of the Genre

Brisk, M. E. (2021). Theory inspired best practices: Elementary teachers appropriate SFL theory to inform their practice. In M. E. Brisk & M. J. Schleppegrell (Eds.), *Language in action: SFL theory across contexts* (pp. 13–32). Sheffield: Equinox.
Brisk, M. E., Tian, Z., & Ballard, E. (2021). Autobiography writing instruction: The journey of a teacher participating in a systemic functional linguistics genre pedagogy professional development. *Systems, 97,* 102429.

References

Brisk, M. E. (2021). *Language in writing instruction: Enhancing literacy in grades 3–8.* New York: Routledge.
Brisk, M. E., Alvarado, J., Timothy, B., & Scialoia, P. (2018). Breaking the linguistic ceiling: Bilingual students appropriate academic English. In J. Sharkey (Ed.), *Transforming practices for the elementary classroom* (pp. 85–98). Alexandria, VA: TESOL International Organization.
Brisk, M. E., & DeRosa, M. (2014). Young writers' attempts at making meaning through complex sentence structures while writing a variety of genres. In L. de Oliveira & J. Iddings (Eds.), *Genre pedagogy across the curriculum: Theory and application in U.S. classrooms and contexts* (pp. 8–24). London: Equinox.
Brisk, M. E., Tian, Z., & Ballard, E. (2021). Autobiography writing instruction: The journey of a teacher participating in a systemic functional linguistics genre pedagogy professional development. *Systems, 97,* 102429.
Butt, D., Fahey, R., Feez, S., & Spinks, S. (2012). *Using functional grammar: An explorer's guide* (3rd ed.). South Yarra, Victoria: Palgrave Macmillan.
Christie, F., & Derewianka, B. (2008). *School discourse: Learning to write across the years of schooling.* London: Continuum.
Coffin, C. (2006). *Historical discourse: The language of time, cause and evaluation.* New York: Continuum.
Derewianka, B. (2011). *A new grammar companion for teachers.* Marickville, NSW, Australia: Primary English Teaching Association.
Eggins, S. (2004). *An introduction to systemic functional linguistics.* London: Continuum.
Fang, F., Schleppegrell, M. J., & Cox, B. E. (2006). Understanding the language demands of schooling: Nouns in academic registers. *Journal of Literacy Research, 18*(3), 247–273.
Humphrey, S., Droga, L., & Feez, S. (2012). *Grammar and meaning.* Newtown, NSW, Australia: Primary English Teaching Association Australia.
Scollon, R., & Scollon, S. B. K. (1981). *Narrative, literacy and face in interethnic communication.* Norwood, NJ: Ablex.

Chapter 5

Fictional Narratives

A narrative is a special kind of story that is highly valued in English-speaking cultures. Narratives tell an imaginative story, although some are based on facts. There are many types of narratives (see "Types of Fictional Narratives" at the end of this chapter). Teachers may focus on a type to reinforce what they are covering in their reading program, such as fables, folktales, historical fiction, and others. For example, in the context of studying about Ghana, students explored and wrote trickster tales, which is a type of storytelling from that culture.

Some of the most useful types for the upper elementary and middle school are fables, historical fiction, realistic fiction, and myths. Fables, where animals act as humans, are easy to integrate because students can use as characters the animals they have researched for their animal unit, a very common topic in elementary schools. History topics provide material for historical fiction projects, while social issues are easily incorporated into realistic fiction. Middle school students usually study myths as well. Table 5.1 describes the main features of these types of fictional narratives.

Narratives are structured to entertain and to teach cultural values. In narratives, normal events are disrupted, and language is used to create suspense until the plot reaches a crisis point. The basic stages of narratives are orientation, complication, evaluation, and resolution (Labov & Waletsky, 1967; Martin & Rose, 2008). Across different cultures, narratives share a similar organization, but what makes for a complicating event and resolution may differ (Martin & Rose, 2008).

Other story genres may involve a disrupting event that is evaluated, but "the 'point' of narrative is how the protagonists resolve a complication in their lives, once they have evaluated the complicating action with some type of attitude" (Martin & Rose, 2008, p. 67). Thus, how characters confront and resolve the crisis teaches the audience about the ways of behaving that are valued in a culture (Rothery & Stenglin, 1997). A narrative may end with a writer's evaluative comment (Butt et al., 2012; Schleppegrell, 2004). For example, a realistic fiction about an Eskimo girl who had a frightening experience concludes with " 'That was my last very first—my very last *first* time—for walking alone on the bottom of the sea,' Eva said" (*Very Last First Time*).

Narratives are a more advanced type of storytelling than personal recounts. Some parents oppose the use of fictional narratives in school because they reflect cultural values. They feel that values should be taught at home, whereas the role of schools is to cover knowledge such as science, math, and history (Dien, 2004). Children come to school familiar with this genre from home experiences of telling or reading stories. These experiences are reinforced in schools when children read or are read more narratives than other genres. Further, a high percentage of the texts in basal readers are narratives (Kamberelis, 1999).

Although children usually enter school familiar with the characteristics and structure of narratives, they may have some difficulty grasping the fictional nature of stories before ages 7 or 8. Preschool children's early interpretation of a story is that something happened in the past and is

DOI: 10.4324/9781003329275-5

Table 5.1 Selected Types of Fictional Narratives Commonly Taught

Type	Definition	Stages/features	Mentor Texts Examples
Fables	A short story that is intended to convey a moral	• Main characters are usually animals • Short, with just one main event and only 2–3 characters • Generally, the main characters are in conflict with each other (good vs. lazy/bad)	Fables From the Sea
Historical Fiction	Imaginative reconstruction of historical events	• Information about the time period must be accurate and authentic (how people lived, ate, dressed, kind of homes, tools, etc.) • Characters imaginary or real from the period • Events real or imaginary (but could have happened)	Baseball Saved Us The Child of Auschwitz Finding Langston My Mother's Secret Heroes Don't Run When My Name was Keoko
Realistic Fiction	Stories that could have actually occurred to people or animals in a believable setting; they resemble real life	• Characters seem like real people; they live in places that are or could be real • Plots highlight social or personal events found in contemporary life (bullying, smoking, cancer, parents' divorce, love, etc.) • Events could happen • Take place in present or recent past	The Name Jar My Name Is Maria Isabel The Hate U Give The Recess Queen
Myths	Traditional stories that explain a natural or social phenomenon	• Typically involve supernatural events or beings • Characters are often non-human (gods, goddess, monsters, etc.) • Often set during ancient historical times • Dualities (night/day, good/evil) are often a central theme	Book of Greek Myths The Gods and Goddesses of Olympus Greek Mythology for ESL: Perseus and Medusa

unchangeable (Applebee, 1978). By ages 7 or 8, most children can differentiate fictional narratives from non-fiction types of writing and know the story organization, such as the need for an initial event introducing the characters, events that follow, and some kind of resolution. They also are aware that most narratives are written in the past tense (Kamberelis, 1999). Between the ages of 8 and 14, children progress to writing longer stories, but use the greater length to elaborate and add more detail rather than to impose more structure on their writing (Donovan, 2001; Langer, 1986).

Development of Units

To develop units, teachers need to consider a number of factors that play a role on what and how to teach and what materials to use. With this in mind, they then plan lessons.

Unit Preparation

To prepare a unit in the chosen recount genre, teachers need to consider the following:

• Grade level
• Connection with content areas

- Mentor texts
- Research resources
- Potential projects, audience, and medium
- Uncoached writing and planning content of the unit
- Lessons to teach purpose, problem, character development, and plot

Grade Level

From a very early age, children have a sense of the narrative genre, but they have difficulty writing stories (McKeough, 2013). Some suggest that "it is the most difficult genre to do well" (Rog & Kropp, 2004, p. 67). Development of characters, taking a third person point of view, creating a problem and a crisis, tracking a number of participants through narrative and dialogue, and building suspense through language and rhetorical devices are all features that make narratives challenging to write. In addition, different cultures have different ways of organizing narratives and expressing different values through them (McCabe & Bliss, 2003), making it difficult for children to acquire new ways of writing narratives, sanctioned by the new cultural context.

Research has shown that children can attempt narratives as young as kindergarten age. In the early grades, they are most likely able to include the basic elements of the text structure, including an initiating event, a sequence of events, and a final event. Students also can use basic language features, such as the use of past tense and temporal connectors as well as participants introduced and tracked through appropriate use of reference ties (Kamberelis, 1999). At this young age, students can become familiar with characters' features and the impact on plot through reading and analyzing stories in dialogue with the teacher (Roser et al., 2007). To develop all of the features, fictional narratives are best attempted from grade 4 through middle school.

A kindergarten teacher carried out a unit on fictional narratives. Although there was variation in students' writing, students started writing pieces closer to personal recount. After coaching, however, they were able to create imaginary stories with problems and resolutions. To a large extent, the students copied from the model that the teacher created with the whole class (Brisk & Zisselsberger, 2011). In another class, McPhail (2009) had 1st graders write in a variety of genres. He found that the boys did better in writing when producing fictional narratives, the genre which they preferred overall. Girls, on the other hand, did better in personal recounts (he calls them *personal narratives*), and only 40% achieved their highest scores in fictional narratives. A 2nd-grade teacher had students research animals and then used them as characters for their fictional narratives. She taught them the different stages of the genre. The most successful pieces were from those children who had been read many stories and were using the patterns they learned to create their own narratives. Other students had difficulty with the sequence of events, tracking participants, and creating a crisis. Their characters were, in general, rather flat (Brisk, 2007).

With upper elementary grades, it may take more than six weeks to address character development. It can take longer if students conduct research on the topic. It is a good genre to do toward the end of the school year because it is a release when students are taking tests, can take advantage of any of the subject area topics already covered during the year, and involves story writing, generally viewed as a fun activity by students.

To adapt narratives to different grade levels, consider the following instructional suggestions:

- *Kindergarten:* Read fictional narratives, identify characters and their attributes, and track plot. Oral retelling of narratives stresses the stages of the genre. Have students draw and write or dictate stories without additional coaching.

- *Grades 1–3:* Read fictional narratives; identify characters; identify external attributes and some internal qualities, such as traits and feelings; and ask students to point at the language that reflects characters' features.

A possible adaptation for 3rd grade is to create a fictional narrative from a personal recount they have already written (see Lesson 8, this chapter).

Mari, a 3rd-grade teacher in a two-way bilingual school teaching in the Spanish side, found the requirement of writing fictional narratives for 3rd graders too difficult. She decided that a good preparation would be to have them write *imaginative recounts* (Brisk, 2015; Derewianka, 1990). The purpose of these recounts is similar to the personal recount in which the writer recounts events but takes the identity of an object or person. For example, the students write from the point of view of the flag in the classroom as students file in at the beginning of the day, or from a child in the 17th century telling what happened one day at sea while sailing to the American continent, with all imagined events (unlike empathetic autobiographies which are based on historical facts). To prepare a unit on imaginative recounts, teachers can follow the lessons for personal recounts (Chapter 3), with the addition of teaching how to write in the first person from another narrator's point of view. This genre is a good literacy activity because it supports children in learning to take another person's point of view, an essential skill needed to comprehend text (Scollon & Scollon, 1981). A good mentor text is *Dirty Laundry Pile: Poems in Different Voices*. Each poem is written from the perspective of a pile of laundry, a broom, and other inanimate objects.

- *Grades 4–8:* Write narratives with attention to character development and other aspects. Encourage writing in third person.

Connection With Content Areas

Writing units are best embedded in content area teaching. Although fictional narratives are typically connected with ELA, research conducted in connection with a content area can be used to inform the topic of a fictional narrative. This research can also help students overcome the challenge of not knowing what to write about. For example, 4th-grade students created animal characters in their fictional narrative based on the information from their research on animals. The characteristics of the animal were considered when choosing the place where their character lived, what they ate, and other details. Further, children can use their knowledge of natural phenomena, such as volcanoes and hurricanes, to write an adventure.

Historical fiction is a form of fictional narrative that can support learning historical content through imaginary stories that use historical figures and events. Writing historical fiction helps students immerse themselves in the events from a period that they are studying. For example, the book *Baseball Saved Us* explores the internment of Japanese communities during World War II through the experiences of a young boy.

Students could be encouraged to turn one of the topics in their persuasive pieces into a fictional narrative. For example, 5th-grade students had written persuasive letters to their principal about the need for bus monitors to make bus rides safer. They could then write a story describing an accident as a result of the lack of bus monitors as a way to make their point.

Fictional narratives can also be used to address social issues connected to social studies or science (realistic fiction). For example, *The Name Jar* and *My Name Is Maria Isabel* address the challenges that immigrant children have with their names when they enter school in the United States. There are a number of children's books that explore current environmental problems. For example, *Garbage Collectors* explores the process of dealing with the excessive amounts of garbage disposed in the United States.

Fictional writing is sometimes used as the only writing done in connection to a discipline. For example, after studying about cellular biology, a teacher had students write stories in which cells were the characters. However, this teacher did not ask students to use their knowledge of cells to write explanations or reports, which would have reinforced their scientific knowledge and language. Starting with fictional narrative writing in an area like science, though, can provide a scaffold to more formal types of scientific writing for students who might be challenged by those genres (Hildebrand, 2001).

Mentor Texts

Mentor texts are written in the genre of the unit and are used to show students the features of the genre. Most classrooms have a good collection of fictional narratives that are familiar to students. It is better to present the features of the genre with short texts that are not difficult to comprehend. For example, in this chapter, the fable *The Moray Eel and the Little Shrimp* is used as the mentor text to illustrate various aspects of the genre because it is short and has all the essential features of the genre. In addition to the mentor texts listed in Table 5.1, there are many more suggestions of texts and Internet resources downloadable from the *Support Material* tab in the book's webpage. Mentor texts for upper elementary classes can also be used with middle school students because the fictional narratives they read are often too long to deconstruct and use as examples. Moreover, students will not be able to create themselves such lengthy and complex products. Selected chapters may be used to illustrate specific features of narratives.

Research Resources

Depending on the type of fictional narrative, students can use different resources to develop background knowledge on the topic. When connected with a content area, these would be the resources used for that content. Thus, information on specific animals for fables, historical facts for historical fiction, social issues or scientific research for realistic fiction, and so on. For realistic fiction, students could interview people with experience in the issue they are writing about (Education Department of Western Australia, 1994).

Middle school students could start a unit by determining what kind of background knowledge the particular type of fictional narrative requires. For example, when studying myths, they might conclude that some are used to explain a phenomenon of the natural world. For example, the myth Arachne the Weaver explains why spiders produce great webs.

Potential Projects, Audience, and Medium

As suggested in the section titled "Connection With Content Areas," students are encouraged to do projects that help them use the content learned in English, science, math, or social studies to write their fictional narratives. Otherwise, students write stories based on the latest video game or movie they have watched.

Children's awareness of audience is usually reflected in their use of asides directed to readers (Edelsky, 1986) or use of the second person addressing the audience directly. These strategies are not always effective in the genre. In fictional narrative the choices are between having a first or a third person narrator telling the story but not addressing the audience directly. Students need to be further aware that audience impacts their choice of topic, amount of information given, and choice of language. Therefore, it is essential that writing be done with the audience in mind and that as students plan and write they are reminded of how the audience affects their choices. For example, a 4th-grade teacher asked the students to write a scary story for the teacher. After the students had written their stories, she asked them to rewrite the same story for kindergarten children. Before changing the language of the stories, students discussed in groups what they would change and why.

The most common medium is a picture book. Other possibilities are story boards, electronic books, comic strips, or puppets acting in a play. Some teachers create magazines containing different class projects including a narrative. Because of the difficulty of creating narratives, some teachers have students working in pairs.

Uncoached Writing and Planning Content of the Unit

Prompt for Uncoached Writing: Write an imaginary story.

Using the Analysis of Student Work forms (downloadable from the *Support Material* tab in the book's webpage), teachers analyze the uncoached pieces to determine what the students already know and what they have not yet mastered. Based on this assessment, teachers identify the lessons that best address their students' needs. Throughout this chapter there are examples of how the analysis form is used to determine needs. Cheryl, a teacher who has been implementing SFL genre pedagogy for 15 years, keeps the uncoached pieces on her desk during the unit to remind herself of things she needs to work on. In order to use these forms, teachers need to know about the purpose and stages of the genre, as well as the essential language features. As opposed to rubrics, where the expected performance is given, analysis of student work requires teachers to identify effective as well as challenging features of students' writing and use this analysis to plan lessons.

Purpose, Problem, Character Development, and Plot: Theory and Practice

This section describes the purpose, stages, and key language of features to be included in lessons. Mastering fictional narratives can be very hard for elementary students. If taught in 3rd grade, it should be done without striving for excellence (see Table 5.2). On the other hand, 4th- through 8th-grade classes can endeavor to produce fictional narratives that have a coherent plot and characters developed, at least to some degree (see Table 5.3).

Purpose of Fictional Narratives

Fictional narratives construct a pattern of events with a problematic or unexpected outcome that both entertains and instructs. There are elements of suspense and disruption. The suspense builds to a crisis point. The characters are a central element of fictional narratives because they are the participants who experience and evaluate the complication, while often expressing an attitude. The crisis is then finally resolved. Fictional narratives teach ways of behaving that are valued in a culture (Butt et al., 2012; Martin & Rose, 2008) or at a minimum, "invite readers to think deeply about ethics, moral choices, and codes" (Roser et al., 2007, p. 548).

Table 5.2 List of Lessons for 3rd grade

1. Purpose of Fictional Narratives
2. Activities That Engage Students With Fictional Narratives
3. Deconstruction of Mentor Texts to Find the Problem
4. Establish the Problem for the Class Narrative and for Students' Individual Narratives
5. Deconstruction of Text to Identify a Character's External Attributes
6. Deconstruction of Text to Identify a Character's Internal Qualities
7. Developing a Character's External Attributes and Internal Features
8. Writing a Fictional Narrative Based on a Personal Recount

Table 5.3 List of Lessons for 4th to 8th grades

Basic Lessons to Teach and Review Over the Grades	Lessons to Choose and Distribute Over the Grades
1. Purpose of Fictional Narratives	
2. Activities That Engage Students With Fictional Narratives	
3. Deconstruction of Mentor Texts to Find the Problem	
4. Establish the Problem for the Class Narrative and for Students' Individual Narratives	
5. Deconstruction of Text to Identify a Character's External Attributes	
6. Deconstruction of Text to Identify a Character's Internal Qualities	
7. Practice Developing a Character's External Attributes and Internal Features	
8. Writing a Fictional Narrative Based on a Personal Recount (Alternative Project for 3rd Grade)	
9. Deconstruct Text to Identify the Plot and How the Characteristics of the Characters Helped to Develop the Plot	
10. Joint Planning of the Plot of the Class Story and Individual/Group Planning of Their Own Story Plot	
	11. Changes in the Character Over the Course of the Story
	12. Learning How to Build Tension
13. Deconstruction of Text—Style of Orientations	
14. How to Write a Captivating Orientation	
	15. How to Write Indirectly the Where and When
16. Joint and Individual Construction of Narratives	
	17. Insert Dialogue in the Narrative

(Continued)

Table 5.3 (Continued)

Basic Lessons to Teach and Review Over the Grades	Lessons to Choose and Distribute Over the Grades
	18. Create Images of Time, Place, and Cultural Group
	19. Teach Students to Incorporate Accurate Facts
20. Deconstruction of Text to Learn About Conclusion	
21. Joint and Individual Construction of the Conclusion	Reference Ties (see Chapter 3, Lesson 24 and Chapter 4, Lesson 3)
22. Title	
23. Create Images for the Text	

The following resources to support implementation of these lessons are downloadable from the *Support Material* tab in the book's webpage:

- Analysis of Student Work: Purpose, Character Development, and Stages (forms/rubrics)
- Graphic Organizers
- Character Development
- Orientation
- Plot
- Mentor Texts That Illustrate the Genre
- Internet Resources With Mentor Texts to Illustrate the Genre

Features of Students' Writing

Students in a 4th-grade SEI class were asked to write an imaginary story in which the main character was a dog. José, a student relatively new to English, wrote:

> I was loss, I went to a house and started barking. When a woman open the door I rolled around and stick my toung out. The woman took me and took care of me. I finnily had a family. Then I went out side to play fetch and I also got a Dog Biscut. I was the perfect dog for that woman. The End.

José has a general sense of what a narrative is supposed to do. His verbs reflect that he is writing about something that has already passed. However, he has some errors typical of L2 learners, such as not adding -*ed* to regular past verbs and not knowing the irregular form. Thus, when he uses *open* and *stick*, he is not switching to the present tense, but is resorting to that verb form knows because he is still learning how to form the past tense in English.

	1	*2*	*3*	*4*	Uncoached Writing Comments
Purpose To construct a pattern of events with a problem, crisis, and resolution			√		Has a sense that it is a story that has a problem and a resolution. No intention to teach anything.
Verb Conjugation (Past, except in direct speech)				√	Didn't put the -*ed* in *open* and wrote *stick*, a verb that requires an irregular past form, both typical errors of L2 learners

Students mostly understand the purpose of stories to entertain, but it is not until approximately age 14 that they become overtly aware that stories can be used to teach something (Langer, 1986). For example, one 2nd-grade student wrote a moral at the end of her report because she said her report taught "an important lesson" (Kamberelis, 1999, p. 432). Thus, the purpose of teaching through narratives is not directly obvious to most children. In middle school, often students are asked to write fictional narratives as a response genre—basing the story on one they have read. Thus, it is hard to gauge if they are fully aware of the features or if they are just imitating.

Lesson 1. Purpose of Fictional Narratives

Goal: To have students understand the purpose of fictional narratives—to entertain and teach about something.

Materials: Mentor texts, especially those already familiar to the students.

Activities

- Read or remind students of the content in the mentor texts that they have already read.
- Ask students what the purpose of the genre in which these texts are written. Emphasize both purposes, to entertain and to teach.
- Point out the specific cultural values that are stressed by the narrative. Contrast with cultural values of the members of the class
- Compare the purposes expressed in these mentor texts with the purposes of genres that have already been covered.

Lesson 2. Activities That Engage Students With Fictional Narratives

Goal: To engage students with different aspects of the story by encouraging them to pay attention to specific information included in the narrative as a way to learn how to include more information about events and characters.

Materials: Depends on the activities chosen.

Activities

When reading stories, teachers can engage their students to comprehend stories by making connections with characters' features and plot (Roser et al., 2007). Projects could include:

- Introducing *realia*, like maps or objects, that are important in the story.
- Having students dramatize aspects of the story. One kindergarten teacher drew masks for the various characters. The children acted out the story wearing their masks. Another teacher used finger puppets to act out the story.
- Have students visualize the characters who are expressing certain emotions or who have certain traits.
- Draw a story map that looks like a board game with students' collaboration to illustrate the stages of a fictional narrative.

Assign students to write about some aspect of the story. For example, after reading *The Name Jar*, students could write or tell about the origin of their names. In a 3rd-grade class, a Chinese child wrote his own name in Chinese and then created name cards with his classmates' names in Chinese.

Development of a Fictional Narrative

Fictional narratives follow a different pattern from other genres because the problem and characters drive the plot, therefore characters need to be able to be established from the start. As mentioned earlier, the first step is for students to become familiar with the topic that provides the background for the story. Thus, the following are the general steps authors follow:

- Research the topic
- Establish the problem (What if . . .? Imagine that . . .)
- Develop the characters':

  - External attributes
  - Internal qualities

- Develop the plot

These steps are not rigid. Authors often comment that their characters further develop as they write their stories.

Fictional narratives are difficult. Writing each aspect for the class project followed by the individual projects can facilitate the process. Teachers may adapt the lessons depending on grade level and experience with writing fictional narratives. To establish the problem, it is easier to have in mind a main character.

The mentor text "The Moray Eel and the Little Shrimp" will be used to illustrate the various steps in developing a fictional narrative.

The Moray Eel and the Little Shrimp (From *Fables From the Sea*, p. 6)

Sunlight drizzled through the water, falling gently upon a rocky reef. A speckled moray eel waited patiently for supper to swim by her cave. With her sharp teeth and speed, she soon caught a small fish. Nearby, a little red-and-white banded shrimp foraged for food. *He's hungry*, the moray thought as she dropped the last bite of her meal in his direction. Grabbing the food with one pincer, the shrimp waved his thanks with another. The moray disappeared back into her home. Months later, the little shrimp recognized the same moray eel rubbing herself carefully against the jagged coral.

"Oh, this terrible itch," moaned the moray eel. The rubbing helped for a while, and then the maddening itch returned. If she scraped any harder, the coral would bite into her soft flesh. Which was worse—the pain or the itch?

The shrimp edged closer. As the poor moray eel twisted in agony, she exposed sharp teeth that could crush a small shrimp instantly. Despite his fear, the tiny shrimp couldn't bear to see the moray eel suffer.

Cautiously approaching the writhing moray, he bowed low. "Perhaps I can help." "How can you help me? You are very little and this itch is very big!" groaned the poor moray eel.

"I can eat the parasites that cause the itch." The shrimp demonstrated by waving and snapping his three sets of pincers.

"Really? You can do that?" the moray asked, astounded. "Why would you do that for me?"

"Once you gave me food. Now you're in great distress and I would like to repay your kindness."

"Well, that's very generous of you."

"I ask only one thing in return."

"What's that, little one?" The moray eel leaned closer toward the shrimp. "Please don't eat me."

"Oh, I can do more than that. All your meals are on me!" Throwing back her head, the moray laughed, tickled by her own joke.

From that day on, the tiny red-and-white shrimp and the moray eel traveled through the maze of coral caves together. The little shrimp never knew hunger, and the moray eel never had another itch.

An act of kindness, no matter how small, should never be forgotten.

Research the Topic

Teaching how to write fictional narratives is time consuming. Teachers can save time by using topics that have been explored in other content areas to be the themes of these narratives. This practice will reinforce what students have learned in another content area, save time, and mirror what real novelists do. Authors use this genre to explore an area of interest or to set forth a cause. For example, the fables included in *Fables From the Sea* are all based on facts about those animals, such as the barber-pole shrimp, which clean off parasites from eels and fish.

One teacher went to the webpage of a children's fiction writer and showed her students the research that the writer used to prepare for topics in her stories. To make the writing task authentic, the teacher should discuss with students how they can use their fictional narratives to teach readers something. For example, students could write a story about an accident when crossing a street against a red light as a way to teach safe behaviors when walking home from school. Students could write about the adventures of an astronaut who goes to all of the planets as a way to teach younger classes about the planets in the solar system. Using the topics from content areas reinforces the learning in those areas, increases student interest, and encourages students to write narratives about topics beyond the plots of movies or TV shows that they watch.

Students who come from different cultures already have a knowledge base, but for particular concepts, their knowledge may differ, which might influence their writing. For example, a 4th-grade teacher had given her students an old prompt from the state test that asked students to tell a story based on what happened when they had a snow day. A student from Central America started her piece with, *Yay! It's snowing and it's Christmas day that means there is no school.* She had no concept of a snow day, when schools are closed because of excessive snowfall. She needed the justification of a holiday such as Christmas.

Establish the Problem

It is essential to establish the problem early on to be able to create the needed characters and guide the plot. The problem is particularly important because "stories are, at their very core, about people and their problems" (McKeough, 2013, p. 78). Authors take their time to develop the problem to build tension and engage the reader. For example, in the mentor text, although it is short, the problem doesn't appear until the second paragraph:

"Oh, this terrible itch," moaned the moray eel. The rubbing helped for a while, and then the maddening itch returned. If she scraped any harder, the coral would bite into her soft flesh. Which was worse—the pain or the itch?

Young students tend to express the problem very quickly. In José's piece he starts directly with the problem: *I was loss.* He is aware of the importance of stating the problem, but by doing it so bluntly, he does not engage the reader slowly into the story, building the need to read more. Middle schoolers tend to build some tension and wait to reveal the problem, although sometimes the early hints of the problem do not always align with the problem and crisis that follows.

Lesson 3. Deconstruction of Mentor Texts to Find the Problem

Goal: Have students decide the problem in fictional narratives.
Materials: Several texts that students have previously read.

Activities

- Choose one text and remind students of what the story was about.
- Discuss what they think the problem is. Ask students how the authors would complete *What if . . .?* Or *Imagine that . . .* when they were planning these texts. For example, in the case of *The Moray Eel and the Little Shrimp*, the author probably thought, *Imagine that an eel was miserable because her body itched a lot.*
- Give groups of students one familiar text per group and have them identify the problem and then share with the rest of the class. (With young students, do the others texts as a whole class activity.)

Lesson 4. Establish the Problem for the Class Narrative and for Students' Individual Narratives

Goals: To establish the problem for the class fictional narrative as well as the individual or group projects.
Materials: Chart paper, notebooks.

Activities

- Choose the main character for the class story; draw on the chart paper.
- Ask students to complete the statement: "What if . . .?" or "Imagine that . . ." giving a couple of potential problems. For example, if the topic is an argument on the availability of cell phones for students in school, students can propose:
    - What if José gets lost on the way back from school?
    - Imagine that José's grandmother is very ill and the family decides to go visit immediately.
- Ask the class to choose one of them to use as the problem for the class story.
- Ask students to follow the same steps to create the main character and problem for their individual/group stories:
    - Draw their main character.
    - Write down a couple of potential problems.
    - Choose one.
- Ask a few students to share their ideas.

Development of Major Characters

Stories have major and minor characters. The major characters drive the story and hold readers' interest. These characters need to be well developed to justify their goals, problems, and challenges, and how they end up resolving their problems. Most stories have one principal character, although there is often at least one other character who needs to be developed, as well. There can be any number of minor characters that do not require much development (Rog & Kropp, 2004). Because "stories are not driven by the plot; the plot is driven by characters" (p. 70), it is important to start writing fictional narratives by creating and describing the main characters. Readers' interest in characters makes the story interesting and exciting. Readers' understanding of characters helps them to understand the story plot (Roser et al., 2007). Thus, first the students will be taught how to develop characters. To develop the characters, students need to have the problem in mind so that they can develop characters that will make sense in the story.

There are three steps to the process of character development:

1. Establish the external attributes: age, gender, ethnicity, and physical features; and internal qualities: traits, interests, abilities, values, feelings, goals or motives, and changes over the course of the story.
2. Choose the language that will help express such features.
3. Choose images that will support the features.

Children's authors use both written descriptions and illustrations to depict the character's external attributes (see Table 5.4). The language resources typically used to create the external attributes include:

- A name that reflects personality: *Mean Jean* (this feature is not always used).
- Age: Expressed through modifiers or images.
- Gender: Expressed through pronouns.
- Physical appearance: Expressed through modifiers as voiced by (a) the narrator and/or (b) the other characters through dialogue.

Table 5.4 External Attributes of the Main Characters

Potential External Attributes	Name the External Attributes	Quote From the Book Illustrating the External Attributes
Moray Eel		
Name	—	
Age	—	
Gender	female	*her* sharp teeth
Physical Appearance	Speckled, fearsome looking, soft flesh	A speckled moray eel, her sharp teeth, soft flesh
Shrimp		
Name	—	
Age	—	
Gender	male	*He* is hungry
Physical Appearance		a little red-and-white banded shrimp

Children's stories support the written descriptions with images. For example, there are two main characters in the mentor text. They both appear in the images.

In the case of these characters, age and name did not play a role.

The internal qualities include traits, interests, abilities, values, feelings, goals or motives, and changes over the course of the story. The left column of Table 5.5 indicates the internal qualities. The middle column names the qualities the author chose for her two main characters, and the third column quotes from the book to indicate the language and rhetorical resources that the author chose to reflect those qualities.

Table 5.5 Internal Qualities of the Two Characters in "The Moray Eel and the Little Shrimp"

Potential Internal Qualities	Name the Internal Qualities	Quote From the Book Illustrating the Internal Qualities
Moray Eel		
Traits	thoughtful, not rash, sure of herself	patiently carefully sunlight *drizzled* through the water, falling *gently* upon the rocky reef
	fearsome	sharp teeth, crush instantly
Feelings	in pain; very uncomfortable	maddening, writhing, groaned moaned, twisted in agony
	Incredulous, Surprised	astounded How can you help me? Really? You can do that? Why would you do that for me?
Abilities	fast	speed
Values		
Interests		
Goals, Motives		
Changes Over Time	no longer uncomfortable	the moray eel never had another itch.
Shrimp		
Traits		
Feelings	grateful	waved his thanks Once you gave me food. Now you're in great distress and I would like to repay your kindness.
	hungry	foraged, grabbing
	scared, hesitant	Edged closer, fear, cautiously, perhaps, please bowed low
Interests		
Abilities	pick small things	The shrimp demonstrated by waving and snapping his three sets of pincers
Values	empathetic	couldn't bear to see eel suffer
Goals, Motives		
Changes Over Time	no longer scared, no longer hungry	From that day on, the tiny red-and-white shrimp and the moray eel traveled through the maze of coral caves together. The little shrimp never knew hunger.

Because these are more difficult for children to express, initially it is best to focus on traits, feelings, and, if relevant, abilities (Brisk et al., 2016).

The internal qualities are usually expressed more indirectly and are thus harder for children to master. The following language and rhetorical resources are commonly used to express the characters' internal features:

- What characters say: "*Oh, this terrible itch,*"
- What characters think: *He's hungry,* the moray thought . . .
- What characters do: *he bowed low.*
- What other characters say about each other: "*Well, that's very generous of you.*"
- The descriptions of the characters by the narrator: *carefully, sharp teeth.*
- How the narrator introduces what characters say: "*Oh, this terrible itch,*" **moaned** the *moray eel.*

Authors directly express features (tell), *he is hungry,* but more often they do it indirectly (show): *groaned the moray eel.* Thus, students need to learn how to write so that readers infer the meaning.

The name or nickname of the character may reveal its personality. For example, in the book *The Recess Queen,* the mean and controlling girl is nicknamed "Mean Jean," while the sweet one is called "Katie Sue."

In picture books, images can reflect internal qualities, as well. For example, in *The Recess Queen,* the images of Mean Jean with gritting teeth, a frown, and later, a big smile, reflect her personality and demeanor, changing over time.

In many stories, characters change over time through their experiences and by their interactions with other characters. In the mentor text, the shrimp changes from being afraid of the moray eel to living in a symbiotic relationship. In *The Name Jar,* Unhei changes her mind from wanting to adopt an American name to using her Korean name and teaching everybody how to pronounce it. In *The Recess Queen,* Mean Jean turns from being a mean and domineering girl to a happy and playful one through the influence of Katie Sue.

Features of Students' Writing

When young children read or write fictional narratives, often "they focus primarily on story actions rather than characters' internal reactions and motives" (Roser et al., 2007, p. 550). This is consistent with the idea that young children focus more on plot than on character development. It takes time for children to learn how to develop characters. As they develop more complex stories, they may have difficulty creating equally complex characters (Villaume, 1988).

Children's characters also tend not to be well rounded. Vardell and Burris (1986) report that 3rd graders often created flat characters (i.e., fixed and easily recognizable), while 6th graders created stereotypical characters reflecting traits of a group or type. Roser et al. (2007) found that 2nd and 3rd graders included external attributes, whereas older students also included internal qualities. Internal qualities are most important to develop in relation to the plot (Roser et al., 2007). Students may be able to identify the changes of a character over the course of a story they are reading, but they may have a harder time accomplishing this in their own stories. Beginning in 3rd grade, children begin to connect internal qualities with the problem. By 4th grade, their characters are more complex. By 5th grade, "their characters' motivations are made clearer in relation to trouble they experience and they behave consistently unless there is a clear reason to change" (McKeough, 2013, p. 83).

José did not describe any external appearance of the dog in his narrative introduced earlier in this chapter. A description of a squalid animal would have reinforced the notion of being lost. He did include one internal quality through what the dog was doing: barking (feeling), rolled around and stuck tongue out (abilities), and what the dog was thinking: perfect dog (trait).

	1	2	3	4	Uncoached Writing Comments
Character Development: External Attributes Name, age, gender, physical appearance	√				None
Character Development Internal Qualities: Traits, feelings, abilities, values, interests, goals/motives, changes over time		√			Showed abilities of the dog ("rolled around and stick my toung out")

Children seem to like characters that are clever and mischievous. They seem to take their clues for developing characters more from movies and TV shows than from books. For example, a 4th grader wrote his uncoached story based on the movie *Alvin and the Chipmunks*.

1   Expressing External Attributes

Students used modifiers to describe characters' appearance, for example, *yung Girl named Starlight, big hairy wolf* (Grade 4), *Chubby chipmunk* (Grade 4). One middle school student, to reveal name and age, had the narrator introduce herself directly talking to the audience: *Hi! My name is sylvia and i'm a freshman in highschool.* Students often do this in personal recounts. It would have been more effective to have the narrator introduce herself to another character to express this information.

2   Expressing Internal Qualities

*   Sometimes, 4th- and 5th-grade students succeeded in describing characters, especially through their actions. For example, a 5th grader showed her character was sad by writing, *They stareded* [started] *crying and crying for a long time.* On other occasions, students showing feelings by naming the feeling, as well. For example, *Kd bite his nails and chatter his teeth because he was nervous.* Yet other students just named the qualities, for example, *She was Smart and talented. He was king but not very powerful* (Grade 3). A middle school student noted the feeling first then expressed this feeling through a saying verb: *scares me, and I scream so loud.*
*   Use of saying verbs to denote feeling. Sometimes, students used a verb to denote the feeling (*She yelled why did you took my stff animals*), while earlier in the story the student named the feeling directly (*Elisabith said angrly . . .*) (Grade 4).
*   Sometimes, the actions are contradictory, giving completely different impressions of the character. For example, a 3rd grader described a chipmunk going to fetch water and taking a long time because *I spilled the water about 5 times*, giving the impression that the chipmunk was clumsy and not too bright. Later in the story, however, the same chipmunk tricks and catches a squirrel that had stolen the chipmunk's nuts, giving the impression that the chipmunk was clever and resourceful.
*   Students used similes, but some were awkward. For example, a 4th grader talking about the mother whale in her fictional narrative wrote, *I would start complaining like a criminal in jail for 12 years* or *I'm beat like running from 3 miles.*

- There were some examples of internal qualities used among 3rd-grade students, but they did not always fit the story (e.g., *Rapunzel started dancing when she was done painting* to denote she was happy). In that example, nothing that the student described was related to the fact that the character was happy. Another student wrote, *the Fox ran away with a evil grin.* Since in the story the Turkey caught the Fox trying to trick him, we might expect a disappointed expression instead.
- Some 3rd-grade stories included many characters, making it difficult to identify the main characters. For example, one story started, *There was a Boy named Johny who lived in Texas. He had a Dog named Lighting.* After the first paragraph, the dog was never mentioned again. *Johny* or *the Boy* can be occasionally tracked through a very involved and almost incomprehensible set of events, each involving different characters. None of the actions or descriptions help to develop this character.
- Students either do not use *dialogue* at all or overuse it. They have difficulty with determining when to use dialogue and how to punctuate it. When they use dialogue, they often omit all of the punctuation, making it difficult for the reader to sort out the dialogue. Moreover, the dialogue they use does not help to build characters. For example, a middle school student in a realistic fiction about the first day of school, the dialogue included, *"Breakfast is ready," Mom yells. "OK. I'm coming down," I said,* missing the opportunity to show that she was excited and anxious. Authors build characters and change the pace of the narrative by adding dialogue. This type of writing can take up to half of the story (Rog & Kropp, 2004). Children need to understand that the dialogue has a purpose. If dialogue is not controlled or becomes random, excessive, and purposeless, the thread of the narrative becomes confusing.

3   Character Changes

Students have difficulty changing the internal qualities of a character as a result of what happens in the story. The trend is to have the character go back to his or her original way. The characters start one way, they change because of what happens in the story, but then they go back to who they were at the beginning. For example, the father whale in a fictional narrative was "non-bothering," then he started bothering the mother-to-be, and finally he goes back to being "non-bothering." In another story, Jenna and Elizabeth start as friends, then they fight, and finally they become friends again.

Lessons to Develop Character

Students in grades 1–3 can work on identifying major characters in fictional narratives, describing as many of the external attributes and internal qualities as they can. The teacher can also show how internal qualities drive the plot. With respect to students' writing, it is best to focus on external features of characters and perhaps feelings, both most accessible to this age group.

In upper elementary grades, students can learn how to develop internal qualities and how these drive the plot. Because it is so difficult for students to develop these qualities, it would be best to start with a few and then build from there. Given that the major characters drive the plot, the lessons in this chapter are designed to help the students work back and forth between developing the characters and sketching the plot. Thus, after developing certain character features, students need to discuss how these features impact the plot and, given the story they want to tell, decide if the major characters' features are appropriate. Because this writing can be very difficult, it is best to illustrate these features through books (mentor texts) and to create fictional narratives as a whole class to reflect the elements included in the lessons. Students should write their own stories as best they can, recognizing that the subtler aspects of this genre take a long time to develop. It is best not to take the fun out of writing by demanding perfection, especially at a young age. As students reach middle school, expectations increase.

One type of lesson to help students learn how authors develop characters is the deconstruction of text for external attributes (Lesson 3) and internal qualities (Lesson 4). These lessons can help students improve their reading comprehension and develop skills that they will need in middle school when encountering the response to literature genre called "Character Analysis," common in the ELA curriculum (Christie & Derewianka, 2008).

When analyzing mentor texts students should notice:

(a) The features, both external and internal.
(b) The language resources the author used to describe this feature.
(c) How this feature impacts the plot.

For example, in the mentor text: *The shrimp edged closer*.

(a) Internal quality: cautious
(b) Verb: edged
(c) It suggests the power relationship between the eel and the shrimp.

Lesson 5. Deconstruction of Text to Identify a Character's External Attributes

Goal: To learn how authors express the external attributes of the major characters.
Materials: Mentor text familiar to the students and in the type of fictional narrative of the unit.

Character Development Graphic Organizer (see *Support Material* tab in the book's webpage) with the image of the character(s) to be analyzed in the middle column of the graphic organizer (see example filled out in Lesson 6).

Activities

- Remind students of the story and ask them, "Who are the two main characters?" If using the images, show them on large chart paper.
- Discuss the type of character given the specific narrative. For example, animal for fable, found in the real world for realistic fiction, imagined and real historical figures for historical fiction, and so on.
- Project and read chunks of the mentor text, and show the illustrations in the text.
- Choose one character at a time and ask students which external features the author includes in each of the chunks.
- As student call out a feature, saying the exact language the author uses to reflect that feature. Write it in a column on the left side of the image (see example filled out in Lesson 6).
- Have students notice that the description of physical appearance is done through noun groups with a variety of modifiers (for review, see Lesson 10.3 in Chapter 4). For example,

  - A *speckled moray* eel
  - Her *sharp* teeth
  - Her *soft* flesh
  - *Sharp* teeth *that could crush a small shrimp instantly*

- If it is a picture book, have students notice what the images show, and note it by putting "image" or "picture" in parentheses.

If an attribute is not mentioned (e.g., "age" in the mentor text), discuss why the author did not believe it was important or necessary to include. If students suggest an internal quality instead of an external attribute, write it to the right of the image.

- Distribute copies of character images in other books with the two columns.
- Have students, working in groups or pairs, identify the attributes of characters in other texts and do the same activities as with the mentor text.

Lesson 6. Deconstruction of Text to Identify a Character's Internal Qualities

Distinguishing individual types of internal qualities is difficult. It is better to name the various types so the students know what to look for but then just identify them and record them as "internal qualities or features."

> **Goal:** To learn how authors express the internal qualities of the major characters.
> **Materials:** Mentor texts used in the previous lesson projected or written on chart paper. Image of the character(s) previously used with the external features filled out (see provided example).

Activities

- Choose the same character(s) from the mentor text and read chunks of the text in which the character is described (directly and indirectly). Ask students to name internal qualities that they glean from the text (traits and feelings are easiest to focus on first), and write them to the right of the image followed by the quoted language from the text (see following example).
- Suggest additional character qualities that students missed but are important to include. As you discuss them, write them down and add the quoted language from the text.

External Attributes		Internal Qualities
	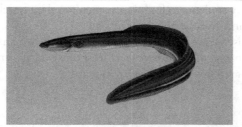 Image credit: Duane Raver/USFWS	
Female: *Her* Physical appearance: *A speckled moray eel* *Her sharp teeth* *Her soft flesh*		Thoughtful, not rash: *patiently, carefully* Feeling in pain: *maddening, writhing, groaned* Fast: *speed* Change: *the moray eel never had another itch*

- Distribute the copies of the images with external features used in Lesson 5.
- Have students, working in groups or pairs, identify the qualities of characters in the same texts used for Lesson 5, and have them complete the Internal Qualities column.

Lesson 7. Developing a Character's External Attributes and Internal Features

This lesson could become a final project for 3rd graders.

> **Goal:** To apply the lessons on analyzing characters for external attributes and internal qualities to have students develop the class character and their own characters.
>
> **Materials:** Image of the class character, chosen in Lesson 4. Chart paper or computer and projector to draw and write features. Students' notebooks with the character they drew when working on the problem. Chart paper with the analysis of the internal and external features of the mentor text's characters.

List of language resources useful to show characters' internal features.

- What characters say.
- What characters think.
- What characters do.
- What other characters say about each other.
- The narrator's description of the character.
- How the narrator introduces what characters say.

Activities

- Show the image of a character chosen for the class narrative. Given the problem, have them suggest external and internal features and write them on both sides of the image.
- Review language resources used to express external and internal features. Ask students to suggest language to describe them and add or revise what was written on both sides of the image. For example, if they gave "courageous" as an internal feature, ask them what would the character do to show courage (keeping in mind the problem).
- Ask the class to compose a short event related to the problem that will show at least one external and one internal feature of the character that they had listed.
- Ask an individual or pair of students to find the character in their notebook that they used to establish the problem and give the character a name.
- Have students think and list a few external and internal features their character should have.
- Have them write a short paragraph that reveals at least one external and one internal feature listed, reminding them to use the language resources.

Planning the Plot

The stages of a fictional narrative include orientation, sequence of events with problem or complication and crisis, evaluation, resolution, and conclusion. Because the mentor text is a fable, it also includes a moral. When planning the plot, it is best to focus on the essential components of orientation, problem, crisis, and resolution. The problem was already developed at the beginning of the process. The conclusion, title, and illustrations can be further developed when the actual writing occurs, as illustrated later in the chapter.

It is also important to show how the characters' features drive the plot. For example, one external attribute and a number of the internal qualities of the shrimp drove the plot in the mentor text (see Table 5.6). Students should be told what encompasses the internal qualities in order to know what to include, but they don't have to identify which quality it is when they suggest them, that is, students can say the character's internal qualities included being *empathetic, grateful,*

Table 5.6 External Attributes and Internal Qualities of the Shrimp and How They Influence the Plot

Potential Features	Name Feature	Quote From the Book Illustrating the Feature	Impact on Plot
External Attributes			
Physical Appearance	small	a little red-and-white banded shrimp	Being small makes it logical for him to be afraid
Internal Qualities			
Traits	empathetic	Couldn't bear to see the moray eel suffer	Will help solve the problem
Abilities	pick small things	The shrimp demonstrated by waving and snapping his three sets of pincers	Will help solve the problem
Feelings	grateful	Waved his thanks "Once you gave me food. Now you're in great distress and I would like to repay your kindness."	Another factor that led to solving the problem
	hungry	Foraged, grabbing	Caused the other character to help
	scared, hesitant	Edged closer, fear, cautiously, perhaps, please Bowed low	Added tension to the actions
Goals or Motives	help the eel	Perhaps I can help	The shrimp approaches the eel even if afraid
Changes Over Time	no longer scared, no longer hungry	From that day on, the tiny red-and-white shrimp and the moray eel traveled through the maze of coral caves together. The little shrimp never knew hunger …	Provides the ending and the moral

and so on. It is too difficult, especially for elementary students, to establish that *empathetic* is a trait and that being *grateful* is a feeling.

A number of rhetorical, linguistic, and content features enhance the plot, such as:

- Building tension
- Orientation style
- Indirect ways of expressing *when* and *where*
- Inserting dialogue
- Making time, place, and cultural features appropriate
- Incorporating accurate facts

Lessons in the chapter address all of them. It is best to include one or two per grade level as appropriate from grade 4 on. By the 8th grade students should have become familiar with all.

The orientation introduces the central character(s) and other characters (when applicable and appropriate), and when and where the story begins. It may also include information that foreshadows the crisis. For example, the following information is included in the orientation in the mentor text:

Characters: Eel, shrimp
When: During the day (sun is shining)
Where: A reef in the sea
Foreshadow: The eel feels sorry for the shrimp and feeds him.

The sequence of events in the story unfolds through narrative and dialogue. These events introduce a problem and follow with complications that culminate in a crisis. Then, characters evaluate the situation leading to the resolution, conclusion, and, in the case of fables, the moral.

Sequence of Events	Mentor Text Example From Fables From the Sea by Leslie Ann Hayashi, p. 6
Problem	The little shrimp is scared of the eel but also indebted to her; "He's hungry, the moray thought as she dropped the last bite of her meal in his direction. Grabbing the food with one pincer, the shrimp waved his thanks with another."
Crisis	The shrimp edged closer. As the poor moray eel twisted in agony, she exposed sharp teeth that could crush a small shrimp instantly.
Evaluation of the Preceding Events	Despite his fear, the tiny shrimp couldn't bear to see the moray eel suffer.
Resolution	Cautiously approaching the writhing moray, he bowed low. "Perhaps I can help." "How can you help me? You are very little and this itch is very big!" groaned the poor moray eel. "I can eat the parasites that cause the itch." The shrimp demonstrated by waving and snapping his three sets of pincers. . . .
Conclusion	From that day on, the tiny red-and-white shrimp and the moray eel traveled through the maze of coral caves together. The little shrimp never knew hunger, and the moray eel never had another itch.
Moral	An act of kindness, no matter how small, should never be forgotten.

The sequence of events in most stories tends to be more complicated than in the sample text. It is helpful to use a simple text that still shows all the stages. Students can then be shown the stages in other stories they know that are more complex. For example, the sequence of events in *The Name Jar* includes:

- Problem: American children have difficulty pronouncing *Unhei*, the main character's name.
- First event: Unhei does not want to tell her class her name.
- Second event: A Korean storekeeper thinks her name is great.
- Third event: Students in her class give her a jar with name cards for her to choose from.
- Fourth event: Grandmother sends her a letter reminding her that her name is beautiful.
- Fifth event: Her friend discovers her real name and its meaning.
- Crisis: The name jar disappears.
- Evaluation: Unhei decides that her name is worth sharing with her classmates.
- Resolution: Her friend brings home the jar, admitting he had taken it away so that she would keep her name.

Features of Students' Writing

From an early age, children have a general sense of the structure of narratives. Kamberelis (1999) found that K–2 children demonstrated greater knowledge of the text structure features than the more detailed language features. Except for the occasional story that reads more like a personal recount, most of the stories that were written by students in grades 2–5 had some, but not all of the elements of a plot. By 5th grade, "many students include a resolution that fully addresses the problems and complications" (McKeough, 2013, p. 83). Children use the past tense, introduce characters, and track them through their stories. By 2nd grade, students use complex temporal connectives and causal connectives to "represent characters' specific internal states" (Kamberelis, 1999, p. 437). However, there are still a number of aspects that slowly develop with age. In addition, Kamberelis found that teachers gave a greater amount of specific feedback with respect to the stages of the text when commenting on narratives than other genres that children were exploring.

In his uncoached piece, José failed to include events that lead to a climax. He mostly developed the resolution.

	1	2	3	4	Uncoached Writing Comments
Sequence of Events (including complication, crisis)		√			Starts directly with the problem and goes quickly to the resolution
Evaluation (optional) Of the preceding events and expecting the following events to be the resolution					N/A
Resolution Problem has been resolved.			√		I finnily found a family followed by one more event showing a happy dog with a normal life

1 *Absence of a Crisis:* The greatest difficulty was building up the events to culminate into a real crisis. For example, a 4th grader wrote about a male whale anxiously asking his pregnant wife if the baby was coming. He bothers her at night while she eats and when she tries to find shelter. Then, he stops bothering her, and he finally apologizes. There is no crisis that led to his change in behavior. In another example, a 5th grader attempted to write a legend where two clouds are unhappy and crying constantly. Other clouds seek the help of a woman who is dressed as a clown and makes the unhappy clouds laugh, causing the rain to stop. There is a problem and a resolution, but not a crisis. For example, the village could have been flooded from the excessive rain or animals could have been drowning.

2 *Logic of the Events:* With the younger students, the sequence of events is often difficult to follow. One 3rd grader wrote a very complicated adventure in which "Johny" encounters a wizard, experiences a hurricane, encounters a "werlock," an old man, a witch, wolves, and Spider Man, and concludes with a large group of superheroes who "Destoryed the vemon People." It is unclear whether "the vemon people" refers to all of the "bad" characters in all of the preceding adventures. New characters appear in each event, but then are not seen again. It is not always clear why one event follows the other. Similarly, a 2nd grader had so many events and characters that it was difficult to figure out the number of characters and what exactly was happening to them.

The 4th and 5th graders' stories were easier to follow, but sometimes the events seemed unexpected. For example, in a story in which four chipmunks barricaded themselves in their home to protect their nuts from a squirrel, they finally let the squirrel in and then "tricked" the squirrel to open the door so that they could run out. There was no indication that the squirrel was trying to harm them, only that it wanted to get their nuts. Therefore, a reader would think that the last thing the chipmunks would want to do is leave their home at the mercy of the squirrel.

3. *Resolutions.* Resolutions are usually quite simple and quick; more akin to an optional type of ending that restores things to a normal or better state of affairs (Kamberelis, 1999). For example, after writing a very elaborate story with major conflict between the two main characters, the narrative ends with, *"I'm sorry elisabith are We friends. Certainly! And they become friends agien. The End!* Becoming friends is a common resolution among children's narrative writing. Middle school students tend to be more dramatic, imitating the content of stories they read.

4. *Building Tension.* Most students had difficulty building tension.

5. Among *middle school students*, there were both unnecessary events that did not help to build tension or character as well as gaps in the events.

Lesson 8. Writing a Fictional Narrative Based on a Personal Recount (Alternative Project for 3rd Grade)

After students have been introduced to a simple version of external and internal features through deconstruction and joint construction of the external and internal features using drawings, they are encouraged to find one of their personal recounts and turn it into a fictional narrative, following these steps:

1. Read the fictional narrative *Alma and How She Got her Name*, including the final page where the author tells about how she got her name, i.e., a personal recount.

2. Ask the students to do something similar, i.e., using a personal recount to create a fictional narrative.

3. Choose the personal recount of one of the students. For example, a personal recount on how last Sunday she went with her family for a walk in the woods.

4. Project it for the whole class to see and have the author read it aloud.

5. Brainstorm with the class a fictional problem based on what they learned in Lesson 3 about how authors do it. For example, if the class has been studying about the weather, they could propose: "What if when I was walking in the woods with my family and friends, a terrible thunderstorm suddenly erupted?"

6. Create a fictional character, for example, Jasmine. Draw her or download an image from the Internet and ask students to suggest a couple of features of the physical appearance. Write them to the left of the picture and one trait that would be relevant given the problem, for example, being courageous (or scared of storms). Write it to the right of the picture.

7. Create a timeline with the original events in the personal recount.

8. Brainstorm with the class what events could be added given the problem and the fact that Jasmine is courageous. Guide them to include a crisis and resolution.

9. Copy the original orientation of the personal recount. Ask them if they want to add/ change anything, perhaps add a foreshadow such as, "There were just a few dark clouds far in the horizon."

10. Write together the story based on the new timeline (or write one or two events together and have groups write one event each and add it to the story).

11. Remind students to use the past tense, avoid repetition of verbs, and use verbs that reveal the personality of the characters. (If needed, use one of the lessons in chapters 3 or 4 that supports these skills.)

12. Ask them to propose a conclusion and add it to the text.

13. Read aloud the finished product. Ask if they want to add or change anything.

14. Type a copy and reproduce it with space to add images. Give one copy to each student, and ask them to add their own images.

15. Decide whether you want them to write individually or in pairs their own fictional narrative following the same steps. This step is not needed if they will be learning fictional narratives in 4th grade or later.

Lesson 9. Deconstruct Text to Identify the Plot and How the Characteristics of the Characters Helped to Develop the Plot

Goals: To learn (a) the features of the plot of the particular type of narrative taught in the unit and (b) how authors develop a plot driven by the features of the main character(s).

Materials: Mentor texts used for character development with the whole class. Additional mentor texts used previously. Large worksheets with the external attributes and internal qualities of the character in the mentor text completed in Lesson 6. Large version of the graphic organizer (uneven sided pyramid downloadable from the *Support Material* tab in the book's webpage). (Note that the pyramid has an extended left side to encourage students to plan a number of events leading up to the crisis, while the resolution tends to be shorter.) Small versions of the graphic organizer for each group.

Activities

- Discuss the type of narrative and features of the plot. For example, in fables there are usually two main characters with opposing features that evoke the conflict. There is a moral at the end (see end of the chapter for description of the various types of fictional narratives).
- Re-read the mentor text using the fictional narrative graphic organizer, and fill in the key points of the plot.
- Have students add a sentence from the text to each point in the plot that shows a feature of one of the major characters.
- Ask students how the descriptions of the eel being big and fearsome and the shrimp being small are important for the plot. Ask the students if the gender is important for the plot. (Note: it would have been important if the author wanted to make a point about power and gender roles, but there is no hint of that in the story.) Continue asking questions to complete the remainder of the graphic organizer.
- Ask students in groups to outline the plot in their graphic organizers of the mentor text the group used in Lesson 6, and notice one feature of the main character that impacts the plot.

Lesson 10. Joint Planning of the Plot of the Class Story and Individual/Group Planning of Their Own Story Plot

Goal: To apprentice students to create the outline of a plot and how it relates to the problem and characters they created.

Materials: Chart paper. Large versions of the character images or worksheets with character features. Large version of the fictional narrative graphic organizer. Computer and projector.

Activities

- Review with students the topic of the whole-class story, the problem and the character features, and the features of the plot of this type of narratives.
- Orally, create a story together with the class.

- Using the fictional narrative graphic organizer on chart paper or a smartboard, fill in the elements of the orientation and the sequence of events, including a problem, crisis, and resolution. The conclusion can be developed later.
- Write in parentheses next to each event the possible feature of the character that they can illustrate in that event.
- Ask if the students would like to make changes or additions to the plot or the characters' attributes for a better match.
- Ask students to apply the same process to enhance their stories.
- As students work on their plans, conference with them to make sure that the problem and their plot align. Check how the features of their characters will help drive the plot.

- Liz MacDonald recalls her experience teaching 2nd graders to write fictional narratives. "My goal in reading *Peter Rabbit* was to have students better understand the elements of a narrative; a genre which they would be expected to write. As I read, I would point out the features of a narrative, including the problem and the solution. I soon discovered that these concepts needed clarification through additional lessons. When we completed reading the book, I asked the students to analyze the text by categorizing the different components in a graphic organizer. Identifying the events posed a challenge for most students. So as all reflective practitioners do, I deviated from that plan, inserting additional lessons to scaffold students' understanding of events in a narrative text. I knew that if students' conceptual understanding of events were not clarified, problems would arise when it was time for them to include events in their narrative piece. One particular lesson that I incorporated was having students order the events of the story of *Peter Rabbit* while viewing an electronic version of the text together on a large screen. The students appeared to have a better understanding of events following the lesson. It was now time for me to move on to teaching students how to gather facts."

Lesson 11. Changes in the Character Over the Course of the Story

With the plan of the plot, students can think how the characters change over time.

Goal: To teach students that characters are not fixed and can change over the course of the narrative because of the events that occur in a story.

Materials: Mentor texts used in earlier lessons. Worksheets or drawings completed with characters' internal qualities.

Activities

- Using one of the mentor texts from previous lessons, discuss internal features that they identified and how they change as the story develops. For example, how the shrimp started afraid of the eel but became close at the end. Repeat with one or two other texts.
- Have students take one of the characters from the class story (e.g., old man, generous, and scared) and have them describe how one of those features might change as the story develops. For example, the old man who was afraid lost his fear over time.

- Have them suggest events to add to the plot that would reflect the changes.
- Repeat the same activity with one of the characters that they had developed earlier with their groups or individually.

Lesson 12. Learning How to Build Tension

Goal: To add an element of tension to students' story plot.

Materials: Graphic organizer with the events in their narratives. Features that build tension listed on chart paper, including the following:

- Adding events before the crisis.
- Deadline or some impending event.
- Setbacks to the main character.
- Something revealed to the reader that the character does not know about.
- Anticipation of a major event.
- Descriptions and actions that reveal tension.
- Insert short simple sentences.

Activities

- Read sections of narratives that you had read with the class before that illustrate the different strategies to build tension. Ask students to identify the strategies.
- With the collaboration of the students, use one or two of the provided strategies to build tension in the class narrative.
- Ask a student to share the events in his or her graphic organizer and, with the class, discuss an event that the author could add to build tension.
- Repeat with another student's work.
- Have students work in groups or pairs to build tension in their narrative plans.
- As the students work, confer with individuals to make sure that their changes or additions make sense.

Creating the Text

With the main characters developed and a plot planned, students are ready to draft their fictional narratives, starting with the orientation; followed by the sequence of events that includes a problem, crisis, and resolution; and ending with a conclusion. The events need to reflect the characters they had planned. Finally, they can think of a title.

Orientation

There are two aspects to consider for an orientation: content and style. Content includes who, where, when, and problem foreshadow, which were already established when planning the plot, but could be reviewed once more.

Structural Elements	Mentor Text Example
	From Fables From the Sea by Leslie Ann Hayashi, p. 6.
Orientation (who/where/when)	Sunlight drizzled through the water, falling gently upon a rocky reef. A speckled moray eel waited patiently for supper to swim by her cave.

Structural Elements	Mentor Text Example
Foreshadow of the problem	With her sharp teeth and speed, she soon caught a small fish. Nearby, a little red-and-white banded shrimp foraged for food. *He's hungry,* the moray thought as she dropped the last bite of her meal in his direction. Grabbing the food with one pincer, the shrimp waved his thanks with another. The moray disappeared back into her home.

The second aspect is the style. The orientation can be written in different styles:

(a) Narrative: "Once upon a time, a long time ago, many animals lived in Puerto Rico" (from *Why the Coquí Sings*).
(b) Dialogue: " 'I can't find Hannibal anywhere, Mom,' David said. 'I thought he'd be home when we got back from the store.' 'I'm sure Hannibal is all right,' Mom answered. 'Cats know more about storms than people do . . .' " (from *Hurricane*).
(c) Actions: "Sunlight drizzled through the water, falling gently upon a rocky reef. A speckled moray eel waited patiently for supper to swim by her cave. With her sharp teeth and speed, she soon caught a small fish" (*The Moray Eel and the Little Shrimp*).

Some authors use a combination of descriptions, actions, and dialogue, as seen in the mentor text *The Name Jar*:

Through the school bus window, Unhei looked out at the strange buildings and houses on the way to her new school. It was her first day, she was both nervous and excited. She fingered the little block of wood in her pocket and remembered leaving her grandmother at the airport in Korea. Her grandmother had wiped away Unhei's tears and handed her an ink pad and a small red satin pouch. "Your name is inside," she had said.

Authors sometimes write the *when* and *where* indirectly. For example, in the mentor text, it says, "Sunlight drizzled through the water, falling gently upon a rocky reef," showing that the sunlight happens during the day and in the ocean (see Lesson 15).

Features of Students' Writing

Students tend to write traditional orientations, beginning with a reference to time, such as *one day*, *once*, *long ago*, or *once upon a time*, followed by the introduction of the main character(s). Sometimes, there is a reference to a place. There is usually no foreshadowing, however there are exceptions, such as the uncoached piece presented earlier where the fact that nobody had noticed the chipmunks becomes an important part of the story.

José skipped the orientation altogether.

	1	2	3	4	Uncoached Writing Comments
Orientation (who, where, when, what, and foregrounding the problem)	√				none

Lesson 13. Deconstruction of Text—Style of Orientations

Goal: To learn to distinguish orientations in different styles to make them more interesting and varied.

Materials: Mentor texts familiar to the students with different orientation styles (traditional, action, and dialogue).

Activities

- Read aloud one of the selected orientations, asking the students to point out the *who, when, where,* and *foreshadowing.* Write their responses under each heading of the orientation graphic organizer. For example, using the material of the mentor text, the teacher would write the following student responses:

WHO	WHEN	WHERE	FORSHADOW
Moray eel, Shrimp	During the day	A reef in the ocean	Eel throws shrimp leftover food

- Show other orientations, repeat the process.
- Discuss how the styles are different but they include the same type of information.
- Distribute the mentor texts among groups in your class.
- Have students describe the style used in the mentor texts that they have used for other lessons in the unit.
- Ask groups to read selections aloud and define which style the author used and the content they expressed.

Lesson 14. How to Write a Captivating Orientation

Goal: To help students write orientations that are interesting and appealing.
Materials: Mentor texts used for the previous lesson. Graphic organizers used in the previous lesson.

Activities

- Show the students one of the orientations and graphic organizers of the previous lesson.
- Write three headings: traditional, action, and dialogue. Choose one of the orientations and ask the students which type it is. For example, choose the mentor text's orientation and write it under "Narrative."
- With the help of the class, convert the orientation to the other two types. Repeat with the other orientations.
- Using the class story, write on the orientation graphic organizer, the *who, when, where,* and *foreshadowing,* together with the students.
- Using the information in the graphic organizer, draft with the students the three types of orientations using the same information. Have the class vote for the orientation that most students prefer for their class story.
- Using the orientation content in their own graphic organizers, ask students to decide which style they each want for their individual story. They might ask other students for their opinions.
- Invite a couple of students to share their orientations.

Lesson 15. How to Write Indirectly the *Where* and *When*

Goal: To learn to express where and when the story took place using descriptions that hint as to the *where* and *when.*

Materials: Select mentor texts that indirectly indicate the *where* and *when*. For example, the mentor text starts with "Sunlight drizzled through the water," indicating that it happened during the day. *Too Many Tamales* starts with, "Snow drifted through the streets and now that it was dusk, Christmas trees glittered in the windows," suggesting that it was during the winter around Christmas and in the northern hemisphere.

Activities

- Read aloud one of the selected orientations, asking the students when or where the story happened. Ask the students, "What did the text say that made them think of the time or place?
- Repeat with the other orientations.
- Ask students to suggest three different times when a story can happen (time). Write their responses on the board. Now ask them to think of sentences that would suggest the time without saying it directly. For example, for the time *fall*, students could have written the sentence, *leaves were falling from the trees whirling around in the wind*.
- Repeat this activity with place. For example, for the place *beach*, students could have written the sentence, *while the children built sandcastles, the mother went swimming*.
- Look at the orientation for the class story. Have students suggest ways to rewrite sections to indirectly indicate the time, place, or both, as needed.
- With students' permission, show one or two of their orientations. Ask the class if something could be changed to indicate indirectly the time, place, or both.
- Have students work on their own pieces. Make sure that they understand that changes in language should be made to make their story more interesting and better written.

Lessons to Draft the Plot of the Narrative

With the plans for the class and individual plots that have been enhanced by learning how to create events that reflect and depend on the features of character, how to build tension, and other enhancing features, students are ready to be guided to writing the various sections of the plot. These lessons include the joint construction of each stage, and students writing the stages for their own stories.

Before students start writing their individual pieces, however, teachers have found it very useful to confer with students to review their plot plans to check whether the connections between the sections make sense, and clarify what they propose to write. This results in writing with fewer inconsistencies. Students are more willing to modify their graphic organizers (GOs) than their drafts. For example, when conferring with 4th-grade students about their fictional narrative GOs, a teacher noticed that there were a couple of GOs where the events did not connect to the problem the students had proposed. After negotiating the changes with the students, they were ready to write.

Lesson 16. Joint and Individual Construction of Narratives

Goal: To write the plot of a fictional narrative based on the characteristics of the character(s) and the plot planned.

Materials: Class and student work already developed, that is, character(s) worksheets, graphic organizers with plot's plan that includes edits.

Activities

- Using the plan of the plot created for the class story, plan the information needed for each event, crisis, and resolution. The developed events should include elements they have learned, such as relating events to a problem, working toward crisis, actions that show personality of characters, and so on.
- Have students orally tell the story based on these plans, and then write down what the students say by using chart paper or projecting it on a screen.

Alternative ways of performing the first two steps;

- Take the first two steps, one event at a time, followed by the next steps to edit what's been written, until all the events, crisis, and resolution have been drafted.
- Do a couple of events together, and then have groups work on the rest of the events of the class narrative and put all of the events together. Then improve the whole narrative by carrying out the steps that follow:
- Review to check if the narrative includes information about the external and internal features of the characters.
- Point at a feature in an event and ask them questions: How can you describe the physical appearance? What can another character say or think about the physical appearance? For the internal features, point to a sentence they suggested and ask: How can we change this sentence to have the character do something that will show this trait or this feeling (pointing at the character plan)?
- Have students read aloud what was written and discuss any inconsistencies or missing information.
- Using the plot plan that students have created for their individual narratives, have them further develop the events of their story by using the graphic organizer.
- Ask students to sit with a partner and tell their story orally.
- Have students add the events, crisis, and resolution following their orientations written earlier.
- Ask students to decide on the medium for their final version.

Lesson 17. Insert Dialogue in the Narrative

Goal: To learn how to build character by using dialogue.

Materials: Mentor texts that are familiar to the students with examples of dialogue that reveal something about the characters. Students' worksheets with external and internal features of their character(s).

Activities

- Read the dialogues of one or two mentor texts aloud.
- Ask the students to describe what their dialogues reveal about the characters.
- Ask a student to show the picture of his or her character and read some of the features, both external and internal.
- Isolate one external and one internal feature of the character (e.g., *old* and *generous*).
- Working with the whole class, construct short dialogues revealing the external and/or internal features that would fit well in the story. For example, for the external feature *old*, the dialogue to be added could be,

"Do you want to walk with me to the top of the mountain?" asked the young man.
"I can't, my heart is not strong anymore and it is difficult for me to walk so much," replied Mr. Jones.

- For the internal feature *generous*, the dialogue to be added could be,

"What a beautiful scarf you are wearing!" commented the young woman. "Would you like it? It would make me happy if you accept it," said Laura.

- Repeat this activity with another student. Point out the need to have meaningful dialogue and not just "Hello" or "See you."
- As you write the examples, point at the punctuation that accompanies dialogue.
- Using the class narrative, point at an external or internal feature of the character included in the text. Ask the class how they could show this feature through a dialogue to be inserted in this section of the narrative.
- Repeat with another feature.
- Following the same steps, encourage students to insert dialogues in their own writing. Remind them of the needed punctuation.
- While students are working, conference with those that may have greater difficulty inserting dialogue. Spot good examples that you want students to share with the class.

Lesson 18. Create Images of Time, Place, and Cultural Group

Fictional narratives create an image of time, place, and cultural background of the characters in which the story occurs. Authors use devices, such as imitating the manner of speech of the time or region. For example, *Mississippi Bridge* takes place in the southern United States, and the characters use the dialect of the region in their dialogue. For example, one character says, "Now I ain't gonna tell y'all again" (p. 45). This can be confusing for bilingual learners who are trying to master a more standard dialect.

Dress, food, drinks, names, tools, and vehicles are other devices used. For example, in the book *Too Many Tamales*, the family is cooking tamales for a party. Tamales are typical in Mexico and Central America and among immigrant families from those regions.

> **Goal:** To enhance the plans for students' narratives with images that reflect the time when the story took place, the place where it happened, and the cultural group involved.
> **Materials:** Fictional narrative texts familiar to the students. Students' graphic organizers. List of items that reflect these features, such as dress, food, drinks, names, tools, language, vehicles, or other devices.

Activities

- Tell students that you (the teacher) will identify if the narratives reflect the time where the story took place, the place where it occurred, and the cultural group involved.
- Show them the list of devices. Point out that the list provides examples of some common devices.
- Read a section of the narrative and ask students to identify when the story took place. Ask them to explain their response.
- Have a student share the plot of his or her narrative. For example, if the students were writing fictional narratives based on a social studies unit about colonial times, you could ask, "What can you do to make the story reflect colonial times?" Possible responses could

include the way the people are dressed, what they eat, features of their houses or residences, and so on.

- Have students work in groups to think about their own writing and plan what they can add to address these features.

Lesson 19. Teach Students to Incorporate Accurate Facts

Goal: To show students that even when a story is fiction, some contextual facts should be accurate and can be helpful to include.

Materials: Mentor text. Class narrative and student work.

Activities

- Point out or circle the factual elements in the mentor text narratives, such as the behaviors of moray eels hiding in the rocks and coming out only to catch food, and of banded coral shrimp that clean parasites off of eels.
- Ask students to identify the facts in the class fictional narrative. Discuss with the students if these facts are accurate.
- Ask the students to identify the facts in their own fictional narrative. Then, have them check these facts against the research that they had done on the topic. Revise facts that are missing and inaccurate facts. For example, one student had a giraffe as her character. In the graphic organizer, she had written South Africa in the "where" box, but failed to write it in the actual story. Fact checking helped her to find this omission. Another student had a penguin as the main character and had him living in the Arctic rather than Antarctica.

Ending

Depending on the type of narrative or author choices, there are different ways to end a narrative. Some, like fables, always end in a moral. The ending of others may vary. For example, realistic fictions end with a feeling, a statement by the main character, an action or closing event, or a summary statement. Deconstructing texts in the type of fictional narrative helps determine the kind of ending. Some examples include:

Conclusion Type	Examples
Fables end with a moral	"An act of kindness, no matter how small, should never be forgotten." (*The Moray Eel and the Little Shrimp*)
Quotation from a character	" 'That was my last very first—my very last first time—for walking alone on the bottom of the sea,' Eva said." (*Very Last First Time*)
Main character's feelings about what happened	"Then Maria couldn't help herself. She laughed . . ." (*Too Many Tamales*)
A summary statement	And to this day Mei talks in Chinese and English whenever she wants. (*I Hate English*)
Legends end with the impact on the present	"And to this day, the *panettone* of Milano is eaten and enjoyed, especially at Christmas." (*Big Book of Favorite Legends*)

Features of Students' Writing

In José's fictional narrative example, shown earlier, the conclusion is quite acceptable, revealing the feelings of the main character.

	1	2	3	4	Uncoached Writing Comments
Conclusion (optional) A moral or other type of conclusion depending on the type of fictional narrative.			√		*I was a perfect dog for that woman.*

Students tend to end narratives by showing that characters that caused the problem changed; for example, *Finally, she did her own work* or *Never again did a fish call KD ugly*. Another common ending is to have characters that start as friends, become separated by conflict, but then restore their friendship, *Then they became friends again*. Thus, although the characters change during the story, what happens in the story does not really affect the character to make them different from where they started. Many middle school students' narratives ended on a final dramatic event, largely imitating the books they read. For example, in a class that had read *The Hate U Give*, a student wrote, *There was no sound coming from him that's when I realize he was dead*.

Lesson 20. Deconstruction of Text to Learn About Conclusion

Goal: To learn the ways authors write conclusions in the specific type of fictional narratives of the unit.

Materials: Mentor texts. Examples of endings on chart paper or ready to project. Handout with examples of endings.

Activities

- Project and discuss the different types of the endings.
- Give each group of students one mentor text. Ask the groups to read and discuss the endings and match it to one of the types of conclusion.

Lesson 21. Joint and Individual Construction of the Conclusion

Goal: To have students learn to write the conclusion on the basis of what they have learned in previous lessons.

Materials: Chart paper. Students' notebooks. Projector.

Activities

- Given what students have learned about conclusions, ask students to give suggestions for a good conclusion for the narrative that they worked on as a whole class.
- Negotiate the conclusion with the class as you write the conclusion on chart paper or project it for the class to see.
- In a group or with a partner, have students work on the conclusion in their own work.
- Confer with the students about their conclusions as they work in groups or pairs.

Reference Ties

Tracking the characters in a narrative is essential to comprehend the story. Characters are usually introduced by name, but then they are referred to by pronouns. It needs to be clear which is the referent of individual pronouns. Students often have narratives with more than one character of the same gender, making it confusing to whom they are referring when using a pronoun. For example, a 4th grader referred to two female characters in her story. In this paragraph she names them initially but then just uses pronouns, making it hard to figure out which of the two she is writing about:

> While elsabith was in **her** house being mad, Jenna went and told everybody the party was cancel. Elizabith was frusteraded **she** was trying to get a way so see how it feels to be robed. **She** got it while **she** sleeps **she** will take **her** favority stuff animals and put them in **her** house.

Another aspect of reference ties that students need to learn both to interpret text and to create text to avoid repetition is the use of different noun groups that refer to the same character (Fang et al., 2006). For example, in the myth *Eros and Psyche*, *Psyche* is referred to not only by her proper name but also as *youngest sister* and *beloved daughter*.

In Chapter 3 there are lessons on reference ties to teach students that pronouns need a referent so the reader can track participants and understand who or what the author is talking about (e.g., Lesson 24) that can equally apply to fictional narratives. In Chapter 4 there is a lesson on reference ties using different noun groups to teach students to name participants in different ways to include variety and show additional information (Lesson 3).

Title

The title usually gives a sense of the topic, as seen in *The Moray Eel and the Little Shrimp*. It can also give a hint that the purpose of the text is a story, such as *My Grandmother's Journey*, and may include features that make the story exciting, for example, *How Many Days to America? A Thanksgiving Story*.

Structural Elements	Mentor Text Example
From *Fables From the Sea* by Leslie Ann Hayashi, p. 6.	
Title	The Moray Eel and the Little Shrimp

José used the name of the genre for the title. With coaching on writing fictional narratives, but not necessarily focusing on writing titles, students wrote titles that revealed the character, such as *Max the Bragger*, or something about the story, such as *Blossom's Day of Fall*.

Lesson 22. Title

Goal: To learn to write an engaging title to interest the reader without revealing too much of the story.

Materials: Mentor texts used throughout the unit.

Activities

- Read aloud and discuss the titles of various mentor texts with the students.
- Brainstorm ideas together with students to show the difference between titles such as *The Frog* and *The Adventures of the Ravenous Amphibian*. Discuss that the title can show: (a) the topic, (b) the purpose/genre, and (c) how the author makes it interesting and intriguing for a chosen audience.
- Take proposals from the class for the title of the class story. Discuss the three elements of topic, purpose, and engagement features. Decide, with the class, on one title for the class story.

- Have students work in groups to decide titles for their individual pieces.
- Have students share their titles with the class.

Lesson 23. Create Images for the Text

In fictional narratives the images are usually drawings or sketches representing the unfolding story. The images reflect the characters' personality.

Goal: To have students learn how to create images that reflect the characters and the plot.
Materials: Mentor texts used during the unit and class and individual narratives.

Activities

- Ask students to look at the images in one of the mentor texts and discuss what they notice in the images.
    - What do you see in the images?
    - How do they help us learn about the characters and the plot?
      For example, the images in the mentor text, *The Moray Eel and the Little Shrimp*, show the two main characters with the eel coming out of the reef and showing her big teeth. The shrimp is catching food with his claws. Both show elements of the plot and the characters.
- Have students work in groups to analyze other texts and answer the same questions about the images.
- Regroup and create criteria for images:
    - Show the characters.
    - Include physical appearance and some aspect of internal features.
    - Reflect aspect of the plot.
    - There can be more than one image, each accompanying and illustrating some aspect of the story and the development of the character.
- Encourage students to work in groups to discuss potential images, and then add them to their narratives following the earlier criteria.

Types of Fictional Narratives

- *Adventure Stories*: "Features the unknown, uncharted, or unexpected, with elements of danger, excitement, and risk" (Harris & Hodges, p. 5)
- *Allegorical Narrative*: A narrative in which a character, place, or event can be interpreted to represent a hidden meaning with moral or political significance.
- *Ballad*: A narrative poem
- *Dystopian Novel*: A narrative used to explore social and political structures. It is often about survival, and their primary theme is oppression and rebellion. The story takes place in large cities devastated by pollution, war, revolutions, overpopulation, and other disasters. It may borrow features from reality, but won't depict contemporary society in general.
- *Fable*: A short, simple story that teaches a lesson. It usually includes animals that talk and act like people.
- *Fairy Tale*: A story written for, or told to, children that includes elements of magic and magical folk such as fairies, elves, or goblins.

- *Fantasy*: A highly imaginative story. Its characters, events, and places do not exist even when believable.
- *Folktales*: A short narrative, handed down through oral tradition, with various tellers and groups modifying it so that it acquired cumulative authorship. Most folktales eventually move from oral tradition to written form.
- *Legend*: A story about mythical or supernatural beings or events. An unverified story handed down from earlier times, especially one popularly believed to be historical.
- *Historical Fiction*: Tells a story that is set in the past. That setting is usually real and drawn from history, and often contains actual historical persons, but the main characters tend to be fictional. Writers of stories in this genre, while penning fiction, attempt to capture the manners and social conditions of the persons or time(s) presented in the story, with due attention paid to period detail and fidelity.
- *Modern Fantasy*: Also known as contemporary fantasy, these stories are set in the putative real world (often referred to as consensus reality) in contemporary times, in which magic and magical creatures exist, either living in the interstices of our world or leaking over from alternate worlds.
- *Mystery*: Literary genre in which the cause (or causes) of a mysterious happening, often a crime, is gradually revealed by the hero or heroine; this is accomplished through a mixture of intelligence, ingenuity, the logical interpretation of evidence, and sometimes sheer luck.
- *Myth*: A traditional story passed down through generations that explains why the world is the way it is. Myths are essentially religious because they present supernatural events and beings and articulate the values and beliefs of a cultural group.
- *Myths and Legends* (seek to explain a phenomenon): A narrative of human actions that are perceived both by teller and listeners to take place within human history and to possess certain qualities that give the tale verisimilitude. Legend, for its active and passive participants, includes no happenings that are outside the realm of "possibility," defined by a highly flexible set of parameters, which may include miracles that are perceived as actually having happened, within the specific tradition of indoctrination where the legend arises, and within which it may be transformed over time, in order to keep it fresh, vital, and realistic.
- *Novel*: A long prose narrative that describes fictional characters and events in the form of a sequential story, usually.
- *Novella*: A fictional prose narrative midway between a short story and a novel.
- *Nursery tale*: A short rhyme for children that often tells a story.
- *Parable*: A simple short story with the purpose of teaching a moral lesson.
- *Play*: A form of literature written by a playwright, usually consisting of scripted dialogue between characters, intended for theatrical performance rather than just reading.
- *Realistic Fiction*: Stories that could have actually occurred to people or animals in a believable setting. These stories resemble real life, and fictional characters within these stories react similarly to real people. Stories that are classified as realistic fiction have plots that highlight social or personal events or issues that mirror contemporary life. They depict our world and our society.
- *Science Fiction*: Imaginary writing based on current or projected scientific and technological developments.
- *Short Story*: Features a small cast of named characters and focuses on a self-contained incident with the intent of evoking a "single effect" or mood. In so doing, short stories make use of plot, resonance, and other dynamic components to a far greater degree than is typical of an anecdote, yet to a far lesser degree than a novel.

- *Tall Tale*: A distinctively American type of humorous story characterized by exaggeration. Tall tales and practical jokes have similar kinds of humor. In both, someone gets fooled, to the amusement of the person or persons who know the truth.
- *Trickster Tale*: "A subgenre of folktales, trouble takes the form of a negative trickster who plagues the hero or a positive trickster who outwits the antihero" (McKeough, 2013, p. 77).

Sources: Harris, T. L., & Hodges, R.E. (Eds.). (1995). *The literacy Dictionary: The vocabulary of reading and writing*. Newark, DE: International Reading Association. Massachusetts Department of Education (June 2001); English language arts curriculum framework. PDF available at www. doe.mass.edu/ela/ and Wikipedia http://en.wikipedia.org

References

Applebee, A. N. (1978). *The child's concept of story*. Chicago: Chicago University Press.

Brisk, M. E. (2007). Enhancing content and language in children's fictional narratives: Tracking the participants. *Paper presented at the American Association of Applied Linguistics conference*, April 21–24. Costa Mesa, CA.

Brisk, M. E. (2015). *Engaging students in academic literacies: Genre-based pedagogy for K-5 classrooms*. New York: Routledge.

Brisk, M. E., & Zisselsberger, M. (2011). "We've let them in on the secret:" Using SFL theory to improve the teaching of writing to bilingual learners. In T. Lucas (Ed.), *Teacher preparation for linguistically diverse classrooms: A resource for teacher educators* (pp. 111–126). New York: Routledge.

Brisk, M. E., Nelson, D., & O'Connor, C. (2016). Bilingual fourth graders develop a central character for their narratives. In L. de Oliveira & T. Silva (Eds.), *L2 Writing in Elementary Classrooms* (pp.88-105). New York: Palgrave/MacMillan.

Butt, D., Fahey, R., Feez, S., & Spinks, S. (2012). *Using functional grammar: An explorer's guide* (3rd ed.). South Yarra, Victoria: Palgrave Macmillan.

Christie, F., & Derewianka, B. (2008). *School discourse: Learning to write across the years of schooling*. London: Continuum.

Derewianka, B. (1990). *Exploring how texts work*. Rozelle, NSW, Australia: Primary English Teaching Association.

Dien, T. T. (2004). Language and literacy in Vietnamese American communities. In B. Pérez (Ed.), *Sociocultural context of language and literacy* (2nd ed., pp. 137–177). Mahwah, NJ: Lawrence Erlbaum.

Donovan, C. A. (2001). Children's development and control of written story and informational genres: Insights from one elementary school. *Research in Teaching of English, 35*, 452–497.

Edelsky, C. (1986). *Writing in a bilingual program: Había una vez*. Norwood, NJ: Ablex.

Education Department of Western Australia. (1994). *First steps: Writing resource book*. Portsmouth, NH: Heinemann.

Fang, F., Schleppegrell, M. J., & Cox, B. E. (2006). Understanding the language demands of schooling: Nouns in academic registers. *Journal of Literacy Research, 18*(3), 247–273.

Hildebrand, G. M. (2001). Re/writing science from the margins. In A. S. Barton & M. D. Osborne (Eds.), *Teaching science in diverse settings: Marginalized discourses and classroom practice* (pp. 161–199). New York: Peter Lang.

Kamberelis, G. (1999). Genre development and learning: Children writing stories, science reports, and poems. *Research in the Teaching of English, 33*, 403–463.

Labov, W., & Waletsky, J. (1967). Narrative analysis. In J. Helm (Ed.), *Essays on the verbal and visual arts* (pp. 12–44). Seattle: University of Washington Press.

Langer, J. A. (1986). *Children reading and writing: Structures and strategies*. Norwood, NJ: Ablex.

Martin, J. R., & Rose, D. (2008). *Genre relations: Mapping culture*. Oakville, CT: Equinox.

McCabe, A., & Bliss, L. S. (2003). *Patterns of narrative discourse: A multicultural, life span approach*. Boston: Allyn and Bacon.

McKeough, A. (2013). A developmental approach to teaching narrative composition. In S. Graham, C. A. MacArthur, & J. Fitzgerald (Eds.), *Best practices in writing instruction* (2nd ed., pp. 73–112). New York: The Guilford Press.

McPhail, G. (2009). The bad boy and the writing curriculum. In M. Cochran-Smith & S. Lytle (Eds.), *Inquiry as stance: Practitioner research for the next generation* (pp. 193–212). New York: Teachers College Press.

National Center on Education and the Economy. (2004). *Assessment for learning: Using rubrics to improve student writing.* Pittsburg, PA: The University of Pittsburg.

Rog, L. J., & Kropp, P. (2004). *The write genre.* Ontario, Canada: Pembroke.

Roser, N., Martinez, M., Fuhrken, C., & McDonnold, K. (2007). Characters as guides to meaning. *The Reading Teacher, 60,* 548–559.

Rothery, J., & Stenglin, M. (1997). Entertaining and instructing: Exploring experience through story. In F. Christie & J. R. Martin (Eds.), *Genre and institutions: Social processes in the workplace and school* (pp. 231–263). London: Pinter.

Schleppegrell, M. (2004). *The language of schooling: A functional perspective.* Mahwah, NJ: Lawrence Erlbaum Associates.

Scollon, R., & Scollon, S. B. K. (1981). *Narrative, literacy and face in interethnic communication.* Norwood, NJ: Ablex.

Vardell, S. M., & Burris, N. A. (1986). *Learning to write: A developmental/literary perspective.* Retrieved from http://eric.ed.gov/?id=ED280073 (ED280073)

Villaume, S. K. (1988). Creating context within text: An investigation of primary-grade children's character introductions in original stories. *Research in the Teaching of English, 22,* 161–182.

Chapter 6

Reports

A report is a factual text used to organize and store information. Reports are fun for children because they like to learn about new things. When a 2nd grader relatively new to the United States was introduced to the report genre, he produced one report after another about insects.

Reports present information clearly and succinctly (Schleppegrell, 2004). There are different kinds of reports: descriptive, comparative, historical, classifying, and whole-to-parts reports (see Table 6.1) (Derewianka & Jones, 2016; Humphrey & Vale, 2020; Martin & Rose, 2008).

Reports can be a good foundation for other genres, as they allow students to become knowledgeable about a topic. This makes it easier to enrich a fictional narrative, form the basis of an explanation, and provide evidence for arguments.

The word *report* is used in other contexts, but it does not always refer to the report genre. Some examples of writing projects that use the word report but are not in this genre are:

- Research Reports
- Lab Reports
- News Reports
- Book Reports

The first two in this list are **macrogenres** because each component of these writing projects has a different purpose. A *research report* expects students to "Conduct short research projects to

Table 6.1 Types of Reports

Type	Purpose	Examples
Descriptive Report	To describe an entity, a species, a class	Report on lions, oak trees, Massachusetts, Canada
Comparative Report	To compare and contrast features of two things or classes of things	Comparison between the Arctic and Antarctica
Historical Report	To inform how things were in a historical period or site	Pueblo Indian cities Leprosy colonies The Middle Ages
Classifying Report	To subclassify members of a general class	Report on different types of wild cats, of invertebrates, of New England States, of Middle eastern countries
Whole to Parts (Compositional Report)	To classify from whole to parts	The circulatory system A flower and its components

DOI: 10.4324/9781003329275-6

answer a question, drawing on several sources and generating additional related, focused questions for further research and investigation" (CCSS, English Language Arts, p. 44; see detailed description in Derewianka & Jones, 2016, chapter 10). In this type of project, the methods section is a procedural recount, while the findings are a report, and the discussion an argument.

Another common macrogenre in the sciences is the *Lab Report*. For example, middle school students wrote Lab Reports testing the speed of descent of small parachutes given the materials used to build them. The lab reports included:

Sections of the Lab Report	Genre Used
Background	A combination of a descriptive report on parachutes with explanations on how they work
Hypothesis	A prediction
How to do the experiment	Procedure
Results	Combination of a report of the results with a procedural recount telling some of the issues they had during the experiment
Conclusion	Argument going back to the hypothesis with evidence from the experiment

The term *report* is also associated with two other different genres that will not be covered in this book: news report and book reports. The *news report* or story, done by journalists, has the purpose of entertaining and highlighting the significance of the story they are telling. It includes the same stages of narratives, but states first the most disruptive events (Butt et al., 2012). *Book reports*, a common practice in literacy lessons, are a response to literature activity with the purpose of checking students' understanding of books they read. They include a summary of the reading and an evaluation of the book.

Development of Units

To develop units, teachers need to consider a number of factors that play a role on what and how to teach and what materials to use. With this in mind, they then plan lessons.

Unit Preparation

To prepare a unit in the chosen recount genre, teachers need to consider the following:

- Grade level
- Connection with content areas
- Mentor texts
- Research resources and how to use them
- Potential projects, audience, and medium
- Uncoached writing and planning content of the unit

Grade Level

Research on the development of the ability to write reports has revealed that students come to school in kindergarten and 1st grade with some basic knowledge of writing that enables them to create reports by drawing, labeling, and making lists (Newkirk, 1987) and distinguish between the genres of stories, poems, and science reports (Kamberelis, 1999). On the other hand, Langer

(1986) found that students in 3rd, 6th, and 9th grades had basic knowledge of report writing but did not improve much throughout the grades. Thus, students had the requisite knowledge and ability, yet, without adequate teaching, only marginal improvement was observed. However, appropriate teaching produces positive results (De La Paz & Graham, 2002). The types of reports and when to teach them follow.

Types of Reports	Grade Level
Descriptive	All grade levels
Comparative	4–8
Historical	5–8
Classifying	6–8
Whole to Parts	Earlier grades as a labeled diagram 6–8

Descriptive reports can be implemented at any grade level. Teachers choose the topic based on the curricular requirements of the grade level and adapt the level of difficulty. Difficulty can be increased or decreased by choosing different mediums that express meaning by balancing the amount of images and text. The more text, the harder it is (see later section titled "Potential Projects, Audience, and Medium" for specific examples).

The other types of reports are challenging because of the different ways of categorizing entities and are therefore more appropriate for upper elementary and middle school. Comparative reports are often included in tests at the upper elementary level, and thus it would be useful to prepare students for the challenge. Historical reports connect well with upper elementary and middle school social studies topics. Classifying and whole-to-part reports are best introduced in the middle school. When done as a labeled diagram, whole-to-part reports are appropriate for elementary students. For example, a diagram of the circulatory system with the organs labeled.

Connection With Content Areas

To be able to write, students need to know the content. Students must acquire the habit of using or seeking knowledge in preparation for writing. They need to be explicitly taught to be researchers (Perry & Drummond, 2002). Because learning and researching the content for writing is time-consuming, it is more efficient to connect writing with content the students have to cover in their various disciplines.

> "Cheryl, a fourth-grade teacher . . . introduced the report genre to her class by telling the students that report writing involved becoming an expert on a topic in order to write about it. She repeatedly stressed the need for students to educate themselves before writing about a topic and informing their audience" (Brisk et al., 2011, p. 4).

Therefore, a report unit should be planned in conjunction with curricular content to be covered in the particular grade. It is important that the various grade teachers plan together or check in with each other in order to connect the report unit with different topics and content areas across the grade levels. The most frequent type of report found in elementary school science is an animal report. Although animals are a good topic to start students on this genre, it is important not to

Table 6.2 Potential Topics

Social Studies	Science	Math
Family	Seasons	Geometrical forms
Community	Animals	Different ways to represent
Holidays (country and world)	Plants	fractions
Form of government	Insects	
States, regions, countries	Solar system	
Indigenous people	Planet earth	
Colonizers	The Moon	
Art and architecture of ancient cultures	Types of rocks	
The Constitution	World deserts, major rivers,	
Laws affecting non-citizens	volcanoes, etc.	
	Gravitational, electric, and	
	magnetic forces	
	Types of organisms	
	States of matter	

repeat it throughout the grades. Table 6.2 illustrates examples of different science, social studies, and math topics that could be covered in reports in the various grade levels. Teachers should check the specific curricular demands of their system to decide on topics to connect with report writing.

Development of content knowledge and teaching the report unit should be webbed together so that the teaching of content and writing reinforce each other. The starting point is the content; however, aspects of the writing unit can be incorporated early on. Teaching of purpose and general organization of stages, including using the graphic organizer (downloadable from the *Support Material* tab in the book's webpage), can be presented when teachers introduce the content of the unit. In this way, the students can use the graphic organizer to begin collecting information related to the content of their reports. For example, if reports were incorporated in a unit about the states of the United States, students could create a descriptive report graphic organizer and start collecting information on the particular state they have chosen for writing.

Mentor Texts

Mentor texts are written in the genre of the unit and are used to show students the features of the genre. Reports can be found in magazine articles, brochures, books, textbooks, and in the findings of a research paper. Following are examples of mentor texts for different kinds of reports.

Type of Report	Mentor Texts
Descriptive	Gallagher, D., & Gallagher, B. (2012). *Ladybugs*. New York: Marshall Cavendish Benchmark. (This is part of a series on insects.)
Comparative	Comparison between the Arctic and Antarctica www.differencebetween.com/difference-between-arctic-and-antarctic/#:~:text=%20What%20is%20the%20difference%20between%20Arctic%20and,ocean%20with%20the%20masses%20of%20other...%20More%20
Historical	Simpson, J., Thomas, D. H., Pendleton, L. S., & Halliday, H. (1995). *Native Americans*. Alexandria, VA: Time-Life Books. (This is a period piece because it contains reports on a variety of topics related to Native Americans only and not in a chronological way like historical recounts.)
Classifying	New England States: https://kids.kiddle.co/New_England (introduction only)
Whole-to-Parts	Stille, D. (1998). *The circulatory system*. New York: Children's Press.

The great majority of reports available for children are descriptive (see downloadable lists in the *Support Material* tab in the book's webpage). Mentor texts need to be written in the specific type of report the students will be learning, but they do not have to be in the topic of what they will be writing. It helps, however, if the topic is close. For example, if the students will be writing a Whole-to-Part report on the circulatory system, a mentor text written as a Whole-to-Part report on the digestive system would be a good mentor text. The type of hierarchal categories will be similar, such as organs.

Often, there is confusion between reports, the genre, and teaching about informational texts used in school. An informational text is a medium that may be written as a report, but it can also include other genres. The following examples of informational texts highlight this distinction. In the book *Saguaro Moon: A Desert Journal*, each page includes several boxes with short reports and one with a diary entry or personal recount. The first half of the book *Massachusetts: The Bay State* contains historical information in the historical recount genre, while the second half is written as a report describing the land, animals, businesses, capital, and tourist sites. The book *Halloween* includes three genres: historical recounts about the origin of the holiday; reports on the various symbols, such as Jack O' Lanterns, black cats, and bats; and procedures on how to construct the various symbols.

Research Resources and How To Use Them

Students obtain information for their reports through teacher presentations, field trips, life experiences, videos, printed material, and Internet resources. With Internet resources, teachers need to teach students how to determine if the resources are reliable. If they are still young, teachers may need to provide students with reliable research sites that were bookmarked in advance. In pre-school and kindergarten, students begin to get a feel for the process of research by exploring material with the teacher and whole class, as Mary did when writing a report on chickens with her 4-year-old students (see box).

Mary and her pre-K class decided to write a report on baby chickens. Mary's colleague, who raised chickens, contributed videos and explanations of how her chicks hatched, what they ate, and others. After further reading about chicks, the students gathered around the easel where Mary had written "chickens" and brainstormed possible subtopics. The children chose food, habitat, and parents. Mary started a web. Then they focused on each of the three subtopics and developed them further, expanding each arm of the web. Together they developed a sentence or two with respect to each subtopic, writing them on a separate sheet per subtopic. Mary then typed the final versions of the sentences on separate sheets, reproduced them, and made individual booklets for the children to illustrate.

With older learners exposed more formally to research, teachers need to:

- Strengthen students' reading comprehension and understanding of the content.
- Teach students to use a variety of sources and take notes.
- Teach students to transform notes to full text.

Strengthen Students' Reading Comprehension and Understanding of the Content

Activities to facilitate this part of the process are carried out during reading and content area time. Specific reading strategies can be used to help students gather research from written sources. Some examples of reading strategies include Reader-Generated Questions, where students are asked to think of questions that will be answered by a text after they are told what the text is about. Students then try to guess answers and finally read the text (Brisk & Harrington, 2007). The Reading to Learn program (Rose & Martin, 2012) suggests that teachers first prepare students for reading by providing background knowledge and overviewing the whole text. Followed by detailed reading of one paragraph, students do joint or individual rewriting of the paragraph using the technical language.

Teach Students to Use a Variety of Sources

Depending on topic, grade level, English language proficiency, and accessibility, there are various research sources available to students. They can use observations, interviews with experts and community members, videos, books, and the Internet to find information for their report (see Stead, 2002, for suggestions on how to secure resources).

Students develop the skills to use different research sources in connection with different report writing projects. With younger grades, teaching how to use one type of research resource at a time is sufficient, while with upper grades, students can tackle multiple types of resources per project. For example, in a 2nd-grade classroom, students learned how to interview people to write about the country of their ancestors. They later learned how to extract information from books to produce their report on animals. On the other hand, students in an upper elementary science class collected information to write reports and explanations related to ecosystems by doing experiments in the indoor and outdoor classrooms, as well as field trips to tidal pools and forest ecosystems. They brainstormed what they knew, discussed misconceptions, conducted experiments, learned to use field guides, recorded observations in their notebooks, and designed models among other things (Hodgson-Drysdale & Rosa, 2015).

As the second example demonstrates, students can obtain information by observing during experiments, field trips, or in other settings. To take full advantage of these observations, it is best to brainstorm what type of information they should be looking for beforehand. After a list of topics or questions is produced, each student should receive a copy (Stead, 2002).

Within the same classroom, teachers may recommend a specific type of research resource to different groups of students based on their students' strengths. For example, one teacher found that interviews with community members were a good alternative to research in books for students new to English.

Teaching Students How to Take Notes

The graphic organizers (downloadable from the *Support Material* tab in the book's webpage) are good tools to collect information from various sources and to help students take notes. These graphic organizers match the stages or text structure of reports. Teachers, the experts on the subject, explore a topic together with the students to demonstrate how to extract information from the sources and note the important information in the graphic organizer. This can be done over time as the particular topic is explored.

> **Steps to Using Genre Graphic Organizers as Research Tools**
>
> - Prepare a large graphic organizer for the type of report of the unit.
> - Explain the topic that you will be studying and link to the type of report that students will be writing.
> - Use a variety of resources to fill in the graphic organizer with information in collaboration with the students. Write the information or have students write it on sticky notes and attach them to the graphic organizer.
> - Depending on the grade level, have students contribute to the class topic with their own research. Have them practice different strategies using their own copy of the graphic organizer to collect the information.
> - Have students add what they find individually to the class graphic organizer.
> - Then groups or individual students can choose their own topic and research and take notes following the same process.

Doing group research helps students because they share the sources found. Thus, each student works with one source, but all contribute to the same set of notes. A 2nd-grade teacher had her bilingual students do research in groups. This group activity was not only helpful with coping with the quantity of information gathered when researching, but also led to animated discussions about the accuracy of the information each found. A 3rd-grade teacher working on descriptive reports gave each group one resource per student and a set of sheets with each subtopic written on the top of the sheet. Students read their resources, took notes on sticky paper about each one of the subtopics, and put the notes on the corresponding sheet. Then each member of the group (or pairs) took one of the subtopics sheets and created a paragraph for their report.

Research resources may be written in the native language of students. However, the challenges of doing research in another language are that students may not be literate in that language, and it may be difficult to find the vocabulary to express themselves in English once they have the information needed in their native language. If students are working with a bilingual teacher, then these language and vocabulary needs can be supported in the classroom. Alternatively, teachers let some students write in their native language and create bilingual books.

Teach Students to Transform Notes to Full Text

Once students have planned their report on the graphic organizer (or whatever note taking tool was used), they need to be taught how to create paragraphs or captions, depending on the medium used for the final product. Often, students have difficulty transforming notes into well-developed, meaningful clauses and coherent text.

Strategies to demonstrate writing from notes:

- Take each note from the graphic organizer, read it aloud, and with the help of the students, create a sentence and write it on a sentence strip. Encourage the use of technical terms and be careful that the content is accurately expressed.
- In collaboration with students, organize the sentence strips to create a paragraph.
- Paragraphs in reports usually include a topic sentence alerting the reader what the paragraph is about. Discuss with the class what the paragraph is about and note it.
- Ask students if the first sentence of the paragraph they currently have indicates what the paragraph is about. If it does not, then work together to create an appropriate topic sentence.

Although topic sentences often appear first, sometimes they do not. Find models of both types to deconstruct and discuss with the class.

Content area teachers can collaborate with grade level or literacy teachers to create reports together. In these cases, the content area teacher teaches the content and plans the report, making sure that the content is accurate. Meanwhile, the grade level or literacy teacher guides the production of the written reports.

Potential Projects, Audience, and Medium

When planning report writing for the class, regardless of the type of report, teachers need to consider the type of the medium, audience, and projects.

Medium

The organization of a report given the medium is different from the organization given the stages of the genre. However, these are often confused. Sometimes, teachers start a report unit talking about the table of contents, subtitles, and glossary, which are features of an informational text (a medium) and not necessarily that of reports (the genre). Reports can be written in the form of posters, brochures, PowerPoints, picture books, infographics, or informational books. The choice of medium is one way to adjust the level of difficulty with posters at one end of the continuum and informational books at the other. The choice of medium depends on the grade level, time of the year, difficulty of the content, and other media that students have already tried (see Table 6.3).

Different grade levels may use the same medium, adjusting for language. For example, in an elementary school, students in pre-K through 2nd grade and also in 5th grade wrote picture books. Pre-K children simply added labels to their images. First graders added one or two sentences to their illustrations, while 2nd graders wrote a short paragraph on each page. Fifth grade reports included several paragraphs of text, occasionally including one general image. Third and 4th graders used different media. Third graders created brochures, while 4th graders designed large posters with images and abundant text.

It is important to differentiate between text organization in relation to the type of report and layout in relation to medium. For example, a classifying report requires a general statement followed by a description of each type, according to chosen criteria, and subtypes, if any. While the medium of infographics requires images and short captions arranged to denote which are types, with subtypes connected to individual types. To teach this distinction and to make sure students do not equate the report genre with informational books, a medium, one 8th-grade teacher exposed students to a variety of mediums when sharing mentor texts to introduce purpose

Table 6.3 Different Mediums Across Grades

Grade/Medium	Pre-K	K	1	2	3	4	5	6–8
Co-constructed posters or books	√							
Picture books			√	√	√			
Group or individual posters				√	√	√	√	√
Brochures		√	√	√	√	√	√	√
Infographics				√	√	√	√	√
Informational books						√	√	√

Audience

As the unit starts and potential projects are discussed, it is important to bring up audience. Writers aim to make their writing comprehensible to their audience by choosing language and structures that will be understood. For example, in these two opening paragraphs on reports about snakes, the language is very different, indicating two different intended audiences.

Text 1

You'd think it would be hard to survive in the wild without legs. But look at snakes! More than 2,500 kinds slither and creep throughout the world. Snakes live just about everywhere except on some islands and near the North and South Poles. They can climb the tallest trees or burrow deep into the earth. Some snakes never leave the water. Others remain forever on land.

(Slinky Scaly Slithery Snakes, p. 3, 4th-grade book)

Text 2

Snakes are elongated, legless, carnivorous reptiles of the suborder **Serpentes** that *can* be distinguished from legless lizards by their lack of eyelids and external ears. Like all squamates, snakes are ectothermic, amniote vertebrates covered in overlapping scales.

(Wikipedia, *Snake*)

Text 1 uses more common technical terms, such as *snakes*, while Text 2 uses *reptiles* and *serpentes*. Further, Text 1 describes the snakes *without legs*, while Text 2 uses *legless*. Text 1 uses a few adjectives, such as 2,500, tallest, North, and South, while Text 2 uses a complex set of modifiers, including adjectives, prepositional phrases, and embedded clauses, that define the noun snakes: *elongated, legless, carnivorous reptiles of the suborder **Serpentes** that can be distinguished from legless lizards by their lack of eyelids and external ears.*

Teachers can assign different audiences to each project to help students become aware of why writers make specific language choices. For example, Holly, a science teacher, had 4th graders create posters about planets to demonstrate to the principal how much they had learned. They also wrote booklets for 1st graders, predominantly using images and short sentences. Teachers can also let the students decide on the audience. For example, students in Liz's 4th-grade class decided to write their reports for their former student teacher that was going to come visit the semester, following his full-time practice. They wanted to show off how much they had learned about a topic that he had started to teach them before finishing his practice (Brisk et al., 2008).

Projects

Teachers have chosen different types of projects depending on the grade level, time of year, and content area to which it is connected. A few examples illustrate the various types in different grade levels:

- In *pre-K*, in collaboration with the science teacher, students created small books about the types of live turtles they had in their classroom. The books included two or three pages with drawings and labels. The teacher created each page on chart paper first, and students produced a similar page for their book, learning the concepts and language all along.
- A *kindergarten* teacher did mini-reports in connection with various content topics. She gave students sheets with a place to draw and a sentence with blanks to be filled. As students

studied about the topic, they filled in the blanks, added illustrations, and assembled their books. With young students, demands can change depending on the time of the year. For example, early in the year a kindergarten teacher produced a big class book on the animal they were studying. Later in the year, the children produced their own PowerPoints on their chosen animal.

- A *1st-grade* teacher started the year asking students to create a book reporting on family members. Each page of the book included the picture of the person and a short description. The topic was very accessible to the students and helped the teacher and students to get to know one another.

- A *2nd-grade* teacher with primarily first- and second-generation immigrant students chose holidays around the world. The students chose a holiday celebrated in their country of origin. Their research consisted of interviewing family members about the holiday, as well as looking for additional information in books. Students worked in groups to produce posters, sharing what they had learned.

- A *3rd-grade* teacher had students prepare brochures in connection to a curricular unit on countries around the world. She gave students a planning sheet divided in four squares with subtopic labels on each and had them focus the research on just those four topics. They then created a brochure with a cover page and three or four pages with topics and illustrations.

- A *4th-grade* teacher decided to do reports in the form of posters as the first unit of the year. Later in the year, when students had mastered paragraph writing, they produced informational books about states.

- A group of *5th-grade* teachers, who wanted to do a short report unit, had students produce group posters. Groups of two or three students shared in the research and writing. Producing posters instead of a book was particularly helpful for bilingual learners who were newcomers to the English language.

- A *6th–8th-grade* science teacher used the tools of reports to help students read and comprehend their texts. She noticed that her students would look for information in their books in the text, but skip what was included in the images or side boxes, which in many cases contained information not included directly in the text. She gave her students the report graphic organizer with the key subtopics to fill out to prompt them to look at all of the material on a given page.

- An ESL *middle school* teacher working with newcomers focused her unit on Boston Historical Buildings. Students did field trips to visit a few of the buildings as part of the research component. She took photos at the sites and taught them how to observe and take notes. Students produced a report using Google slides to share with 2nd and 3rd graders in their partner school.

Uncoached Writing and Planning Content of the Unit

The unit starts by having the students write an uncoached piece to gauge students' knowledge of the features of the genre, which guides the planning of instruction (Stead, 2002).

Prompt for Uncoached Writing: *Write about an animal or a family member.* The prompt should not include the word *favorite* because students will write a persuasive piece to justify why the animal or person is their favorite one. For example, to avoid students' persuasive writing, a 5th-grade teacher asked her students to write a report on their school.

Teachers analyze the writing that emerges from the prompt using the Analysis of Student Work: Purpose, Stages, and Language form (downloadable from the *Support Material* tab in the book's webpage) to determine what the students can already do and what their challenges are. Based on the overall trends of the class, the teacher then designs the unit to focus on the aspects that address students' needs in areas that are developmentally appropriate and match grade level standards.

Purpose, Stages, and Language: Theory and Practice

This section describes the purpose, stages, and key language features to be included in the lessons. Analysis of student work in relation to each aspect illustrates the challenges students have. Lessons on purpose and stages are combined with lessons on language, with the goal of emphasizing language development from the start of the unit lessons. Table 6.4 suggests the order of the

Table 6.4 Teaching Language Parallel to Purpose and Stages

Lessons on Purpose and Stages	*Lessons on Language*
1. Purpose	2. Teach Formation of Third Person Singular in Present Tense and Past Tense (for L2 Learners in Particular)
3. Deconstruction of Text to Learn About Stages	4. Teach to Write in the Third Person *If the only aspect of language that will be formally covered in the unit is noun groups, start with the first activity included in Lesson 9 here, and distribute the others throughout the unit.*
5. Plan a Report • Choose subcategories • Order subcategories • Research and take notes	6. Teach Students to Use Appropriate Academic Language—Noun Groups
7. Teach How to Organize the Text Given the Medium (Grades 4–8)	
8. Writing the Subcategories • Write topic sentence • Transfer notes in graphic organizer to paragraphs • Create a cohesive paragraph (Chapter 8, Lesson 24)	9. Expanding Noun Groups by Using Pre-Nominal Modifiers (Grades K–8) and Post-Nominal Modifiers (Grades 4–8)
10. Joint and Group/Individual Revision of Paragraphs (Grades 1–8), With the Theme/New Information Tool (Grades 6–8)	and the Use of Modifiers (Grades 1–8)
11. Teaching How to Write the Opening General Statement	12. Participants (Generalized vs. Specific; Beings vs. Institutions) *(If needed, teach formation of plural in English)* Remind them of third person in relation to audience and voice
	13. Use of Clause Complexes to Make Meaning (Grades 4–8) 13.1. Clause Complex Puzzles 13.2. Deconstruct Clause Complexes 13.3. Revising Clause Complexes
14. Teach to Write Concluding Paragraph (Optional)	

Lessons on Purpose and Stages	Lessons on Language
15. Production of the Published Reports • Joint and Individual Revision of the Final Draft (see Chapter 4, Lesson 20) • Choosing the Title (see Chapter 3, Lesson 31) • Inserting Factual Images (see Chapter 4, Lesson 18) • Dissemination	

The following resources to support implementation of these lessons are downloadable from the *Support Material* tab in the book's webpage:

• Analysis of Student Work: Purpose, Stages, and Language
• Graphic Organizer
• Mentor Texts That Illustrate the Genre
• Internet Resources With Mentor Texts to Illustrate the Genre

lessons on purpose and stages and when to introduce the various aspects of language. When planning a unit, teachers will choose just two to four aspects of language to teach based on the background of the students and what the students have already learned when studying other genres. After introducing the chosen aspects of language, as suggested in the table, teachers will have the students practice it throughout the unit.

In spite of all the lessons on aspects of language, students do not always apply them to their individual writing, requiring additional lessons and encouragement to use the features in their writing. For example, Pat had made great effort during deconstruction and joint construction to teach students to use modifiers, mostly adjectives, to better describe what they were writing about. During joint construction, the students suggested a number they had learned from the texts they had deconstructed. However, when writing their own paragraphs, they barely used them. He then added a lesson on joint revision, where he showed students a list of nouns they had used in their reports and had them look at published texts for adjectives authors had used to describe those nouns. As a class, they then chose those that would go with the nouns in the list. The students went back to revise their own pieces, adding adjectives to enhance their descriptions (Brisk et al., 2018).

Purpose of Reports

Understanding the purpose is essential for students to achieve the goal of the genre, organize the text appropriately, and use language effectively. A report "is a factual text used to organize and store information. . . . Students at school are often expected to write information reports to display what they have learned" (Butt et al., 2012, p. 270). As we saw at the beginning of the chapter (Table 6.1), there are five different types of reports with different purposes. The choice for a particular unit will depend on the topic and grade level. For example, a report on organs is a descriptive report and can be done at any grade level, while a report on the circulatory system is a Whole-to-Part report more appropriate for upper elementary and middle school levels.

A 5th-grade class decided to do biographical reports on explorers. Instead of organizing the life of the person in a timeline like a biographical recount, they organized it by subtopics, including personal background, motives, sponsors, route of exploration, details of explorations, and impact. Teachers may find this organization easier to apply to most historical figures, rather than creating a different timeline for each subject. However, it is much easier for students to write about a historical figure in the form of a chronological biography (see Chapter 4).

Features of Students' Writing

Reports tend to be implemented after students have worked on genres that organize information chronologically, such as personal recounts and procedures. Moving from organizing text chronologically to categorizing or classifying topics in a logical order is a challenge for students (Brisk et al., 2008; Christie & Derewianka, 2008). As the following vignette illustrates, the teacher had to repeatedly stress that students were not writing a recount of their field trip, but a report about the exhibits.

The kindergarten class was preparing to start animal reports when Jeannette Sullivan's class went on a field trip to the Children's Museum. When they returned, Jeannette told the children that they were going to write a brochure with information about the exhibits in the museum. She had to stress that the report was not a personal recount about their visit, but that it was something that they would give to somebody who wanted to visit the museum and wanted information on the different types of exhibits. Using folded papers, the children drew the different exhibits that they remembered visiting and labeled them with Jeannette's assistance. The drawings appropriately illustrated the exhibits. Only occasionally did the drawings appear more story-like with an image of the writer visiting the exhibit. Jeannette pointed this more story-like element out to the children so that they could revise the images for their final version. Given that the children had made such a great effort to conceptualize the writing as a report, Jeannette thought that just labeling the exhibits was enough because as soon as longer text was attempted, the children wanted to write stories.

Another challenge students encounter, especially in younger grades, is their initial tendency to write using the purpose of the genre that they have just finished learning about. For example, Fred, a 2nd grader, wrote a report about Thanksgiving. The beginning of his writing showed the purpose by giving information, but it soon turned into a personal recount of his own experiences at Thanksgiving. Even after coaching, sometimes students are unclear of the purpose of reports. For example, one 1st grader wrote a procedure of how to take care of a hamster, instead of a report on hamsters. A 3rd grader started his report on cheetahs with a sentence more appropriate for a story (*It's a dark night in the savvan sound are all around you all a sudon something orange flashes by it a cheetah*). One 5th grader ended his report with, *that is the end of my story*, using inappropriate metalanguage, which may be the consequence of often hearing teachers talking about their writing as stories (Martin & Rose, 2008).

Older students have no trouble with the purpose. Students in 5th grade were given the prompt, *Write about the [Name] School*, for the uncoached piece at the beginning of the unit. Alicia wrote:

In the [name] school there are healthy snacks like brocoli, pinapple, Cubecumbers, oranges, apples, pears, Asian pears and others. Here we got smart and needs improvement students. There are education, subjects like math, writing, reading, and social studys.

There are grades from ko to 5 grade. Ko, k1, k2, 1st grade, 2nd grade, 3rd grade, 4th grade, and 5th grade, then your off to middle school 5th grade is hen you graduate form Elemantry school to middle school.

There are hobies like art, computers, science, (P.E.) gym. In art you can do creative things like clay pots and others. In computers you can (find) search up what you need. In science, all students learn scientific nature and learn more of are solar system. In gym (PE.) we get some good exersise like jugging, running, walking, football and others.

Purpose Depending on the type	√	The whole piece is a descriptive report on the school. At the very end, switches the focus to the author and other students.
Verb Conjugation (present, past in historical)	√	Present tense

This uncoached report has room for improvement, but Alicia shows that she has a clear idea that the purpose of reports is to give information about something organized in subtopics, and it is all written in the present. This student learned about written reports in 4th grade, so she was able to apply the knowledge into the next year. The prompt indicates that the topic is not about a class of things (e.g., schools), but about a particular member of that class.

While the difficulty of mastering the purpose of the genre varies by grade, other features such as organization and keeping the subtopics to one topic are challenging for all students. Language is particularly challenging because the need to express more complex ideas and relationships requires mastery of more complex language features.

Lesson 1. Purpose

Although to be able to write reports students need to start by doing research and developing content knowledge, it is a good idea to establish early on in the unit the purpose of what they will write and also start talking about potential audience. In this way the students have a sense of the reason for researching and learning so that they can write about it.

> **Goal:** To teach the purpose of reports and distinguish them from whichever genre or type of report with which the uncoached piece showed evidence of confusion. (If students are familiar with descriptive reports from earlier grades and the type of report for this unit is different, you may need to contrast the type of report students will be writing with descriptive reports, rather than another genre.)
>
> **Materials:** Mentor texts in the type of report of the unit. Examples of the contrasting genre or report with which the students showed confusion. Chart paper or projector.

Activities

- Brainstorm the purpose of the type of report as you look at books, brochures, and other texts written in that type of report.
- Show contrasting examples of the unit report and the source of confusion and discuss the differences.
- Discuss potential class and/or group/individual projects they will carry out.

Audience

In collaboration with students, teachers should determine the audience or audiences. This is essential because, as explained later, the language of a report is greatly influenced by the choice of audience.

Lesson 2. Teach Formation of Third Person Singular in Present Tense and Past Tense (for L2 Learners in Particular)

Reports are usually written in the present, because they are about how things are. In the case of historical reports, which are about how things were in the past, the past tense is used. Conjugation of the present is not a problem except for the third person singular. If the report is about one entity, expressed in third person singular (e.g., Willy the Whale), it becomes a source of difficulty for second language learners, with many students skipping the "s" (*the whale swim* instead of *swims*). Many reports are about a category or generalized participant, such as killer whales or invertebrates, and use the third person plural. In addition, because reports include the verbs *to be* and *to have*, students need to know the specific formation in those two verbs. Formation of the past in historical reports also presents difficulties.

A. Formation of Third Person Singular

Goal: To learn how to form the third person singular form of the verb.

Materials: Projector. A paragraph of a report on Antarctica, includes verbs in third person singular except in the next to last sentence, for example,

> Antarctica **covers** an area of 14 million square kilometres (5.4 million square miles). It **is** the 5th largest continent after Asia, Africa, North America, and South America.
>
> Antarctica's climate **is** harsh and unforgiving. It **is** cold, dry, and frequently swept with hurricane force winds. There **is** very little precipitation on Antarctica. In the interior, it **falls** as snow, and averages 2 inches (50 mm) per year.
>
> Most of the people who **live** on Antarctica **are** scientists and support staff. Antarctica **has** no indigenous peoples. (source: www.activewild.com/antarctica-facts-for-kids/)

Chart to Add Examples of the Various Forms

Verbs *to be* and *to have*	Verbs that add -s	Verbs that end in s, x, ch, sh, or o add -es	Verbs that end in -y preceded by a consonant add -ies	Verbs that end in -y preceded by a vowel add -s
Is has	covers falls	watches	carries	pays

Activities

- Project the paragraph, and with the whole class circle or highlight the verbs.
- Read aloud the first verb with the noun: *Antarctica covers*. Ask the students how they would say it if it was "I" or "Clouds." Discuss the difference between *Antarctica covers* and *Clouds cover*.
- Add *covers* to the chart in the proper column. Tell the students that other verbs change in different ways. Give a few examples to add to the various columns in the chart. As students encounter other forms, encourage them to add them to the chart.

Follow Up

- Remind students when jointly and individually constructing text whether the report requires third person singular.
- Bring it up during joint revision of drafts, if it shows to be an issue.

B. Formation of the Past Tense

Refer to Lesson 3 in Chapter 3.

Stages of Reports

Reports consist of two main stages: a general statement that gives the main topic and an indication to the type of report followed by the information categorized in subtopics, which vary depending on the type of report (see Table 6.5). The order in which the information is presented

Table 6.5 Stages of Different Types of Reports

Type of Reports	Stages	Example
Descriptive	General statement (Classification)	Lions are a type of wild cat found in Africa
	Description through subtopics	• Physical characteristics • Habitat • Diet/prey • Predators etc.
	Summarizing statement (optional)	
Comparative Report	General statement with features to be compared and contrasted	The Artic and Antarctica are located on the poles of the planet earth. Antarctica is a continent while the Artic is a sea of ice.
	Features Feature 1 Feature 2 Etc.	Contrast with respect to: • Human habitation • Fauna • Temperature
	Summarizing statement that brings the two topics together	Both Antarctica and the Arctic are threatened by global warming.
Historical Reports	General statement with time or place	Pueblo Indians built cities throughout the state of New Mexico.
	Descriptive subtopics	Location of the cities Features and function of the buildings Etc.
	Conclusion (optional)	
Classifying	General statement with classification system	There are about 40 species of wild cats, some are large and others are small.
	Description of each type based on criteria Description of subtypes for one or more of the categories, i.e., Type A Type B Type B.1 Type B.2, etc.	The seven large cats include ... while there is a greater number and variety of small cats. They can be further classified given ...
	Conclusion (optional)	

(Continued)

Table 6.5 (Continued)

Type of Reports	Stages	Example
Whole-to-Part (Compositional)	Description of the entity	The digestive system breaks down food to allow the body to absorb it.

	Description of each component and their function. A component may have additional subcomponents.	Organs and their function
		  Mouth
		  Esophagus
		  Stomach
		  Small intestine
		Juices and their function
		  Saliva
		  Stomach acid
		  Small intestine juices

	Conclusion (optional)	Statement about differences with other mammals

Sources: Derewianka and Jones (2016), Humphrey and Vale (2020), Martin and Rose (2008)

and consistency of information within each cluster are features of a clear report. Although students are often encouraged to write a concluding statement, published reports rarely include such conclusions (Butt et al., 2012; Martin & Rose, 2008).

In classifying reports, the classification can be based on different criteria. For example, wild cats can be classified based on size: large and small; based on status of the species: endangered and not endangered; and so on. It depends on the goal of the report. There can also be subclassification. For example, among the endangered, there could be almost extinct and vulnerable.

The following mentor texts have been deconstructed into their stages. The first one, *Meet the Sonoran Desert*, a descriptive report, has a general statement, three subtopics, and a final summarizing comment. The first two subtopics are included as one paragraph because the piece is rather short. An important aspect of the stages in a report is that they are logically connected to the topic of the report. To create a report that is clear to readers, writers indicate the topic of the whole report (macrotheme) in the initial general statement and the subtopics of each paragraph in the topic sentence (hypertheme—**in bold**).

Stages		Mentor Text
Title		*Meet the Sonoran Desert*
General Statement (Identification and classification of the topic; what and how this is classified in the universe of things)		There are four major deserts in North America: the Chihuahuan, the Great Basin, the Mojave and the Sonoran. Together they cover roughly 5,000,000 square miles in the southwestern part of the United States and northwest Mexico.
Information organized in bundles (or categories, subtopics) by topic	Climate	The Sonoran is the only desert in North America that does not have cold winters. This makes it **a tropical desert**.
	Size	It covers 100,000 square miles and expanded to its present size only about 8–10,000 years ago, which makes it **a medium-sized**, but very young desert.

Stages		Mentor Text
Title		*Meet the Sonoran Desert*
	Vegetation	The Sonoran Desert is also thought of as an **arborous desert**, which may seem like a contradiction, since "arborous" means trees. It is not that the Sonoran Desert is covered with forests, but there are tall cacti and many trees—it is more like a sparse woodland.
Summarizing Comment (optional)		Scientists have recorded more different types of animals and plants in the Sonoran than in any of the other North American deserts, making it a truly exciting place to explore.

Source: Pratt-Serafini, K. J. (2002). *Saguaro moon: A desert journal.* Nevada City, CA: Dawn Publications, p. 3.

Descriptive reports such as the example are most appropriate for the elementary grades. The other types of reports are more appropriate for the middle school. Comparative reports, like the following example, are often demanded in tests, including in the upper elementary grades. These reports are similar to the descriptive, but students need to find the categories of differences and similarities, making them more challenging.

Stages of a Comparative Report		Mentor Text: The Senate and the House of Representatives Source: www.eslbee.com/comparison_contrast_essays_models.htm
General Statement		The government of the United States is made up of three branches: the legislative branch, the executive branch, and the judicial branch. The legislative branch, called Congress, is responsible for making laws. Congress is made up of two houses: the Senate and the House of Representatives. In this essay, you will learn the differences and similarities between these two houses of Congress.
Features	Feature 1	There are many differences between the Senate and the House of Representatives. The Vice President of the United States is the head of the Senate. He must vote in the Senate if there is a tie. On the other hand, the House of Representatives' leader is called the Speaker of the House. The representatives elect him or her.
	Feature 2	Another difference is that the Senate is made up of 100 senators, two from each state. The House of Representatives, however, is made up of 435 representatives. The number of representatives from each state is determined by that state's population. The greater the population in a state, the more representatives that state will have in the House.
	Feature 3	A third difference is that senators are elected to six-year terms, while representatives are elected to serve two-year terms. Every two years, the nation holds an election for members of Congress. At that time, all members of the House of Representatives and one third of the Senate are up for re-election.
	Feature 4	There are also similarities between the Senate and the House of Representatives. For example, both houses of Congress are made up of men and women. Both senators and representatives are members of Congress who must work together toward the same goal: to create, discuss, debate, and vote on bills, some of which eventually become laws. In the U.S. Capitol Building in Washington D.C., senators and representatives often meet with each other and in smaller groups to discuss laws. Before the President can sign a bill into law, it must first be approved by a majority of members in both the House and Senate.
Conclusion		Although Congress is made up of two types of lawmakers, they must work together for the benefit of all Americans.

Most reports conclude with one last element of the categories included in that type of report. For example, a descriptive report on telescopes concludes with:

> Some telescopes are launched into space. These telescopes gain clearer views. And they can collect forms of electromagnetic radiation that are absorbed by the Earth's atmosphere and do not reach the ground.
>
> (CCSS.ELA/Appendix B, p. 75)

Some descriptive reports for children conclude with an advisory or engaging statement to keep the interest of the children, as we saw in the earlier example of the *Sonoran Desert* mentor text. Comparative reports often conclude with a statement that brings both elements together, as shown in the text about the American Congress.

Features of Students' Writing

Students have great difficulty with the introduction of reports signaling the main topic and classifying, comparing, or meeting the demands that type of report usually includes. With coaching, students tend to include these initial, general statements. For example, Christine (Grade 2) appropriately started her report with *A penguin is a kind of bird*. Middle school students' reports included rather complete introductory paragraphs. In Alicia's piece describing her school, she failed to introduce her school; instead, she just named it and went on to develop one subtopic.

	1	2	3	4	Comments
General Statement (a) Topic is introduced (b) Content depends on the type	√				(a) Doesn't introduce the topic (b) Doesn't classify the topic
Information organized in bundles depending on type. Each bundle: (a) covers one aspect (b) relates to the topic of the General Statement (c) includes a topic sentence		√			Six topics unevenly developed. No sense why the particular order. (a) some paragraphs do, others do not (b) all except the last paragraph switches the focus to students rather than the school (c) no topic sentences
Conclusion (optional)					No conclusion

The information that follows in Alicia's piece also presents difficulties with respect to (a) introducing the topic, (b) developing the topic, and (c) staying on topic. Alicia succeeded in introducing some subtopics, but for others she just wrote about them. The first paragraph has a combination of topics. The sentence's topics were snacks (first), type of student (second), and subject matters (last). Paragraphs with multiple instances of unrelated information are common in students' writing, especially in the uncoached pieces. In the younger students' writing and older students new to English, the pieces are often too short for topics and subtopics to be introduced and developed.

Topic sentences are the hardest for students to include because they require abstracting the topic of the paragraph and naming it. For example, a paragraph from a 5th-grade report on jaguars starts, *What Jaguars eat is Deer cause the size of their horns. Also they may sometimes eat elephants . . .* The student goes on to list each prey in a different sentence. However, he did not indicate that he was going to write about the jaguars' diet or type of prey at the beginning of the paragraph.

Even when coached and following a set of questions, 2nd graders often went directly to giving information about a topic, or as in the case of one student, starting a report about pigs with *pigs are omnivore so they eat chicken*. The first clause, *pigs are omnivores*, would have been a good topic sentence for a paragraph on diet, but the second clause limits the topic.

With coaching, middle school students become aware of the need to name the topic of the paragraph but still show some difficulties. For example, one student writing a report about a Community Center started a paragraph with: *The programs at the Community Center are* . . . and went on to write about the various programs. Another paragraph includes the topic sentence: *One of the well-known events held at the Community Center is* . . ., but then the student wrote about two different events. Yet, another paragraph had no topic sentence.

Although in reports there is flexibility as to the order of the information, certain information tends to make sense to put first. Alicia's order of presentation seemed random, starting with the food they eat at school, followed by the grades the school covers, a logical first subtopic, and ending with what students study. One 5th grader started with a paragraph about what jaguars eat, followed by where they live. Only in the third paragraph, just before the conclusion, did he describe the features of a jaguar. A more logical order would have been the exact reverse. Students in pre-K through 3rd grade organized topics in a logical manner because the teachers coached the students on the order of the subtopics through modeling or questions. It became more challenging when the students chose their own order.

Alicia's uncoached writing did not include a conclusion, which most published reports do not include either. Students' reports include them when they are coached to do it.

Language Features of Reports

In a report, topic development is very demanding because it requires knowledge of the topic and knowledge of language to adequately express meaning. In order to convey factual information in a precise manner, report writers employ technical vocabulary to form clauses that include verbs, complex noun groups, and adverbials. Often, ideas expressed in individual clauses are connected to form clause complexes or sentences to express different logical relations.

Verbs are not very complex in reports; they are mostly relational and action verbs, usually in the present tense. Relational verbs describe characteristics and varieties. For example, the verbs *be*, *have*, and *seem* are used to show features of the Sonoran desert in the mentor text. Action verbs describe behavior or activity, as in *cover*, *make*, and *record*.

Adverbials of place, time, manner, reason, and others express circumstances providing important information about the topic, for example, "8–10,000 years ago," "in North America," and "roughly." Students also use adverbials in their writing, especially of time, place, and reason, for example, *since 1972*, *into caves*, and *for their warm skin*.

Although reports do not usually use text connectives, children tend to start sentences with new information by using *also*. Using the Reformulation Approach (see Brisk & Harrington, 2007), in which the teacher rewrites the piece without *also*, students realize that use of *also* is not necessary.

This section on language will address those areas that reflected the greatest challenges in students' writing, including participants and the ability to pack information through noun groups and clause complexes. In addition, in order to provide clear information about the topic of the report, writers need to create paragraphs with a well-defined topic sentence and clauses that connect to each other when developing the subtopic.

Tenor: Audience and Voice

Language choice depends not only on topic, but also on audience. Depending on the age and language proficiency of the audience, authors control the difficulty of the technical terms and complexity of clause elements and clause complexes. For example, the following excerpt comes from a 4th-grade book about snakes. It includes several uncomplicated clauses and sentences.

You'd think it would be hard to survive in the wild without legs. But look at snakes! More than 2,500 kinds slither and creep throughout the world. Snakes live just about everywhere except on some islands and near the North and South Poles.

(from *Slinky Scaly Slithery Snakes*, p. 3)

The second excerpt, geared for adults, comes from Wikipedia, and consists of just one 25-word sentence with complex noun groups and adverbials, as well as a subordinate clause.

Snakes are elongated, legless, carnivorous reptiles of the suborder Serpentes that can be distinguished from legless lizards by their lack of eyelids and external ears.

(Wikipedia)

In the case of children's writing, their language maturity plays a role in how technical the language can be regardless of audience.

Because reports are used to provide factual information about a subject, they generally present the author as an expert on the topic. Therefore, the tenor, or relationship between writer and audience, is formal, and the text is written in the third person. The use of first or second person is not common. Occasionally, in the introduction of reports, authors use second person to address the audience directly. The texts are directed to young students, as in the 4th-grade mentor text shown earlier. If any of the mentor texts shows this feature, it is important to discuss with students the author and audience. In the case of that mentor text, an adult wrote for children trying to get them interested by directly connecting with them. The rest of the book is all in third person. Therefore, students need to consider their audience when writing. If they are writing reports to their classmates, older students, or adults, it would be better to write in third person, reflecting the voice of an expert. When writing to younger students, they may still do so in third person, as many authors do, or use second person in the introduction and third person in the rest of the report.

Noun Groups

Noun groups are abundant in reports. They carry a great deal of the report's information and tend to be complex. The structure of noun groups used in school materials increases in complexity with grade level. In turn, what students are capable of producing does, too (Brisk, 2021). For example, in the first 36-word paragraph of the mentor text cited earlier in the chapter, "The Sonoran Desert," only seven words (20%) are not part of complex noun groups (in bold):

There are **four major deserts in North America: the Chihuahuan, the Great Basin, the Mojave and the Sonoran**. Together they cover roughly **5,000,000 square miles in the southwestern part of the United States and northwest Mexico**.

Nouns and modifiers tend to be technical terms denoting specialized meaning, adding to the authoritativeness of the voice (Fang et al., 2006). These nouns and adjectives reflect the topic of the report. For example, the mentor text on the Sonoran Desert includes such nouns as *desert, miles, Sonoran, Great Basin, trees, forests, cacti, woodland, animal,* and *plants*. They also include adjectives, such as *four major, northwest, tropical arborous,* and *exciting*. Interestingly, the adjective *exciting* is the only generic adjective, and it is used at the end when the author tries to generate interest in the topic.

A noun group includes a head noun and modifiers before or after the noun, or both (see Table 6.6). These modifiers define and describe the noun. Determiners and adjectives precede the noun. Prepositional phrases, appositions, and embedded clauses with conjugated or

Table 6.6 Types of Pre-Nominal and Post-Nominal Modifiers (bold)

Type		Example
Determiners (a/an/the)		**The** Sonoran Desert
Pointing Word (this/these; that/those)		**These** properties include hardness …
Adjectives	Possessive	**My** pet snake
	Quantity	**Four** major deserts
	Opinion	It is truly an **exciting** place to explore.
	Factual	A **medium-sized**, very **young** desert
	Comparing	The Sahara, the **largest** subtropical desert in the world, covers …
	Classifying	It makes it a **tropical** desert
Prepositional Phrase		The only desert **in North America**
Apposition		The Sahara, **the largest subtropical desert in the world**, covers …
Embedded clause with conjugated (finite) verb (also called relative clause)		The only desert in North America **that does not have cold winters**
Embedded clause with non-conjugated (non-finite) verb	*To* clauses	an exciting place **to explore**.
	-ing clauses	in the Sonoran than in any of the other North American deserts, **making it a truly exciting place to explore**.
	-ed clauses	The structure **formed by the atoms clicking into place** is called a lattice.
Adjective group after a relational verb		The shell of a snake's egg is **tough and leathery, not hard like a bird's egg**.

non-conjugated verbs follow the noun (Derewianka, 2011). The adjectives are factual and precise.

These complex noun groups are also found within adverbials, making adverbials complicated structures. For example, the adverbial "in *the southwestern part of the United States and northwest Mexico*" includes a complex noun group (*italics*) [determiner + adjective + noun + prepositional phrase].

Participants

The participants that are the focus of the report are usually generalized, that is, they represent a class of things, such as *deserts*. To indicate this kind of participant, the noun is in the plural. There are reports, also called descriptions, that are about one participant, such as *the Sonoran Desert*. Having to write about a category or generalized participants rather than an individual is a new experience for children who are used to writing recounts about specific participants. In addition, L2 learners need to learn plural forms of nouns, both regular and irregular. For example, a student wrote *mouses* for *mice*. They need to learn to add not only the "s" to the singular form, but also "es" in some cases (*classes*), as well as the irregular plural forms (e.g., *feet*, *lives*) and a number of other variations. (For a complete list of rules on plural formation, see www.myenglishpages.com/site_php_files/grammar-lesson-plurals.php#.Ukv2heDipvY.)

Verb Groups

Reports include mainly relational verbs and action verbs (Derewianka & Jones, 2016). Relational verbs are different from others because they do not have their own meaning, but they are used to relate one piece of information with another. The most common relational verbs are *to be* and *to have*. Others include: *mean, become, seem, appear, represent, symbolize, equal, turn into, possess, own, include, comprise, encompass,* and *lack* (Derewianka, 2011). In reports, relational verbs are used to describe and to define. The distinction between describing (*The carpenter ant is large and black*) as opposed to defining (*The carpenter ant is an insect*) is important for students to understand. In the chapter's mentor text there are instances of relational verbs to describe (*there are tall cacti and many trees; the only desert in North America that **does not have** cold winters*) and to define (*This **makes** it a tropical desert*). Action verbs are mainly used to show behavior (*they **cover** roughly 5,000,000 square miles*). Reports on living beings have more action verbs, as well as other types. For example, a report on penguins includes such action verbs as *live, eat, drink, swallow, swim,* and *waddle*. It also includes sensing verbs, such as *see, vocalize,* and *hear*. A number of the verbs are technical words that may be unfamiliar to students. For example, a report on insects includes such verbs as *breed, swarm, dwell, sting,* and so on.

Clauses and Clause Complexes

In the early stages of writing development, students express most of their ideas through simple clauses. In the upper elementary and middle school grades, students start to express complex ideas that require sentences with multiple clauses—clause complexes—connected to denote different meanings. The texts they encounter also use these complex structures to make meaning. Even those for younger students include some clause complexes.

The grammatical categories that form a clause are verb groups, noun groups, and adverbials, the focus of previous sections. Clauses contain one verb group to express what is happening (process). They indicate who/what is taking part (participants) and the circumstances surrounding. Not all clauses contain all three of these meanings, but verb groups are essential.

Clauses come together to form clause complexes, which can be categorized by their structure and by the meaning relationship. The latter is essential to teach to help students make meaning in their writing. Teachers are masters at interpreting students' writing, but students need to learn to make their intended meaning clear to a general audience.

Structurally, sentences can be compound, complex, or compound/complex, depending on the level of dependence:

Compound (each clause stands on its own): *A cobra's front ribs are especially long, and they can fan out to the sides.*

Complex (one clause can only be together with another): *When two or more atoms bond together, they form a molecule.*

Complex/Compound (combination of both): *Because rocks are often made of several minerals, it is difficult to use these properties to describe or identify a rock.*

Members of a clause complex are formed with a conjugated verb (finite) or non-conjugated verb (non-finite) (Derewianka, 2011; see Table 6.7). Non-finite clauses (italics) contain a verb (bold) that is not conjugated.

Non-finite clauses help compact the writing. Thus, instead of adding a separate clause—The fangs inject deadly poison—the use of *injecting* allows the writer to create a clause complex.

These non-finite clauses have a variety of functions, such as indicating a circumstance of time ("When threatened, it lifts and . . .,") or acting as the subject of a sentence. For example, a 4th grader wrote, *Making the pamphlets* was fun.

Embedded clauses, which are a type of modifier as we saw in the Noun Group section, are structurally similar to clause complexes, with conjugated or non-conjugated verbs (see Table 6.8), but their function is to modify a noun. They tend to appear later in students' writing.

The other way to analyze clause complexes is by the relationship that they express. The two basic types of relationships are *projection* and *expansion* (Halliday & Matthiessen, 2004). Projections were addressed in Chapter 5 because they are more likely to occur in recounts or narratives. In expansions, one clause expands what is expressed in the other. There are many different possibilities to build on the meaning, often signaled by a connecting word (a conjunction or other types of connectives). Table 6.8 illustrates the relationships most commonly found in reports (for a full range and analysis of logico-semantic relations, see Brisk & DeRosa, 2014).

Table 6.7 Clause Formation: Finite and Non-Finite Verbs

Type of Structure		Example
Finite verb		These properties **include** hardness, color, density, and cleavage.
Non-Finite Verb	**To** clauses	it is difficult to use these properties **to describe or identify** a rock.
	-ing clauses	. . . the fangs swing out and pierce the prey, **injecting** deadly poison. (from *Slinky, Scaly, Slithery Snakes*)
	-ed clauses	When **threatened**, it lifts and flattens its neck, and hisses. (from *Slinky, Scaly, Slithery Snakes*)

Table 6.8 Clause Complexes: Types of Relationships

Type of Relationship	Connecting Words	Examples From the Children's Texts Slinky, Scaly, Slithery Snakes *and* Rocks and Fossils
Temporal (When? How long? How often?)	*Then, next, afterwards, as, just then, at the same time, while, until, before that, soon, after a while, meanwhile, all the time, until then, now, every time, whenever*	A snake has no limbs to get in the way *when it's chasing after tunneling ground squirrels and burrowing mice.* Snakes' bodies make S shapes *as they glide along.* (*Slinky, Scaly, Slithery Snakes*)
Causal (reason, purpose)	*Because, as, since, so, then, consequently, therefore*	Even the fastest snake has a hard time escaping from an animal with four legs, *so some snakes have ways of tricking their enemies.* (reason) Other snakes use their color *to hide.* (purpose)
Conditional	*If, as long as, in case, on condition that* (positive); *unless, without* (negative)	*If that doesn't work,* the snake violently twists its body about . . .
Manner (How?)	*By, through, with Thus, and + in that way, so, and + similarly, as if, as though, as, like*	Sidewinders seem to swim over the surface of the desert, *looping their way quickly from place to place.* (non-finite clause that is not connected by a conjunction)

(Continued)

Table 6.8 (Continued)

Type of Relationship	Connecting Words	Examples From the Children's Texts Slinky, Scaly, Slithery Snakes and Rocks and Fossils
Comparative	Likewise, similarly, in a different way	A method good for measuring ages in millions of years is of no use on an object that is only a few thousand years old. Likewise, a method that works well for a short time span is undoubtedly worthless for much longer periods. (Rocks and Fossils)
Concessive	But, yet, still, despite this, however, even so, nevertheless, although, even though, even if, while, whereas, much as	Snakes can't hear well, but they easily feel vibrations through the ground.
Extending by adding something new	And, as well (additive)	When threatened, it lifts and flattens its neck, and hisses.
	But, while (adversative)	Many kinds of snakes can swim, but sea snakes are swimming champions
	Or, instead of, besides, instead of, without, rather than (variation or replacement)	Some snakes attract their prey instead of ambushing it.
Elaborating without introducing something new	In other words	Certain types of materials, such as uranium, are radioactive. In other words, they give off radiation.
	For example, for instance, in particular	That picture, however, is incomplete. For example, creatures with soft bodies, which easily decay, are not very likely to leave fossils behind.

Sources: Brisk and DeRosa (2014), Eggins (2004), Halliday and Matthiessen (2004), Thompson (2004).

Thus, when combining clauses, writers need to decide the desired meaning to be expressed and the connective that will signal the type of expansion.

Cohesive Paragraphs

Two features help develop clarity in paragraphs for reports. One is that paragraphs include a topic sentence introducing the subtopic of the paragraph, and the second is the internal flow of the paragraph. The topic sentence is often, but not always, at the beginning of the paragraph to guide the reader as to what the paragraph is about. Thus, a paragraph about crystals, starts, "A crystal is an orderly arrangement of atoms and molecules" (Foss, Earth History, p. 61), introducing and defining crystals. Student writing often includes the content of a subtopic but misses the introduction to the content, which often requires an abstraction.

Within paragraphs, clauses relate to each other. Each clause starts with the theme or what the writer is writing about and ends with the new information, what the writer is saying about it. The term theme refers to a grammatical category and not to the "theme" or "deep meaning of a literary work" used in literary analysis (Fang & Schleppegrell, 2008, p. 98).

The theme usually consists of the initial part of the sentence until the verb of the main clause. After the initial sentence of a paragraph, the themes of clauses that follow either connect to the new information of the previous sentence or to the original theme. Authors choose the information included in the theme position to direct the reader to the focus of the writing. For example, in recount genres, the initial theme of paragraphs tends to include an adverbial of time to denote passage of time, for example, "Soon after he . . .," "About four months after he . . .," and "In 1985 his autobiography, *The Narrative of the Life of Frederick Douglass, An American Slave* . . ." (from *A Picture Book of Frederick Douglass*). In reports, the initial themes relate to the focus of the subtopic of the paragraph. Following themes provide more detailed information about the initial. For example, in the CCSS text "Telescopes" (CCSS.ELA/Appendix B, p. 75), analysis of the third paragraph shows the strategies used by the writer.

Theme	New Information
There	are many different types of telescopes, both optical and non-optical.
Optical telescopes	are designed to focus visible light.
Non-optical telescopes	are designed to detect kinds of electromagnetic radiation that are invisible to the human eye.
These	include radio waves, infrared radiation, X rays, ultraviolet radiation, and gamma rays.
The word "optical"	means "making use of light."

The writer presents the concepts of optical and non-optical as new information in the first sentence, elaborates on optical in the second, and non-optical in the third sentence, with optical and non-optical in the theme position. In the third sentence, the author introduces "kinds of electromagnetic radiation" referred to as "these" in the theme of the fourth sentence and described in the new information. The fifth sentence goes back to the theme of optical, which signals that it could have been placed as a second sentence when the concepts of optical and non-optical were introduced.

It is important for the reader to know what the writer is referring to when a topic, idea, or information is introduced more than once. For example, in the aforementioned passage, the theme of the fourth sentence has a weak reference when the sentence starts with "these" because a theme can refer to the "kinds of electromagnetic radiation" or the previous theme, "non-optical telescopes."

Features of Student Work

The following example from a 5th grader writing on leopards illustrates the language strengths and challenges students experience when writing reports. Timothy writes,

> Leopards are real interesting animals because leopards climb trees to sleep and protect their food from other animals. Did you know that one kind of leopards is snow leopards? These leopards live in the mountains and grassland of centorial Asia Snow leopards have been listed as endangered since 1972. Female snow leopards give birth to two to four cubs at a time.
>
> Some live in Africa like these dark colored leopards live in the warm Amazon dark rain forest. They are only a few left in the world because people hunt for their warm skin. Also because there forest is gettin felled little by little. Leopards eat goat, hores, deer and bunny's. They climb trees to protect their food by climbing trees, and also they sometimes camouflage to eat/protect. Also that when they sometimes take them into caves. Also Some not all go where they live and hunt them/eat them there.
>
> Leopards are very but very cool and interesting animals!! More than people think they were. The Leopards are cool and interesting. Cause where there from. Like where they live, eat. Even how they protect their food from other people and anmails.

Audience Information and language level of difficulty and amount appropriate for the audience and level of maturity of writer.	√	Unclear audience, language structures more due to student's ability than audience
Voice Body of text in 3rd person General statement and conclusion voice may vary for young audiences.	√	Mostly statements in 3rd person. One question.
Noun Groups: Modifiers to pack information • adjectives • prepositional phrases • embedded clauses with finite or non-finite verbs • adjective group after a relational verb	√	Uses some adjectives, some repeated. In addition, several in adjective groups connected by a relational verb. No prepositional phrases or embedded clauses.
Noun groups: Technical language Uses technical language related to the topic for nouns and modifiers	√	Some technical terms: grassland, camouflage, cubs. "Interesting" and "cool" are generic adjectives not reflective of the topic.
Participants (generalized, specific) If generalized, they are consistently used.	√	There is no clear switch from talking about snow leopards and back to leopards in general.
Verb Groups (a) relational verbs to describe and define (b) action verbs to show behavior		(a) Some generic and not factual description (b) Climb, hunt, live
Clause Complexes to pack information Meaning, conjunction, order	√	Difficulty combining and separating information in sentences. Excessive use of *also*. Some problems with connecting words.
Cohesive Paragraphs (topic sentences; Theme/New Information)	√	Generic topic sentences, themes not related to new information introduced, mixes topics in each paragraph.

THEME/NEW INFORMATION
(1st paragraph of Timothy's report)

Theme	New Information
Leopards	are real interesting animals because *leopards climb trees to sleep* and *protect their food* from other animals.
Did you	know that one kind of leopards is snow leopards?
These leopards	live in the mountains and grassland of centorial Asia.
Snow leopards	have been listed as endangered since 1972.
Female snow leopards	give birth to two to four cubs at a time.

Tenor: Audience and Voice

There is no intentional use of language given audience and the voice the writer wants to reflect without instruction. Moreover, the technicality of the language and complexity of structures are more related to maturity than to audience. In contrast, well-coached 2nd-grade animal reports were written in an authoritative voice, using declarative sentences in the third person. The structures and language were as expected of that level of maturity, regardless of audience. Students used a lot of simple sentences with relational verbs describing their animal. Similarly, middle school students who were coached through their projects to share with other middle school students as well as adults in a published book wrote in declarative sentences and third person. Their structure and language were appropriate for their audience. In the case of beginners in English, the pieces tended to be short and with structures students could produce at their stage of language development. Timothy's report includes a question at the beginning just because students in the school, before starting to teach using SFL genre pedagogy, were taught to start most writing with a question, without clarifying the impact on their writing. It is not clear who his audience is, but the lack of complexity of the structures makes it appropriate for a younger audience.

Noun Groups

Children in general use very few modifiers, and the level of technicality of the words in noun groups is initially limited. The pre-K texts have illustrations with labels to inform the reader about the participants. For example, Michael's report on turtles started with the image of a turtle labeled with *HEAd*, *claw*, *FEET*, and *sheLL*. Throughout the grades, the description of participants (nouns) is limited. If description is found, it is mostly as adjectives as part of the noun group, as in *sharp teeth* (grade 3), *a snakes tail* (grade 4), or *The most biggest and dangerous cat* (grade 5), or connected by relational verbs, especially *to be* and *to have*. For example, *Venus is the hot planets* (kindergarten), *it's cold* and *freezeing* (grade 2), and *some of them are huge large* (grade 3) demonstrate this element in student writing. The adjective groups after the relational verb are not complex structures like those found in books. They could easily join the noun to make a complex noun group. For example, a 2nd grader's sentence, *Their body is round and soft*, could become the beginning of a sentence (*Their round and soft body . . .*) that tells what octopuses do with their body. Another 2nd grader, when researching the attributes of penguins, located the relevant information, but had difficulty creating noun groups. She wrote, *The belly color is yellow at the top* instead of *The top of the belly is yellow*.

Timothy also uses only adjectives and a few technical terms. Some 5th graders could write relative clauses to further describe the noun: *Their paws have really sharp claws that allow them to climb trees and open all sorts of containers for food*. The use of the embedded clause is a sign of maturity (Christie, 2012).

With coaching, middle school students used a greater variety of modifiers and more complex noun groups. For example, *the most important person*; *books for all ages*; *a well-rounded, artistic experience*; *a program that helps students to write more quickly*. By doing research, they appropriated more technical terms than most of the younger students. For example, *identification number*, *mobile market*, *nutritious*, *access*, *civil rights organization*, and so on.

Other challenges encountered by students with their noun groups included:

- Difficulty with ordinal numbers: *earth is the three pnt* [planet] (kindergarten).
- Omission of the determiner: *a habitats of a penguin is* [the] *tundra* (grade 2).
- Inappropriate use of the: *the sharks have sharp teeth* (grade 3).
- Inclusion of the plural "s" marker when it was not needed: *a habitats of a penguin* (grade 2); *low incomes* (6th grade).
- Omission of the plural "s" marker when it was needed: *snake come* (grade 4).
- Omission of the apostrophe to indicate a possessive: *snakes pray* [prey] (grade 4).
- Formation of the possessive as a prepositional phrase rather than by using the possessive: *a habitats of the penguin* (grade 2).
- Use of prepositional phrase instead of pronominal adjectives: *people with low incomes* (6th grade).
- Formation of the comparative structure: *most biggest* (grade 5).

These challenges could be developmental or second language difficulties because all of these students spoke a language other than English at home. These are challenges typical of second language learners. Some L2 learners have first languages where the adjectives usually follow the noun, and they may tend to apply that structure to English noun groups. L2 students also need to learn the formation and use of comparison adjectives: *better, best; more expensive, most expensive.* Students need to learn when to use and not to use "more."

A peculiar English structure is the possessive modifying a noun (*the desert's vegetation*), a prenominal construction representing a prepositional phrase (*the vegetation of the desert*). Indeed, some languages use a prepositional phrase, and students tend to transfer that to English (*a baby penguin drink milk from its mother*, rather than *his mother's milk*). Another difficulty of the possessive is using the apostrophe after the "s" in the case of plural nouns. Thus, a 3rd grader wrote, *Whales enemies are people*, without the apostrophe. Once they learn the possessive form, however, students may over use it (*is gonna be yours falut* [fault]).

Generalized Participants

Although meaning to express a generalized participant, students often alternated between appropriately using the plural form and the singular form. For example, a 5th grader wrote his first draft about tigers with the title in plural, while references to tigers in the first paragraph were singular, and all references in remaining paragraphs were plural. However, omitting the "s" at the end of a plural noun is a common error for L2 learners, even if the student intends it to be plural (Brisk, 2012). When coached by teachers, students can keep the generalized participants consistent as illustrated in Timothy's writing analysis shown earlier. A 2nd grader writing about octopuses used octopus because he did not know the plural form because he was new to English. In other reports, he used the plural forms. Thus, when teaching about generalized participants, teachers need to supplement with lessons on formation of the plural.

Verb Groups

To use relating verbs to describe and define as well as to use action verbs to show behavior, students need to appropriate the information from research. Timothy does not have many factual descriptions or definitions. He does use a few technical action verbs describing behavior. Young writers use relational verbs mostly to describe. For example, *Octopus have 240 suckers. Their body is round and soft.* To counteract this tendency, in one second grade class, the teacher taught them to start with a definition: *A penguin is a kind of bird.* Young writers also tend to use few action verbs, such as *eat, drink*, and *live*. In upper elementary school and even middle school, relational verbs still predominate, yet the use of action verbs increases, provided they have done research and learned the technical terms.

Clause Complexes

Clause complexes are mostly found in 4th grade through middle school students' writing, both in compound and complex sentences. Of the non-finite constructions, the most frequent is *to + verb* to indicate cause, for example, *The snakes use there powerful muscles to move around freely* (grade 4). The most common of the finite constructions were temporal, causal, and additive; for example, *When predators come the snake waves around in a circle then vomits* (temporal, grade 4); *An animal does not have these things since animals do not make their own food* and *New Jersey nickname is the Garden state because it has so much garden and trees* (causal mostly of reason rather than purpose, grade 4); and *If their prey is bigger they often hunt in groups and they work together to kill the prey* (additive, grade 5). Other relations expressed in children's reports were conditional (*If snake venom gets in your bloodstream you'll die*, grade 4); concessive (*If snake venom gets in your bloodstream you'll die, but if you swallow venom it cures bad health*, grade 4); and adversative (*An animal cell has all of these things, but a plant cell has a cell wall and chloroplast*, grade 4).

Students sometimes had difficulty expressing the relation that they intended. Daniel (grade 4) wrote on his poster about "Snakes," *When snakes slither they make the letter S so they can swim.* The source book included the following sentence: "Snakes' bodies make S shapes as they glide along. This kind of movement also helps snakes swim" (Patent, 2000, p. 6). Therefore, the connection is not one of cause (glide/slither) and effect (swim), as Daniel puts it, but rather that gliding and swimming are both helped by the S-type movement. He also wrote, *Certain Snakes live in water but never leave their habitat.* "And" would be a more appropriate conjunction since he is adding information. Oscar (grade 5) used multiple complex sentences that were difficult to understand or made ambiguous connections. For example, he wrote, *What Jaguars eat is Deer cause the size of their horns*, leaving the reader to wonder what it is about the size of the deer's horns that allows jaguars to eat.

Timothy shows some of the difficulties found in upper elementary students. For example, he includes two concepts in the same sentence without clearly connecting them: *Some live in Africa like these dark colored leopards live in the warm Amazon dark rain forest.* In other cases, he separates concepts which are connected: *They are only a few left in the world because people hunt for their warm skin. Also because there forest is gettin felled little by little.* There are multiple uses of *also* to add new information. The use of the connecting word because in the sentence, *Leopards are real interesting animals because leopards climb trees to sleep . . .*, does not denote a factual reason, expected in a report, but the writer's own feelings.

Given the clause complexes that elementary students attempt to create on their own, writing instruction should be initially limited to those types illustrated in the examples of students' writing. When students encounter the other types while reading texts, teachers should explain the meaning and structure. This instruction should be done with 4th to 8th graders and should include creating clause complexes as well as revising their writing to pack simple sentences and express the correct relationships.

Cohesive Paragraph

In the early grades, children tend to write short reports or picture books with images accompanied by one or two sentences. These sentences can be related to the topic, especially if guided by the teacher, but the information or ideas in the sentences do not necessarily relate to each other. For example, a page from a 2nd-grade report on spiders read, *A spider is a carnivore. Young spiders are often cannibals. Also to catch up prey they jump out of no where.* From 3rd grade up, students start writing longer pieces that include paragraphs for each subtopic. The Theme/New Information analysis of the first paragraph in Timothy's leopard report starts by giving specifics about leopards; however, the first paragraph is not limited to one subtopic. In the first sentence, he introduces that leopards climb trees to sleep and to protect their food. However, the following themes are all related to snow leopards, instead of further developing the new information in the first sentence. Only later does he write about the initial theme. Although the sentences that follow are all related to snow leopards, they read like a list with leopard in the theme position and the new information following. None of the new information is further developed. Christie and Derewianka (2008) found similar characteristics in children's writing collected in Australian schools.

Elementary students may have difficulty writing a topic sentence abstracting the topic of the paragraph and keeping the paragraphs to one main topic. The 2nd graders in one class had topic sentences due to their teacher's coaching. For example, *A spider is a carnivor.* Timothy's topic sentences, when included, are generic. For example, he starts the piece with, *Leopards are real interesting animals*, which does not lead to the content of the paragraph. By middle school, with coaching, they have an easier time with topic sentences. For example, *The programs at the Community Centre are . . .* After listing the programs, the student explains them further.

Lessons to Learn About Stages and Language of Reports

Initial lessons present the stages in a general way and direct students to create their graphic organizers for their report. Later, each stage is presented in more depth by including a description of the stage and the possible challenges for students. Initially, it is best to present good examples of the genre and deconstruct them with the students to allow them to see how authors accomplish the goals of the genre. Graphic organizers can help to visually show the text's various stages. It is always important to point out both the genre's standard features and how authors vary within the standard structure.

After this general introduction, lessons first present how to develop the subtopics then offer suggestions for how to write the opening and closing statements (if included) and title. Students often have an easier time with the text's body than with the opening statement. This type of statement requires abstraction, making it rather difficult for children to construct. In the case of posters or brochures, opening and closing statements are not necessary. With pre-K students, teachers jointly construct the text without going into too many explanations of the stages of a report. Audience and voice will be addressed in connection to each of the stages.

> "The science teacher, who taught about live turtles, helped the four-year-olds write a four-page book about turtles. He taught the content at the same time that he modeled each page on chart paper, and the students followed the model as they drew and wrote on their own papers. One of the pages included the picture of a turtle with the body parts labeled. To focus on the food eaten by turtles, he gave them a page with four numbered squares and the question, 'What do Diamondback Terrapin Turtles eat?' The students drew and labeled a type of food in each of the squares. Two more pages included turtles' nests and turtles' habitats with labels such as *baby turtles, beach,* and *moon* to indicate they hatch in the evening" (Brisk et al., 2011, p. 4).

Lesson 3. Deconstruction of Text to Learn About Stages

Goal: To familiarize students with the stages of the genre.

Materials: Reports of the type chosen for the unit (preferably short, even from a lower reading level from the grade). Large graphic organizer on chart paper. Copies of the small version of the graphic organizer for the students (see graphic organizers for different types of reports downloadable from the *Support Material* tab in the book's webpage).

Note about topic of mentor texts: Mentor texts can be

(a) Of the same topic as the unit, the advantage being that the subcategories will be similar to the report the students will be writing;

(b) Of a different topic: the advantage is to show students that one can write reports in a variety of topics.

Activities

- Read the reports aloud.
- Show a graphic organizer that reflects the stages of the chosen type of reports. As you read the different reports, point to the place in the graphic organizer in which that section of the report belongs.
- Divide students into small groups and distribute reports among them, giving each a graphic organizer.
- Ask students to fill in the graphic organizer with the stages of the report that they have.

Cheryl, a 4th-grade teacher "provided mentor texts that were written as reports but at a lower level than the fourth-grade books they usually read. Cheryl presented a graphic organizer on chart paper with the components of a [descriptive] report including the general statement, subtopics, and an optional concluding statement . . . As she read the book on bats and discussed the components with the students, they filled in the graphic organizer. Cheryl read aloud a number of these books, and for each book the students had a similar graphic organizer to complete, based on the information in the teacher's read-alouds. Some students had difficulty with the graphic organizer because they needed to think not only about the information they would write, but also, to consider the topic to determine the column in which the information would be written. She gave these students a . . . web that provided space for the information to be written without the need to categorize it at the same time. Later, they grouped the information into categories" (Brisk et al., 2011, pp. 4–5).

Lesson 4. Teach to Write in the Third Person

Goal: To teach students to use the third person because the author and the audience stay hidden while the topic of the report stands out.

Materials: Mentor texts. Videos or short passages about a topic to stimulate quick writing (for example, if the unit is on comparative reports, have short videos on desert plants and rainforest plants). Projector.

Activities

- Report samples written only in the third person. Ask students what the reports are about. Circle the topic and the subjects of the clauses in a short chunk of the text. Tell the students the author is writing in third person because s/he wants the reader to pay attention to the topic in order to learn about it.
- Tell the students that you are going to show a video on rainforest plants and another on desert plants.
- Divide the class in groups of four, and give each pair a large sheet of paper or have them work together using a computer. Tell them that after watching the videos, one pair in the group will write a short description of rainforest plants and the other pair on desert plants.

- When they are finished, choose the writing of one pair that used third person and project their piece and read it aloud. Point out how their piece focuses on rainforest plants and information on them, circling the subject of sentences.
- If there is a pair that used first and/or second person, ask them to share their writing. Discuss the presence of the author or audience.
- Have the class suggest revisions.

> "One aspect of language that required repeated discussion was the students' tendency to insert themselves into their writing. They often started sentences with I *think*, I *believe*, or I *learned*. Cheryl pointed out that the report was not about the author but about the topic they were researching. Often, she had students read through the mentor texts to see if they could find such clauses" (Brisk et al., 2011, p. 5).

Follow Up

- Raise the question of choice of person when jointly constructing pieces.
- Remind students when drafting their pieces.
- Address, if needed, during joint revision.

Lesson 5. Plan a Report

Any time during this lesson, when working with grades 4–8, take a break to decide on the medium for the report (see Lesson 7).

> **Goal:** To teach students to plan the stages of their report with focus on the subcategories. Students will learn to:
>
> - Choose topic of the report
> - Choose subcategories
> - Order subcategories
> - Research and take notes
>
> **Materials:** Chart paper with graphic organizer (downloadable from the *Support Material* tab in the book's webpage), and graphic organizers for students. Mentor texts written as the type of report of the unit. Research resources in the topic of the reports.

Activities

- Choosing class and individual/group reports topics

  - Discuss the class report topic that the students will jointly construct, and then have students choose their own group or individual reports topics. To facilitate access to available research resources, limit the choice of topics. For example, students in a 4th-grade class chose their own state for the class report. For their individual/group projects, they were given the choice of states in the region where they lived. An exception was made for students who had moved from a different region. They could choose to write about the state where they were born.

- Choosing and ordering subcategories

There are three ways to go about choosing subtopics for reports: (1) teacher defines the subtopics, (2) students brainstorm subtopics, and (3) teacher and students read through reports on the type of subject and agree on the topics that tend to be covered in that subject. In all styles, try to use the technical language that defines the category.

1. Teachers define the subtopics (pre-K–Grade 3). It can be done in two ways:

    a. On chart paper, draw a graphic organizer with four squares labeled with the subtopics. For example, a 1st-grade graphic organizer for an animal report had *body*, *habitat*, *food*, and *predators*.

    b. On chart paper, write 3 to 5 questions (depending on the grade level) that represent the topics in an order that makes sense. For example, 2nd- and 3rd-grade teachers, working on descriptive animal reports, gave questions such as *What do they look like? Where do they live? What is their diet? Who are their enemies?*

2. Students brainstorm subtopics (Pre-K–Grade 5). To use this approach, students first must be familiar with the topic.

    - Ask students what subtopics would be of interest to explore with respect to the topic of their report.
    - Create a web and note student suggestions.
    - Group any subtopics that belong together.
    - Ask for further suggestions for each subtopic, and expand the web. With upper elementary students, transfer this information to the report graphic organizer (downloadable from the *Support Material* tab in the book's webpage).

3. Students use mentor texts to define subtopics (Grades 4–5).

    - Prepare a large version of the report graphic organizer.
    - Ask students to scan various readings about the topic on which they will write. For example, if students are going to write a report on states, students can work in pairs or groups to go through books on different states.
    - As a whole class, discuss the suggested subtopics, write them down in a web, group related information, and number the subtopics in the order in which they will be written. Different books may have a different order, but there usually is information consistently found early in the texts.
    - Write the subtopics into the report organizer in the order that was agreed on.
    - Review the whole-class graphic organizer for logic and organization.
    - Have students write the subcategories in their own graphic organizer for their individual/group reports.
    - Confer with students for logic and organization of their own report graphic organizers.
    - Researching subcategories and taking notes in the graphic organizer.
      Expose students to the content of the topic's subcategories through field trips, videos, books, Internet, and other resources to find information and take notes in their graphic organizers or in their notebooks, organized with the categories in the graphic organizer. These activities are done as a whole class and/or individually or in groups, depending on the grade level. For example, Mary researched together with her 4-year old pre-school students through field trips, videos, read alouds, and giving students iPads to look at images with information. She brainstormed with them and took notes on chart paper. They used these notes to create a class report. Occasionally,

some students chose to produce their individual reports with drawings and short captions.

Other teachers encouraged group research, where group members shared the resources, collaborating to add information to a common graphic organizer. Then individual members of the group took charge of writing one of the paragraphs based on the collective notes. The group then revised the draft together. Pat and Beverly, upper elementary teachers, had long discussions about how best to teach students to do research and decided to start by doing it together with the students to help them navigate the research resources, decide and organize the subcategories, learn the technical language, take notes, and finally draft their reports.

Beverly and Pat, working with their 5th-grade classes, started the research process for their descriptive reports on presidential candidates as a whole class and then had the students work on their own reports. Some of the strategies they used were:

- Looking at the resources and listing the subtopics with the more important ones on top.
- Isolating a paragraph, reading it, underlining technical terms, discussing the meaning to find more familiar ways to express the idea, and then deciding whether they could use the alternate term or if they needed to learn the term used in the paragraph. Students practiced in groups with additional paragraphs.
- Choosing one subtopic and creating together with the class a graphic organizer with notes and a side column with technical noun groups, which they discussed to ensure understanding.
- Students were encouraged to plan their own reports using the same process with the subtopics they had chosen (Brisk et al., 2018).

Lesson 6. Teach Students to Use Appropriate Academic Language—Noun Groups

Most of the information in reports is included in noun groups. For example, this 25-word noun group from one of the mentor texts analyzed earlier in the chapter summarizes the work of the U.S. Congress: *members of Congress who must work together toward the same goal: to create, discuss, debate and vote on bills, some of which eventually become laws.* When teaching students to use appropriate academic language, focus on the entire noun group. It is not only the technical noun but all the descriptors that contain this information and, in turn, include more technical language.

> **Goal:** To have students become familiar with the language of the topic they are studying, particularly noun groups, in order to use it with understanding and construct informative noun groups in their own writing.
> **Materials:** Texts that have been used to introduce the topic (or the genre, if in the topic of the unit). For example, the text presented earlier, *The Senate and the House of Representatives*, when studying about the branches of government. Chart paper. Copies of texts to be used for the students.

- Project a paragraph of the chosen text, with the noun groups in bold or highlighted. Discuss it with respect to (a) the meaning of the language used and (b) the structure of the noun groups. For example, using the following paragraph with noun groups in bold:

Both senators and representatives are **members of Congress who must work together toward the same goal: to create, discuss, debate and vote on bills, some of which eventually become laws**. In **the U.S. Capitol Building in Washington D.C.**, senators and representatives often meet with **each other and in smaller groups** to discuss **laws**.

(a) Focus on meaning and information

- Read it aloud with students following.
- Discuss the ideas expressed by the noun groups, and clarify any meaning that is unclear to students, or have them look words up. For example, What are senators and representatives? What is their job? What is the U.S. Capitol Building? Where is it located? (Note: *in Washington D.C.* indicates place, but it is part of the noun group and not an adverbial because it gives more information about the Capitol Building. *In the U.S. Capitol Building, in Washington D.C.* is the adverbial that indicates where they meet.)

(b) The structure of noun groups

- After showing how much meaning these noun groups carry, then show the function and forms of the noun groups. For example, in the earlier paragraph there are (for more types of modifiers, see Table 6.6):

- Noun groups as the subject: *Both senators and representative*
- Noun groups following the verb *to be*, describing or defining the noun preceding it: *members of Congress who . . . .*
- Noun groups as part of an adverbial prepositional phrase: *in the U.S. Capitol Building in Washington D.C.*
- Noun groups including just noun(s): *laws; senators and representatives*
- Others including complex structures: noun + prepositional phrase + embedded clause with conjugated verb: *members of Congress [who must work together toward the same goal: to create, discuss, debate and vote on bills, some of which eventually become laws]*.

- Have students propose which information from what they learned in this paragraph to add to the notes, either for the class project, individual projects, or both. If they resort to the use of everyday language, discuss which technical language they just learned would be more effective, and make changes accordingly.
- Give groups of students other sections of the research resources on the topic to identify the noun groups, discuss the information they get, and clarify the meaning of words they may not know. Add the information to their notes, using technical language if they understand it and including the whole noun group.
- With younger students, use images to support this activity. For example, write the noun group *snakes with striped bodies* and ask them to draw it where they take notes and copy the phrase. Alternatively, show them an image of a striped snake and ask them what it is; then have them write it down in their notes. Repeat with additional noun groups. For example, a kindergarten teacher had prepared booklets for the students with the subtopic titles typed on each page. The students drew and labeled their drawings in post-it notes and attached them to the corresponding page, using them afterwards for illustrating and writing their subtopic on the same page.

As students perused texts for structure and content, Cheryl reminded them to think about language, which needs to be descriptive to educate their audience on the subject. She used the mentor texts and the descriptive language in them as examples. On an overhead projector, she compared parts of the mentor texts with and without the author's descriptive language, and the students were asked which piece was more informative and why. The students all came to the same answer: The descriptive knowledge helped to serve the author's purpose, which is to inform the reader. Cheryl also discussed with them the role of the illustrations to complement the written text and reflect important information (Brisk et al., 2011, p. 5).

Lesson 7. Teach How to Organize the Text Given the Medium (Grades 4–8)

For younger grades, teachers guide the students through the production, given the medium. For example, a 2nd-grade teacher gave students a template of the informational books that included a title page, table of contents, set of pages with room for writing and illustrating for each subcategory, and pages for a glossary, bibliographic information, and about the author. A 3rd-grade teacher gave students folded pages in thirds to imitate a brochure. Another teacher, writing reports on countries in the form of posters, chose her own country and showed the students how she organized her poster. Students drew ideas from it but also made their own decisions. For upper grades, this lesson can be done as a break, anytime during the planning process (Lesson 5).

> **Goal:** To teach students how to organize the text in the medium chosen for their reports.
> **Materials:** Samples of reports or other genres in the particular medium.

Activities

- Review a number of examples of reports in different media and have students identify features. For example, Cheryl walked around the school with her students looking at all of the posters and discussing their features in preparation to produce reports as posters.
- With your students, plan how you will organize the report that you will write together.
- Working in groups, have students draw the layout of their own report.

Lesson 8. Writing the Subcategories

The specific subcategories differ depending on the type of report. Use the process described in this lesson, adjusting for each report type. The biggest challenge for students is understanding the type of classification. Thus, the choices depend on grade level.

Descriptive (K–8)	*Subtopics Describing the Entity*
Comparative Report (4–8)	Compared and contrasted features of the entities being compared Feature 1 Feature 2 Etc.

Descriptive (K–8)	Subtopics Describing the Entity
Historical Reports (5–8)	Descriptive subtopics of the time or place reported
Classifying (6–8)	Description of each type based on criteria for classifying the entities. Some entities may be further subcategorized Description of subtypes for one or more of the categories., i.e., Type A Type B Type B.1 Type B.2, etc.
Whole-to-Part (6–8) Early grades labeled diagram	Description of each component of the entity and their function (a component may have additional subcomponents)

This lesson includes a number of activities necessary to create good paragraphs. It should take a minimum of a week or more depending on the daily time allotted to writing.

Goal: To apprentice students to write the subcategories. To create paragraphs for these subcategories, which requires:

- Write topic sentence
- Transfer notes in graphic organizer to a text
- Create a cohesive paragraph (Theme/New Information) (see Chapter 8 "Creating a Cohesive Text," and Lesson 24).

Materials: Paragraphs from mentor texts. Class and individual graphic organizers. Chart paper or projector.

Activities

For each of the subtopics, follow the same process.

- Project and read aloud one paragraph from the mentor text. For example,

Minerals are made of only one substance. They have properties that allow us to identify them. These properties include hardness, color, density, and cleavage. Because rocks are often made of several minerals, it is difficult to use these properties to describe or identify a rock.

Ask students what this paragraph is about (properties of minerals as identifiers).

Is there a sentence that expresses that concept? (They have properties that allow us to identify them.) Tell the students that this is the topic sentence and usually comes at the beginning of the paragraph or soon after. It prepares the reader for what they are going to read.

Choose the subtopic from the graphic organizer, and ask students to describe what it is about.

- Create a topic sentence for the paragraph on the basis of student responses.
- Ask students what information they have written in their graphic organizer about this subtopic. Write sentences that reflect their responses on chart paper or by using the projector. Reinforce the notion of writing in the third person. Negotiate the construction of the sentences with the students so that they are well formed and carry the meaning intended. With 3rd through 5th grades, start modeling clause complexes (see Lesson 13). For example, if students propose to write the following on the basis of their notes in the graphic organizer:

Snakes can't hear well or *Snakes feel vibrations through the ground*, suggest that these sentences could be combined because they are related in meaning and changed to *Snakes cannot hear well, but they feel vibrations through the ground*. Let the students try first to combine the sentences. If they struggle, provide assistance.

- Re-read and make any revisions.
- Have students work in groups or pairs to work on their group or individual pieces.
- Repeat with the next subtopics. All can be addressed, or, after modeling a couple, students can draft the remainder of the subtopics on their own.

After planning the report as described in Lesson 5, Pat and Beverly:

- Used the notes and the language in the graphic organizer to jointly construct each paragraph. After reading together, the teachers underlined everyday terms students had suggested for substitution with the technical language they were learning.
- Students were encouraged to do the same process with the subtopics they had planned for their own reports.

(Brisk et al., 2018)

Lesson 9. Expanding Noun Groups by Using Pre-Nominal Modifiers (Grades K–8) and Post-Nominal Modifiers (Grades 4–8)

If only one aspect of language is going to be included in the report unit, this one *must* be the lesson because most of the information in reports is found in noun groups that include modifiers. As the grades advance, the noun groups' complexity increases, both in the texts students encounter and what they produce. Mentor texts usually use noun groups that are more complex than students are ready to produce. Therefore, texts of a lower grade level can be used to learn and practice noun groups. Modifiers to describe nouns, as we saw earlier, can occur before (pre-nominal) and after (post-nominal) the noun. Through 3rd grade it is enough to teach students to use pre-nominal adjectives to describe and give specific information about the entity that is the focus of the report. From 4th grade on, post-nominal modifiers should be added, not only to give information but also to pack language and make it look more like written language. The goals, materials, and activities of Lessons 9 and 10 need to be adjusted to the grade level. Depending on what the uncoached writing shows, middle school teachers may skip Lesson 9 or may do it with a group of students who need practice.

> **Goal:** To teach students to identify and understand the function of pre-nominal and post-nominal modifiers and be able to use them.
> **Materials:** Mentor texts and research resources appropriate for the grade level. Set of questions to elicit adjectives. Chart paper or projector.

Questions (example in parentheses)

> Noun: *bones*
> Which ones?/Whose? (*Those* bones/*Her* bones)

How many? (*Those three* bones)
What like? (qualities: facts) (*Those three white* bones)
What kind? (*Those three white lamb* bones)

Note: Adjectives in reports are factual. Young students often write opinion adjectives. For example, in a report on wolves a student wrote: *Wolves are* **enormous** *and* **gigantic**, rather than indicating how tall and heavy they are.

Activities

Depending on the age group, do one or more of these activities as initial or follow up activities. Use entities that students will write about and types of modifiers that need practice. In the following examples, animals, which are a typical topic of reports in the early grades, are used to teach language, with the focus on pre-nominal adjectives. Comparable lessons can be done with other topics and other types of modifiers. For example, the Senate and the House of Representatives for a comparative report to teach post-nominal modifiers (*The legislative branch,* **called Congress**, *is responsible for making laws. The nation holds an election* **for members of Congress**).

Activity 1

- Project a drawing that needs coloring with a sentence underneath where the adjectives for colors are missing, and give the students paper with the same information. For example, a coyote with the sentence from the mentor text *Coyote*: Coyotes have _____fur on their backs and _____ bellies.
- Read aloud the sentence and ask the students: What color should I paint the fur on the back? What about the belly? Discuss with the students what is missing in the sentence, and talk about adjectives, words that describe the things, animals, or people we are talking/writing about.
- Read aloud the sentence with the adjectives, and ask the students what you should add in each blank.
- Have the students add the adjectives and color their drawings accordingly.
- Give groups of students an image of an animal of those that someone in the class will write a report about and a comparable sentence for them to fill out the blanks using the image as a reference. For example, Eagles have _____ feathers on their backs and wings and _____ ones on their bellies.

Activity 2

Project and read aloud the mentor text *Coyotes*. Have students help you identify adjectives and start a noun group anchor chart for the different animals the class will write about. Do the same with additional books. For example,

Coyotes	Capybaras	Etc.
Wild dog	Ten capybaras	
Reddish-brown legs and feet	Family groups	
Big, pointed ears	Large heads	
Etc.	Red-brown coats	
	Etc.	

Show videos of the same topics; stop occasionally to ask if they heard additional adjectives or the same they already have.

Have students create lists for their topic in their notebook. If students are writing about the same topic, they can create their lists together looking at different sources.

For Upper Elementary and Middle School

In addition to practicing pre-nominal adjectives, older students need to practice post-nominal ones (see Brisk, 2021, chapter 3, for complex noun groups).

- Read the following examples from mentor texts and/or research resources used. Ask students what they learned about the desert, and explain that these prepositional phrases or embedded clauses that follow the noun give the reader a lot of information.

  - Prepositional phrases: *The Sonoran is the only desert **in North America.***
  - Embedded clause with conjugated verbs: *The Sonoran is the only desert in North America **that does not have cold winters.***
  - Embedded clause with non-conjugated verbs: "*. . . a truly exciting place to explore.*"

- Have them add post-nominal examples to their anchor chart of the topic they are researching.

Lesson 10. Joint and Group/Individual Revision of Paragraphs (Grades 1–8), with the Theme/New Information Tool (Grades 6–8) and the Use of Modifiers (Grades 1–8)

Goal: To learn to revise paragraphs based on what was taught to the particular grade level, including the use of modifiers.
Materials: Samples of student work.

Activities

- Choose one or two students to share their pieces with the whole class. It is best to choose students who can use the extra help.
- Read it aloud or have the author read it aloud in chunks.
- Focus on a couple of specific aspects that were taught during the unit that seem challenging to most students. Have students help each other check on the same feature in their writing.
- Choose another student's writing, focusing on another general challenge, and repeat the process.
- Have students work on their subcategories, while you conference with individuals.

For middle school students, use the Theme/New Information tool to edit a paragraph that has been jointly constructed and one of the students' paragraphs.

- Demonstrate Theme/New Information analysis with the paragraph used earlier.

	Theme	New Information
1	**Minerals**	are made of only one substance.
2	They	have **properties** that allow us to identify them.

	Theme	New Information
3	These **properties**	include hardness, color, density, and cleavage.
4	Because **rocks**	are often made of several **minerals**,
5	it	is difficult to use these **properties** to describe or identify a **rock**.

- Show the analysis with the new information covered, and ask the students what they think the paragraph is about. The words in the theme position give the reader the notion that the author is writing about *minerals*, *properties*, and *rocks*.
- Show the students how the author develops the concepts slowly by introducing them in the theme position and then expanding. The sentences slowly build the connections by introducing and expanding each. Sentence #1 introduces *minerals* in its theme position, which is stated again in the theme of #2 to further expand, stating the core concept of the paragraph. Sentence #2 introduces *properties* in its new information, which is picked up in the theme of #3 to further develop. Sentence #4 introduces *rocks* in the theme position. By placing sentence #4 before #5, the writer switches the attention to *rocks*, appearing in the theme position. Rocks is the important topic in the last sentence. In sentence #5, the new information connects *properties* and *rocks*, both concepts that had been introduced earlier separately.
- Analyze one paragraph in the jointly constructed report and ask:

  - Is there a topic sentence?
  - If we cover the new information, do the themes tell us what the paragraph is about?
  - Are the concepts introduced in the theme position further developed?
  - Are any edits needed?

- Take one paragraph from a student work and analyze it with the Theme/New Information tool. For example, this paragraph on *habitat* in a report on grizzly bears:

1	Grizzly Bears	live in Asia, North America and Europe.
2	They	live not in [?] one place.
3	They	live in open fields.
4	Some	live in mountain lands.
5	Not much	live in dens.
6	Grizzly Bears	live in woods that are deep.
7	There	are many more places.

- Ask the students:

  - What is the paragraph about? (habitat)
  - Is there a topic sentence indicating that?

- Let's create one given the information there. For example: *Asia, North America, and Europe offer suitable habitats for grizzly bears*. The other edit that this sentence achieved is to eliminate one of the verbs *live*, which is repeated in almost every sentence.
- Ask the students if the themes give any indication that the paragraph is about habitat (only grizzly bear is in the theme position, but that is the topic of the whole report).
- Ask the students if they notice any words repeated (*live*).

- To avoid repetition, (a) teach synonyms or words with appropriate meaning. For example, for *live*, students could use *inhabit, roam, hide*; (b) teach that sentences can be combined, and other verbs can be used instead. Have them work in groups or pairs to come up with some ideas. For example,

  - 3 and 6 could be combined and two new verbs used: *Some <u>roam</u> open fields while others <u>hide</u> deep into woods.*
  - 2 and 7 could be combined: *Grizzly bears <u>inhabit</u> many different types of places.*

- Have students, working in pairs, take one of their paragraphs and do a comparable analysis to see if it leads to some revisions. Give them a checklist:

  - Is there a topic sentence?
  - Do the words in the theme position reveal what the paragraph is about?
  - Are there lots of pronouns in the theme position that hide what I'm writing about?
  - Are there words repeated? Can I combine sentences? Can I replace repeated words with some more specific?

Joint and Group/Individual Revision of Paragraphs for Use of Modifiers

After students have drafted their subcategories, do joint and group/pair revision of their work.

- Take one paragraph of one student.
- Identify the main nouns, especially the focus of their report.
- Ask the class if there is any modifier describing or telling us more about the noun.
- Brainstorm what could be added by consulting with their anchor charts or the texts they have used.
- Add suitable ones.
- Have students working in pairs or groups, help each other to add one or two modifiers where needed.

For Upper Elementary and Middle School

In addition to the earlier revision activity, revise to pack language with post-nominal modifiers.

- Identify sentences that could be packed by creating a complex noun group using modifiers.
- Ask the students, could we change these two sentences and make them one? For example, a student wrote, *These leopards live in the mountains and grassland of centorial Asia Snow leopards have been listed as endangered since 1972*, could be written using an embedded clause with a non-conjugated verb: *These leopards, listed as endangered since 1972, live in the mountains . . .*
- Have students working in pairs or groups help each other pack the language in one or two examples that you have underlined in their work.
- Have a couple of students share good examples of packing language.

Lesson 11. Teaching How to Write the Opening General Statement

As shown in Table 6.5, reports start with a general statement introducing the entity or entities (in the case of comparative reports) and place it in context. The voice is authoritative, except some authors choose to use a more familiar voice in this section of the report, especially when writing for children.

> **Goal:** To learn how to write opening statements appropriate for the type of report through deconstruction and joint and individual/group construction.
>
> **Materials:** Introductory section of several mentor texts in the type of report of the unit. If students have learned a separate type of report in earlier units, have mentor text in that type as well to compare. Chart paper, students' notebooks or computers to project and produce text. Class and individual drafts of the subcategories produced earlier.

Activities

- Read aloud or give students reports with different types of beginnings, and ask them to describe them.
- Project or show on chart paper examples of two or three different opening statements from the mentor texts.
- Discuss the type of beginning, the appropriate audience that matches, and why.
- Show the class project so far and ask students: What have we written about?
- Have students think of the intended audience and the type of opening statement that they want for their class report.
- Jointly construct an opening statement with the class, reminding them of the features of those in the mentor texts.
- Have students think of a different audience and propose a different opening statement.
- Working in pairs or groups, have students discuss what their reports are about. Call on a student to share.
- With the whole class, help the student construct on chart paper or the computer (projecting).
- Remind students of the audience that they had decided on for their reports.
- Have the rest of the students write their opening statement on the basis of the models discussed, given topic and audience.
- Have students read the opening statement of their report aloud to their group or to each other if working in pairs.
- Have students discuss whether it is an appropriate opening statement given the type of report and their audience.
- Walk around listening to student discussions.
- Have one or two groups or students share their decision with the class. Choose individuals or groups that you heard giving appropriate responses to model for the other students.
- Have one or two students that you think need revision present. Have the class react and suggest revisions.

Lesson 12. Participants (Generalized vs. Specific; Beings vs. Institutions)

> **Goal:** To teach students the difference between writing about a category and an individual. For middle school: teach that participants are sometimes institutions, rather than people. For example, Congress vs. legislators (see Chapter 4, Lesson 10.5).
>
> **Materials:** T-chart. Chart paper or projector. Students' draft reports. List of review questions on chart paper: *Have they written about a generalized or a specific participant? If generalized, is the noun in the plural form (unless it is a collective noun like water)? Is the information appropriate for that type of participant?*

Activities

- Draw a T-chart with a whole category on one side, for example, *volcanoes*, and an individual participant, for example, *Vesuvius*, on the other.
- Discuss when you would write one type versus the other.
- Point out that the generalized participant is written in the plural form.
- Brainstorm the kind of information that you would include in one type or the other. For the generalized participant, the information will be in categories, for example, *components of a volcano*. For individuals, the information will be specific, for example, *height*.
- Project one student sample. Point at each of the questions on the list, and solicit comments from the class.
- Working in groups or pairs, have students review what they have written, assisted by the list of questions.

Note: Some students will need lessons on the formation of the plural in English. In that case, start an anchor chart and have students keep it also in their notebooks, and add examples as they emerge in mentor texts or in use. For example,

Regular		Irregular	
+ "s"	Spelling Change	Form Change	No Change
Horses	Parties (party—consonant before "y")	Feet (foot)	People
Plays	Classes (class—words that end in s, x, ch, sh, or o add -es)	Mice (mouse)	Water
		Lives (life)	

Lesson 13. Use of Clause Complexes to Make Meaning (Grades 4–8)

Usually beginning in 4th grade, students want to express more complex ideas where clauses are combined with a connecting word expressing the relationships. The following are a series of lessons to learn and practice clause complexes. Choose given the needs and level of linguistic maturity of your students (see Brisk, 2021, chapter 3).

Lesson 13.1. Clause Complex Puzzles

Goal: To learn how different conjunctions signal different relations.
Materials: Sentence strips with clause complexes from a report cut up to separate each clause and the conjunction. Envelopes with sentence strips inside similarly cut up and taken from the report texts that you are using for the given subject area. The sentences can all be the same or be different. Chart paper or projector.

Activities

- Project the conjunctions or put them up on the board or chart paper.
- Working with the whole class, read aloud or have students read aloud the sentence strips. For example:

The shell of a baby tortoise does not completely harden + until + it turns 5 years old.
Their life span is about 35 to 40 years, + but + some can get to be 100 years old.
Turtles spend more time in the water, + so + their feet are better for swimming.

- Pick one sentence strip, and ask the students to pick a conjunction and another sentence that, when put together with a conjunction, makes sense.
- Have students read aloud the new sentences to test that they make sense. Have students explain the meaning in the new sentences.
- Repeat with other sentence strips and conjunctions.
- Ask if students can make different combinations of sentences (and related meaning).
- Give each group of students one of the envelopes and have students carry out the same activity with the small sentence strips. Have students share their sentences and explain what each means. (This activity helps students appropriate the language of books. By manipulating sentences from books, children can internalize the structures of written language.)

Lesson 13.2. Deconstruct Clause Complexes

Goal: To learn how to express ideas through clause complexes from authors.

Materials: Page of a report with examples of clause complexes. Chart paper or projector. Copies of a page or two of a report that has examples of clause complexes. For both examples, choose sections of the text(s) that have essential content needed to understand the topic being studied.

Activities

- Project the chosen text and have students identify the verbs. Ask students if the clauses are simple or if they are combined to express a relation. For example, the sentence "**When** *threatened*, it *lifts* **and** *flattens* its neck, **and** *hisses*" has four verbs (the first one is non-finite), and the clauses are all connected.
- Ask students what connects the verbs and clauses and what the conjunctions tell you about the relation signaled. In the example, the first is temporal (telling when the snake shows these behaviors) and the other two are additive (*lifts* and *flattens* are connected with each other in relation to *neck*, and *hisses* is connected to both previous behaviors). You can also show how the commas help to group the meanings.
- Repeat this analysis with other clause combinations. Discuss their meanings and content.
- Give the student groups the copies of the text. Have them do the same activity and go around working with individual groups as they work. Make sure that students pay attention to both form and meaning.

Lesson 13.3. Revising Clause Complexes

Goal: To teach students to revise their work to include clause complexes that reflect their intended meaning.

Materials: Selected pieces of student work. Projector. Students' drafts with one or two sentences underlined that could be combined or that have an unclear relation.

Activities

- Project one of the students' pieces. Have the student author read it aloud. Depending on what the writing needs, ask the author for the meaning in the sentences or how they could be combined.
- Ask the author and the class to suggest revisions, and write the suggestions on the board or smartboard. Then, discuss which suggestion seems to best express the author's meaning.
- Repeat with one or two more examples.
- Have students work in groups and do the same activity with the underlined sentences in their drafts. Have students first propose revisions, then discuss with the group and make a final choice. Students may not end up with the best choice alone, so it is important for you to walk around and help out, as needed.

Lesson 14. Teach to Write Concluding Paragraph (Optional)

In general, reports conclude with a subcategory that belongs at the end and rarely has a summarizing statement. Therefore, if teaching this lesson, show students the optional nature of this stage.

> **Goal:** To have students learn how to write concluding paragraphs given the type of report.
> **Materials:** Mentor texts with concluding paragraphs that just include a final subcategory and others include a summarizing comment. Projector. Class and individual report drafts.

Activities

- Read the mentor texts aloud while projecting them for the students to see.
- Discuss with students what the authors do in these final paragraphs, and compare the different endings.
- Discuss the intended audience and the grammatical structures, such as person or type of sentence, that signal the intended audience. Were these written for different audiences? Which type would be appropriate for older readers? For younger readers? Why?
- Have students decide what kind of final paragraph they want to write given the audience. For example, ending with a summarizing comment or one last subtopic. For the latter option, have them decide which would be most appropriate.
- Jointly construct a closing statement with the class.
- Read and revise if needed.
- Have students work in groups or pairs.
- Have students read their reports aloud.
- Have students discuss whether the current ending is an appropriate ending for their report given the audience, or if they want to add a different ending. If students want to change their ending, have them explain why.
- Walk around and listen to student discussions.
- Have one or two groups or students share their decision with the class. Choose individuals or groups who have appropriate endings to model for the other students.
- Have one or two students that you think need revision present. Have the class react and suggest revisions.

Lesson 15. Production of the Published Reports

The final steps in the production of the final report follow the same process as with other genres. Check the suggestions in the other chapters using mentor texts to identify the specific features of a report. For example, images in reports are conceptual rather than narrative. Conceptual images represent "participants in terms of their more generalized and more or less stable and timeless essence, in terms of class, or structure, or meaning" (Kress & van Leeuwen, 1996, p. 79). These are typical of reports and explanations. They convey concepts in the form of diagrams and other abstract designs, as well as factual images such as photographs or technical drawings. Students need to be taught the distinction between this type of images and those from fictional narratives. For example, a 4th grader illustrated her report on snakes with narrative images, such as the parent snakes kissing each other. Mary, a pre-school teacher, told her students that when drawing a diagram on the life cycle of a chicken, they could not color their chicks pink. She stressed that they were not producing a story, but rather a cycle explanation of what really happens.

The steps to finalize a report include:

- Joint and individual revision of the final draft (see Chapter 4, Lesson 20)
- Choosing the title (see Chapter 3, Lesson 31)
- Inserting factual images (see Chapter 4, Lesson 18)
- Dissemination

Once all the students were satisfied with their final products, they had a publishing party that was open to the school. Cheryl gave her students a set of questions for the authors to ask as they viewed the posters. These questions were all related to process. The students were told that they must provide feedback that was relative to the elements of a report. For example, they could not respond with, "This is very good. I liked it." Their feedback responses had to show their knowledge of the genre as well. For example, one student said, "Your use of the words *predator, habitat, prey* show that you have done your research on the snake." Another said, "Your word choice 'The slithery, sneaky, venomous cobra' captured my attention and showed me that you were thinking of word choice for effect" (Brisk et al., 2011, p. 5).

Professional Articles that Describe Instruction of the Genre

Brisk, M. E., Alvarado, J., Timothy, B., & Scialoia, P. (2018). Breaking the linguistic ceiling: Bilingual students appropriate academic English. In J. Sharkey (Ed.), *Transforming practices for the elementary classroom* (pp. 85–98). Alexandria, VA: TESOL International Organization.

Brisk, M. E., Hodgson-Drysdale, T., & O'Connor, C. (2011). A study of a collaborative instructional project informed by systemic functional linguistic theory: Report writing in elementary grades. *Journal of Education, 191*, 1–12.

Gort, M., & Hamm-Rodríguez, M. (2022). Centering language and communicative purpose in writing instruction for Bi/Multilingual learners. *The Reading Teacher, 75*(6), 693–706. http://doi.org/10.1002/trtr.2098

Snow Balderas, M. B., Hamm-Rodríguez, M., Santiago Schwarz, V., & Gort, M. (2022). Resisting high-stakes educational reform through genre writing in a multilingual classroom. *Language Arts, 99*(3), 179–191.

References

Brisk, M. E. (2012). Young bilingual writers' control of grammatical person in different genres. *Elementary Education Journal, 112*, 445–468.

Brisk, M. E. (2021). *Language in writing instruction: Enhancing literacy in grades 3–8.* New York: Routledge.

Brisk, M. E., Alvarado, J., Timothy, B., & Scialoia, P. (2018). Breaking the linguistic ceiling: Bilingual students appropriate academic English. In J. Sharkey (Ed.), *Transforming practices for the elementary classroom* (pp. 85–98). Alexandria, VA: TESOL International Organization.

Brisk, M. E., & DeRosa, M. (2014). Young writers' attempts at making meaning through complex sentence structures while writing a variety of genres. In L. de Oliveira & J. Iddings (Eds.), *Genre pedagogy across the curriculum: Theory and application in U.S. classrooms and contexts* (pp. 8–24). London: Equinox.

Brisk, M. E., & Harrington, M. M. (2007). *Literacy and bilingualism: A handbook for all teachers* (2nd ed.). Mahwah, NJ: Lawrence Erlbaum Associates.

Brisk, M. E., Hodgson-Drysdale, T., O'Connor, C. (2011). A study of a collaborative instructional project informed by systemic functional linguistic theory: Report writing in elementary grades. *Journal of Education, 191*, 1–12.

Brisk, M. E., Horan, D., & MacDonald, E. (2008). Scaffolding teaching and learning to write: The rhetorical approach. In L. S. Verplaetse & N. Migliacci (Eds.), *Inclusive pedagogy: Research informed practices for linguistically diverse students.* Mahwah, NJ: Lawrence Erlbaum Associates.

Butt, D., Fahey, R., Feez, S., & Spinks, S. (2012). *Using functional grammar: An explorer's guide* (3rd ed.). South Yarra, Victoria, Australia: Palgrave Macmillan.

Christie, F. (2012). *Language education throughout the school years: A functional perspective.* Chichester, West Sussex: Wiley-Blackwell.

Christie, F., & Derewianka, B. (2008). *School discourse: Learning to write across the years of schooling.* London: Continuum.

De La Paz, S., & Graham, S. (2002). Explicitly teaching strategies, skills, and knowledge: Writing instruction in middle school classrooms. *Journal of Educational Psychology, 94*, 29–304.

Derewianka, B. (2011). *A new grammar companion for teachers.* Marickville, NSW, Australia: Primary English Teaching Association.

Derewianka, B., & Jones, P. (2016). *Teaching language in context* (2nd ed.). Melbourne: Oxford University Press.

Eggins, S. (2004). *An introduction to systemic functional linguistics* (2nd ed.). London: Continuum.

Fang, Z., & Schleppegrell, M. J. (2008). *Reading in secondary content areas: A language based pedagogy.* Ann Arbor, MI: University of Michigan Press.

Fang, Z., Schleppegrell, M. J., & Cox, B. E. (2006). Understanding the language demands of schooling: Nouns in academic registers. *Journal of Literacy Research, 38*(3), 247–273. http://doi.org/10.1207/s15548430jlr3803_1

Halliday, M. A. K., & Matthiessen, C. M. I. M. (2004). *An introduction to functional grammar* (3rd ed.). London: Hodder Arnold.

Hodgson-Drysdale, T., & Rosa, H. (2015, February). Go with the flow: Fifth grade students write about the flow of energy and matter through an ecosystem. *Science and Children*, 32–37.

Humphrey, S., & Vale, E. (2020). *Investigating model texts for learning.* Sydney: PETAA.

Kamberelis, G. (1999). Genre development and learning: Children writing stories, science reports, and poems. *Research in the Teaching of English, 33*, 403–463.

Kress, G., & van Leeuwen, T. (1996). *Reading images—the grammar of visual design.* London: Routledge.

Langer, J. A. (1986). Reading, writing, and genre development: Making connections. In M. A. Doyle & J. Irwin (Eds.), *Reading and writing connections* (pp. 32–54). Newark, DE: International Reading Association.

Martin, J. R., & Rose, D. (2008). *Genre relations: Mapping culture.* London: Equinox.

Newkirk, T. (1987). The non-narrative writing of young children. *Research in the Teaching of English, 21*, 121–144.

Patent, D. H. (2000). *Slinky scaly slithery snakes.* New York, NY: Walker & Co.

Perry, N., & Drummond, L. (2002). Helping young students become self-regulated researchers and writers. *Reading Teacher, 56,* 298–310.

Rose, D., & Martin, J. R. (2012). *Learning to write, reading to learn: Genre, knowledge and pedagogy in the Sydney School.* Sheffield: Equinox.

Schleppegrell, M. (2004). *The language of schooling: A functional perspective.* Mahwah, NJ: Lawrence Erlbaum Associates.

Stead, T. (2002). *Is that a fact?: Teaching nonfiction writing K-3.* Portland, ME: Stenhouse.

Thompson, G. (2004). *Introducing functional grammar* (2nd ed.). London: Arnold.

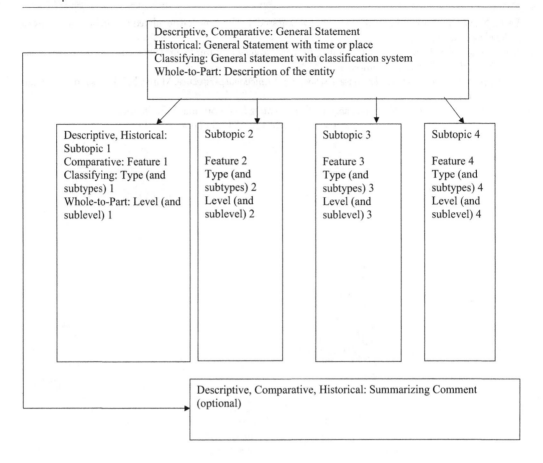

Chapter 7

Explanations

Explanations share a number of features with reports. The major difference is that, while reports have chunks of information that stand on their own and the author chooses which ones to include, explanations have chunks of information that are connected with each other and cannot be omitted. Ignoring any part of an explanation will make it inaccurate. For example, in the sequential explanation on how recycled paper is made (included in this chapter), skipping a step will make the explanation incomplete. Further, in the systems explanation about the branches of government (another example included in this chapter), all three branches and their relationships need to be included. The writer cannot decide to skip one because the explanation would then be truncated. On the other hand, when writing animal reports, teachers typically encourage students to describe the animal and write about diet, habitat, and predators. There are many other things that one could write about animals, but a report can stand alone with just those few.

Explanations seek to explain *how* or *why* things come to be the way they are or to analyze *how* things work. There are a variety of types of explanations (see Table 7.1): sequential, causal, cyclical, systems, factorial, consequential, and conditional (Christie & Derewianka, 2008; Coffin, 2006; Derewianka & Jones, 2016; Martin & Rose, 2008; Veel, 2000). Explanations are found mostly in science and history texts. Table 7.1 shows at which grade level to introduce each type. Once introduced, they are used at all levels depending on the topic.

Explanations are found in some texts within a report. For example, a report on volcanoes included a short causal explanation of how a volcano erupts. They can also be the concluding section of a lab report. This was the case in a lab report on whether objects sink or float in water, which concluded with a conditional explanation stating which conditions allow an object to float and which to sink (Humphrey & Vale, 2020).

Sometimes, explanations can be confused with recounts or procedures. In cases where children are asked to "explain" how they solved a math problem, they are actually being asked to write a procedural recount because they are describing what they did one time when solving a math problem. In these situations, it would be better to ask them to "tell" how they did it. Similarly, if they are giving instructions on how to solve the problem, then they are writing a procedure. Even adults confuse these three genres—when a teacher requested examples of books that included procedures, a librarian included the book *How Are Sneakers Made?*, which is not a book of instructions describing how to make sneakers, but an explanation of how they are made in a factory.

There are two approaches to teaching explanations: (1) oral explanations with labeled diagrams and (2) written explanations in which students learn the stages and language of various types of explanations. Oral explanations for diagrams are good projects for the early grades. For later grades, diagrams accompany written explanations. The remainder of the chapter first offers suggestions for how to teach oral explanations, followed by how to teach students to write explanations of various types.

DOI: 10.4324/9781003329275-7

Table 7.1 Types of Explanations

Type of Explanation	Purpose	Example
Lower Elementary Grades		
Sequential	Explain phenomena in a linear sequence	How recycled paper is made; how a bill becomes a law
Causal	Explain phenomena in a linear sequence showing how one step causes the next	How a volcano erupts; solar eclipse
Cyclical	Explains phenomena in a cyclical way, where the last step is also the beginning of the cycle	The life cycle of a frog; the water cycle
Upper Elementary Grades		
Systems	How a system works; includes description of the components and how they relate and interact with each other	How the desert works as an ecosystem How the branches of government work
Factorial	Factors that contribute to an event or outcome	Factors that create the conditions for a tornado Factors leading to WWII
Middle School		
Consequential	Effects of a phenomenon	Consequences of deforestation Consequences of the war in Sudan
Conditional	Variable conditions for a phenomenon	Temperature on the ground and the atmosphere impact that type of precipitation

Oral Explanations (Pre-K–8)

This lesson's suggestions assume that children have not been exposed to explanations previously. This lesson will be illustrated using the life cycle of a frog. Similar lessons can be done with other topics and other types of explanations.

Lesson 1. The Life Cycle of a Frog

Goal: To teach students how a cyclical explanation works by manipulating and talking about the components.

Materials: YouTube animation: www.youtube.com/watch?v=7NhA9SHunKs. Mat With the Life Cycle of a Frog: www.communication4all.co.uk/Screen%20Shot%20Images/ Frog%20Life%20Cycle%20Word%20Mat.png. PowerPoint for Grades 2–3 and up: classroom.jc-schools.net/sci-units/frog-cycle.ppt; Printable Book: www.enchantedlearn-ing.com/subjects/amphibians/books/froglifecycle/. Chart paper with the statement of the phenomenon on top: "A frog goes through four stages from egg to adult." For older students, the statement should be more technical: "The metamorphosis of a frog includes four stages." Depending on the students' level (1) labeled cards with images illustrating each event in the cycle: adult frog, eggs, tadpoles (with and without legs), and froglet, as well as arrows; (2) cards that include only the images with space for the students to label; or (3) blank cards for students to draw the images and label them. Chart paper. Jamboard to create the puzzle online.

Activities

- Show the video on the life cycle.
- Alternatives depending on grade level:

  a Show the labeled cards and discuss with the students.
  b Show the cards with images and have students label them.
  c Have students create their own cards and labels.
  d Have students create their own cards and write a short sentence for each stage of the cycle.

- Create the cycle on the chart paper with input from the students using the statement of the phenomenon and the cards and the arrows.
- Reproduce the life cycle mat. Cut it as a puzzle with each stage having a separate section. Give the pieces to student groups to put together. The puzzle can either have the labels left blank, requiring students to label them, or students can write sentences, depending on age.
- Ask a few students to show their puzzle and orally explain the life cycle of the frog. Make sure that students express themselves accurately, and encourage the use of technical terms, making sure that students understand them. For example, Mary's pre-kindergarten bilingual student showed her frog cycle and explained, "First the Egg, then the tadpole, then the tadpole gets feet, then it is like a baby frog, then it turns it into a grown up."

Development of Written Explanation Units

To develop units, teachers need to consider a number of factors that will play a role on what and how to teach and what materials to use. With this in mind, then they can plan lessons.

Unit Preparation

To prepare a unit in the chosen explanation genre, teachers need to consider the following:

- Grade level
- Connection with content areas
- Mentor texts
- Research resources and how to use them
- Potential projects, audience, and medium
- Uncoached writing (3–8 only) and planning content of the unit

Grade Level

Explanations are a difficult genre. In the earlier grades, most explanations in school science are based on events that children can observe or visualize. As they grow older, explanations become based on cause-and-effect relationships and, eventually, very complex theories (Veel, 2000). Sequential, causal, and cyclical explanations are the types that children typically encounter and acquire in the elementary grades (Christie & Derewianka, 2008; Derewianka & Jones, 2016). These explanations require the information to be presented in a temporal sequence, making it easier for young learners to understand and practice. Systems and factorial explanations are appropriate for the upper elementary grades. Consequential and conditional can be taught in middle school. These other types require categorization and relationships, which are more difficult cognitive skills for children.

Table 7.2 Types of Explanation by Grade Level

Type of Explanation	Content Area	Oral + Labeled Diagram			Written + Labeled Diagram		
		Pre-K–2	3	4–5	3	4–5	6–8
Sequential	Science	√	√	√	√	√	√
	History			√		√	√
Cyclical	Science	√		√	√	√	√
Causal	Science		√	√		√	√
Systems	Science			√		√	√
	History			√		√	√
Factorial	Science			√		√	√
	History			√	√	√	√
Consequential	Science						√
	History						√
Conditional	Science						√

Before 3rd grade, it is best to do oral explanations accompanied by labeled diagrams. Later, it is best to write and diagram whole class projects. Individual or group writing of explanations in grades 4–8, especially scientific ones, should be done only when the students really master the concepts (see Table 7.2). A way to initially ease the difficulty of writing individual explanations is to choose a young audience. Diagrams with captions accompanied by oral explanations would best suit this audience.

Connection With Content Areas

Explanations fit with a number of topics included in the science curriculum, as well as some of the social studies curriculum. This chart shows some possible topics that can be used to write explanations, by subject.

Science Topics	Social Studies Topics
• Life cycle of plants and animals • Water cycle • Animal adaptations • How a volcano erupts • Circulatory system • Ecosystems • Factors that create the conditions for a thunderstorm • Consequences of deforestation • Weather conditions for different types of precipitation	• How a bill becomes law • Government system • Factors that led to the Vietnam War • Consequences of the Sudan War

Teachers will have to choose from their district's curriculum. The topics themselves distinguish the level of difficulty. The level of technicality can be adapted to facilitate understanding among children.

In addition to suggesting what type of explanation to introduce at each grade level and in which mode (oral, written, or both), Table 7.2 suggests in which subjects to introduce this genre in the different grades. Science explanations, especially of familiar phenomena, are probably easier for younger children than explanations related to historical topics, which are more abstract and difficult to demonstrate. Within science explanations, explaining *how* is easier than explaining *why*. Science specialists and classroom teachers in elementary school could collaborate by team teaching. Alternatively, the classroom teacher can support the drafting and revising of the final product, while the science teacher teaches the content and plans and diagrams the initial draft.

Mentor Texts

Mentor texts are written in the genre of the unit and are used to show students the features of the genre. The Internet and science and social studies textbooks are good sources of explanations (see Table 7.3 and lists downloadable from the *Support Material* tab in the book's webpage).

Table 7.3 Sample Topics and Mentor Texts

Type of Explanation	Content Area	Example	Mentor Text
Sequential	Science	The process followed to recycle Respiratory system (how air travels through the system)	www.factmonster.com/ipka/A0934633.html *(Includes glass, plastic, aluminum, and paper)* www.ehow.com/how-does_5387071_human-respiratory-system-works.html
	History	How a bill becomes a law	http://kids.clerk.house.gov/grade-school/lesson.html?intID=17
Cyclical	Science	The life cycle of a frog The water cycle Carbon cycle Electricity circuit	www.tooter4kids.com/Frogs/life_cycle_of_frogs.htm www.sciencekids.co.nz/sciencefacts/weather/thewatercycle.html http://eo.ucar.edu/kids/green/cycles6.htm www.youtube.com/watch?v=VnnpLaKsqGU (Video of the electric circuit)
Causal	Science	How a volcano erupts Solar eclipse	www.ask.com/question/how-do-volcanoes-erupt www.hko.gov.hk/gts/event/event-solar-eclps11_e.htm
Cyclical	Science	The life cycle of a frog The water cycle Carbon cycle Electricity circuit	www.tooter4kids.com/Frogs/life_cycle_of_frogs.htm www.sciencekids.co.nz/sciencefacts/weather/thewatercycle.html http://eo.ucar.edu/kids/green/cycles6.htm www.youtube.com/watch?v=VnnpLaKsqGU (Video of the electric circuit)
Systems	Science	Circulatory System Ecosystems Electric Circuit System	www.childrenscolorado.org/wellness/info/parents/20540.aspx (The first part explains the various parts of the system and how they relate to each other) http://education.nationalgeographic.com/education/encyclopedia/ecosystem/?ar_a=1 (General and specific explanations of ecosystems) http://kids.discovery.com/tell-me/curiosity-corner/science/how-do-electric-circuits-work (Short explanation) www.petervaldivia.com/technology/electricity/moving-charges.php (Electric circuit diagram with explanation)

(Continued)

Table 7.3 (Continued)

Type of Explanation	Content Area	Example	Mentor Text
	History	Checks and Balances in the Constitution	"14.7. Limiting Power: Checks and Balances" in *History Alive: America's Past* (p. 148)
Factorial	Science	Factors that create the conditions for a thunderstorm	www.uwec.edu/jolhm/eh/barnier/tornado.htm *(the factors for a thunderstorm are included in the first paragraph within a larger sequential explanation of thunderstorms that may turn to tornados)*
	History	Factors that led to WWII	www.historyonthenet.com/WW2/causes.htm *(Difficult)* www.johndclare.net/RoadtoWWII7a.htm
Consequential	Science	Consequences of deforestation	https://byjus.com/questions/what-are-the-consequences-of-deforestation/#:~:text=%20Consequences%20of%20deforestation%20%201%20Increase%20in,wood%20for%20heating%20and%20cooking%20purposes.%20More%20
	History	Consequences of WWII	www.ducksters.com/history/world_war_ii/after_ww2.php
Conditional	Science	Precipitation	See full text at the end of the chapter

The greatest challenge in locating mentor texts is that the texts frequently include a mixture of genres to facilitate learning of the content required for understanding the explanation. For example, Gail Gibbon's book *Hurricanes* includes an explanation of how hurricanes form, a historical recount of the impact of hurricanes, and another more specific historical recount on some hurricanes throughout history. Various reports are also inserted in between the other genres, such as general information about hurricanes, each of the five categories, and how hurricanes are measured.

The book *Magnetism and Electricity* in the Foss series, includes historical recounts on how discoveries were made, procedures for experiments, various explanations, biographies of scientists, and reports on various types of machines. To work with such texts, teachers could play a "find the purpose game." First, discuss the purpose of the various genres used in the book. Then have students label the various genres throughout the book with sticky notes and share their decisions. Finally, they can just focus on the explanation.

Sometimes explanations are mixed with asides ostensibly to help the students understand. However, it could add confusion. In the middle school text *Earth History*, the explanation on erosion has references to activities students did in experiments. These sentences interrupt the explanation with recounts in a different voice (in bold), such as that in the section on Ice Wedging (*Investigations 2: Weathering and Erosion*, 2004) which reads,

> When ice freezes, it expands with tremendous force. **You saw what happened when water in a jar froze and expanded. The force shattered the jar!** Ice expansion naturally causes physical weathering.

(p. 17)

The section continues with the explanation of weathering due to impact of ice filtering into rocks. To facilitate reading comprehension of a text such as the one shown earlier, and to learn the features of the explanation genre, teachers in collaboration with the students can distinguish what is the explanation and what are the asides. Then they can just write the explanation part to use it as a mentor text.

Research Resources and How To Use Them

Resources used in science and social studies classes are the best sources to use in order to connect the writing with content area development. In addition, students need to learn how to conduct research and take notes (see Chapter 6 for an extensive description of these tasks). Students can get immersed in the content knowledge of science through field trips and experiments using research tools comparable to those of scientists (Hodgson-Drysdale & Rosa, 2015). With social studies, it is harder for students to have a personal connection with the content unless the topic is local or they have access to people who have experienced the historical times.

Potential Projects, Audience, and Medium

As shown in Table 7.2, students do not actually write explanations before 3rd grade. They either are given diagrams to label or create and label the diagrams. They do the projects as a whole class using a large diagram and then creating the same one on their own. These activities are followed by an oral explanation. One pre-K teacher worked with her class on an explanation of the life cycle of a chicken after doing a report on chickens. By the time the class labeled the cyclical diagram, they knew all the technical language to easily label the explanation.

By the upper elementary grades, they start writing their own projects, but they still need a lot of instruction to learn the concepts, the technical language, and how to express themselves accurately. One way to facilitate the transition to writing explanations is to choose a young audience. That way the projects need to include lots of diagrams and images and less language.

Hodgson-Drysdale and Rosa (2015) found that extensive experience with the content through field trips and classroom research helped students create systems explanation models in large posters. In addition, they found that first writing a report on the components facilitated writing the explanation itself.

Middle school teachers agreed that factorial and consequential explanations helped their students understand historical events. For example, Alice and Steve created a unit on consequential explanations where students wrote about how tribal warfare caused the formation of the Lost Boys of Sudan.

The lessons described here illustrate how two 4th-grade classes carried out explanations in their classroom. In the first, a classroom teacher and literacy coach carried out the project. In the second, a science teacher taught the unit.

Liz, a literacy coach, and Mia, a 4th-grade teacher, followed these steps to teach explanations:

1   *Explanation immersion for several days:* In pairs, the students read multiple texts and discussed their purpose at the end of the lesson. During the next lesson, they read more explanations and explored the stages. The last activity was to define the stages and the language features of the water cycle explanation.
2   *Class rubric:* On the basis of what students had explored with purpose, stages, and language, the students created a class rubric.

3   *Instruction on stages, language, and type of explanation using everyday themes:* This step included a number of lessons. The first lessons worked on identifying themes, oral rehearsing, and writing. Then, lessons addressed the specific stages: statement of the phenomenon, type of explanation, organization of the body of the explanation (either by a series of events with or without causality, events in a cycle, and factors), and finally the conclusion. To teach these stages, Liz and Mia had the class revise a few students' pieces, highlighting the various stages in sample explanations, and then putting together cut-up explanations. They also taught modifiers, adverbials, and text connectives in connection to different types of explanations. Students prepared one explanation for publication and added a diagram to it.

4   *Instruction using scientific explanations:* To carry out the instructions for scientific explanations, the teachers followed similar steps as the previous set of lessons, but also included time dedicated to research once students had selected topics from a bank provided by the teacher. While doing research, the students were taught how to take notes in an explanation graphic organizer and write scientific words and their definitions at the bottom of the graphic organizer. While writing their explanations, they turned the definitions into appositions (Harris, 2011).

Features of Ed Ballard's Explanation Unit on Electricity (4th Grade)

1   **Developed content knowledge** by introducing a new concept every week through written resources and experiments. For example, to teach which materials are good conductors and which can serve as insulators, he read aloud the book *Conductors and Insulators* and had his 4th graders create an electric circuit to test different materials for being either conductors or insulators of electricity. Students noted their findings in their notebooks.

2   **Taught the structure of an explanation** starting with the statement of the phenomenon followed by the explanation sequence, by modeling explanations orally and reading mentor texts.

3   Noted the **difference between explanations and procedures**, already familiar to students.

4   **Jointly constructed** explanations with the students.

5   **Taught selected aspects of language**, specifically action verbs to be used in the present and generalized participants, pointing out that they do not describe what happened one time, but how it works.

6   **Taught technical language** throughout the lesson by creating a word bank with the words and a simple definition and diagram. He also used oral discussion to deepen the understanding of the terms. Both teachers and students created labeled diagrams, while the students used new terms in theirs.

7   **Students independently wrote** a full explanation with the accompanying diagram at the end of the unit (Hodgson-Drysdale & Ballard, 2011).

Uncoached Writing (3–8 only) and Planning Content of the Unit

The unit starts by having the students write an uncoached piece to gauge students' knowledge of the features of the genre, which guides the planning of instruction (Stead, 2002). It is important to carefully construct the prompts because, if written unclearly, they may lead students to write in a different genre.

Prompt for Uncoached Writing

Write an explanation based on the diagram on the board. The diagram represents an explanation covered in an earlier lesson that has only been done orally. The explanation should be of the same type as the one the students will write.

There are genres, especially in the upper grades, where it becomes harder to do an uncoached piece because of the need for content knowledge. Therefore, the teacher will need to draw on previously taught content or something very familiar to students. Students can also watch a video and write based on the content of the video. For example, if the prompt is "Write about two or three factors that caused the Vietnam War," students could interview a family member that experienced the war as homework and then respond to the prompt in school. Alternatively, they could watch a chunk of a video addressing the topic and then respond to the prompt. In reviewing the resulting writing, teachers should focus on the features of the explanation and not on the accuracy of the facts.

Teachers analyze the writing that emerges from the prompt using the Analysis of Student Work: Purpose, Stages, and Language form (downloadable from the *Support Material* tab in the book's webpage) to determine what the students can already do and what their challenges are with respect to their ability to write an explanation and not their knowledge of the content, which can be addressed separately.

Purpose, Stages, and Language: Theory and Practice

Before establishing the purpose of the type of explanation the class will write, students need to start developing the content knowledge. Simultaneously, teachers should start identifying and clarifying the meaning of technical action verbs, noun groups, and adjectives students will need to write precisely. For instance, to understand the mentor text for the systems explanation introduced later in this chapter, students need to understand noun groups such as *Constitution, impeachment, branches of government, a system of checks and balances, Congress, Senate, Legislature,* and *Supreme Court*; verbs such as *pass/veto a law* and *challenge a law in court*; and adjectives such as *unconstitutional, federal,* and *judicial*. Further, difficulty emerges from multiple meanings of words. Students may be familiar with one meaning of a word but not with the one used in social studies or science. In the context of this example topic, the word *branch* will most likely be associated with trees and not with components of a system. Unlike the science explanations, the language in social studies explanations is difficult to introduce because it cannot be as easily demonstrated with hands-on activities.

When planning a unit, teachers will choose just two to four aspects of language to teach based on the student's background and what the students have already learned when studying other genres. After introducing the chosen aspects of language, as suggested in Table 7.4, teachers will have the students practice them throughout the unit.

The remainder of the chapter describes the purpose, stages, and key language features to be included in the lessons; illustrates challenges students have; and includes lessons alternating those for purpose and stages with language lessons, as shown in Table 7.4. The purpose and stages

Table 7.4 Teaching Language Parallel to Purpose and Stages—Written Explanations

Lessons on Purpose and Stages illustrated with a Sequential and a Systems explanation	Lessons on Language
Multiple lessons for development of content knowledge of the science or social studies unit.	2. Technical Language: Action Verbs, Nouns, and Adjectives
3. Purpose of the Type of Explanation of the Unit	4. Verb Tense (present, science; past, history)

5. Stages of an Explanation
   5.1. Teach Cause and Effect
   5.2. Interrelationships of the Components of a System Explanation
	6. Passive Voice
	7. Adverbials
	  • Place
	  • Time
	  • Manner
	  • Extent
	  • Reason

Development of content knowledge specific to the topic of the class and individual products. Use of graphic organizers to take notes.	*Further practice and learning of technical verbs, nouns, and adjectives.*
8. Joint and Group/Individual Planning and Diagraming the Stages of the Explanation	9. Expanding Noun Groups by Using Pre-Nominal Modifiers (Grades K–8) and Post-Nominal Modifiers (Grades 4–8) 10. Nominalizations (see Chapter 4, Lesson 10.7; Grades 6–8)
11. Joint and Group/Individual Construction of the Stages	12. Generalized Participants 13. Relational Verbs Defining and Describing (Grades 5–8)

14. Joint Revision of the Body of the Explanation	15. Clause Complexes
	   15.1. Create Clause Complexes (Grades 4–8)
	   15.2. Pack Simple Sentences Into Clause Complexes
	   15.3. Revise Students' Sentences
	   15.4. Overuse of "And"

16. Introduction Given the Type of Explanation	17. Audience and Voice (Tenor) *Additional practice lessons, given what was salient during joint revision.*
18. Write Full Explanations (for Individually or Group-Produced Explanations)	

The following resources to support implementation of these lessons are downloadable from the *Support Material* tab in the book's webpage:

• Analysis of Student Work: Purpose, Stages, and Language
• Graphic Organizer
• Mentor Texts That Illustrate the Genre
• Internet Resources With Mentor Texts to Illustrate the Genre

in the following lessons are illustrated through two different explanations: a sequential and a systems explanation. These exemplify the two major types of explanations, one a chronological type (such as cyclical, sequential, and causal) and the other a categorical type (such as systems, factorial, consequential, and conditional). Examples and resources are included for all types of explanations. Adaptations will be needed when implementing the types of explanations not illustrated here. Although the language aspects are included in the lessons for written explanations, students can be taught some of these aspects when doing oral explanations. The specific aspect will depend on the level of maturity of the students and experience they already have from previous genres.

Lesson 2. Technical Language: Action Verbs, Nouns, and Adjectives

This lesson will take place simultaneously with content development occurring in class. The important caveat is that this should not be a lesson on vocabulary pre-taught but rather focus on language as the concepts are introduced, thus providing the context for students to understand the meaning and use of this technical language (Brisk & Zhang-Wu, 2017).

> **Goal:** To teach the technical verbs, nouns, and adjectives the students need to express accurately the concepts of the explanation. To teach the technical language and the content simultaneously.
> **Materials:** The same materials used to teach content.

Activities

As you teach the concepts, teach the language.

Learn technical language through field trips. For example, for a science explanation on ecosystems, do a field trip to an ecosystem.

- Collect organisms in the system. As you and the students collect them, show them to the whole class and discuss the name (*muscles, barnacles, substrate*), and have the students write them in their field guides. If the organisms have important attributes, teach the adjectives that describe those attributes (*small acorn barnacles*).
- When describing the relationships between these organisms in the system, teach students the technical action verbs that describe those actions (*feed, scrape*).

Learn technical language from research resources and mentor texts, if they are on the topic of the unit. Even if they are not, students still need to learn the technical language to understand the mentor explanation. For example, for the mentor text *How Recycled Paper Is Made*, students need to know the meaning of *fibers, pulp, vat, chemical, debris, screen* (nouns); *pulping* facility, *recycled* paper (adjectives); and *spit out* (action verb).

- If a procedure is available, do the procedure in anticipation to the unit. For this topic, students can create recycled paper in class (see instructions at http://voices.yahoo.com/recycled-paper-project-fun-kids-adults-3082080.html). In this procedure, the process described is similar to how recycled paper is produced at a plant, and terms like *pulp, recycle,* and *screen* are introduced in more tangible ways.

Alternatively, have visuals or a video that illustrate the noun groups or verbs.

- Read chunks of the text with support of the visual; name the object, attribute, or action; and have students locate it on the text. Discuss the meaning. (As you saw earlier, Liz had them write a definition.)
- If watching a video, stop it after the terms are revealed and have them identify them on the text.

Follow Up

This follow up lesson should be done with Lesson 14 in units where students or groups do their own writing.

> **Goal:** To teach students to use technical language in order to reflect the explanation topic. The use of technical terms assists the preciseness of the concepts explained.
>
> **Materials:** Students' drafts with everyday language with the words that would best be substituted with technical terms underlined. For example, one student explained evaporation as *the warm air toches* [touches] *the water*, rather than *the warm air heats the water*. Another wrote, *The water go up* instead of *rises*. Mentor texts that include the technical terminology. Large sticky notes.

Activities

- Distribute texts on the topic that students have used before among groups of students.
- Show a draft of student work with the everyday terms underlined.
- Ask students to work in their groups, consulting the texts, to find terms that would be more effective to replace the underlined words. Ask students to write the replacement words on the sticky notes and place the suggestions sticky notes above each corresponding word on the larger class copy.
- Once all groups have contributed, look at the suggestions for each word, group those that are identical, and read them aloud. If all of the students came up with the same solution, discuss that suggestion's accuracy. If there is more than one suggestion, discuss the differences and how the different words change the meaning.
- Have students look at their own drafts and decide whether their terms also need to be substituted with more precise language.

Purpose of Explanations

Different types of explanations have different purposes (see Table 7.1). The differences between sequential and cyclical explanations are minimal. They both explain the phenomenon in a sequence, but in the cyclical, the last event becomes the first event to complete the cycle. Causal explanations add cause to the explanation sequence. The purpose of systems, factorial, consequential, and conditional explanations are quite different from each other and from the other three. To help a group of middle school teachers clear the confusion between factorial and consequential explanations, the diagram in Figure 7.1 was developed.

The difference between factorial and consequential explanations is the direction of the cause–effect relationship.

The verbs in scientific explanations are usually in the present tense. If an explanation is about something that no longer exists (e.g., dinosaurs), the verbs will be in the past tense (Knapp & Watkins, 2005). For example, in the explanation of the evolution of reptiles to birds, all of the verbs are in the past tense: "Some scaly reptiles **began** climbing trees to escape from enemies"

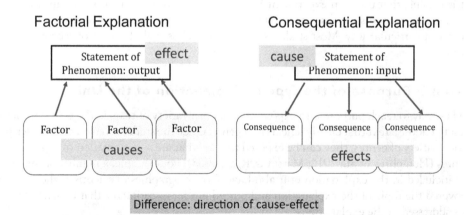

Figure 7.1 The difference in the direction of the cause–effect relationship between factorial and consequential explanations.

(*How Birds Fly*, p. 4). Historical explanations are in the past. Since the factors that led to the Vietnam War have all already occurred, it makes sense that the past tense be used to explain them.

Features of Students' Writing

Students understand that they have to explain the ideas in their writing. Their writing usually includes the word "because" to do so. However, without instruction, it is difficult for students to write good explanations. To elicit the uncoached piece, a 4th-grade teacher carried out an experiment with students putting one piece of moist bread and one piece of dry bread in separate plastic bags. They observed how long each piece of bread took to decay. On the basis of this experiment, the teacher asked students to write why the bread decayed. Rachel wrote:

Why?

I think that the dampbread decayed faster because the water couldn't take the water and the bread couldn't fight it. It also needed air to stay fresh. Since it was sealed for 8–9 days, It was hard for the bread to not decay. It decayed because the bread said "I cant take it!" Thats why it decayed.

Purpose (Varies depending on type)	√	Reflects elements of procedural recounts, such as documenting observations, and of a narrative, such as dialogue and personification inanimate objects
Verb Tense Scientific mostly present. Historical past.	√	Mostly past tense, consistent with the recount genre, rather than a scientific explanation

Instead of explaining why the pieces of bread decayed, Rachel described what happened. Her attempt to give reasons was not accurate. She also personified the bread. Knapp and Watkins (2005) found similar switches of purpose in children's explanation writing.

It is possible that using an experiment in connection to the explanation prompt caused students to write recounts because they naturally want to write about what happened rather that why it is a particular way. Most students in the same class had elements of recounts in their writing.

Lesson 3. Purpose of the Type of Explanation of the Unit

The best way to teach purpose is to expose students to a variety of texts in the genre. Initially, it is best to choose a text that clearly reflects that genre. Once the students have a clear understanding of a variety of genres, they can be exposed to texts that are a combination of genres or macrogenres (Humphrey et al., 2012; Martin & Rose, 2008). For example, a number of the science texts included in the explanation unit also have short biographies of scientists who studied or discovered the topic of the explanation and procedures for experiments that enhance the concepts addressed in the explanations.

> **Goal:** To understand the purpose of a particular type of explanation by being exposed to examples. To let the class know that, as a whole class, they will produce an explanation related to the topic they have been studying for a particular audience (and if appropriate, in groups or individually as well).
> **Materials:** Texts, diagrams, and videos illustrating the type of written explanations that students will write and diagram.

Activities

- Read aloud and discuss the purpose. Include explanations that students have encountered before in various content area lessons. In the case of scientific explanations that are demonstrated through an experiment, distinguish between the procedure followed in the experiment and the explanation of how or why things happen repeatedly and not just in this one experiment.
- Explore texts with diagrams and videos.
- Discuss the purpose of this particular type of explanation.
- Discuss the difference in purpose with genres that the students have encountered, especially recounts and procedures.
- Discuss the project that the class will produce.
- Define the audience and discuss how the audience will affect the features of what they write. For example, if it is for a younger audience, they will produce a diagram with annotations, while if the audience is adults or classmates, they will include written text.

Lesson 4. Verb Tense

This lesson may not be needed if students have been taught formation and use of verb tense in other genres. Decisions should be made based on the uncoached writing. As we saw earlier, Rachel confused the purpose and thus switched tense several times.

> **Goal:** To teach students the choice and formation of the verb tense given the purpose and type of explanation.
> **Materials:** Mentor texts used in Lesson 3. A sentence or two from an explanation text written on chart paper and the equivalent sentence if it were a procedure or any other genre appearing in students' uncoached pieces. For example, for the explanation text "One end

of the filament connects to the side of the metal screw base on the bulb" (*Magnetism and Electricity*, p. 33), a procedure would be written, "Connect one end of the filament to the metal screw base on the bulb." Student work.

Activities

- Show students a chunk of one of the mentor texts. Have them identify the verbs by circling or highlighting them.
- Ask them what tense the text uses and why? (Present: indicates how things are; past: indicates how things used to be or an action that already occurred.)
- Show them a concept diagram created during content lessons with the technical action verbs developed in Lesson 2.
- Working in groups, ask students to write a sentence explaining one aspect of the diagram.
- Have them share and comment on the verb tense. Edit if needed.
- Show the students the sample sentence from the published explanation and the equivalent as a procedure or any other genre that appeared in the uncoached pieces. Discuss the difference in purpose in the sentences.

Follow Up

- When jointly constructing the explanation, remind students of verb tense if anyone suggests use of a different tense.
- If students have created individual/group explanations that show problem with verb tense, make it a focus of joint revision.

Stages of Explanations

The structure of explanations differs depending on the type and the content area (see Table 7.5). All explanations include an introduction and the explanation proper. Sometimes there is also a conclusion. Explanations start with a statement to identify the historical event or introduce the scientific phenomenon by describing or classifying it (Knapp & Watkins, 2005). A statement of the phenomenon could read, "With the aid of pumps, fluids—gases such as air, and liquids such as water and oil—are able to transmit great power and drive machines" (*How Things Work*, p. 38) or "Wind turbines use the power of moving air currents to spin their propellers. These are huge windmill-like blades on top of a tall tower. As they spin, generators inside the turbines make electricity, which is sent via cables underground" (*How Things Work Encyclopedia*, p. 66).

In historical explanations, in addition to the identifying statement, there is some historical background that provides the context. In the following factorial explanation there is historical information highlighting the importance of the topic, followed by the identifying statement (in bold),

> The effects of the Great Depression were huge across the world. Not only did it lead to the New Deal in America but more significantly, it was a direct cause of the rise of extremism in Germany leading to World War II. **A combination of domestic and worldwide conditions led to the Great Depression.**

The body of an explanation differs depending on the explanation type, with each type demanding different skills. Sequential, causal, and cyclical explanations all require events following each other. However, causal explanations involve one event causing the next, while

Table 7.5 Type of Explanation and Stages

Type of Explanation	Stages	
	Science	History
Sequential	• Phenomenon Identification • Explanation Sequence	
Causal	• Phenomenon Identification • Explanation Sequence (indicating causality)	
Cyclical	• Phenomenon Identification • Cyclical Explanation Sequence	
System	• Phenomenon Identification • System Description • System Explanation and Interaction (among components) • Generalization	• Identifying Statement (with historical background) • System Description • System Explanation and Interaction (among components) • Generalization
Factorial	• Outcome (effect) • Factors (causes) • General Statement	• Outcome • Factors • Reinforcement of the Factors
Consequential	• Phenomenon Problem (cause) • Consequences (effects)	• Identifying a Historical Phenomenon (that will lead to consequences/changes) • Consequences • Reinforcement of Consequences
Conditional	• Phenomenon • *Multiple possible outcomes* (if . . . then)	

Sources: Coffin (2006), Derewianka and Jones (2016), Martin and Rose (2008)

cyclical explanations have the last event mark the beginning of the cycle. Systems, factorial, consequential, and conditional explanations require students to sort out elements that are not organized in a sequence, but in specific categories. In addition, the conclusions differ depending on the explanation.

The following two mentor texts have been deconstructed for their stages. The first one, a sequential explanation, illustrates the stages of a chronologically organized text, and the second, a systems explanation, shows how an explanation organized in categories works.

Sequential Explanation: How Paper Is Recycled

Stages	Mentor Text (Adapted from www.factmonster.com/ipka/A0934633.html)
Title	*How Paper Is Recycled*
Phenomenon Identification	Recycled paper is made from used paper. Paper is made of tiny fibers. Because these fibers eventually become weak, paper cannot be recycled forever.
Explanation Sequence	• The paper is sorted out in the recycling center and transported to a pulping facility. • The paper is soaked and heated in huge vats, becoming pulp. Chemicals in the liquid separate the ink from the paper.

Stages	Mentor Text (Adapted from www.factmonster.com/ipka/A0934633.html)
Title	How Paper Is Recycled
	• The pulp is screened and cleaned to remove glue, other debris, and the remaining ink. • The pulp is refined and beaten to make it ready to become paper again. • The pulp is fed into a machine that spits out the pulp onto a flat moving screen where it forms sheets. • The sheets are rolled and dried and ready for their new life.

Since the text is for children, the explanation sequence is facilitated by writing it as a bullet list.

Systems Explanation: Checks and Balances in the Constitution

Stages	Mentor Text
Title	Limiting Power: Checks and Balances In History Alive!: America's Past, p. 148.
Historical Background	The men who wrote the Constitution wanted a strong and lasting government. One way that they tried to achieve this goal was by designing a system of "checks and balances."
Identifying Statement	The Constitution gives each branch of government the power to "check" (stop) certain actions of the other branches. It also balances each branch's powers with the powers of the other branches.
System Description	Appeared earlier in the textbook.
System Explanation Interaction Between Components (a labeled diagram showing this interaction accompanies the text)	Checks and balances help to make sure that no one branch becomes too powerful. For example, Congress can pass laws, but the president approves or vetoes them. The president's power is a check on the power of Congress. What if congress and the president agree on a law that disagrees with the Constitution? If the law is challenged in court, the judicial branch has the power to decide whether it is unconstitutional. The court's power is a check on the power of the other two branches. How are the powers of the different branches balanced? Suppose the president wants one thing and Congress wants another. Congress cannot make laws without the president's signature, and the president needs Congress to pass the laws he wants. Their powers balance each other. And even though the courts can declare laws unconstitutional, federal judges are appointed by the president with the approval of the Senate. Another example of checks and balances is impeachment. Suppose members of the executive or judicial branch try to abuse their power. Congress can impeach them and remove them from office.
Generalization	In these ways, the Constitution tries to make sure that no one branch of the government becomes too powerful.

This text is missing the system description because each branch was thoroughly described earlier. Teachers could create with their class three sentences describing each branch of government and insert them where indicated.

Features of Students' Writing

When students like Rachel switch the purpose, they typically do not include the stages of an explanation. There was no statement of the phenomenon or explanation sequence in Rachel's piece, nor in the writing of other students who wrote something closer to a recount. Both Harris (2011) and Hodgson-Drysdale and Ballard (2011) found that students had difficulty writing the statement of the phenomenon, even after instruction. In one writing sample, "the student begins 'A circuit can make a lightbulb turn on,' which would be a more complete initial statement if it were phrased as 'Electricity flowing through a complete circuit can make a lightbulb turn on,' " (Hodgson-Drysdale & Ballard, p. 40). Even when students attempt an explanation sequence, their writing sometimes reveals limited understanding of the scientific phenomenon or a sequence with gaps. Thus, instruction needs to constantly focus on content as well as structure and be carefully scaffolded, as will be shown in the following lessons.

Language Features of Explanations

An important language aspect of explanations, especially scientific explanations, is that the language to express the ideas needs to be specific and accurate in order to convey the meaning of the particular topic. For this reason, the writing needs to be carefully scaffolded. A variety of language aspects with specific functions help express ideas, including verb groups, noun groups, adverbials, and clause complexes. Students need to pay attention to audience and voice, which usually call for authoritative voice to focus on the phenomenon or historical event being explained and not on the writer or audience.

Many of these language features are comparable to those of reports. One feature of language that distinguishes explanations from reports is the connecting words. In explanations, each component of the explanation sequence or each category is related to the other. Thus, the connecting words help to indicate sequence, cause, effect, and condition, depending on the type of explanation.

Verb Groups

There are three issues to attend in relation to verbs: tense, types of verbs, and use of passive voice. Explanations are written in the present because they tell how things are or why they are the way they are. Factorial and consequential historical explanations use the past tense because they are referring to things that already occurred. In contrast, the systems explanation included in this chapter uses past tense in the historical background, but the explanation itself is in the present tense. It explains how the structure of the government is.

Verbs in explanations are mostly action verbs that develop the topic. Thus, for the most part, they are technical words. Causal, factorial, and consequential explanations often include verbs indicating causality, such as *produces*, *led to*, *causes*, and so on (Derewianka & Jones, 2016; Humphrey & Vale, 2020). Relational verbs are also used to describe or define. Passive voice is often used because the focus is on the scientific phenomenon or historical event and not the persons carrying out the actions.

- Action verbs in the present: *At night, temperatures **fall**, and the water **freezes**, **expands**, and **presses** against the surrounding rock.*
- Action verbs in the past and indicating causality: *The stock market crash of October 29, 1929 was one of the major causes that **led to** the depression.*
- Relational verbs to describe: *Fibers eventually **become** weak.*

- Relational verbs to define: *Physical weathering **is** the breaking down of rock into smaller pieces.*
- Passive voice: *Paper **is made** of tiny fibers.*

Adverbials

Explanations need adverbials of a variety of types to add specificity to mainly the actions described by the verbs and, in some cases, adjectives. They express circumstances of place, time, manner, accompaniment, extent, and others. Circumstances of time are common in chronological explanations, such as sequential, cyclical, and causal. They are used to connect the steps in the explanation sequence. Circumstances of reason are common in factorial and consequential explanations. Students have encountered these types of adverbials in other genres, such as procedure and recounts.

- Place (Where?): *Electricity flows **through the electromagnets**.*
- Time (When?): ***At night**, temperatures fall, and the water freezes, expands, and presses against the surrounding rock.*
- Manner (How? What with?): *It also balances each branch's powers **with the powers of the other branches**.*
- Extent (How much?): ***Too** powerful.*
- Reason (Why?): *Russia was excluded from joining The League of Nations **for fear of Communism**.*

Noun Groups

Similar to reports, noun groups in explanations carry a great deal of information. Nouns expressing concepts related to the topic, often technical terms, are important to understand and use. This is evident in the mentor text *How Paper Is Recycled*, which includes nouns such as *recycling center*, *pulping facility*, *huge vats*, and *chemicals* that are all connected with the paper recycling topic. A variety of modifiers define the noun (appositions) or give specificity to it (adjectives, prepositional phrases, and embedded clauses). Often the modifiers are also technical terms. For example, in an explanation about how hurricanes form, the author writes about *cumulonimbus* clouds. Thus, it is a specific type of cloud described with a term not commonly used when referring to clouds (see Table 6.6 for a detailed explanation of modifiers).

Explanations are usually about generalized participants representing the whole category, for example, *paper*, *pulp*, and *president*. The explanation is not about a specific president, but the office of the president in general. An explanation of the circulatory system will include things like *heart*, *vein*, and *artery*, referring to any person and not those specific to a particular person.

Another feature of noun groups that students need to learn as they mature is nominalizations, where verbs or adjectives are turned to nouns in order to put focus on the action, as well as evaluate actions and pack language (see Brisk, 2021, for complete explanation). In the sentence *The spinning of the air accelerates*, by nominalizing the verb *spin*, the writer was able to place the idea in the theme position (what the author is writing about) of the sentence. Children would write instead, *The air spins faster and faster*, where *air* rather than *spinning* is what the writer is writing about.

- Technical nouns: *A baby bird is called a **hatchling**.*
- Technical adjectives: ***Cumulonimbus** clouds.*
- Prepositional phrases: *The other end of the filament attaches to the metal tip **at the foot of the socket**.*

- Embedded clauses with conjugated verb: *Many believe erroneously that the stock market crash **that occurred on October 29, 1929** is one and the same with the Great Depression.*
- Embedded clauses with non-conjugated verb: *A special hard structure **called the egg tooth** forms on the beak.*
- Appositions: *Neville Chamberlain, **Prime Minister of Britain**, believed that the Treaty of Versailles had treated Germany badly.*
- Generalized Participants: *All **hurricanes** form over tropical waters.*
- Nominalizations: *The warm moist air spins upward, creating a draft that sucks up more moisture. The **spinning** of the air accelerates.*

Clauses Complexes

In the upper elementary grades, both the texts that students encounter and those that they compose begin to include clause complexes, where ideas are combined in sentences with multiple clauses, often using connecting words that signal specific meanings (see Table 6.8 for a full list of types of relationships). Students have difficulty with these clause complexes, and it is hard to tell whether ideas, grammar, or both create the challenges. Some types of these clause complexes and connecting words are more common in certain explanations. Both explanation mentor texts, introduced earlier, include clause complexes expressing different types of relations (see Table 7.6; separation between clauses is shown with | |).

How Paper Is Recycled is an easier text and has few of these complex constructions. Additive and causal relations are often the first type that children start to write. The more difficult text,

Table 7.6 Types of Relations in Complex Clauses in the Mentor Texts

Type	How Paper Is Recycled	Limiting Power: Checks and Balances
Projection: Idea		Suppose || the president wants ... Suppose || members of the executive or judicial branch try ...
Additive	The sheets are rolled || and dried || and ready for their new life	the president wants one thing || *and* Congress wants another Congress cannot make laws ..., || *and* the president needs Congress ... Congress can impeach them || *and* remove them from office
Variation		the president approves || *or* vetoes them
Concessive		Congress can pass laws, || *but* the president approves
Causal Non-finite	to remove glue ... ink (purpose) to become paper again (result)	
Causal Finite	| *Because* these fibers eventually become weak, | paper cannot be recycled (reason)	
Conditional		*If* the law is challenged in court, || the judicial branch has ...
Concessive		*even though* the courts can declare laws unconstitutional, || federal judges are appointed ...

Limiting Power: Checks and Balances, has greater number and variety of these sentences. The purpose of using these structures is to pack more information and express relations between ideas.

Some types of clause complexes and connecting words are more common in certain explanations. For example,

- Clauses indicating time (sequential, cyclical, and causal explanations): **When the circuit is closed**, *electricity flows through the filament.*
- Conditional clauses (conditional explanations): **If the temperature is around 30 F (−1 C)**, *a fairly low relative humidity (less than 30 percent) is needed for good snow-making conditions.* **If the temperature is less than 20 F (−6.7 C)**, *snow can be made fairly easily even if the relative humidity is 100 percent.*
- Words and connecting words indicating causality (factorial and consequential explanations): **In addition to the untold consequences for military families due to the massive loss of 58,000 American lives during the conflict, the Vietnam War led to the end of the military draft in the United States, a reduction in the voting age to age 18, and restriction of a sitting president's ability to send military forces into combat.**

Audience and Voice

An explanation will be more or less complex depending on the audience. For example, the following two explanations on how corals are formed differ in the amount of information and the number of steps and technical terms included. The first one is short and very general, accompanied with simple diagrams. The second includes more information, variation, and technical terms. A short excerpt from each illustrates the differences:

> Coral reefs begin to form when free-swimming coral larvae attach to submerged rocks or other hard surfaces along the edges of islands or continents.
> (http://oceanservice.noaa.gov/education/kits/corals/coral04_reefs.html)

> Coral reef formation is only made possible by the cumulative efforts of millions of individual organisms working over very long periods of time. When we consider that the growth rate of the most abundant Caribbean "hard" coral (*Montastrea annularis*) is only in the range of about 3–9 mm/year, it becomes quite evident that coral reefs are built over decades and centuries—not weeks or months.
> (www.coral-reef-info.com/coral-reef-formation.html)

Considering the mentor texts included in the lessons in this chapter, the recycled paper text is written simply, has very few technical terms, and includes only the major events in the process. This makes it likely to be intended for a younger audience. The text on the balance of powers among the branches of government has more complex concepts, relationships, and language. This renders the text more appropriate for a slightly older, more knowledgeable audience.

The voice in an explanation is typically authoritative. The sentences are all declarative and written in the third person, and the language is factual and devoid of judgment. Occasionally modal verbs are used, as seen in the mentor text on the branches of government, which often uses *can* to indicate what the various branches can or cannot do. This text also uses some questions, which is more typical of texts written for children. It is important that students do not feel that they need to always include questions in their own writing. Some texts for children also use the second person to create familiarity with the reader, such as this causal explanation on sneezing: "Sneezing, also called sternutation, is your body's way of removing an irritation from *your* nose" (http://kidshealth.org/PageManager.jsp?lic=1&article_set=10317&cat_id=124). However, using the third person signals to the students that an event happens with everybody and not just them.

Consequential explanations may include evaluative language to show attitude toward phenomenon (Humphrey & Vale, 2020). This is seen in this excerpt, where the author uses evaluative language and graduation (bold) to show attitude toward the painful impact of the Vietnam War: *In addition to the **untold** consequences for military families due to the **massive loss** of **58,000** American lives during the conflict.*

Features of Students' Writing: Language

Denise, a 4th grader, wrote the following piece after the students had learned to write explanations—with focus on purpose and stages only—in the context of an electricity unit.

Prompt: Explain how electricity in a circuit can cause a light bulb to light.

> The D-cell battery holed's [holds] the
> Electricity, the wire's are conected [connected]
> to the positive or Negative
> end's. Onets [Once] the wire is conectied [connected]
> to the end's of ether [either] the positive
> or negative, the wire must be
> atached [attached] to the tip of the Receiver
> A.K.A lite bolb . . . The pathway (A.K.A
> The Wire) should be conected [connected] to the
> metal jacket. Onets [Once] the path way is conekted [connected] to the metal jacket
> the wire should be cunected [connected] to
> the positive or Negative end
> then the lite bolb [light bulb] will start to
> heat up and lite up! like so.

Verb Groups

Denise uses action verbs. She repeats *connects* in most sentences. Alternative verbs to use would be: *attaches* or *flows*. She does not use passive voice. The real problem with her verbs is the tense because she describes or reports what the elements look like using the present perfect (*the wire is conectied* [connected]) rather than explaining how it works in the present (the wire conducts the electricity). Like with Rachel, writing an explanation after watching an experiment leads Denise to write a mixture of description of what she sees (*the wires are connected*) and a procedure (*the wires should be connected*), rather than *the wires, connected to the positive and the negative sides of the battery, conduct electricity from the battery to the light bulb and back to the battery.* What causes the light bulb to light up is the wires *conducting* electricity, a concept not included in the piece. Teachers need to be clear that experiments are carried out to understand how things work, but when students write an explanation, the focus needs to be on explaining how things work and not what happened in the experiment.

Adverbials

Denise uses several adverbials of place, *to the positive or Negative end's* in the form of prepositional phrases. *Then* is the only adverb of time.

Noun Groups

Denise uses a few technical nouns associated with the electric circuit, such as *wire* and *pathway*. As in other genres, children tend to not use many modifiers. Denise is no exception. She uses a few technical adjectives (*D-cell, positive, negative*) and appositions: The pathway (*A.K.A [also known as] The Wire*).

Denise does not use generalized participants, but talks about the things that were used in the experiment. She writes about *the wires, the D-cell battery,* and *the light bulb,* but not about wires, batteries, and light bulbs in general to create an electric circuit.

Clause Complexes

Denise included a few of these constructions in her writing. She uses clauses to indicate time: *Onets [Once] the wire is conectied [connected] to the end's of ether [either] the positive or negative,* and one to indicate addition: *and lite up!*

Other common problems found in students' writing is the overuse of *and* and *because*. Students often string sentences together using *and*. Sometimes *and* is used appropriately to indicate an additive relation between the clauses, but other times it is unnecessary. Still, other times the sentence could be changed to express the relation more accurately. For example, these two sentences written by 4th graders could benefit from changes: (1) *We have two bread. and one is dry and the other is wet.* (2) *and the bread stayed for 5 day and then it grew mold in a plastic bag.* The first *and* can be eliminated. The second *and* in the first sentence indicates an additive relation. The second indicates a temporal relation. The latter could be more clearly expressed with a dependent clause: *After 5 days in a plastic bag, the bread grew mold.* (See Brisk & DeRosa, 2014, for a thorough analysis of clause complexes.)

Most times, *because* is appropriately used to indicate reason, even if the reason is not accurate (e.g., *the damp bread decayed faster because it couldn't take the water*). However, some students started their explanations with *because* (e.g., *Because when you stretched the rubber Band it will go Faster.*). The *because* is not necessary and is more typical of oral language. The reason or cause is not explained, and only the facts are given.

L2 writers have difficulty with the use of adverbial phrases of time that should start with *as* (e.g., the sentence, "As the corals grow and expand, reefs take on one of three major characteristic structures—fringing, barrier or atoll."). Instead of using *as*, L2 students sometimes use *when*, giving the sentence a different meaning.

Audience and Voice

Children tend to include writing features that connect them closer to their audience. They frequently use interpersonal themes, such as **I think** *that the damp bread decayed faster . . . .* It is best to encourage students to avoid these features because they place the focus on the writer rather than the topic of the explanation. Students also use the second person to address the audience directly (e.g., *because when you get a magnet and a nale* [nail] *and put the nale on the magnet the nale will become a magnet*).

Knapp and Watkins (2005) noted that children include judgments in their explanations. For example, at the end of the water cycle explanation, a child wrote, "I like rain. Rain is good for you" (p. 129). This would be a more appropriate ending for a personal recount and not for an explanation.

Denise had difficulty with being clear in her purpose and sentence construction, affecting the tenor. The language is simple enough to be appropriate for other children. However, the explanation sequence is not clear enough for children to understand. In addition, she uses strong modals (*must be*, *should be*), making it sound more like a procedure on how to create a circuit. She uses an exclamation at the end, not common in explanations, even for children.

Lessons to Teach Stages and Language

The lessons on stages apply to all types of explanations. When implementing, apply to the specific characteristics of the stages described earlier. Some lessons are specific to certain types of explanations.

Explanations share a number of language features with reports. Therefore, students may already master them. After analysis of student work, teachers can decide in which of the areas included in this section students need additional instruction. They can also use similar lessons from the report chapter to focus on the various language features.

Lesson 5. Stages of an Explanation

Goal: To familiarize students with the stages of the type of explanations featured in the unit.
Materials: Mentor texts used in Lesson 3. Purpose. Large version of the graphic organizer for the unit's explanation type (downloadable from the *Support Material* tab in the book's webpage). When working with 3rd grade, the graphic organizer should include the introductory statement. For 4th through 8th grade, it should not because students will learn how to write it in later lessons.

Activities

* Show the graphic organizer and introduce the stages.
* Read aloud the mentor text.
* As you read, point to the graphic organizer to indicate from which stage of the explanation you are reading. Engage the students in deciding which stage it is.
* Repeat with other explanations of the same type.

Lesson 5.1. Teach Cause and Effect

Factorial, consequential, and conditional explanation require the understanding of cause and effect when teaching the stages.

Goal: To distinguish between cause and effect and show the direction of the relationship.
Materials: An example of a familiar topic to illustrate the cause–effect relationship of the type of explanation of the unit.

Activities

In anticipation to Lesson 5, teach cause and effect with a topic familiar to the students.
For example, if you are teaching factorial explanations,

* Tell the students: "Our school won an award for its music program. What caused it?" Brainstorm ideas.
* With students working in groups, ask them to name an effect (outcome) and then give two or more things that caused it. For example, "this weekend I got sick with a bad cold." Some

of the reasons were: "I went out to play with my friends without a coat, and it was cold." "Several of my friends had colds."

Added Activity for Lesson 5

In Lesson 5, as you read and identify the stages in one of these types of explanations, ask the students which were the causes or which were the effects.

- Factorial: Introduction (effect); Factors (causes).
- Consequential: Introduction (cause); Consequences (effects).
- Conditional: As conditions change (causes), results (effects) change.

Lesson 5.2. Interrelationships of the Components of a System Explanation

> **Goal:** To show students that what makes a system is the interrelationships between its components.
> **Materials:** Three 8 × 5 cards per group of students. Six arrows per group, with one interrelationship (e.g., "can veto bills") written on each (see *Limiting Power: Checks and Balances* mentor text).

Activities

- Group students and give each group three cards.
- Re-read the system description in the mentor text and discuss how the system works.
- Have student groups draw each component of the system on a separate card, for example, president, Congress, the Supreme Court (they can also download pictures from the Internet).
- Re-read the interaction between components of the system and discuss.
- Give each group the six arrows, each describing one interrelationship, and ask the students to arrange the arrows so that each arrow points from one branch of government to another to show an interrelationship. Students can paste the cards and the arrows to a sheet of paper.
- Ask one or two groups to orally present their results to the whole class.

Lesson 6. Passive Voice

> **Goal:** To understand the function and form of passive voice.
> **Materials:** Mentor texts used to teach other aspects of the genre that include passive voice. T-chart with column emphasis on doer and on things done. Sentences with passive voice and the equivalent active voice.

Activities

- Show the students one or more of the passive voice examples from the mentor text *How Paper Is Recycled*. For example, *The paper **is sorted out** in the recycling center*. Ask the students, "What is sorted out at the recycling center?" "Who sorts out the paper?" Since they cannot give the answer, ask "Does it matter that the explanation doesn't tell us?" "What are we talking about? What is important in this explanation?" The answer is "the paper." It is what the author is writing about. The author is not writing about the people who make the paper, but about paper.

- Show the T-chart with some sentences in passive and some in active indicating the focus of each. For example,

Sentences where the focus is on what is done	Sentences with focus on the doer
Recycle paper is made from used paper.	
	The workers make paper of tiny fibers.
Paper cannot be recycled forever.	
The paper is soaked in huge vats.	
	Farmers irrigate crops every day.
	Congress passed a major legislation.

- With the help of the class, change the first two examples to the opposite construction.
- Ask students, working in groups, to propose the opposite construction in the rest of the T-chart. Discuss the way passive voice is structured: verb *to be* + *past participle*. The verb *to be* is in the present or past depending on the tense of the piece.
- Show students these two clauses:

  - *Crops are irrigated every day.*
  - *Crops are irrigated every day by the farmers.*

- Ask, What is the difference? Then explain that sometimes you want to name the doer but in a secondary position. To do this, the phrase with "by" is added at the end.

Lesson 7. Adverbials

Goal: To demonstrate to students adverbials' power of adding essential information.
Materials: Paragraph with adverbials crossed out and verbs in bold or circled. Chart paper or projector.

Activities

- Project a paragraph with verbs in bold or circled and adverbials covered. For example, The paper **is sorted out** ~~in the recycling center~~ and **transported** ~~to a pulping facility.~~
- Read it aloud and ask students to try to explain what you just read.
- Uncover the adverbials and ask, "Can you now tell me what it means?"
- Using examples of additional adverbials in the mentor texts, first identify the verb or adjective (in bold), then ask a question to locate the type of adverbial (italics) and add them to a chart. For example,

Type of Adverbial	How Paper Is Recycled	Limiting Power: Checks and Balances
Place (Where?)	The paper **is sorted out** *in the recycling center* and **transported** *to a pulping facility.*	Congress can impeach them and **remove** them *from office.*
Time (When?)	fibers *eventually* **become** weak	
Manner (How? What with?)		It also **balances** each branch's powers *with the powers of the other branches.* ... federal judges **are appointed** by the president *with the approval of the Senate.*
Extent (How much?)		*too* **powerful**

Follow Up

After students have produced drafts:

- Project sample student work and have the class identify the verbs (what is happening). Ask, "Are there adverbials adding precise information? Do they need adverbials to be more precise?"
- Have students work with their own writing in pairs or groups, identifying verbs and discussing whether they should revise. Confer with individuals or groups as they are doing this work.

Lessons to Develop Content Knowledge and Language for the Writing Projects

Having been introduced to the purpose and stages of the genres, the students are ready to start working on the writing projects. Teachers need to hone in on the specific content of these projects by facilitating the research (see Chapter 6, Lesson 5) and teaching the technical verbs, nouns, and adjectives students will need to write about these topics (see Lesson 2). Until the students master the content, especially in science, the written projects will be produced as joint construction with the whole class collaborating in order to ensure that the explanation is scientifically accurate. Another way to initially scale down the difficulty of individual/group writing is to choose a young audience and have students produce diagrams with short captions, comprehensible to the young audience. The projects are then presented with additional oral explanations. Eventually students are challenged with fully written explanations, using the diagrams as a complement.

Lesson 8. Joint and Group/Individual Planning and Diagraming the Stages of the Explanation

Goal: To learn how to plan an explanation with a supporting diagram.

Materials: Texts or videos with explanations used to teach the topic and technical language for the joint and individual/group projects; large version of the graphic organizer for the specific explanation (downloadable from the *Support Material* tab in the book's webpage); images and labels in either the same large cards or in separate cards (more difficult) as well as images of arrows; additional videos or texts with explanations; copies of small versions of the graphic organizer and small cards with captions and images (together or separate).

Activities

- Read aloud the explanation or show a video.
- Using the graphic organizer, create a diagram of the explanation by reading the cards with the captions and with the images and deciding which one goes where. Then have the students choose arrows and paste them where they belong. For more advanced levels, have the students working in groups create cards and labels to add to the class diagram. (See example from a 5th-grade class working on systems explanations, Hodgson-Drysdale & Rosa, 2015, p. 34.)
- Divide the class into groups and provide them with a graphic organizer and the resources for them to research other explanations (from ones already previewed in other lessons). Ask them to produce a diagram with labels or captions. Then, have each group explain the diagram orally to the class. Encourage accuracy and use of technical terms.

Lesson 9. Expanding Noun Groups by Using Pre-Nominal Modifiers (Grades K–8) and Post-Nominal Modifiers (Grades 4–8)

After teaching technical adjectives, there is need to teach additional adjectives and other modifiers that help describe accurately what the explanation is about. By the time they do an explanation unit, students would have had lessons on modifiers for other genres. Therefore, the focus is on the function of modifiers for explanations, that is, to provide accurate descriptions of the entities explained. Through 3rd grade, it is enough to teach students to use pre-nominal adjectives. From 4th grade on, post-nominal modifiers should be added, not only to give information but also to pack language and make it look more like written language.

> **Goal:** To teach students to identify and understand the function of pre-nominal and post-nominal modifiers used in explanations.
>
> **Materials:** Mentor texts and research resources used in previous lessons and to develop content knowledge; set of questions to elicit adjectives; chart paper or projector.

Activities

- Project and read aloud a chunk of one of the texts.
- Ask students help you find the nouns (bold), and then ask questions to help identify adjectives (3rd grade and up) and other types of modifiers (4th grade and up) and start a noun group anchor chart with the different types. For example, show the following chunk and ask, What kind of paper? What kind of fibers? Which fibers? How do the fibers become?

  - *Recycled* **paper** is made from *used* **paper**. **Paper** is made of *tiny* **fibers**. Because *these* **fibers** eventually become *weak*, **paper** cannot be recycled forever.

- In the following example, circle or highlight *branch* and *power* (in bold).

  - The Constitution gives each **branch** *of government* the **power** *to "check" (stop) certain actions of the other branches*. It also balances *each branch's* **powers** *with the* **powers** *of the other branches*.

- Ask the students the following questions, and as they answer, underline or highlight,

  - What else do you learn about branch? (of government)
  - What else do you learn about power? (to "check" or *stop* certain actions of the other branches; each branch's; of the other branches)

With this chunk, ask the students, What kind of machine? What kind of screen? (answers in italics).

> The pulp is fed into a **machine** *that spits out the pulp* onto a *flat moving* **screen** *where it forms sheets*.

- Discuss with the students how much more information they get from the use of modifiers. You could also have them draw a picture of the machine and the screen.
- With the whole class, go over the diagram they created during Lesson 8 and see if it would be effective to add modifiers.
- Have them do the same with those they created in groups.

Follow Up

- Joint revision of class draft project if needed.
- Joint and individual revision of students' drafts if they have produced these.

To teach children how to add definitions by using appositions, Liz Harris (Harris, 2011) included a box at the bottom of the Explanation graphic organizer where students wrote key terms and their definition. Then, she had students choose a couple of terms in their explanations that they thought should be defined. Using the definitions from their graphic organizers, the students added the definitions in their explanations without the relational verbs, i.e., as appositions. For example, one student wrote "A tornado forms by a thunder storm [,] called a super cell" (p. 235).

Lesson 10. Nominalizations

There is a lesson on nominalization in Chapter 4, Lesson 10.7 that can easily be adapted to explanations, using examples from science and social studies explanations. For example,

> **Adaptation** is all about survival. When the environment changes dramatically, some animals die, others move to another location, and some develop **adaptations** over generations that help them survive.
>
> (www.generationgenius.com/animal-and-plant-adaptations-video-lesson-for-kids/)

and from the systems explanation mentor text,

> [f]ederal judges are appointed by the president with the **approval** of the Senate.

Lesson 11. Joint and Group/Individual Construction of the Stages

As discussed earlier, until the students become more able to handle the content and processes of explanations, it is best to highly scaffold the writing of explanations. The activities will be illustrated through a series of levels, diminishing the scaffolding. Teachers choose at which level they want to start and how far they want to move with their class. The specific information for the content of the explanation should be the one developed in Lesson 8.

Goal: To jointly write an explanation with students, followed by students individually or in groups producing their own explanations.

Materials: Graphic organizer and diagram developed in Lesson 8. Sentence strips (in hard copy or using a software program such as Jamboard) with the identifying statement or statement of the phenomenon and the chunks of the explanation sequence or categories, and a conclusion when needed. These should include the amount of language appropriate for the level of scaffolding. Projector.

Activities

Level 1

- Display the graphic organizer and diagram they developed in Lesson 8.
- Read aloud and display the sentence strips.
- Have students working in groups decide which is the statement of the phenomenon and which should be the order of the rest of the strips.
- Ask a group for the statement of the phenomenon.
- As you move it up to the top position, ask the class to give their opinion as to whether it is right or not.
- Ask another group to share which sentence they placed after. Move it to second position, and check what the rest of the class thinks.
- Continue until the whole explanation is put together.
- Read the whole explanation. Discuss whether it is clear and how it compares with the diagram.

Level 2

- Read aloud sentence strips that include the introduction of the explanation and half of the steps in the sequence or categories.
- Have the class match those strips with the diagram to determine what is already written and what needs to be written.
- Jointly construct the sentences missing with the whole class.
- Read the whole explanation together.

Level 3

- Jointly construct with the whole class the whole explanation, using the graphic organizer and diagram as a guide.

Level 4

- Jointly construct the introduction and a few sentences.
- Have students working in groups create the other sentences.

Levels 1–4

- At the end of the last level or levels you choose to do,

    a) Do a joint revision of the whole piece, making edits as necessary, including issues of audience and voice recommended in Lesson 17.
    b) Ask students to write their version of the whole class explanation, imitating what was done and designing their own diagram. It is fine if they copy the sentences from the work done together because you want them to be accurate in what they write.

Level 5

- Have students write their own individual/group explanation based on the individual/group plans and diagram created in Lesson 8.

Lesson 12. Generalized Participants

This lesson is appropriate to do after the students start drafting explanations on their own. When doing joint construction activities, the teacher mentions the need and reason for using generalized participants.

Goal: To help students understand the reason for using generalized participants and revise their writing accordingly.

Materials: A sentence or two from an explanation text written on chart paper and the equivalent sentence as if it were a procedural recount, which is what students were doing in their explanations. For example,

- "*Wires* conduct electricity from the battery to the bulb and back to the battery." (explanation)
- "Once *one wire* was connected to the bulb and the positive side of the battery and *the other* to the negative side of the battery, the light bulb lit up because *the wires* conducted the electricity through the circuit." (student work)

Activities

- Show the two sentences. Point at the participants in the texts and ask the students what the difference is between the term *wire* in the two texts. The explanation uses the term *wire* in general, while the procedural recount talks about the specific wires used for the experiment.
- Ask the students what the sentence about wires is about. Point out the grammatical features that indicate that one sentence is generalized and the other specific (such as use of plural form and not using "the" the first time the participant is referred to).
- Choose a few student sentences, point to the participants, and discuss whether they refer to the objects in general or to particular ones. Make modifications if necessary.
- Have students work with a partner or in groups to modify the participants, if needed.
- Help groups with their work, as needed.

Lesson 13. Relational Verbs Defining and Describing (Grades 5–8)

Goal: To have students understand that the verb *to be* either describes attributes or defines.

Materials: Examples of sentences with the two functions as shown.

Activities

- Give the class a few examples of sentences with both functions of the verb *to be*. For example,

  - The circle is small.
  - A circle is a shape consisting of all points in a plane that are at a given distance from a given point, the center.
  - The volcano is dormant.
  - A volcano is a mountain or hill, typically conical, having a crater or vent through which lava, rock fragments, hot vapor, and gas are being or have been erupted from the earth's crust.

- • The Supreme Court is politicized.
- • The Supreme Court is the highest federal court in the U.S.

- • Discuss the differences.
- • Divide the class in groups. Have each group think of a pair of sentences with the same subject and the two functions. They can use objects in the class or something they have recently learned.
- • Ask one group to share one sentence. For example, "A sweater is a knitted garment typically with long sleeves, worn over the upper body," or "Snow is white."
- • The class then has to come with the parallel sentence with the other function of the verb to be, i.e., "The sweater is red;" "Snow is ice crystals (frozen liquid water) that falls from a cloud."

Lesson 14. Joint Revision of the Body of the Explanation

This lesson is applicable only to the work of students who wrote individual/group explanations (Lesson 11, Level 5).

Goal: To learn to revise paragraphs based on what was taught to the particular grade level.
Materials: Samples of student work.

Activities

- • Choose one or two students to share their pieces with the whole class. It is best to choose students who can use the extra help.
- • Read it aloud or have the author read it aloud in chunks.
- • Focus on a couple of specific aspects that were taught during the unit that seem challenging to most students. Have students help each other check on the same feature in their writing.
- • Choose the writing of another student, focusing on another general challenge, and repeat the process.
- • Have students work on their explanations while you conference with individuals.

Lesson 15. Clause Complexes

Students attempt to use clause complex structures as their thinking becomes more complex. It is best to teach clause complexes in connection to students' own work. Because the formation of these structures is connected with expressing themselves accurately, some of these issues might have been already addressed when revising the graphic organizers for accuracy of content. If there are more issues remaining, it is best to review the students' work and decide which of the following lessons are needed. In Table 7.6 there are examples of clause complexes from the two mentor texts that can be used in the ensuing lessons.

Lesson 15.1. Create Clause Complexes (Grades 4–8)

Goals: To match clauses that form a clause complex (a combination of clauses) to make sense.
Materials: Clause complexes written in sentence strips and cut up to divide each clause. Include sentences that describe everyday topics as well as sentences from the texts on the topic that students are studying. Have one large set of sentences to work with the whole class and then smaller sets for the students to work on in their groups. Or use a computer with a program that allows movement of chunks and project it to share with the class.

Choose sentences from the explanations that will help to reinforce concepts. Sample sentences could include the following:

When I am late,	my mother gets angry.
When the circuit is closed,	electricity flows through the filament.

Sentence starters that include the first clause in the clause complex and a conjunction that begins the second clause (e.g., "Congress proposed a bill and . . ."). Worksheet with similar types of sentence starters from concepts addressed in the explanation unit.

Activities

- Display all of the first clauses from the sentences, and have the class read them aloud.
- Show one of the second clauses, and ask the students which clause it matches with to form a sentence. Once students choose a first clause to match, have them read the whole sentence and explain its meaning.
- Give students the packets with small sentence strips.
- Have students work in their groups to match the sentences.
- Show students one of the sentence starters that ends in a conjunction (e.g., "Congress proposed a bill and . . .").
- Have students complete the sentence.
- Then, change the conjunction (e.g., "but") and have students complete the sentence again. Do the same activity with other sentence starters to work with the whole class.
- Give each group one worksheet with sentence starters and ask them to complete it.
- Have one group share their responses from the worksheet.

Lesson 15.2. Pack Simple Sentences Into Clause Complexes

Goal: To help students create sentences that combine ideas using clause complexes in order to show relationships between the ideas and to pack the writing.

Materials: Students' drafts with simple sentences underlined that could be turned into a clause complex.

Activities

- Show one of the student examples to the class. For example,

  a) The House standing committee approves the bill. The committee reports it to the House floor.

  b) The sharp edges and corners of rocks wear away. This happens because the rocks are hit by windblown sand. This is called abrasion.

  Brainstorm how the ideas could be combined, expressing the relationships. For example,

  a) After the House standing committee approves the bill, it is reported to the House floor.

  b) Abrasion happens when windblown sand hits the rocks.

- Show another student example. Have the students propose a combination.
- Repeat with another example.
- Have the students work in groups to practice with other drafts.

Lesson 15.3. Revise Students' Sentences

Goal: To help students express complex ideas clearly using clause complexes. (This activity can help review difficult concepts that students are having a hard time expressing.)

Materials: Students' drafts with a few problem sentences underlined. For example, in Denise's piece I would recommend choosing, *[Once] the wire is conectied [connected] to the end's of ether [either] the positive or negative, the wire must be atached [attached] to the tip of the Receiver A.K.A lite bolb.* The explanation for how electricity flows through the circuit would read something like, "Electricity flows from the battery to the receiver or light bulb and back to the battery through the wires connected to the positive and negative side of the battery." Her sentence currently reads more like a procedure describing how to create a circuit (use of the temporal clause "once . . ." + clause signaling the next step).

Activities

- Show one of the student examples to the class. Demonstrate how you would revise the clause.
- Show another student example. Have the students propose revisions.
- Repeat with another example.
- Have the students work in groups revising the sentences you have underlined in the rest of the drafts. If the problem is individual or with just a few students, skip the whole-class lesson and confer with those students.

Lesson 15.4. Overuse of "And"

Goal: To teach students to eliminate unnecessary use of *and* or to replace it with conjunctions that express the relationship between words or ideas more accurately.

Materials: Projector. Student drafts with excessive or inappropriate use of *and*. For example, this string from the uncoached piece shown earlier could be used:

We have two bread. and one is dry and the other is wet.
and the bread stayed for 5 day and then it grew mold in a plastic bag.

Activities

- Ask students to circle all the "ands" in their drafts.
- Choose one or two drafts to work on with the whole class.
- Project the text and ask the students how "and" affects the meaning that connects the two clauses. Discuss possible modifications with the class.
- Repeat with other sentences.
- Have the students work in groups to examine the rest of their drafts.
- Walk around to help students and to ensure that they do not eliminate all "ands," as some may be appropriately used.

Lesson 16. Introduction Given the Type of Explanation

For grades K–3, it is better just to give them the introduction appropriate for the type of explanation. For the other grades, it is best to develop it together given the difficulty students usually have abstracting the information to develop the introduction.

Goal: To teach students how to write the introduction given the type of explanation of the unit (see Table 7.5 for various introduction types).

Materials: Graphic organizers with the explanation sequence produced from previous lessons.

Activities

- Show the graphic organizer produced during Lesson 5 as a result of the deconstruction of the mentor text(s) with the introduction blank.
- Ask the students for the phenomenon, the focus and historical background, the outcome, effect, and so on, depending on the type of explanation. For example, in the case of each of this chapter's mentor texts, you would ask students what phenomenon the sequence explains in *How Paper Is Recycled*, that is, "recycled paper is made of used paper." And in the mentor text *Limiting Power: Checks and Balances*, you would ask what system is being addressed and what historical background the explanation gives (see earlier analysis of this mentor text for the answers).
- Write the introduction at the very top of the graphic organizer, editing as needed and comparing with the original.
- Ask groups which explanation they worked on during Lessons 8 and 11, showing the graphic organizer and/or the written explanation produced during those lessons.
- Have them orally propose the introduction.
- Discuss if the statement needs revisions.
- Have students write the final version at the top of their graphic organizers from the joint construction in the designated space they have in their notebooks.

For Students Who Wrote Individual/Group Explanations

- Share the graphic organizer with one of the explanations produced by an individual or group.
- Have them tell the class about their explanation, supported by the graphic organizer and a diagram.
- Have the author(s), with the support of the class, propose an introduction.
- Repeat with another, especially if you feel another student or group would need extra help.
- Then have the rest work on their own, writing it on their graphic organizer. Check what they produced through sharing and/or conferencing.

Lesson 17. Audience and Voice (Tenor)

In the jointly constructed pieces, these issues should be addressed at the end of the process of joint construction or even during it. The lesson proposed here is for individually or group-created explanations.

> **Goal:** To help students revise their work to achieve an appropriate tenor.
> **Materials:** Student work that includes tenor issues that you want to address in this lesson. Mentor texts that exemplify good models of tenor with similar context of situation as the students' writing.

Activities

The following are typical issues in students' writing that impact the tenor:

- Use of technical terms instead of everyday language.
- Level of complexity depending on the audience.
- Use of declarative sentences (some questions may be appropriate when writing for a younger audience).
- Use of third person.
- Avoidance of interpersonal themes, such as *I think, I learned.*
- Avoidance of judgment.

Choose the particular tenor issue that you want to address and do the following:

- Read mentor texts and discuss the specific issue in that text.
- Show a sample of student work, and ask the class what they notice with respect to the particular tenor issue.
- Ask students to propose revisions.
- Repeat with another sample student text.
- Have students work in groups to revise their texts for the same feature.

Lesson 18. Write Full Explanations (for Individually or Group-Produced Explanations)

Goal: To add the introduction and fully develop/edit written explanations using scientific language that clearly expresses the ideas.

Materials: Individual/group-completed graphic organizers with explanation sequence, diagrams or images, and drafts of the body of the text produced during Lesson 11, with any modifications resulting from language lessons.

Activities

- Have students start their final versions by writing the edited introduction they have in their graphic organizers.
- Ask them to follow it with a clean version of the rest of the text as developed in Lesson 11 and edited since.
- Ask them to insert the diagram or images where they see fit.
- Have selected students share with their group and beyond as planned at the beginning of the unit.

Conditional Explanation Mentor Text

6th Grade Science
Coached Student Work

Precipitation

Precipitation refers to any form of water that falls from the atmosphere to the earth's surface. The type of precipitation that falls depends on temperature. Water in the atmosphere cools and condenses to form clouds, collections of tiny water droplets and ice crystals. Precipitation falls when clouds are too big or too heavy.

If it's above 0 degrees Celsius beneath the clouds, then ice crystals melt and water droplets fall as rain, drizzle, or glaze. Rain, mid-size water droplets, form at moderate temperatures. A drizzle, tiny water droplets, form at very warm temperatures. A glaze, also called freezing rain, falls as liquid water but freezes when it hits ground that is below 0 degrees Celsius.

If the temperature directly beneath the clouds is below 0° Celsius, then crystals of ice combine to form snowflakes. If the temperature of the ground is cold, then the snow is dry. And if the ground is above 0°Celcius then the snow is wet.

References

Brisk, M. E. (2021). *Language in writing instruction: Enhancing literacy in grades 3–8*. New York: Routledge.

Brisk, M. E., & DeRosa, M. (2014). Grades four through eighth students attempts at making meaning through complex sentence structures. In L. De Oliveira & J. Iddings (Eds.), *Genre pedagogy across the curriculum*. London: Equinox.

Brisk, M. E., & Zhang-Wu, Q. (2017). Academic language in K-12 contexts. In E. Hinkel (Ed.), *Handbook of research in second language teaching and learning* (3rd ed., pp. 82–100). New York: Routledge.

Christie, F., & Derewianka, B. (2008). *School discourse: Learning to write across the years of schooling*. London: Continuum.

Coffin, C. (2006). *Historical discourse: The language of time, cause and evaluation*. New York: Continuum.

Derewianka, B., & Jones, P. (2016). *Teaching language in context* (2nd ed.). Melbourne: Oxford University Press.

Harris, E. (2011). *Portraits of writing instruction: Using systemic functional linguistics to inform teaching of bilingual and monolingual elementary students* (Unpublished doctoral dissertation). Boston College, Chestnut Hill, MA.

Hodgson-Drysdale, T., & Ballard, E. (2011). Explaining electrical circuits: A unit structured around inquiry activities teaches students to share results through written explanations. *Science and Children, 48*(8), 37–41.

Hodgson-Drysdale, T., & Rosa, H. (2015, February). Go with the flow: Fifth grade students write about the flow of energy and matter through an ecosystem. *Science and Children*, 32–37.

Humphrey, S., Droga, L., & Feez, S. (2012). *Grammar and meaning*. Newtown, NSW, Australia: Primary English Teaching Association Australia.

Humphrey, S., & Vale, E. (2020). *Investigating model texts for learning*. Sydney: PETAA.

Knapp, P., & Watkins, M. (2005). *Genre, text, grammar: Technologies for teaching and assessing writing*. Sydney: University of South Wales Press.

Martin, J. R., & Rose, D. (2008). *Genre relations: Mapping culture*. London: Equinox.

National Center on Education and the Economy. (2004). *Assessment for learning: Using rubrics to improve student writing*. Pittsburg, PA: The University of Pittsburg.

Stead, T. (2002). *Is that a fact? Teaching nonfiction writing K-3*. Portland, ME: Stenhouse.

Veel, R. (2000). Learning how to mean—Scientifically speaking: Apprenticeship into scientific discourse in the secondary school. In F. Christie & J. R. Martin (Eds.), *Genre and institutions: Social processes in the workplace and school* (pp. 161–195). London: Cassell.

Chapter 8

Arguments

SFL researchers consider argument an umbrella term for a cluster of different types of writing that have as the purpose to persuade (see Table 8.1). The types include: exposition (hortatory and analytic), discussion, and challenge (Coffin, 2006; Derewianka & Jones, 2016; Humphrey, 2017; Rose & Martin, 2012). This chapter covers one-sided arguments, appropriate for the elementary level, and one-sided arguments with rebuttal, as well as two-sided arguments, known also as discussion, which can be attempted at the middle school level. The term *argument* instead of *exposition*, commonly used in SFL literature, is used because the term *exposition* is often confused with expository writing, traditionally considered a form of composition that includes arguments, narratives, and descriptions (Harris & Hodges, 1995). The CCSS uses the word *opinion* to refer to this genre in the early grades. However, research on writing consistently refers to the genre as

Table 8.1 Types of Arguments

Name	Purpose	Examples
One-sided argument to do something	To persuade to do something	The school should provide lockers for all students. Families should go to the Dominican Republic for vacations. Whales should be protected.
One-sided argument to do with rebuttal	To persuade to do something	For all the earlier examples, the counter opinion is briefly stated.
One-sided argument about something	To persuade about something	Zoos are good places for wild animals. Zoos are not good places for wild animals. Chocolate milk is not a healthy drink
One-sided argument about something with rebuttal	To persuade about something	For all the earlier examples, the counter opinion is briefly stated.
Two-sided argument	To present more than one side of an issue and conclude in favor of one	Zoos are good places for wild animals./ Wild animals should not live in zoos but in the wild. Video games waste children's time./ Video games are educational for children.
Challenge	To rebut a position on an issue	The government has taken X position with regard to global warming. X position is a bad idea.

DOI: 10.4324/9781003329275-8

Table 8.2 Oral Arguments and Games to Practice Argumentation

Oral Arguments

1. Learning to Give Reasons to Support a Thesis Statement or Appeal (Grades K–2)
2. Learning to Give Reasons to Support a Thesis Statement or Appeal (Grades 3–8)
3. Taking a Stand in Relation to a Reading (Grades 4–8)
4. Putting an Argument Puzzle Together (Grades 4–8)
5. Role Playing Arguments (Grades 3–8)
6. Short Public Speech or Announcement (Grades 6–8)
7. Short Oral Debates (Grades 6–8)

argument (Bunch et al., 2014; Ferretti & Lewis, 2013) and never uses the word *opinion*. The definition of opinion does not include the concept of persuasion. Therefore, it is strongly recommended to refer to this genre as *argument* no matter which grade. Another difference in naming is reasons and evidence, which are called *argument* by some researchers (Derewianka & Jones, 2016; Humphrey & Vale, 2020). In this book, the terms *reasons* and *evidence* will be used to avoid confusion with the name of the genre.

An argument unit can take up to six weeks, depending on the number of projects. It is good to start the unit with oral activities before teaching to write arguments. Oral dialogue "is essential for the development of reflective argumentative writing" (Ferretti & Lewis, 2013, p. 114). Young learners continue practicing orally throughout the unit. Children are skillful in arguing orally, but written arguments are very difficult. In the United States, argumentation was not taught until middle and high school, but currently the standards demand them at a much earlier age. Written arguments can be in the form of PowerPoints, brochures, posters, letters, and essays. Essays are the hardest and should not be attempted until upper elementary grades.

Oral Arguments and Games (Grades K–8)

Table 8.2 lists lessons covering oral arguments and games included in the chapter. These activities help practice argumentation without having to write them. These are a good way to start a unit for any age. Young students could continue to do this as they start lessons on books with dilemmas (Lesson 9).

A good first activity is to take a stand, where students only need to give reasons to a given thesis statement. Other activities include choosing different reasons for given audiences, taking a stand in relation to a reading, an argument puzzle, role-playing arguments, and debates.

Lesson 1. Learning to Give Reasons to Support a Thesis Statement or Appeal (K–2)

> **Goal:** To learn to give reasons to persuade about something given a thesis statement and an audience.
> **Materials:** Chart paper.

Activities

* Write a thesis statement on chart paper with two columns below, one titled *Agree*, the other *Disagree*.

- As students come in at the beginning of the day, have them sign their name under either *Agree* or *Disagree* depending on their opinion toward the thesis.
- Call the name of a few students on each side to provide a reason for their selected opinion.
- Do this activity daily or weekly for a period of time. Have a different thesis statement each time, and have different students give reasons for their stance.
- You may choose to write the reasons given by the students at the bottom of the columns (Stead, 2002).

Example:
Thesis: X book is better than Y book.

AGREE	DISAGREE
Why?	Why?

Lesson 2. Learning to Give Reasons to Support a Thesis Statement or Appeal (Grades 3–8)

Goal: To learn to give reasons to persuade about something or to do something given a thesis statement/appeal and an audience.

Materials: Chart paper.

- Suggest a thesis statement/appeal for the students to consider (e.g., *longer breaks are good for students*; *Give students longer breaks*).
- Put the following signs around the room: "strongly agree," "agree," "disagree," and "strongly disagree" (see Figure 8.1).
- Have students stand by the sign that matches most closely to their belief, forming a group at each sign. Let students confer.
- Have them share the reasons why they took that position.

Thesis statements/appeals can be chosen from topics from a content area that students are studying or from a book or article that they are reading. For example, if students are studying about the American Revolution, the thesis could be "American revolutionary forces achieved independence from the British swiftly and easily." While studying the colonies, students wrote letters to Europeans appealing them to come to the colonies: "Come settle in the colonies." Students would demonstrate knowledge of content by the reasons they give.

Lesson 3. Taking a Stand in Relation to a Reading (Grades 4–8)

Goal: To learn to take a position in relation to the content of a reading.

Materials: Anticipation guide prepared in relation to a reading. For example, Peggy, a 4th-grade bilingual teacher, passed out the following anticipation guide in Spanish to her students prior to reading *La Moneda de Oro* by Alma Flor Ada.

Take a Stand Game

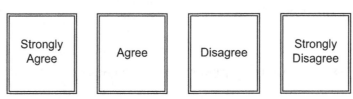

Figure 8.1 Charts for take a stand game.

Anticipation Guide

	Me	My Partner and I	Author
1. To be rich means having a lot of money.	Yes ____ No ____	Yes ____ No ____	Yes ____ No ____
2. People who do bad things can't change.	Yes ____ No ____	Yes ____ No ____	Yes ____ No ____
3. It is important to have a lot of money.	Yes ____ No ____	Yes ____ No ____	Yes ____ No ____

(Brisk & Harrington, 2007, p. 124)

Activities

- Have students take a position on the statements related to a reading that you prepared. The statements should reflect important themes inferred from the reading.
- Have students fill in the "Me" column based on their beliefs.
- Working with a partner, have students explain why they checked *yes* or *no*.
- Have students come to a consensus and fill the second column.
- After reading the selection, have them fill out the "Author" column.

This strategy should be done in connection to the reading curriculum. It helps students practice taking a stand and activates their background knowledge to support reading comprehension (see full description of the strategy in Brisk & Harrington, 2007).

Lesson 4. Putting an Argument Puzzle Together (Grades 4–8)

This is a good lesson to do early in the unit to get students to manipulate the stages of the genre without having to write.

> **Goal:** To learn the stages of an argument with sensitivity to audience so that students understand that the reason and evidence choice vary with audience.
> **Materials:** These materials can be prepared in hard copy or by using an App, such as Jamboard, which would be much easier to create.

Prepare the pieces of the puzzles, which consist of:

- Four arguments, broken up into separate cards or notes if using Jamboard, each with an audience, thesis (1 and 2) or appeal (3 and 4), each reason followed by each evidence and four reinforcement of statement, as follows:

Argument 1

Argument 2

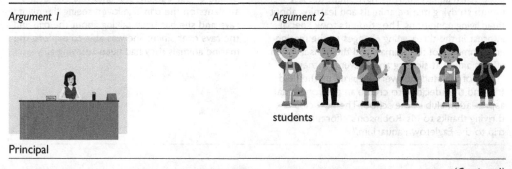

Principal

students

(Continued)

Argument 1	*Argument 2*

Students need lockers.

Students carry heavy textbooks around all day, which can be physically strenuous. Access to lockers will prevent stress.

"The incidence of back pain in early adolescence approaches that seen in adults. This study identifies 2 factors associated with self-reported back pain in early adolescents that are amenable to change: availability of school lockers and lighter backpacks" ("Back pain and backpacks in school children," www.ncbi.nlm.nih.gov/pubmed/16670549).

Students can secure their valuable items in personal lockers to prevent theft in the school.

Since the beginning of the school year, there have been three thefts of personal belongings in students' backpacks in the school.

Having lockers will solve current problems.

Students need lockers.

Lockers provide a space for students to leave all of their things (textbooks, jackets, lunches, athletic equipment) throughout the day. Students do not have to lug as many things around.

There have been a lot of complaints from students about carrying all that weight.

It is fun to decorate the inside of the locker. Locker decorations allow students to express themselves and create a personal space in the school.

At my sister's school, students have lockers and they love to be able to decorate them.

Having lockers will make students happy.

Argument 3	*Argument 4*

students

Principal

Students should take a field trip to the aquarium.

A visit to the aquarium can inspire students to take interest in marine animal care and conservations efforts.

Story from *The Eagletown Times*: "Last Thursday, Ms. Emma Robinson's 3rd-grade class visited the Eagle-town aquarium. They have spent the last month studying marine animals and learning about their living conditions. The students took special interest in the threatening changes to the marine environments of the animals and the conservation efforts aimed at slowing and preventing them. "Many of the students were inspired by the field trip, and they decided to create an environmental appreciation club at the school. The new club is thriving thanks to Ms. Robinson's efforts and the trip to the Eagletown aquarium."

Students should take a field trip to the aquarium.

Students can see the different marine animals they have been learning about in class up close.

There was a similar field trip planned and executed a few years ago, and the older sister of one of our current students was one of the students on the trip. She loved seeing the manta rays, and she has been talking about the trip and the rays ever since! She was able to explore the marine animals they had been studying all year.

Argument 3	Argument 4
Students need "real-world" exposure to the topics they are studying in class. A visit to the aquarium will provide them with this real-world experience, and they will bring that knowledge back to the classroom.	Students can spend the day exploring outside of the classroom and have fun.
"Field trips provide students with a window to the real world that they don't get in the classroom, and they can help students understand real-world applications of seemingly abstract topics in math and science,' she [teacher] says. For example, engineers may often use formulas taught in Algebra II, calculus, and chemistry classes" ("Teachers, Don't Overlook Value of Field Trips." www.usnews.com/education/blogs/high-school-notes/2011/12/12/teachers-dont-overlook-value-of-field-trips).	Last year, we made two field trips and they were a lot of fun because we were able to observe our favorite marine animals that we had been learning about! We saw penguins interact with each other, and we watched the aquarium workers feed the sharks. Their teeth were huge, and we were able to buy real shark teeth to bring back to the classroom from the gift shop. We loved seeing everything up close, as we were only separated from the animals by a thin layer of glass.
Field trips fulfil important educational functions.	Field trips are great.

Depending on the class needs, these cards may or may not have the labels "reason" and "evidence," or the different stages may be color coded. Without the labels, it could be good practice to have the students figure out the difference between reasons and evidence.

This activity can be done as a large version to work with the whole class, or as a small version to work with each group. Laminating the pieces and putting a fabric hook-and-loop fastener on them can allow the teacher and students to move the pieces around and put them in place, while holding up other pieces to view. If using Jamboard, it can also be done as a whole class, where the teacher projects the computer, or students could work in groups, with each group having a computer or using breakout rooms if using a video conference system.

Activities

- Play the game with the whole class or in small groups.
- For the whole-class version, display the appeal/thesis statements and the audience icons.
- Divide the class into a few small groups, and give each group an equal amount of reasons and evidence cards or notes.
- If the cards are not labeled or in different colors, then have the students first sort the cards into reasons and evidence. If the cards are labeled or colored, skip this step.
- Have the students choose the two reasons that would go with their particular thesis statement/appeal and audience. Have the students post the cards in order of significance, leaving space to place the evidence under each reason.
- Have students choose the evidence cards that seem best suited to support each of the reasons given the audience. Have students place the chosen evidence under each reason.
- Read the final product and discuss whether the placement of the reasons and evidence are accurate. Make any changes if necessary.
- Alternatives:
  - Start with a thesis statement/appeal and the reasons, and ask the students to choose the audience and the evidence.
  - Start with thesis and evidence and have the students choose reasons.
  - For the small-group version, have each group do the same activities in their groups and then share the results with the class.

- Since they have had experience at this point, you may, for example, leave one of the reasons blank and as a whole class or in groups have them brainstorm what they could write as a reason given the evidence and the audience.

Lesson 5. Role Playing Arguments (Grades 3–8)

This lesson is adapted from Wagner (1999).

> **Goal:** To have students practice oral argumentation in specific contexts.
> **Materials:** None needed.

Activities

- Explain the task and facilitate an initial discussion to provide background information for a selected context and inspire students to think about different perspectives.
- Give pairs of students different roles. For example, one student could act as a student, while the other could act as the principal.
- Give students a thesis statement (e.g., *students need lockers*; *students need longer breaks*; *students need sweet snacks*) or appeal (*Save endangered species*; *Add monitors to school buses*).
- Have students act in character and engage in a dialogue with their partner, giving reasons for their stance and disputing the reasons their partner offers.
- Have students switch roles, and then give them another thesis statement/appeal.
- Have students reflect (or journal) about their role-playing experience and what it was like to argue from different perspectives.

Lesson 6. Short Public Speech or Announcement (Grades 6–8)

This is a short informal practice lesson appropriate for middle school students to introduce them to arguments to do something. A public speech can also be a medium for a fully developed and longer argument done carrying out the lessons developed for written arguments. A well-constructed speech is always written and revised following the same process as a written argument.

> **Goal:** To learn how to prepare a call to action argument to be given orally.
> **Materials:** Chart with stages of an argument to do something; video or transcript examples of call to action speeches, for example, Leonardo di Caprio's appeal to the United Nations on Climate Change. www.youtube.com/watch?v=ka6_3TJcCkA

Activities

- View one video with the class.
- Review the stages of this type of argument on the left column.
- View the video again, stopping to insert notes in the right column as appropriate by asking students their suggestions.

Stages	Notes From Example
Introduction Background Thesis/Appeal	
Reasons and Evidence	
Reinforce Call to Action (in general) (Optional: add specific suggestions)	

- Working in groups, have each group view an additional video and notice additional features or ways of implementing the stages. Have them share.
- Brainstorm topics that they have been studying or reading about as the basis to create a short speech or public announcement. List them.
- Divide the class into groups, and ask each group to choose a topic.
- Using the same organizer as earlier, have them plan and draft their short speech. They can check resources they have used when working on those topics.
- Conference with the groups.
- Have them create a short video where a member of the group does the presentation (maximum 3.5 minutes).
- Have them share with the class, followed by a discussion on the good features and any changes that would make the appeal more powerful.

Lesson 7. Short Oral Debates (Grades 6–8)

This lesson is an informal short lesson to introduce students to oral debates. To create a fully developed debate activity, they would have to create it in writing following the lessons for two-sided arguments and prepare all the materials in writing before carrying out the debate. Fully developed oral debates are similar to two-sided written arguments. However, instead of one author writing both sides, there are two people or teams involved, and each side takes one of the positions, giving the reasons and evidence that supports their side.

> **Goal:** To learn how to support a point of view against an opponent.
> **Materials:** Graphic organizer with the stages of a debate; videos illustrating debates. Choose short videos, or chunk longer videos. For example, this is a video of two 5th graders debating about food: www.youtube.com/watch?v=aGxOS2RdVBc

Activities

- View one or two videos. Discuss what and how opponents presented their point of view.
- As in Lesson 6, review stages looking at the graphic organizer and, while viewing one of the videos in chunks, make notes.

Stages	Notes From Position A	Notes From Position B
Introduction Background Thesis/Appeal		
Reasons and Evidence		

- State a controversial topic related to what students are studying or to a current issue in the school.
- Have the students think of the two opposing views, giving a thesis statement/appeal for each view.
- Divide the class in two groups, and give each group one of the thesis statements/appeal for them to defend.
- Have each group think of a minimum of three reasons supported by evidence. Everyone in the group should take notes.
- Have each group choose as many group representatives as reasons they have.
- Have the representatives of each group sit facing each other; the rest of the members of each group can stand behind in case their representatives need support.

- Have the first student state the background and thesis statement/appeal the group is defending and state the first reason supported by evidence, followed by a member of the other group refuting and giving their reason.
- Have a different student from the second group give an additional reason, followed by a member of the first group disagreeing and given their reason.
- Follow the same way until all the reasons and evidence have been stated.
- Tell students that if they feel the other side convinced them of their position, they can move over to the other side. Discuss why they moved or how convincing reasons and evidence were and why.

Children tend to be more intuitive and better at oral argumentation. Lessons 6 and 7 are meant to awaken those skills. Thus, it is best not to be over critical of their performance, but rather, let them discover the skills needed. Later, in the lessons for written argument, they will learn to perfect reasons, evidence, and the language to make their arguments persuasive.

Development of Units for Written Arguments (Grades 3–8)

To develop units for written arguments, teachers need to consider a number of factors that play a role on what and how to teach and what materials to use. With this in mind, they have to plan lessons. As teachers start the argument units, they can incorporate some of the oral activities or games recommended earlier.

Unit Preparation

To prepare a unit in the chosen argument type, teachers need to consider the following:

- Grade level
- Connection with content areas and everyday life
- Mentor texts
- Research resources
- Audience
- Medium
- Potential projects
- Uncoached writing and planning content of the unit
- Lessons to teach purpose, stages, and language

Grade Level

Persuasive genres are difficult but extremely useful in real life and essential in a democratic society (Ferretti & Lewis, 2013). Children "have an intuitive understanding of the importance of argumentative discourse" (Ferretti & Lewis, 2013, p. 113). However, students have great difficulty finding reasons that support the argument and evidence that gives credence to the reasons offered. Although research claims that elementary school children are not ready for persuasive writing, Anderson (2008) argues that they are. She maintains that a lack of exposure to persuasive writing in school is to blame for limited mastery of the genre. With instruction and peer support, elementary school children can become more effective in their persuasive writing (Wollman-Bonilla, 2004). Moreover, the learning features of arguments engage students in academic writing, which they can apply to other genres (Gebhard et al., 2007).

Children enjoy persuasive writing because it gives them an opportunity to express their opinions. One 5th grader reflected,

> I feel like I like it better because my grades are higher, and persuasive writing is powerful, it can help me get a better education and I can tell people what I think to change their minds.
> (Sánchez Ares, 2012, p. 31)

Gradually introducing different types and aspects of arguments can support students eventually when tackling the hardest types (see Table 8.3).

With students in early grades, it is sufficient just to teach them how to take a stand using oral language and finding reasons from their everyday topics or stories. Some teachers have had students write simple letters at this early age with a claim and a reason or two. Kate, a 2nd-grade teacher, had students add evidence in jointly constructed letters only. By 3rd grade, projects, including creating brochures to attract visitors or writing a class letter to the principal, are doable.

Table 8.3 Argument Instruction Across Grades

Type/Grade	Stages of Arguments	K–2	3	4–8
Using stories that pose dilemmas	Thesis/Appeal	Provided		
	Reasons	√		
	Evidence			
	Reinforcement			
Commonsense arguments	Thesis/appeal	Provided	√	√
	Reasons	√	√	√
	Evidence	2nd grade jointly with teacher	Provided or √	√
	Reinforcement		√	√
Using historical context	Thesis/Appeal			√
	Reasons			√
	Evidence			√
	Reinforcement			√
Science arguments	Thesis/Claim			√
	Reasons			Provided or √
	Evidence			√
	Reinforcement			√
Arguments with rebuttal and two-sided arguments				Grades 6–8
Medium		Oral, Games, Letters	Oral & Written Brochures, Posters	Oral & Written Brochures, Posters, Essays

Key: "Provided": the teacher creates; "√": the students create.

Essays are better to attempt in upper elementary grades and beyond. These students also benefit from the activities recommended for younger learners in preparation to writing argumentative essays. For example, a 4th-grade teacher used a book with a dilemma as the introductory activity for her argument unit where students produced essays.

In the early grades or when initiating students to argumentation through oral activities and games, the teacher should provide the thesis statement/appeal and then ask students to give reasons for the stance. When using literature that poses dilemmas, the teacher should provide the thesis statement/appeal, while expecting the students to find the reasons in the text. As students start to write their own arguments, the teacher should allow the students to develop their own thesis statements/appeals and reasons, and help only with the evidence for common-sense arguments. In scientific arguments and response to literature writing, the teacher action is reversed, with the teacher helping students with the claims and reasons, while the students write the evidence. By 4th grade and beyond, the students are expected to create and progress through all of the stages by themselves. Arguments with rebuttal or two-sided arguments are recommended for middle school.

Another important consideration related to grade level is the various aspects of language authors need when writing an argument. Writers make language choices based on audience and voice, that is, *tenor*. The voice is achieved through grammatical choices (see Table 8.4). Depending on the grade level, some or all of the aspects are targeted for lessons. Others are taught through deconstruction of mentor texts and editing.

Table 8.4 Key Aspects of Language to Teach

Aspect of Language	Grade Level to Teach	Example
Evaluative language	All grades	Iguanas are *cute*. (positive) That is a *ridiculous* idea proposed by the *foolish* children. (negative)
Graduation (a) Turns up or down the intensity of the evaluative language (b) Narrow or widen focus	(a) All grades (b) Middle school	Iguanas are *really* quiet. (up) Cats make *excellent* house pets. (up) I make a *tiny* puncture. (down) Families harvest *only* 40% of the crops (narrow). Athletes receive *some sort* of compensation (widen)
Grammatical person First person (familiar, solidarity, letter writing) 2nd person (familiar, personal) 3rd person (authoritative)	Grades 4–8 For younger students, help edit for consistency	*I* think they are much cuter than hamsters. *We* need more parks in Australia. (solidarity) But since *you* are men of genuine good will … ("Letter from Birmingham Jail," M. L. King, Jr.) *Advocates of year-round schools* cite increased performance.
Type of sentence: • Statements (more authoritative) • Questions (open door for other opinions, less authoritative) • Exclamations (playful, less authoritative or very authoritative)	Grades 4–8 For younger students, help edit for consistency	• Cats are civilized members of the household. • Did you know that iguanas are really quiet? • So please hold still at this juncture, while I make a tiny puncture! • Solve our school heating problem immediately!

Aspect of Language	Grade Level to Teach	Example
Modality (obligation, probability, or possibility) Verbs (high to low)	Grades 4–8	A year-round schedule *might* reduce absences. (low) Children *must* go outside at break times. (high)
Modality (other grammatical forms: adverbials, adjectives, clauses)	Grades 5–8	Plastics *definitely* create an environmental hazard in the oceans.
Engagement (open or close doors for other opinions)	Rhetorical questions, modality, Grades 5–8	Isn't year round schools a great invention? I think schools should operate year round. (open)
	Concession, Grades 6–8	Although school year with long summer vacation has advantages, schools that operate year round are the best. (open–close)
Engagement (introduce others' points of view through the quoting verb)	6–8	The doctor assured me, "He is not sick." (supports the doctor) The doctor claimed, "He is not sick." (creates distance with the doctor's opinion)

Evaluative language and graduation are essential for argument writing, otherwise students' arguments sound too factual. Students enjoy the use of these words, although they can easily overdo it. Pat would have students who added too many read aloud their drafts. They quickly realized they needed to cut down on using such terms as *tremendously* on every sentence. (For detailed coverage and lessons of all aspects of language, see Brisk, 2021.)

Connection With Content Areas and Everyday Life

Arguments are good to teach not only embedded in content areas but also in relation to school and community life as well as current events. Teachers take advantage of things that are happening in the school or community for ideas for arguments. For example, at the Russell school, the principal decided to turn the cafeteria into a gym and have the students have lunch in the classroom. One 4th-grade teacher had students take sides, and they jointly constructed arguments either supporting keeping the cafeteria or switching to a gym. Another time the heating system was not working well in the middle of the winter. Rosemary, another 4th-grade teacher jointly constructed with her class a letter to the superintendent to address the problem.

When arguing within content areas, it is very important to develop the content in order for students to have believable reasons and strong evidence. When planning to write an argument in connection with a scientific experiment, the students should carry out the experiment and discuss the content in anticipation of writing the full persuasive piece. Similarly, in math, it is best to solve the problem that will provide the evidence and discuss the mathematical reasoning before students actually write. In everyday arguments and those based on historical content, students need to research the topic to develop well-supported reasons and evidence. When writing the evidence, students will need technical terms. Thus, as they research the topics, it is important to constantly build the language needed to develop the topic.

Arguments are used in all content areas (see Table 8.5). In ELA, arguments usually relate to students' everyday life (e.g., a group of 3rd graders wrote to their principal requesting lockers).

Table 8.5 Elementary and Middle School Arguments in Various Content Areas

Content Area	Example of Elementary Projects	Example of Middle School Projects
ELA	Kindergarten teacher used the Great Kapok Tree. Students took the side of the animals and found reasons in the book.	Students should/should not wear masks to school.
Social Studies	Students wrote letters to Europeans trying to persuade them to move to the colonies.	Letter to the Montgomery Bus Line to persuade the company to abolish its segregationist policies.
Science	To persuade that human activity is causing climate change.	Persuasive slide presentation to museum donors to continue to fund excavations and exhibits for fossils in natural history museums.
Math	Two dozen eggs at $5 is a better buy than one dozen at $2.75.	Analyze graphs representing public transportation company use, cost, and location, and write a letter to the CEO arguing whether they think the cost of public transportation should be free, lowered, or increased.

With young children it is easiest to use books with dilemmas, that way the reasons are all contained within the book. For example, in the book *Hey, Little Ant*, students can argue on the boy's or the ant's side, finding all the reasons in the story. In science, scientific arguments are at the core of scientific inquiry (Zembal-Saul et al., 2013). For example, 5th graders constructed a scientific argument when they were given a diagram with four houses on different types of terrain and asked to argue which terrain would be the safest place to build a new house. In math classes, students are often asked to make judgments, for example, Is it better to accept a poor paying job or continue to receive unemployment benefits? (Marks & Mousley, 1990). Students solve the problem to obtain the reason and evidence and make a claim. Table 8.5 includes examples of projects for elementary and middle school, several of which were proposed and tested by teachers.

Teachers use historical topics as the content to write arguments. For example, 5th-grade teachers had students write letters as if they were colonials trying to convince Europeans to come to America. These arguments are very different from historical arguments, which argue "the case 'for' or 'against' a particular interpretation of the past and foreground the debatable nature of historical knowledge and explanation" (Coffin, 2006, p. 77). Historical argumentation is probably the most difficult type of persuasive writing and usually not encountered until high school (Christie & Derewianka, 2008; Coffin, 2006).

Reading tests often include questions that require students to look for evidence in a text to support a given claim. For example, a prompt on a standardized test read, "Why does reading to the class make Ida feel both happy and scared at the same time? Support your answer with important details from the chapter" (Massachusetts Comprehensive Assessment System, 2009). This type of writing is considered Response to Literature. Using stories to create arguments is different from doing character analysis or thematic interpretation, which are more appropriate for older students (Christie & Derewianka, 2008).

Mentor Texts

Mentor texts are written in the genre of the unit and are used to show students the features of the genre. Choice of mentor texts depends on the age of students and the chosen medium. For kindergarten and grade 1 students, there is no need for a mentor text written as an argument.

Teachers will guide the students through their writing of short letters as a result of working with texts with dilemmas. For example, a 1st-grade teacher read with the students *Hey, Little Ant*, and together they found reasons for the boy to squish the ant and the ant not to be squished. Students were given a choice, and they all took the point of view of the ant writing letters to the boy asking him not to squish it, choosing reasons from those they had listed.

For elementary students grade 2 and older, fictional narratives where the characters argue work very well. The books are written as fictional narratives, but the letters or dialogues within are arguments. For example, in the book *I Wanna Iguana*, a child writes letters to her mother trying to persuade her to take home his friend's iguana while his friend travels, and the mother responds with counter claims. Because there are characters reacting to the argument, the students also get a sense of the importance of audience in the choice of language. The letters illustrate the use of language to show voice. For example, in *Dear Mrs. LaRue*, the point of view from the dog, who wants to convince his owner that obedience school is awful, is made stronger by the use of high modality, while that of the vet is made weaker by low modals:

> "**I had to** be taken to the vet/Dr. Wilfrey claims that he **can't** find anything wrong with me, but **I am certain** I have an awful disease. **I must** come home at once."

In the book *Can I Keep Him?*, the mother's language, all in statements, is more authoritative than that of the child, who asks many questions.

> " 'Mom, I found this dog sitting all by himself. Can I keep him?'
> 'No, Arnold. Dogs are too noisy. He would bark all the time . . .' "

For upper elementary through middle schools, arguments written as essays, as the one used later to illustrate the stages of the genre, are good additional mentor texts because they show the type of writing students will have to write. The following charts provides suggestions for mentor texts of the various types of essays.

Name	Mentor Text Sample
One-sided argument to do something	Adopting a Pet from the Pound https://k12.thoughtfullearning.com/studentmodels/adopting-pet-pound
One-sided argument about something	Playing games is important for both children and adults www.testmagic.com/test/ViewDtlEssay.asp?EssayID=29&TopicID=60
One-sided argument about something with rebuttal	Malaria: One of the Oldest Diseases (full text at the end of the chapter)
Two-sided argument	College Sports (full text at the end of the chapter)

The magazine *Time for Kids* has texts that claim to be persuasive; however, they are not always clear or well developed. They should be reviewed carefully before being selected as mentor texts.

In addition, if students are writing persuasive brochures and advertisements, they should analyze these types of text to see how they are organized differently from an essay or letter. For suggestions of all these various types of mentor texts, check lists downloadable from the *Support Material* tab in the book's webpage.

Research Resources

As mentioned earlier, for young learners only one book is needed when using books with dilemmas. For students 2nd grade and up who come up with their own claims, research is important in arguments to find reasons and evidence. The Internet, books, and videos are good sources. As the students review these to come up with particular evidence, they should also identify and learn technical terms to express the evidence. In some cases, surveys are appropriate, for example, when getting the opinion of students about a school concern. In science, experiments or research resources provide the evidence, and the students need to know the science to express the reason. For example, in this argument, students need to consult resources to find the evidence (italics), but they had to have studied about animal adaptation to write the reasoning (bold):

> Polar bears can live in the Arctic, because they have adaptations for the environment. *Their webbed paws allow them to swim through the water to catch seals. Their claws also allow them to catch seals. Their fur keeps them warm in the cold environment.* **Adaptations are characteristics that allow an animal to survive in its environment. Getting food and staying warm are both necessary for an animal to live.**
>
> (McNeill & Krajcik, 2012, p. 82)

Similarly, in math, solving a problem shows the evidence, but the reasoning comes from knowledge of math.

Because usually the sources to look for evidence are written as report, students have become confused and ended up writing a report on the topic rather than an argument. For example, a 4th grader, while trying to write a persuasive essay about protecting endangered species, carried out research on a few animals and ended up writing a report on four endangered species.

To avoid this problem, conference with students once they have created their graphic organizer and also while they start to draft.

Audience

Of all the genres, arguments are most impacted by audience. Audience influences writers' decisions on stages and language. For example, the amount of background, the choice of reasons, and the type of evidence all depend on audience. In addition, audience and voice influence language choices. Therefore, before planning reasons and evidence, students must identify the audience for their arguments and discuss why it is important.

Pat is reading *Should There Be Zoos?: A Persuasive Text* by Tony Stead & Judy Ballester that includes a number of arguments written by a 5th-grade class in the Bronx. As he reads, he discusses features of arguments found in the text. After he reads an example where the author compares making kids stay inside to do their homework with keeping animals in cages, Pat asks,

TEACHER: What is he [the author] trying to tell us?
STUDENT: That the animals should have more time outside of their cage.
T: What is Christian [the author] using as an example and who do you think his audience is?
S: The reader.

T: Who is the reader, though? Me? You? Your mom? Who?

S: Everyone.

T: The whole world?

S: No, I think kids in school.

T: You have to know your audience. The way I talked to the football team last night when they weren't doing well is different from how I talk to you. Very different language . . . Depending on audience, you have to use a different example.

Kroll (1984) argues that it is easier for children to adapt their writing to an audience if the audience is a specific person (e.g., *my cousin, Richard*) rather than a category of persons (e.g., *children*). For this reason, letters written to specific people, such as the principal or a parent, are easier for younger students to write than letters sent to the editor of a newspaper with whom they do not have direct connection. The latter are more appropriate from 5th grade up.

Moreover, audience awareness is reflected by clarifying culture-specific topics. In the modern world, children write for people of different cultures within their country and, using social media, across the continents. Their audience may not be familiar with their experiences and content of their writing. Therefore, students may need to be more explicit about what they write.

Medium

Essays are the traditional medium for arguments, but they are also the hardest to write. Argumentative projects also include letters, posters, brochures, public service announcements (PSA), and different forms of advertisements. The specific medium chosen will make producing arguments easier or harder. Thus, 3rd-grade teachers, although they taught purpose, stages, and some elements of language, did not have their students produce individual essays. Fifi, a 3rd-grade SEI teacher, co-constructed with her students a letter to the principal asking for more time at the school library. Students worked in groups to brainstorm reasons and evidence and shared their contributions with the whole class. The teacher then wrote all of their ideas on chart paper. Then, as a class, they chose a few of the reasons and the evidence that best supported those reasons. The students worked in English and Spanish, helping each other with the language to be incorporated in the argument. They explored persuasive language to include in the letter. Michelle, another 3rd-grade teacher, had students do short projects after reading *Can I Keep Him?* such as writing a letter to their mothers asking for a pet. Their big project was to write a three-fold brochure convincing people to visit their state or country of origin. Michelle gave the students a worksheet divided into four squares titled *climate, food/culture, attractions*, and *fun facts*. Students used these worksheets to guide their research and to take notes. She found that initially, without the worksheet, the students were overwhelmed and did not know what information to gather. As a class, they discussed what kind of information would be of interest to people wanting to visit and made recommendations about what to include in the brochure. For example, the class recommended that a Sudanese student omit a sentence listing the various wars that occurred, as that information would not likely persuade someone to visit.

Students in the upper grades can also benefit from attempting different media. For example, Angela, a 5th-grade teacher, carried out an 8-week unit in which students produced a variety of arguments. For science, her students had to invent a machine. Then, the other students in the school voted for their favorite machine. Angela's students wrote advertisements about their science machine inventions and posted them around the school to encourage other students to vote for theirs. Later in the unit, students complained that there was misbehavior on the school buses, and Angela suggested they write a letter to the principal arguing for the need for bus monitors. In addition, students read *The True Story of the Three Little Pigs* and wrote letters to the "judge" supporting either the side of the wolf or of the pigs. To end the unit, the class brainstormed community issues and wrote essays to persuade community members about double parking, trash collection, the pay scale of the local police, and other concerns.

The medium will necessitate consideration of the structure and language. For example, an *essay* includes the traditional stages of title, thesis/appeal, preview of reasons, reasons with evidence, and reinforcement of the position. An *advertisement* includes the stages in short sentences, mixing language and images. Although essays and editorials will be written in the third person, letters can be written in the first and second person, and advertisements will often include use of the second person.

Potential Projects

It is important to consider how authentic students' products will be. Having students produce written artifacts that approximate what they see in real life increases the motivation and care with which they write and, therefore, the quality of their products (Edelsky & Smith, 1984). For example, a teacher had her students create posters on places to visit as part of her argument unit. The teacher asked a local travel agent to exhibit them in their store windows. This authentic task contributed to students' understanding of the language and content choices they needed to make (Stead, 2002).

Table 8.6 shows examples of units planned by teachers of various grade levels.

Table 8.6 Projects From Different Grade Levels

Grade Level	Content Area	Mentor Texts	Projects
K	Science	*The Lorax*	Argument given thesis and a reason: *The Once-ler should not cut the tree because the Lorax living there.*
1	ELA	*Hey, Little Ant*	Daily Take a Stand game. Final Project: Students wrote letters to the boy from the point of view of the ant to spare her life.
2	Science	*I Wanna Iguana* by Karen Kaufman Orloff *One Word From Sophia* by Jim Averbeck *Hey, Little Ant* by Hannah Hoose and Phillip Hoose *Earrings* by Judith Viorst *The Big Bed* by Bunmi Laditan	Within a unit on pollination: Project 1: Students developed a poster to argue the importance of bees to the school community. Project 2: Students made a video message arguing the importance of pollinators to gardeners to persuade them to include plants that attract pollinators in the garden.
3		*I Wanna Iguana*	Letter to parents asking for a pet.
5	Social Studies	*Give Bees a Chance* by Bethany Barton *Dear Mr. Blueberry* by Simon James "Toward a More Perfect Union"—speech by Barack Obama	In the context of a unit on voting rights: Students wrote an essay on whether voting should remain optional in the United States, or become mandatory as it is in Australia and other countries.

Grade Level	Content Area	Mentor Texts	Projects
6	ELA	*Wonder Video:* Principal giving out/explaining the rationale for a student's award (from the movie *Wonder;* starts at 1:00) *Video:* Michael Jordan gets the presidential medal of freedom from President Obama *Video:* Obama Get Out the Vote Video *Video:* Why Oprah Winfrey won a lifetime achievement award	Mock elections for class president of the two main characters in two books they read: *The Lightning Thief* and *Bud, Not Buddy.* Project 1: Group campaign ad (poster, video) for Percy, Bud. Project 2: Individual argumentative speech in character's voice in favor of either character as a candidate for class president.
8	Social Studies	• "Is it time to pass tough gun control laws?" adapted by Newsela staff from *The Tribune* (published by McClatchy). • "Should Congress stop funding sanctuary cities?" by Tribune News Service, adapted by Newsela staff • "Is it time for public schools to put religion back into schools?" by Tribune News Service, adapted by Newsela staff	In the context of a unit on gun control (second amendment): 1. Group debate about the second amendment. 2. Independently write a paper discussing your argument for or against gun control, supported by research.

Uncoached Writing and Planning Content of the Unit

At the beginning of the unit, give students a cold prompt to find out how much the students know about writing arguments. The uncoached piece of writing provides the initial information about the students' familiarity with purpose and stages of the genre and the aspects of language that are still challenging.

> • Use the uncoached writing as data to inform instruction only.
> • The prompt should be a test of the genre and NOT of the content.
> • Skip this step with kindergarten and first grade students.

The prompt should be simple and without guidance. The content of the writing should be familiar to the students and not a test of students' knowledge of the content of the unit. For upper elementary and middle school students, think of prompts related to current issues of interest, either internal to the school or to the community and society at large. Possible prompts are:

There should be school rules.
Students should have longer breaks.
Parents should pick up children from school when they are sick.
Cats make better pets than dogs.
Teachers should not assign homework over the weekend.
Write a letter to your teacher persuading her/him about what kind of brain break to use during remote learning. (Options may include yoga, freeze dance, drawing time.)

Write an argument persuading readers that face masks should or should not be required to be worn outside of their homes.

Everybody should/should not get the COVID vaccine.

Using as a guide the Analysis of Student Work: Purpose, Stages, and Language forms, download-able from the *Support Material* tab in the book's webpage, teachers determine what students can already do and what their challenges are. The results help the planning of lessons.

Purpose, Stages, and Language: Theory and Practice

With all of the preparation described earlier on hand, teachers need to think about the actual lessons they will carry out to teach about purpose, audience, stages, and the aspects of language they have chosen to teach. They also need to include lessons on medium if using one unfamiliar to the students. Moreover, they will need to teach students how to do research and how to use software applications, if the teaching has to be done online. Table 8.7 shows a potential order of lessons. Depending on grade level, teachers choose a specific set of lessons to cover.

Table 8.7 Lessons to Teach Purpose, Stages, and Language in Written Arguments

Lessons on Purpose and Stages	Lessons on Language
8. Persuasion in Students' Environment and Introduction to the Purpose of Arguments	
9. Using Books With Dilemmas to Introduce Students to Arguments	
10. Review the Purpose of Arguments and Distinguish Between Persuading to Do and Persuading About	11. Introduction to Evaluative Language and Graduation
12. Deconstruction of Text to Learn About Stages *(these lessons will lead to creating a class argument in the form of an ad, brochure, essay, or other mediums)*	13. Reinforce Evaluative Language and Graduation (for All Grades)
14. Development of Thesis Statement/ Appeal and Background for a Whole Class Argument	And Make Decisions on Generalized Participants, Type of Sentences, and Person to Use
15. Specific Audience Calls for Different Reasons	17. How the Language Changes Given Audience and Voice (Grades 4–8)
16. Specific Audience Calls for Different Types of Evidence	
18. Teach students to Research, Identify, and Take Notes on Supporting Reasons and Evidence *(For middle school: Take notes on the opposite position in order to write a rebuttal or a two-sided argument)*	Collect Language That Reflects Expertise on the Topic *(Reinforce evaluative language and graduation and distinguish between the two)*
	19. Learn How to Moderate the Argument by Using Modality (Grades 5–8)
	20. Learn How to Moderate the Argument by Using Concessive Clauses (Grades 6–8)
21. Teach Students to Quote Evidence	Use Verbs to Introduce the Quoted or Reported Evidence (Grades 6–8)

Lessons on Purpose and Stages	Lessons on Language
	22. Text Connectives
23. Write Planned Thesis, Reasons, and Evidence for the Whole Class Project	Review Language Features Learned in Previous Lessons
	24. Review Paragraphs With the Theme/New Information Tool (Grades 6–8 essays)
25. Reinforcement of the Position	
26. Produce Individual, Pair, or Group Argument	27. Joint Revision of Aspects of Language
28. Images That Accompany Arguments	

The following resources to support implementation of these lessons are downloadable from the *Support Material* tab in the book's webpage:

• Analysis of Student Work: Purpose, Stages, and Language
• Graphic Organizer
• Mentor Texts That Illustrate the Genre
• Internet Resources With Mentor Texts to Illustrate the Genre

Purpose of Arguments

Although one purpose of all arguments is to persuade, different types of arguments have slightly different aims (see Table 8.1). Arguments that present one point of view may aim at persuading to do something or about something. Arguments that present both sides have as a goal persuading on a position after presenting the opposing points of view. Challenges aim at rebutting a position on an issue. Arguments that present one point of view are recommended for elementary students. Middle school students start with these as well, may add a rebuttal, and then move on to the type that presents both viewpoints. Challenges are recommended for high school level.

As in narrative genres, arguments use a variety of tenses, but it can vary in specific arguments. Usually the background and thesis/appeal are written in the present. The latter may include modal verbs. The reasons are in the present except when it is a prediction of what would happen, where the future or conditional (*will* or *would*) are used. For example, in an argument against teachers and students befriending on Facebook, a student wrote, *Finally, the student would not finish there homework!* Evidence is often in the past, but when describing how things are, it is in the present. In the reinforcement, the present is used, sometimes with modals. When there is a call to action, then the imperative appears.

Features of Students' Writing

A 4th-grade teacher wrote the question *Should there be school rules?* as a prompt for the uncoached piece. The students decided to write a letter to the teacher to respond and to attempt to persuade her. Selena, one of the students, wrote the following piece. After she wrote the letter, Selena decided to distinguish each reason (written as a command) by adding the word *like* on the margin before each. In addition, she added two hearts, four stars, and "Love, [name of the student]!" to the top of the second page. She may have felt that she was being too daring with her assertions and wanted to soften the message.

> Dear, Mrs. [Name of Teacher],
> Yes! I think we sould have school rules because If we Did,nt had nd rules we will be like crazy and we will never get the part to learn.
> Let My give you some Exzapeles

like: Protet you from getting hurt and stol.
Like: follow them you will handel them.
Like: Don,t be crazy or you will be lazy.
Like: Don,t be bad or the teacher will get mad

So if you are gonna be bad I don,t know what the teacher is gonna say when se or he is MAD!
So think be-for you do somthing or somthing will happen Don,t think it is the teachers foult it is gonna be yours falut.
NEVER Ever BE BAD OR you Will not get a EDUCATION. If you make the teachers happy the whole school is happy
yours truly, [Name of student]

	1	2	3	4	Uncoached Writing Comments
Purpose To persuade to do something or about something		√			Starts with a thesis and preview of reasons, but then it turns into instructions for the students.

Selena seems to understand the purpose of the genre to persuade, but switches her purpose to give instructions on behavior (protocol). The topic might have confused her because school rules are usually written as a protocol or a series of instructions to always be followed (Butt et al., 2012). The use of the imperative signaled the switch in purpose.

Middle school students also were clear of the purpose. Their arguments were consistent in purpose, but sometimes they had difficulty with keeping the message consistent across thesis, reasons, and evidence. For example, one student started an argument claiming that Facebook makes users lonely and changed to argue about loneliness in the United States. Another feature occasionally found in students' writing is to refer to the process. For example, an 8th grader wrote, *Today, I have read an article about the immigration . . .* telling the reader how he went about writing his argument. Luis, another 8th grader, wrote with great passion an argument about immigration. Although the purpose was to argue, it was confusing as to whether he was writing to allow immigration (arguing to do) as opposed to immigration being something important for the country (arguing about). His piece read as follows:

WE SHOULD ALLOW IMMIGRATION BECAUSE WE HAVE A BAD ECONOMY

Aren't sure about where you stand on immigration? Do you think immigration is a good choice or a downfall to the country? Read on to find out. My opinion is that we should let immigration be allowed in our country. Why? People keep reading to find out.

We should let immigration be allowed because it is important to candidates. It is important to candidates because they rely on the huge amounts of immigrants that may vote for them. The candidates may scam the immigrants so they can get many votes and win the election.

Immigration is also important because it helps build complex communities. If immigration was banned form our country then everything might be plain and boring, [but there are advantages like having no shootings, having peaceful nights, no more screaming in the middle of the night, and not having any one coming over to ask if they can use your ldder at 2 am in the morning. When there are advantages there are almost always disadvantages. Some disadvantages of not having a complex community would be hardly any parties, super quiet communities (it may be an advantage and a disadvantage because some *people like quiet and some people just don't). They also wont have any people to play or hang out with, and most of all no social skills.] (all crossed out)*

Lastly immigration is also good because with the baby boomers retiring, the immigrants can easily replace them. That way many companies don't go out of business and the jobs that the immigrants get may be good jobs. So they will be able to support themselves and support others.

We should allow immigration because this is America, the country of freedom. I think that it is up to us to do it. So if you're a real citizen then you'd do the same as I would.

	1	2	3	4	Comments
Purpose To persuade to do something or about something			√		Persuade to allow immigration (to do) but then talks about why immigration is important (about). Unclear audience. Who is "we," the country? The government? It couldn't be the citizens because they don't have direct control.

When working with kindergarten and 1st-grade students, it is best to start directly with Lesson 9, which uses books with dilemmas. Activities in this lesson and oral activities should be the focus of the unit for those grade levels.

Lesson 8. Persuasion in Students' Environment and Introduction to the Purpose of Arguments

Goal: To understand the purpose of persuasive writing. To have students identify persuasion in their own lives so that they realize how prevalent the genre is.

Materials: TV, magazine advertisements, brochures, PSAs, and other media of persuasion found in the community (e.g., students could examine brochures handed out by an animal shelter to convince people to adopt adult cats).

Activities

- Have students watch advertisements on TV or the Internet or look for ads in magazines as homework.
- The following day, discuss the following:

  - The purpose of the advertisements.
  - What information was included in each.
  - How the ads were trying to persuade their audience.
  - Who is the intended audience and what in the advertisement suggests a particular audience.

- Repeat the activities with the other persuasive materials.
- Explain to the students that in this unit they will learn how to write persuasively, i.e., they will learn argument writing.

Lesson 9. Using Books With Dilemmas to Introduce Students to Arguments (Grades K–1; Other Grades Optional)

This is actually a series of lessons to use books with dilemmas to teach argumentation to kindergarten and 1st-grade students. Together with the oral activities, it is sufficient instruction on argumentative writing for this age group. One 1st-grade teacher did the Take a Stand game for 5 minutes before each of the lessons related to working with these books.

For other grades, it is a good warm-up activity when introducing the genre or in connection to learning reasons.

Goal: To teach students that persuasion requires reasons; to teach students to identify reasons in the source book that support a thesis statement/appeal.

Materials: Books with dilemmas, such as *Hey, Little Ant* or *The Great Kapok Tree*. Both these books have Spanish versions. For other ideas, check the *Support Material* tab in the book's webpage.

Activities

The activities are illustrated through the use of *Hey, Little Ant*. They can be done with any book with a dilemma. For example, a kindergarten teacher used *The Great Kapok Tree* because her class had been studying about trees and plants.

- Read and discuss *Hey, Little Ant*.
- Identify the two arguments: The boy should squish the ant/The boy should not squish the ant. Write them on a T-chart.
- Read the book aloud again, and ask the class to let you know as you read if they hear a reason for one or the other side. If you can project the book so that the students can follow as you read aloud, it is easier for bilingual learners.
- Ask students which thesis statement the given reason belongs.
- Write it on the appropriate column on the T-chart.
- Prompt them if they missed any reason.
- Tell the students that they are going to choose one of the thesis statements and write a letter using some of the reasons listed. For example, they can write a letter to the boy asking him not to squish the ant or a letter to the ant asking her to let the boy squish her. (Most young children take the side of the ant.)
- After they choose the thesis, students choose some reasons from the T-chart and draft a short letter.
- Teach a lesson on evaluative language and graduation (adapt Lesson 11 for this age group).
- Have them edit their letters to apply the use of negative or positive words and turning up or down the volume to help their argument. For example, one 1st grader changed *the baby ants will be **unhappy*** to *the baby ants will be **miserable***.

Lesson 10. Review the Purpose of Arguments and Distinguish Between Persuading to Do and Persuading About

Goal: To review that the purpose of arguments is to persuade an audience. To teach students that arguments generally either persuade to do something or to believe something.

Materials: Chart paper and paper strips. Travel brochures, magazine advertisements, and additional materials, such as those listed in the *Support Material* tab in the book's webpage. (Make sure that some are persuading to *do* something, e.g., visit the Dominican Republic or buy Crest toothpaste, and others *about* something, e.g., the Dominican Republic is the best vacation spot in the Caribbean; Crest is the best toothpaste.)

Activities (Grades 2–8)

- Choose one or two of the resources (materials) and read each aloud, or, in the case of a video, show it to the students.

- Discuss what the author is trying to do or what the character in the story is trying to do. (In the list of mentor texts downloadable from the *Support Material* tab in the book's webpage, there is a list of fictional narratives in which a character is trying to persuade another character to do or believe something.)
- Write it down on paper strips.
- (4th grade and up; optional for 2nd and 3rd grades.) Go over the statements that you wrote down and discuss with students if they see patterns. Lead the discussion to notice the difference between persuading to *do* and persuading *about* something.
- Using chart paper, the board, or computer with projector, create two columns ("to persuade to do" and "to persuade about").
- Move the paper strips to the corresponding column.
- Distribute the rest of the materials among the student groups, and have them decide whether the author or character is trying "to persuade to do" or "to persuade about."
- Have students write them on paper strips and add their responses to the appropriate columns on the chart paper.

Lesson 11. Introduction to Evaluative Language and Graduation

In this lesson, evaluative language and graduation are introduced together to show the function they play in arguments. In later lessons they can be explained individually in more detail.

> **Goal**: To show that the function of evaluative language is to express a positive or negative attitude toward what the author is writing about in order to enhance the argument, and the function of graduation is to increase or decrease the intensity of that attitude.
>
> **Materials**: Short passages with examples of evaluative language and graduation with both positive and negative, as well as turning up and turning down the volume. These should be taken with arguments that have been used in the lesson of purpose so that the students are familiar with them, and there are no problems with comprehension. For example, letters in *I Wanna Iguana* or *The Mosquito Song*.

Activities

- Project the letter in *I Wanna Iguana*:

  Dear Mom,
  Did you know that iguanas are really quiet
  And they're cute too. I think they are
  Much cuter than hamsters.

  > Love,
  > Your adorable son.
  > Alex

- Ask students: Do you see any language in this letter that shows positive or negative attitude toward the iguana, i.e., what the boy is writing about?
- Circle the answers: *quiet, cute*
- Ask them: Do you think these words help Alex's argument?
- Explain: This is called positive language that helps enhance the argument.
- Go back to the letter and ask them: Is there language that increases or decreases the intensity of the attitude?

- Circle the answers: *really, much* cuter
- Ask them: Do you think that turning up the volume of the attitude helps the argument the boy is doing to his mother?
- The argument can also be helped by negative language. For example, Alex's mother, who does not want the iguana, writes back: *By the way, that iguana of Mikey's is uglier than Godzilla.*
- Ask the students: Is there positive or negative language about the iguana?
- Circle *uglier* and confirm it is negative with the volume turned up because it helps the mother's argument, who does not want that iguana.
- Show/read aloud *The Mosquito Song* and ask them if they can find words that turn down the volume.

The Mosquito's Song by Peggy Leavitt
I sing. You slap
I mean no harm
There is no cause
for your alarm.
A **little** drop
Is all I ask.
It really is
a **simple** task.
So please hold still
at this
juncture,
while I
make
a **tiny**
PUNCTURE!

- Circle the answers: *Little, simple, tiny.* Explain that sometimes turning down the volume is more helpful for the argument.
- You may start a list of positive and negative words to help students when they write their own arguments.

Positive	Negative
Quiet	Ugly
Cute	

- Encourage them to add to the list when they are looking at other arguments in later lessons.

Follow Up: Lessons 13, 17, 24, and 25.

Stages of Arguments

Attention to the structure and content of the argument are important. Organization depends on the type of argument (see Table 8.8) and the medium. While all arguments include an introduction followed by reasons supported by evidence and a conclusion, the specifics of each varies.

The conclusion of arguments to do something may include a call to action (Derewianka & Jones, 2016). By the middle school level, students are instructed to include a rebuttal to their

Table 8.8 Stages of the Different Types of Arguments

One-Sided Argument		Two-Sided Argument
Persuade to Do	*Persuade About*	
Introduction, including background, thesis statement or appeal, preview of reasons (optional).	Introduction, including background, thesis statement, preview of reasons (optional).	Issue and background to the issue.
Reasons supported by evidence. *Option for middle school level:* add a rebuttal	Reasons supported by evidence. *Option for middle school level:* add a rebuttal	Position A supported by evidence. Position B supported by evidence. (Each position may include rebuttal.)
Reinforcement of the statement (may include a call to action).	Reinforcement of the statement.	Recommendation (for A or B given the strength of the evidence).

reasons and evidence. The rebuttal states the opposing view and gives evidence that does not support this view (see mentor text *Malaria—One of the Oldest Diseases* at the end of the chapter).

The introduction of two-sided arguments raises the issue to be debated. Then the reasons and evidence for one position and then for the opposite one are stated. The essays conclude with a recommendation for the position the author supports (see mentor text *College Sports* at the end of the chapter).

To prepare his upper elementary students to eventually write arguments with rebuttals or arguments with both points of view, Pat has students writing arguments taking one point of view and then writing another with the opposite point of view. Although students write defending just one point of view, more appropriate for elementary grades, they learn how to take the opposite view, which in turn, helps improve the writer's reasons and evidence.

The medium also calls for different organization. Essays include several paragraphs containing the introduction, various reasons supported by evidence, and a conclusion. The paragraphs include topic sentences that establish what the paragraph is about and in turn connect to the main topic (Coffin, 2006; Halliday & Matthiessen, 2004). A persuasive brochure, poster, announcement, or advertisement contain the same stages but laid out in different ways with images supporting text.

Regardless of the way it is laid out and organized, most important is that the thesis/appeal, reasons, evidence, and conclusion make sense together. The reasons should support the thesis/appeal, and the evidence should support each reason. In the following argument, the topic of the text is that dogs are good pets. Then, each paragraph describes a quality that makes a dog a good pet. The last sentence connects back to the overarching topic of the piece.

Stages	*Example*
Introduction: • Background • Thesis Statement or Appeal • Preview of Reasons (optional)	*Why Dogs Are Better Than Cats* Dogs are often called "man's best friend" and make ideal pets.

(Continued)

Stages	Example
Series of reasons, each supported by evidence (In science, math, or response to literature, the evidence is often stated before the reasons.) The content of each paragraph relates to one reason and all reasons relate to the thesis/ appeal.	The most attractive quality of a dog is its faith in its owner and its loyalty. They always greet us when we come home and they will never leave us even in a dire situation. For example there was a sick man and the dog barked and barked until the rescue team arrived.
	Furthermore dogs are strong animals that will protect us. Houses with dogs are considered much safer than even those with burglar alarms. Not only will they stop thieves, but they will also guard against fire. For example there was a serious fire and a dog managed to pull its owner out.
	And finally dogs can be trained to help people. Dogs can do a number of things that people can not. For example they can sniff out drugs, find bodies, illicit DVDs and hunt down prisoners. They're also used to help the elderly and disabled.
Reinforcement of Statement of Position (relates to the original thesis/appeal)	To sum up, dogs are really friendly, civilized and loyal companions.

Source: www.jamesabela.co.uk/exams/dogsvscats.pdf (Downloaded 8/11/11)

At the end of the chapter there are two additional mentor texts appropriate for middle school level. One, *Malaria—One of the Oldest Diseases*, is an argument in support of preventive measures with a rebuttal in favor of treatment. It has extensive background information before stating the thesis, followed by a couple of reasons and evidence. Before a short conclusion reinforcing the thesis, the rebuttal paragraph reads,

Some policy makers believe that treatment is the solution. However, a major program launched by the WHO failed. The number of people in Sub-Saharan Africa who contracted malaria as well as the number of malaria deaths actually increased over 10% during the time the program was active. The participating countries could not afford such an expensive program and the widespread use of chloroquine created drug resistant parasites which are now plaguing Sub-Saharan Africa.

The first sentence (bolded) states the opposing view, but what follows is all evidence that treatment was not very successful in curing malaria, strengthening the thesis of the essay.

The second mentor text, *College Sports*, for middle school is a two-sided argument about whether college athletes should be paid. After stating the issue, the essay has two sets of reasons and evidence for each position. The essay concludes by stating: *While both sides have good points, it's clear that the negatives of paying college athletes far outweigh the positives.* Thus, recognizing the value of both positions but recommending one.

To successfully compose the individual stages of an argument, students need to learn:

- *To take a position and give reasons*: Students need to learn to express an opinion about something or persuade the audience to do something. Although it is their own, they need to learn to express it as a general opinion (e.g., *Students should be allowed to have cell phones in the classroom*). Sometimes, the writer is just trying to persuade for himself or herself. For example, a student might write a letter to a parent trying to persuade him or her to buy something. The thesis statement/appeal needs to be accompanied with reasons that support the position. There is no need for a fixed number of reasons, which may vary depending on audience.

- *To support reasons with evidence*: Evidence can appeal to the intellect or to emotions (Rog & Kropp, 2004). Writers should choose their evidence depending on the audience. Evidence that appeals to the intellect includes:

  - Facts that can be proven
  - Statistics that offer scientific support
  - Expert opinions or quotations
  - Exhibits, including visual or auditory evidence (pictures, artifacts, recordings)

  Evidence that appeals to emotions includes:

  - Examples that are powerful illustrations of the point of view
  - Anecdotes that illustrate an incident, often part of the writer's personal experience
  - Emotional appeals that include carefully chosen words to sway the reader's emotion in a desired direction

- *To differentiate between fact and opinion*: Persuasive writing uses facts to support an author's opinion or point of view (reasons). For example, in the mentor text, being helpful and protective are opinions about dogs. However, the examples of dogs aiding the disabled or pulling their owner from a house on fire are facts (evidence).
- *To take the opposite position in order to create a rebuttal or two-sided argument (middle school)*: Taking the opposite position is developmentally difficult. Although it is appropriate to teach it at the middle school level, it is still difficult for these students.
- *To consider audience when writing each stage*:

  - The thesis statement/appeal needs to be preceded by background information. The amount will depend on the audience. For example, the mentor text discussing dogs as pets may first need some background information if the audience included children in cultures that do not have dogs as pets, but rather as working animals.
  - Reasons are also carefully chosen depending on the audience. For example, when students wrote to the principal attempting to persuade him or her to install lockers, they gave *security* as a reason, which they believed would appeal to an adult. If the audience had been other students, they may have chosen *being fun to decorate*.
  - Evidence is chosen given the audience. Certain people may be better convinced with statistics, whereas others may prefer anecdotes and real-life examples. The mentor text seems to be directed to the general public with appealing examples of what dogs can do for their owners.

Features of Student Writing

Following is the analysis of the sample uncoached piece by Selena with focus on the stages:

Feature	1	2	3	4	Comment
Stages follow the organization of an argument and the content relates to the thesis or appeal	√				Starts with a thesis and couple of reasons, but then it turns into a protocol and concludes with a topic not quite related with the thesis.
Introduction: • Background • Thesis Statement or Appeal • Preview of Arguments (optional)	√				Instead of starting directly with the thesis statement, she inserts "Yes" and "I think" at the beginning. Previews: being crazy and not learning

(Continued)

Feature	1	2	3	4	Comment
Reasons Supported by Evidence Evaluate for both structure and meaning	√				Doesn't develops the reasons she previews.
Evidence Content supports corresponding reason Types of evidence appeal to the audience	√				What would have been the evidence turns into a protocol of appropriate behavior, changing the support of having rules to the topic of appropriate behavior.
Reinforcement of Statement of Position Reinforces, does not repeat Includes a call to action in "to do" arguments	√				Concludes with encouraging students to make the teacher happy, unrelated to the initial reasons.

Often, when the prompt is a question, students, instead of writing a thesis statement, write *yes* or *no*, depending on which point of view they choose to argue. The student stated her thesis preceded by an interpersonal theme (bold): **I think** *we sould have school rules.* Children do not realize that the use of these interpersonal themes weakens the claim, especially with a phrase with medium intensity as *I think* (Droga & Humphrey, 2003). Because the student switches to giving instructions or advising, she does not provide reasons supported by evidence, failing to reinforce her position.

One great source of difficulty for elementary students is to write the thesis statement in the third person, when addressing a general audience and wanting to be authoritative. As seen in the uncoached piece, even if the teacher had written the prompt in the third person (*Should there be school rules?*), the student chose to use the first person to focus on her opinion and her classmates (*I think we should have school rules*).

Fourth graders writing persuasive pieces struggled to state convincing evidence (Bermúdez & Prater, 1994). By 6th grade, students showed the ability to make appropriate changes in the content and language of persuasive pieces when writing to different audiences. For example, Martínez et al. (2008) showed that when students wrote to the principal about the need to do something about the school police, they said the police treated them like criminals. However, when these same students wrote to other students, they wrote that, "They're [the school police] stupid and they bug" (p. 421).

Middle school students usually have more experience with argumentation and tend to have all the stages, but sometimes they have difficulty expressing their ideas clearly. Luis's argument shown earlier had all the stages that stayed with the topic, but his wording was not always clear, and he kept adding reasons without developing them. Following is the analysis of the stages in his writing:

Stages follow the organization of an argument and the content relates to the thesis or appeal	√				All the reasons and evidence relate to the thesis.
Introduction: Background Information Thesis Statement or Appeal Preview of Reasons (optional)	√				Has a thesis but no background (it should say something about immigration being restricted). Probably a better thesis to go with her reasons would be "immigration is important for the US." Previews one reason, but it is not one of the ones she elaborates.
Reasons Evaluate for both structure and meaning	√				Has 5 reasons. There are two more reasons; one in the introduction and one in the conclusion, which are not developed.

Evidence Content supports corresponding reason Types of evidence appeal to the audience	√	Three of the reasons in the body of the text are supported by evidence. Although it is speculative and not based on research. For one of the reasons, the student gives first the counter evidence, which brings a negative tone to the argument she is trying to make and never quite fixes it. No evidence for the two other reasons.
Reinforcement of Statement of Position Reinforces, does not repeat Includes a call to action in "to do" arguments	√	The reinforcement is actually an additional evidence and a call to follow her point of view.

Without instruction and scaffolded planning, students, as the one in the earlier example, have difficulty keeping the argument coherent. For example, a 5th grader wrote a piece against television sets in children's rooms. The focus of her argument switched back and forth between television sets and children (*Children get unhealthy because it damages children's eyes and causes obestiy. Lastly, television prevents them from doing well in school . . .*). Since the essay was about television sets, the first sentence should have read, "Televisions are unhealthy because they damage children's eyes and cause obesity."

Other issues that students have with respect to the stages are:

- A study of 9-year-olds writing persuasive pieces showed that students had trouble giving sufficient background information (Kroll, 1984).
- Students sometimes have difficulty giving a variety of reasons and repeat the same reason with slightly different wording.
- Students tend to repeat the thesis statement when writing the conclusion.
- Students in upper elementary through middle school have difficulty clearly wording the content in the stages.

Language Features of Arguments

Language choices writers make heavily influence the success of their arguments. In arguments it is important that authors are consistent in the choice of participant—generalized or specific. They need to show expertise on the topic and awareness of audience and voice. Additionally, well-developed paragraphs and measured use of text connectives (also called transition words) contribute to the clarity of the text.

Generalized Participants

Arguments commonly center on generalized participants, sometimes including beings like *dogs* in the mentor text, but they often include generalized issues, such as pollution, smoking, and school uniforms. Occasionally, arguments can be written to support a specific situation (e.g., *your dog needs obedience school*). Children have difficulty with the use of generalized participants. As seen in the uncoached piece, although the prompt had a generalized participant (*Should schools have rules?*), the student immediately changed it to a specific school, theirs (*Yes! I think we sould have school rules . . .*). As they mature, they argue more about issues. By middle school, they are quite capable of using generalized participants.

Language That Reflects Expertise on the Topic

Much of the evidence on arguments written in late elementary and middle school comes from research that helps support the reasons and thesis/appeal. This language is technical and discipline specific. It is not simply vocabulary but often includes complex noun groups and nominalizations. For example, in the three mentor texts included in the chapter, we find such evidence as:

> Technical terms: *elderly*, disabled, *chloroquine, eligibility*
>
> Complex noun groups: *insecticide-treated bed nets; those [houses] with burglar alarms; people who argue against the idea of paying college athletes*
>
> Nominalizations: *reducing* the number of people who contract malaria; *participating* countries; *proponents* of the idea; *payment* to college athletes

The technicality of the vocabulary used in arguments will be relative to the level of the writer's language maturity and the audience. Even if older students are writing and are capable of using complex technical language, they need to consider their audience. If their audience is young students, they need to choose language that will be understood by them.

Audience and Voice (Tenor)

Tenor "is concerned with the interpersonal in language, with the subjective presence of writers/speakers in texts as they adopt stances toward both the material they present and those with whom they communicate" (Martin & White, 2005, p. 1). Writers constantly make language choices depending on the intended audience and the voice they want to reflect through their writing. Children have an idea that their audience can differ, but they do not always adjust their language to show it. Kroll's (1984) research showed that children can adapt to different audiences, but this occurs to different degrees.

The notion of voice has been interpreted as writers expressing their personality and their excitement about what they are writing. This has led to indiscriminating use of language that is sometimes inappropriate, especially in non-fiction disciplinary writing (O'Halloran & Schleppegrell, 2016). SFL theory proposes that there are a number of grammatical resources, including evaluative language, graduation, type of sentence (mood system), person, and modality that help create voice (Humphrey et al., 2012). Depending on the genre, the audience, and the discipline, the voice is entertaining or authoritative. Students need to learn how the grammatical resources play a role in creating different voices and realize that there are no fixed rules, but, given the context, a particular voice may be more effective. Their use of the grammatical features must be intentional given the voice they want to present.

Evaluative language and graduation are essential in persuasive writing, otherwise students' writing sounds too factual. For young learners, it would be sufficient to teach this aspect of language when introducing argumentation. Students need to be taught the impact of using the different types of sentences and to be consistent with the use of person and modality to avoid constant changing of voice. When students reach middle school, they can be taught how certain structures open or close the door to other opinions and how to introduce the opinion of others to show the writer's stance toward those opinions.

In addition, spelling can be framed for children within voice. Starting approximately with the 20th century, accurate spelling has been viewed as important, and poor spelling has been associated with a lack of education. Thus, being careful with spelling in specific situational contexts is advantageous for the writer. Oral arguments tend to use a greater variety of each of these grammatical elements, mostly due to the fact the audience is in the presence of the speaker (Derewianka & Jones, 2016).

Evaluative Language

Writers use positive or negative evaluative language to

(a) Express feelings (Affect): The athlete sustained a *serious* knee injury (negative). He *enjoyed* playing for Duke (positive).
(b) Make moral judgments of behaviors (Judgment): Zoos make animals *crazy* (negative). Dogs will *protect* us (positive).
(c) Assess quality (Appreciation): The program to prevent malaria was *effective* (positive). A major program to cure malaria *failed* (negative).

This language is essential in argument writing to enhance the author's point of view. Students do not naturally use it, especially at the elementary levels. However, once they discover it, they tend to overuse it, which can defeat its purpose. It is important to teach not only the literal meaning of the words, but also how they can show the author's perspective (Humphrey et al., 2012). For example, an L2 student asked for the meaning of the word *nasty*. The teacher gave the definition, but needed to add that by using it, the student would also show the writer's point of view with respect to the particular person she was describing.

Graduation

Writers use graduation to increase or diminish the intensity of meanings and to increase or open up the focus of it (Derewianka & Jones, 2016; Humphrey et al., 2012). The evaluative words can be made to stand out more by increasing or diminishing the level of intensity through the choice of synonyms, intensifiers, and others (see detailed description in Brisk, 2021).

- To increase the intensity:

  - College sports are *hugely* popular.
  - Iguanas are *really* quiet. They are *much* cuter than hamsters.
  - *Six million* adults die every year due to smoking.

- To decrease the intensity:

  - A *little* drop; a *tiny* puncture (*The Mosquito's Song*)

When presented with the notion of graduation, children automatically want to increase the intensity. Thus, it is good to expose students to a text such as *The Mosquito's Song* poem (quoted earlier) to demonstrate that lower intensity can also be effective in certain circumstances.

The focus of the intensity can be narrowed to increase the focus or widened to soften the focus.

Narrow focus: Compensation will *actually* encourage athletes to stay in college.

Malaria-afflicted families typically harvest *only* 40% of the crops.

Widened focus: Athletes should receive *some sort of* compensation.

Roughly 20% benefited from the drug therapy.

Types of Sentences

There are four types of sentences:

1   Statements or declarative sentences (Dogs are too noisy.)
2   Questions (Can I keep him?)
3   Exclamations (I can keep him!)
4   Commands (Take him back.)

Statements are more assertive, focusing on the topic of the argument rather than on the audience and writer. Questions, exclamations, and commands inherently show a relationship between writer and audience and as a consequence are more common in arguments to do something. Questions are the least assertive way to address an audience because they open the door to other opinions. Questions also signal that the writer knows more than the reader, consequently they can be inappropriate in certain contexts. For example, a 6th grader wrote to the producer of a film that included actors smoking. He starts the argument with the question *"Did you know that every cigarette a person smokes takes seven minutes off their life?"* (CCSS, 2010, Appendix C, p. 36). This is a child treating an educated adult as ignorant. A statement with the same information included in the evidence would have been more appropriate. Exclamations are used to express surprise or make an emphatic statement (Derewianka, 2011; Derewianka & Jones, 2016). Children tend to overuse exclamations to express what graduation does more precisely (Brisk, 2021). In oral arguments, speakers use a greater variety of types of sentences because there is greater need to connect with the audience.

Grammatical Persons

There are three grammatical persons: first (I, we), second (you), and third (she, he, it, they). The first and second persons overtly express the presence of the writer and the audience. The third person places the focus on the topic at hand, hiding the writer and gearing the piece toward a generalized audience, making the voice more authoritative and impersonal or "professional" as Pat, one of the teachers, kept telling his students. The three mentor texts included in this chapter use the third person because they are arguing about general issues. The one on support for dogs as pets uses the first person plural a couple of times to make the audience feel closer to the issue. For elementary and middle school students, it is more natural to use first and second person without intentionally wanting to make the writing less formal and closer to oral language where the first and second are more naturally used. Luis starts his essay using *we* (first person) and then goes on to use third person. Often students start their thesis with "I think that . . ." and although they use third person with the reasons, they tend to use the second person with the evidence. For example, one student wrote: *Video games are tremendesly educational. Such as FIRST in Math because it helps you in your math skills*. It is important to stress that all three persons can be appropriate depending on the audience and the voice the author wants to reflect. The choice must be intentional and consistently reflected in the writing.

Modality

Modality indicates obligation (I **must** come home at once.), probability, and possibility (There **may** be particular cases in which home tutoring **would** be advantageous. Student athletes **could** earn income from endorsements.). Modality allows writers to express commitment to a position to varying degrees (Vaccines are *definitely* effective. Vaccines *may be* effective.). Modal verbs or

Table 8.9 Modality

	High	Medium	Low
Verbs	Must, need, has to	Will, would, supposed to	Can, may, might
Adverbials	Certainly, definitely, absolutely, undoubtedly	Probably, usually, likely, apparently, presumably	Possibly, perhaps, maybe
Adjectives	Certain, definite	Probable, usual	Possible
Nouns	Certainty, necessity, requirement	Probability	Possibility
Clauses and Phrases	I believe that Everyone knows that	I think that In my opinion,	I guess that

Sources: Derewianka and Jones (2016), Humphrey et al. (2012).

auxiliaries and adverbials or modal adjuncts are most commonly used. Other grammatical resources to express modality are adjectives, nouns, and clauses or phrases. Modals express different degrees of obligation or uncertainty (see Table 8.9).

Modality greatly depends on audience and discipline. For example, 2nd graders, when requesting from the principal a pet for their classroom, use low modality to recognize the difference in authority. Instead of writing: *You **must** give us permission to have a pet*, they would write: *You **may** consider giving us permission to have a pet*. Scientist write the results of their research in factual terms. However, in the interpretation, they use modality to make the interpretation more cautious, giving room for the possibility of different interpretations (O'Hallaron & Schleppegrell, 2016).

Engagement: Opening the Door to the Position of Others

To engage the reader or build solidarity, the authors may show openness to other points of view. Several of the language resources reviewed serve to expand the possibilities of points of view (Humphrey et al., 2012). For example, different types of modals and questions serve this role. When an author writes, *Is year-round school really where the money should go?* the possibility of the opposite position is on the table. Sometimes authors open the door but close it immediately with the use of concessive sentences. For example, *Malaria treatment is not the best way to reduce the disease. In spite of heroic efforts to cure malaria, preventing the disease is a much more affordable solution.* First the author allowed for the other position and then refuted it.

On the other hand, negatives or statements with positive or negative language do not open the possibility for other positions. For example, *This is not a good book. This is the best book ever written. This is a dreadful book.*

Engagement: Introducing Others' Point of View

Middle school students begin to encounter in their readings expressions of other people's opinion. The way these are introduced show the author's perspective on the opinion of the quoted or reported statement. For example, when the dog writes, *Dr. Wilfrey claims that he can't find anything wrong with me,* by introducing what the doctor said with the verb *claim*, the dog shows doubt in what the doctor said. While by writing, *Studies have shown that, for every 100–1000 more nets being used, one less child dies of malaria,* the author affirms what the studies reported by using *shown*.

Creating a Cohesive Text

Earlier in the chapter, the overall cohesion of the text through the development of stages was addressed. There is a further need to ensure that the clauses in individual paragraphs work together, helping the paragraph to flow clearly. Paragraphs can be broken down into theme (what the author is talking about) and new information (what the writer is saying about the theme or topic). Text connectives, reference ties (see Chapter 3), and technical language related to the topic are additional language features that help the text come together.

Theme/New Information

The *theme* is located at the beginning of sentences and helps the reader identify what the author is writing about. The *new information* usually starts with the verb of the main clause. In the following chart, find an example of an analyzed paragraph from the mentor text on malaria included with resources at the end of the chapter:

	Theme	New Information
1	One of the cheapest and most effective ways of preventing malaria	is to implement insecticide—treated bed nets (ITNs).
2	These nets	provide a protective barrier around the person or people using them.
3	While untreated bed nets are still helpful, those treated with insecticides	are much more useful
4	because they	stop mosquitoes from biting people
5	and they	reduce mosquito populations in a community.

The first sentence introduces in the theme position what the paragraph is about, that is, preventing malaria. The #2 theme picks up the concept of "nets" introduced in the new information of the first sentence and expands it. The third theme starts with a subordinate clause, so the whole clause is part of the theme, followed by the theme of "treated nets" (same as #2) to further expand this concept. The theme in #4 and #5 is the pronoun "they," which has a referent "treated nets," further expanding the information on the nets. In this paragraph, after introducing the concept of treated nets in the first sentence's new information, the theme of nets is repeated to reinforce the argument in favor of those nets. Repetition of the theme—without using the exact same words—is one strategy used in paragraph formation. As we saw in the example in Chapter 6, the themes in the report picked up from the new information to start new themes, what is called zigzagging (Fang & Schleppegrell, 2008). Themes should help the reader learn what the author is writing about. In this example, just looking at the themes we learn that the paragraph is about preventing malaria as well as treated and untreated nets.

In this text, all the themes are *experiential* (what you are talking about: *prevention, nets*). In the mentor text about dogs, there are also *textual themes* (words that help connect the text: *for example*). None of the three sample mentor texts included in this chapter have what are called *interpersonal themes*, which help connect the writer and reader, for example, <u>I think that</u> college athletes should be paid. The mentor texts do not include them because they were written with an authoritative voice rather than a more familiar voice. Children commonly use the interpersonal themes. Experiential themes always follow textual and interpersonal themes.

To help students organize their paragraphs use the Theme/New Information table included at the end of the Analysis Forms (downloadable from the *Support Material* tab in the book's webpage). It is recommended to do just one paragraph in the body of the text to help them practice and improve their writing. Although teachers with students as young as 3rd grade have done lessons on theme/new information, it is a practice most recommended for the middle school level. With younger grades, it is sufficient to make them notice if there is a lot of repletion or just use of pronouns in the theme position.

Another point to raise with respect to the choice of theme is the reason the author has to start with a particular theme. For example, in the clause: **In May 2020** *a major COVID outbreak took place in New York City*, the author pays attention to time when it occurred by starting with the date. If the author wanted to stress the place, the clause would have read: **In New York City** *a major COVID outbreak took place in May 2020*. The outbreak itself is the focus in the clause: **A major COVID outbreak** *took place in New York City in May 2020*.

Text Connectives

These textual devices help connect chunks of text, sequencing ideas, offering alternatives, clarifying information, and so on (for a complete analysis see Derewianka & Jones, 2016 and Humphrey et al., 2012). Table 8.10 illustrates the meaning signaled by text connectives with examples of common connectives. There are two challenges students face when using connectives. One is to be clear of the meaning, and the second is that they tend to overuse them (Hinkel, 2002). Authors tend to use them sparingly. For example, neither of the two middle school sample texts included at the end of the chapter uses them. The mentor text *Why Dogs Are Better Than Cats* includes: *for example, furthermore, and finally*, and *to sum up*.

All the aspects of language covered so far are illustrated in the mentor texts (see Table 8.11).

Table 8.10 Text Connectives

Type of Connection	Examples
Sequencing	*Firstly, in the first place, to summarize, in conclusion*
Alternative	*Alternatively, on the other hand, instead*
Clarifying	*For example, in other words*
Addition	*Moreover, furthermore, in addition*
Causality	*As a result, therefore, consequently*
Contrast/concession	*However, instead, on the contrary*

Source: Adapted from Derewianka and Jones (2016)

Table 8.11 Language Features of Arguments in Mentor Texts

Language Feature	Why Dogs Are Better Than Cats (elementary)	Malaria—One of the Oldest Diseases (middle school)
Generalized Participants (dogs, zoos, animals)	*dogs*	*programs, malaria*
Language that reflects expertise on the topic (technical terms, complex noun groups, nominalizations)	*sniff out drugs, find illicit DVD, hunt down prisoners, help elderly and disabled*	*...parasites that are transmitted to people* *...preventing infection* *productivity of the region* *chloroquine* *drug resistant parasites* *plaguing*

(Continued)

Table 8.11 (Continued)

Language Feature	Why Dogs Are Better Than Cats (elementary)	Malaria—One of the Oldest Diseases (middle school)
Evaluative Language To express attitude	ideal, attractive, strong, friendly, civilized, loyal, serious (positive) dire, sick (negative)	cheaper, effective (positive) expensive, plaguing, failed (negative)
Graduation	ideal, very sick, much safer, most attractive, really friendly (turned up)	cheapest, most effective, 12 billion, much more affordable, stronger only (narrow the focus) nearly, roughly (widen the focus)
Types of Sentences	All statements	All statements
Grammatical person	3rd person, 1st person plural in first paragraph	3rd person
Modality	will (medium), can (low)	must (strong), can, could (low)
Opening or closing doors to other positions (middle school)	Assertive, does not open door to other opinions	Closes doors: could not afford Open and then closes: Some policy makers believe that treatment is the solution. However, a major program launched by the WHO failed.
Introducing others' points of view (middle school)	NA	Some policy makers believe (sides with the people—but in the next sentence critiques belief)
Cohesive Paragraphs: 1. Theme/New Information (Analysis of the paragraph in the following table and commentary here.) 2. Text Connectives	1. Mostly has dogs in the theme position. In sentence #5, the author could have written "For example, a serious fire," using fire to tie the theme with the previous new information. 2. for example, furthermore, and finally, to sum up	Full analysis of the paragraph appeared earlier. 1. Some themes are extensive. Focus is nets, which the author is advocating. 2. No text connectives.

Number	Theme	New Information
1	Furthermore dogs	are strong animals that will protect us.
2	Houses with dogs	are considered much safer than even those with burglar alarms.
3	Not only will they	stop thieves
4	but they	will also guard against fire.
5	For example, there	was a serious fire
6	and a dog	managed to pull its owner out.

The paragraphs in the *Malaria* mentor text are cohesive with themes that clearly state with the author is writing about. There is a good example of the zigzag structure where the new information in one sentence becomes the theme in the next (see bold):

One of the cheapest and most effective ways of preventing malaria is to implement **insecticide treated bed nets** (ITNs). These **nets** provide a protective barrier . . ."

Features of Students' Writing

The following 5th-grade student text, written after the class received instruction on the purpose and stages, will be used to illustrate major challenges that students have with the aspects of language particularly significant for arguments. In addition, students will need conferencing, as determined by other language needs. For example, Isabella constructed some of the future tense incorrectly.

Here are two paragraphs of Isabella's first draft of her argument against zoos.

We shouldn't have zoos!
Why we should have zoos? Zoos are abusive to animals. When a animal dose a confusing trick wrong, the cruel trainer will hit, kicked or shocked the animal very baddly and possibly kill the harm less animal. It's horrible what these repulsive trainers are doing—would you like if you were abused? Anmals belong in the wild not in zoo.

Table 8.12 shows the features of Isabella's and Luis's language. They were successful in using certain features and challenged by others.

Table 8.12 Features of the Elementary and the Middle School Students' Language

Aspects of Language	√ Isabella X Luis				Isabella	Luis
	1	*2*	*3*	*4*	*Comments*	
Generalized Participants (dogs, zoos, animals)				√ X	The thesis statement is written in first person, but that was given to the students. The rest of the piece uses generalized participants: zoos, animals, trainers.	immigration
Language That Reflects Expertise on the Topic	√ X				Abusive, trick, cruel trainer, the wild	This language appears in the reasons (*complex communities, baby boomers, retiring, a downfall*) but not in the evidence.
Evaluative Vocabulary			X	√	Negative when referring to zoo staff: *Abusive, cruel, repulsive, hit, kicked, shocked, kill, badly* Confusing referring to the trick given to the animals, a sign of maliciousness toward the animals. Positive when referring to the animals: *Harmless*	Positive: *good, important, huge, win, real, advantages* Negative: *downfall, plain, boring, disadvantages* Uses a negative, *scam*, that breaks the positive image the student was creating for one of the reasons and evidence.
Graduation • Turns up or down the intensity • Narrow or widen the focus			X	√	• *Repulsive, very badly, horrible* (volume up) • NA	• Huge • NA

(Continued)

Table 8.12 (Continued)

Aspects of Language	√ Isabella X Luis				Isabella	Luis
	1	2	3	4	Comments	
Types of Sentences			√		Exclamations and questions. The voice considers the audience: other children. There is no need for exclamation in the thesis statement. It is strong enough as it is. There is no need of the question: *Why we should have zoos?*	Although the student writes mostly in statements, he starts the argument with questions that make the voice familiar.
			X			
Use of Person	**X**	√			Uses 1st person plural and 2nd person. Most is 3rd person.	There is inconsistency in the voice. It starts with 1st person plural, which builds solidarity but takes away the focus of immigration. It uses 2nd person in the questions, addressing directly the audience. Then goes on to mix "we" with 3rd person throughout the essay. At the end uses 1st person singular and 2nd person, addressing the audience directly.
Modality		**X**	√		Uses of *should*, strong modality appropriate when a child addresses children. Also *will*, medium modality. Uses *possably* [possibly], a low modality adverbial to soften the verb *kill*, a rather strong assertion. This makes it more believable.	Uses mostly verbs (*should, would, will, may, can, might*) from strong to low modality. The low ones weaken the strength of the argument. Uses two phrases: *My opinion* and *I think*.
Opening or Closing Doors to Other Positions (middle school)		**X**				Inconsistent and use unintentional. The initial questions open the doors for other positions, while the reasons in the form of statements, closes them. Use of *My opinion* and *I think* open the doors to other opinion, also weakening the argument.
Introducing Others' Points of View (middle school)						NA He doesn't quote or report on any of the sources.

Generalized Participants. Initially Isabella, as other students, did not always use generalized participants in arguments of general interest. After learning about the purpose and stages of the genre, Isabella mastered the use of generalized participants. For middle school students, this was not an issue.

Language That Reflects Expertise on the Topic. Isabella used a few technical terms, while Luis used them mostly on the reasons while the evidence was expressed with everyday language.

Language to Create Voice. Isabella's draft exhibits language choices appropriate when writing to children. Isabella understands the power of positive and negative language as well as graduation and modality to support her point of view. Her choice of negative words to describe zoos and trainers reflects her strong opinion on the treatment of animals in zoos, whereas animals are *harmless*. There are some inconsistencies in her choice of types of sentences and person. Both take a while to learn which choices are more effective. Although Isabella seems to be on point with her use of language given her audience, the concern is whether it was planned or intuitive. To test her abilities, she should be given opportunities to write to a different audience to see if she makes different choices and is aware of them.

Some of the other elementary students were not as successful in maintaining a consistent voice. For example, in an argument directed to teachers, some students switched between first and third person. Their choice of words, reflecting their perspective, was sometimes respectful, but also included language that would be appropriate to use only with a close friend.

Although Luis's argument is longer and more elaborate than Isabella's, it shows similar issues with respect to voice. There is inconsistency between a familiar and authoritative voice due to the switching of person, use of questions and phrases such as *I think*, and the range of strength in the modality. Although he makes good use of evaluative language, in one case it did not help the argument. He does not quote or report other people's thinking to support his evidence, making it sound like he just thought of it, and thus, less authoritative.

Both elementary and middle school children need to be taught about creating voice with grammatical features given their audience rather than just using the grammar because that is the way they talk.

Creating a Cohesive Text (Mode)

Earlier in the chapter, the overall cohesion of the text through the development of stages was addressed. When planning to write the whole text, students need to review the stages to determine if the components make sense together. For example, each paragraph in the mentor text presents a reason supported by evidence that dogs make good pets.

There is a further need to ensure that the clauses in individual paragraphs work together, helping the paragraph to flow clearly. Each clause should start with a Theme followed by new information (see Chapter 3). The theme in the following clauses either connects with the original theme or with the new information. For example, in the second paragraph of the mentor text, most of the themes relate to the original "dog" by using pronouns or repeating the word. The pattern is broken only in the fourth sentence when "example" becomes the theme.

Isabella's second paragraph has some good features and some problems.

Number	Theme	New Information
1	Why **we**	should have zoos?
2	**Zoos**	are abusive to **animals**.
3	When an **animal** dose a confusing trick wrong, the cruel **trainer**	will hit, kicked and shocked the animal very badly
4	and [the **trainers**] possably	kill the harm less animal.
5	**It**	[is] horrible what **these repulsive trainers** are doing
6	Would **you**	like if you were abused?
7	**Anmals**	belong in the wild not in zoo.

The themes contain topics that are at the heart of her argument, such as *zoos*, *animals*, and *trainers*. Others relate to the interpersonal function, or the relation between the writer and audience (e.g., *we*, *you*). If the questions with these themes were eliminated, then the clause, *Zoos are abusive to animals*, her first reason, would become the topic sentence. The second question removes the focus on animals. Sometimes, authors writing to children use this strategy to engage them, but it can also break the flow of the argument.

The pronoun *it* at the start of the fifth sentence relates to the previous new information and would be better expressed with a nominalization, such as, *cruelty to ANIMALS*, language that children at this stage are unlikely to naturally produce. Using the nominalization would eliminate *these repulsive trainers* from the new information position, because it would no longer be new to the reader.

The last clause refers back to the central topic of the whole argument, *animals*, and the new information relates to the argument, in general, and does not extend the notion of cruelty, the focus of this paragraph.

Luis's paragraph chosen for Theme/New Information analysis looks more like oral language with themes consisting of mostly pronouns and most of the information contained in the new information. A reader looking only at the themes would not know what the paragraph is about.

Number	Theme	New Information
1	We	should let immigration be allowed
2	because it	is important to candidates.
3	It	is important to candidates
4	because they	rely on the huge amounts of immigrants that may vote for them.
5	The candidates	may scam the immigrants
6	so they	can get many votes
7	and [they]	[can] win the election.

The topic sentence (repeated #2 and 3) follows the unnecessary restatement of the thesis, which is often seen in students' arguments.

Lessons to Teach the Stages and the Language of Arguments

Before beginning these lessons, it is to be assumed that students will have practiced the activities in the Oral Arguments section earlier in this chapter, either in previous grades or during the year. Before starting the standard process of deconstruction, joint construction, and group/individual construction of the various stages in order to create their own written arguments, students will need a number of lessons to practice giving reasons and evidence.

In scientific and response to reading arguments, giving reasons can be a difficult task. In scientific arguments, the reasons must be accurate, reflecting knowledge of science. The evidence, however, is present in the science experiments. When reading literature, the reasons often have to be inferred from the text, whereas the evidence is spelled out in the text. Thus, for science and responses to literature, it is best to teach evidence first and then reasons. For scientific arguments, teachers would begin by carrying out an experiment to collect evidence. For response to literature arguments, students would read the text first. This activity can be done during reading time, using reading strategies to facilitate comprehension.

In commonplace arguments and those using historical contexts or addressing social or current issues, it is easier to state the reasons first. The evidence needs to be researched from a variety of sources. For example, for the thesis statement *People should not smoke*, students can easily come up with the following reasons: *It is bad for people's health* or *People can die of lung cancer*. However, the evidence to support these reasons would be in medical studies that they would need to research. The lessons that follow are ordered for an everyday type of argument, which are the easiest for students and a natural starting point. Lessons should be adapted when teaching other types of arguments.

Lesson 12. Deconstruction of Text to Learn About Stages

With all grade levels, it is best to start with one-sided arguments. For middle school, follow with arguments with rebuttal and eventually with two-sided arguments. Follow the same steps as the lessons included here for one-sided argument, using the appropriate mentor texts.

> **Goal:** To teach the stages of the argument genre so that students learn to organize the text.
>
> **Materials:** Mentor texts, including video and magazine advertisements, brochures, letters, and student work from previous years. Make sure there are arguments written for different audiences (check the types of mentor text needed in Lesson 14 and 15, and include all of them in this lesson, too). Audiovisual equipment. Large version of the argument graphic organizer (downloadable from the *Support Material* tab in the book's webpage). Copies of some of the mentor texts. Highlighters.

Activities

- Read a few mentor texts and show the videos.
- Using a large version of the graphic organizer, identify the stages in the mentor text, connecting them with the graphic organizer. Highlight in different colors: background, thesis/appeal, reasons, evidence, reinforcement of the thesis/appeal. Discuss if any are missing. For example, a 3rd-grade teacher showed her students that the letters in *I Wanna Iguana* included only reasons.
- Group students and give them copies of additional arguments.
- Have students highlight the stages of arguments.

Lesson 13. Reinforce Evaluative Language and Graduation (for All Grades)

> **Goal:** To identify positive and negative language with or without the intensity turned up or down. To apply it in their own arguments.
>
> **Materials:** Chunks of mentor texts familiar to the students with different examples of evaluative language and graduation. Groups of word cards with words that increase or decrease from neutral grading (in bold). Examples include *drenched, soaked, **wet**, moist, damp; stunning, gorgeous, **pretty**, nice-looking; petrified, terrified, **afraid**,scared, upset, worried; pleasant, polite, **nice**, **friendly**, amiable, charming;* and *loathsome, revolting, **ugly**, awful, bad-looking.* Include groups that would work with the images. Images of people who look scared, images of ugly objects, pretty objects appropriate for girls and for boys of your grade level. For example, the latest model of a cell phone, an ugly pair of girl's shoes, of boy's shoes, a pretty dress, and so on.

Activities

- Project one of the mentor texts. Ask the students to identify positive or negative language and any with the volume up or down. Add to the anchor chart started during Lesson 11. Tell them that they will refer to this chart when writing the class and individual arguments.
- Give groups (for young students continue as a whole class) one mentor text each, and ask them to find and highlight additional forms of this language.
- Show students a list of words and discuss how within graduation there are different levels. Show the image of the scared person and discuss which one of the following words: *petrified, terrified, afraid, scared, upset, worried*, would apply to that picture.
- Working in pairs, have each member draw a picture reflecting one of the words in the scared scale. Ask the partner to guess which one it is. Then reveal the chosen word. Have a few pairs share.
- Show the picture of a cell phone. Ask the students how they would describe the phone to convince their parents to buy it for them.
- Give groups samples of the other images and have each student or pair/group choose one. Tell the group to discuss how they would talk about it to their parents to get them to buy it or not buy it (if they consider it ugly).
- Have them write a short letter making the request. Have them underline the examples of evaluative language or graduation they used. Have a couple of students who did a good job share their letters.

Lesson 14. Development of Thesis Statement/Appeal and Background for a Whole Class Argument/and Make Decisions on Generalized Participants, Type of Sentences, and Person to Use

There are two ways to organize the lessons to jointly write a whole class argument and have students write their individual, pairs, or group argument projects.

1. Write the entire whole class argument, followed by the individual ones.
2. Write each aspect of the argument with the whole class, followed by each aspect by the individuals.

The first way is better with older students and the second one with younger students. The lessons that follow illustrate the first way, but they can easily be adapted for the second way.

For two-sided arguments, instead of a thesis statement or appeal, the issue is stated. For example, *As college sports continue to be popular, people have revived the debate on whether college athletes should get paid*. Thus, the lesson should be adjusted to fit this goal.

Goals:

- To teach students to develop the background given the audience.
- To teach students to create thesis statements that express an opinion about something or write an appeal to try to persuade someone to do something.
- To teach students to decide on the use of generalized or specific participants (full lesson in Chapter 6, Lesson 12), types of sentences, and person to use given audience and voice (tenor).

Materials: Vetted Internet resources and books useful for the topic and appropriate for the grade level that illustrate both types of persuasion. Create a note-taking tool in anchor charts and in the students' notebooks by designating a page for background and thesis/appeal, several pages for one reason each with supporting evidence, and a page for the reinforcement of statement. The reasons and evidence pages should have one broad column for the notes and a smaller column to the right for language (specific aspect of language targeted). This tool will be used for all the lessons designed to create an argument.

1. For one-sided argument

2. Argument with rebuttal

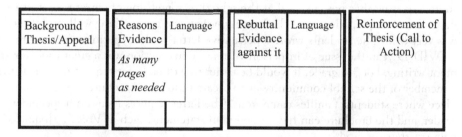

3. For two-sided argument

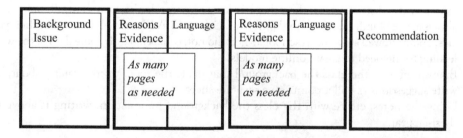

Activities

- Remind students of the thesis/appeal used in oral activities practiced earlier in the unit.
- Project a couple of texts in the type of argument you are teaching and identify:
  - Thesis statement (*Programs that focus on preventing malaria are more effective than those that aim at curing it.*)
  - Appeal (*There is an urgent need to increase the number of National Parks in Australia.*)
- Working with the whole class, decide on the thesis/appeal for the class argument. Ask students for suggestions. Give them feedback and ask questions until deciding the final thesis

statement/appeal. As you are planning the wording, discuss the language and review examples of mentor texts:

- Should we write about participants in general (e.g., *Students should visit Plymouth Plantation*) or a specific participant (e.g., *Our class should visit the Plymouth Plantation*)?
- Should we write in first or third person (e.g., *We should visit Plymouth plantation* or *Students should visit Plymouth plantation.*)?
- Should we write it as a statement, a question, or a command (e.g., *Students should go on a field trip to Plymouth plantation; Don't you think that students should go on a field trip to Plymouth plantation?; Take students on a field trip to Plymouth Plantation!*)?

Discuss how the writer, the audience, or the medium can help us decide which would be the most effective thesis/appeal. For example, if students in a class are writing a letter to a Foundation to get support for field trips, they should use generalized participants (*students*), but if they are writing to their principal to have their own teacher and not outsiders take them on the trip, they should use a specific participant (*Mrs. Miller*). For these two examples, they may use statements to make their arguments more authoritative, but if they are writing a brochure, they may choose a command: *Visit Plymouth Plantation.*

- Write the final version on the lower part of the first page of the chart paper. It is best to find an issue that has emerged at the school or something of current interest to students. For example, one winter the heating system was not working well, and the school was very cold. The students wrote a persuasive letter to the superintendent. During the COVID-19 year, the issue of in-person vs. remote instruction was a great topic for argument writing. For 3rd grade, it would be easier to write a letter requesting something of a member of the school community or to create posters or brochures about visiting the place where students' families came from. The letter requires focus on a specific writer/reader, and the brochure can have a common statement, such as *Visit . . .* [name of the country, state, or city].
- Show students the background information related to the thesis/appeal in a few mentor texts. Tell them this is the information that sets out the need to argue for something. For example, the district where the school is located controls the heat centrally and is not always aware of individual schools' problems. During COVID, schools differed in their policies. Some allowed students in school, others did not; others did only some days of the week, leading to the need to create online models.
- Brainstorm with the class the background that made the topic worth arguing about, and write suggestions as bullet points on a separate sheet.
- Using the notes, create with the class the background information, writing it above the thesis/appeal.

You can have students write their own version of this class project in their notebooks. This is particularly useful when writing the whole class project first. If the students are staggering the class and individual/group projects, then at this point they would work on their own projects before going to the next step.

Lesson 15. Specific Audience Calls for Different Reasons

Goal: To learn to give reasons to persuade given the audience and voice.
Materials: Book *One Word From Sophia*; Chart paper or computer with projector.

Activities

- Read aloud *One Word From Sophia*, or with older students, divide in groups and give each group a couple of pages to read. Discuss why she chooses a particular reason for a particular person. **With grades 6–8,** divide the class in groups and give each group a couple of pages of the book. Tell them that you are giving them pages of a children's book to see if they can figure out what the author is teaching children about argumentation. If the students do not guess, steer the discussion about giving different reasons to different audiences. Tell the students that now they are going to practice how to be as smart as Sophia in choosing reasons.
- Refer back to the thesis or appeal for the class project.
- Brainstorm with students:

  - Who they are trying to persuade in the class project, choosing more than one audience.
  - What they are trying to persuade them to do or about what.

- Have students give reasons that would appeal to each of the chosen audiences.
- Write them underneath the thesis statement/appeal on the chart paper. For example,

STUDENTS NEED TO GO ON FIELD TRIPS

Principal	Students
Educational	Fun
Builds community	Skip being in the classroom
Learn concepts first hand	Get to talk with friends

- Decide on which audience they want to choose for the class argument. Note it on the side of the graphic organizer.

Follow Up: Remind students to think of the audience when planning reasons for the class project (Lesson 18) and for their individual arguments (Lesson 26).

Lesson 16. Specific Audience Calls for Different Types of Evidence

Goal: To recognize that an author chooses different types of evidence deemed most effective given the audience.

Materials: Sets of mentor texts and videos used in previous lessons directed to different audiences with different types of evidence. For example, one TV ad for children and another for adults. One brochure to attract families to a theme park with testimonies of families who had attended and another with statistics and expert opinion to convince adults to take a vitamin complex. One letter directed to students to support having lockers and another directed to the principal requesting lockers for students. Anchor chart with examples of the different kinds of evidence, including facts, expert opinions, statistics, examples, and anecdotes.

Types of Evidence

Facts: *The NCAA brings in roughly $1 billion revenue a year to colleges.*
Expert Opinion: *Researchers state that the cheapest and most effective way of preventing malaria is to use treated nets.*

> Statistics: *Malaria-afflicted families only harvest 40% of the crops that healthy families harvest.*
> Examples: *They can sniff out drugs, find bodies, illicit DVDs and hunt down prisoners.*
> Anecdotes: *There was a very sick man and the dog barked and barked until the rescue team arrived.*

Activities

- Working with one contrasting set of arguments, show each one to the class and together with the students identify the reasons and the evidence. Refer to the type of evidence anchor chart and ask them which type it is.
- Discuss with the students how the reasons and evidence are different in each argument.
- Ask them who they think the audience is for each and why? Steer them to the notion that authors choose the reasons and evidence that they think will be most persuasive for a certain audience.
- Give groups sets of the other arguments for them to identify reasons and evidence and guess the audience.
- Given the audience decided for the class argument, discuss which types of evidence would be appropriate. Note it on the graphic organizer.

Follow Up: Remind students to think of audience and voice when planning evidence for the class project (Lesson 18) and for their individual arguments (Lesson 26).

Lesson 17. How the Language Changes Given Audience and Voice (Grades 4–8)

This lesson can be adapted and repeated over the course of the unit. For example, instead of covering all aspects of language listed in the following table, you may cover one or two aspects of language first and then repeat the lesson adding more aspects.

Goal: To show students that authors use different language features when writing to different audiences.

Materials: Sets of mentor texts used in Lesson 12 directed to different audiences and reflecting different voices. For example, one TV ad for children and another for adults. One brochure reflecting an entertaining voice to attract families to a theme park and another with an authoritative voice to convince adults to take a vitamin complex. One letter directed to students to support having lockers and another directed to the principal requesting lockers for students. Checklist:

Language/ Text	Text 1	Text 2	Text 3	Text 4	Text 5	Text 6
Statements						
Questions						
Commands						
Exclamations						
1st person						
2nd person						
3rd person						

Language/ Text	Text 1	Text 2	Text 3	Text 4	Text 5	Text 6
Positive language						
Negative language						
(with/without volume up or down)						
High modality						
Medium modality						
Low modality						

Activities

- Show the two videos.
- Ask students who they think is the audience for these videos and how they know.
- Show the students the two brochures and ask them the same questions.
- Ask them whether the voice in each brochure is entertaining or authoritative and how they know and why it is different.
- Show the two letters with the addressee covered, i.e., Dear _____.
- Tell them one of the letters is for the principal and the other for students and ask them which one is for the principal and which one for students and how they know.
- As you discuss each set of mentor texts, mark things the students mention in the checklist projected or written on an anchor chart. Depending on the grade level, you may steer the discussion to features they did not notice and go deeper in the discussion of each language feature, or you may just tell the student that over the course of the unit, they will learn how language features help create either a familiar, entertaining, or more formal authoritative voice.
- Divide the class in two or four groups (depending on size). Based on what they have learned in Lessons 15 and 16, have one or two groups create an advertisement on a product directed to children, and the other groups create the advertisement on the same product for adults.
- Have them share and identify good features of their ads. (Because the students still need to learn a lot more to write good arguments, there is no point on worrying about errors at this point.)

Follow Up: Review this lesson when drafting and revising the class project as well as their individual projects.

Lesson 18. Teach Students to Research, Identify, and Take Notes on Supporting Reasons and Evidence/Collect Language that Reflects Expertise on the Topic

Note-taking varies with grade level. For kindergarten and 1st grade, as the students look for reasons in books with dilemmas, the notes are taken as a whole class in anchor charts for the students to use later. In 2nd grade, since looking for evidence is done as a whole class, the note taking can also be as a whole class from different sources. From 3rd grade on, the notes for the whole project are done as a whole class, followed by group or individual note taking for the group or individual projects. The lesson that follows is geared to have students research a variety of sources to find reasons and evidence.

> **Goal**: To teach students how to identify information in a variety of sources that makes for good reasons and effective evidence to support the thesis statement/appeal; to have them identify language related to the topic to use when writing evidence and learn the meaning.

To teach students to identify information that supports the opposite position with respect to their thesis to write their rebuttal: the opposing view and evidence that this view does not work (for middle school).

Materials: Same research resources and note taking tool they started using with Lesson 16. There are many examples from the Internet of "reasons to . . ." articles. For example, a travel brochure for Latin America has 10 reasons to travel with the company (www. statravel.co.uk/the-world-brochure.htm; Latin America 2013.pdf, p. 6). Some animal shelters post reasons to adopt an adult cat. Some are simple and just give the reasons (e.g., www.petfinder.com/pet-adoption/cat-adoption/10-reasons-senior-cats-rule/), while others are lengthier and add information to support the reasons (www.catsontheweb. org/10-reasons.htm). Reports are good for finding evidence. Information to support the rebuttal (for middle schools). Chart paper.

Activities

These activities take several days. It is important not to rush so that the students understand the meaning of the language used and learn how to distinguish reasons and evidence.

- Read aloud a couple of sources that will inspire the class to find reasons to support the thesis. Give copies to pairs of students to have them follow along. (This is particularly helpful because listening comprehension is harder than reading comprehension. Therefore, seeing the text at the same time as hearing it makes it easier to understand and draw ideas from it.)
- Brainstorm with the whole class possible reasons drawn from the first text, keeping in mind what they learned in Lesson 15, and write them on chart paper. At this point, also encourage students to give reasons they may have based on personal experience. In addition, students could interview experts in the topic to get information that will help with reasons and evidence.
- Have the students, working in pairs or groups, identify others from the other reading(s); then have them share, and add them to the chart paper. Students can also include reasons based on their own personal experience.
- Go over what is written on the chart paper and decide which ones would make good reasons given the audience. There is no "magic number" for reasons. (Pat, a 5th-grade teacher, at this point, would take a quick look at the various sources with the students and star the reasons that had more supporting evidence in the sources. Those would be chosen for sure. The others were optional. It cut down on the frustration of not finding evidence and taught students a good strategy to decide on reasons.)
- Have students decide the order to present the reasons, and write them on a fresh sheet of chart paper. Check with the class that they all support the thesis and that they are not repeated or very similar. (It is best to end up with a few reasons that can be well developed and multiple that cannot or that would take too long to develop.)
- Write each agreed upon reason on a different sheet of chart paper. Have the students do the same in their notebooks. You could let the pairs or groups choose their own additional reason.
- As you write the reasons, include evaluative language and graduation found in the text sources, and remind students of their function.
- Take the first reason, and review sources again to find evidence to support that reason. Make notes underneath the reason and discuss whether this evidence is appealing to their audience and clearly supports the reason, keeping in mind what they learned in Lesson 16 about types of evidence. Note content language to describe the evidence in the language column. Check that the students understand the meaning of the language. Have students do it in their notebooks. Repeat the process for each reason.

- As you write the evidence, include evaluative language and graduation found in the text sources, and remind students of their function.

Lesson 19. Learn How to Moderate the Argument by Using Modality (Grades 5–8)

This lesson is recommended for upper elementary and middle school. For younger grades, modality can be edited as the class is jointly constructing arguments as well as when revising, especially if they overuse *can* or use modality that is inconsistent or ineffective for the chosen audience.

Goal: To have students learn how they can control the certainty of opinions or recommendations by using modality.

Materials: Sentences 1–6 (see "Activities") written on chart paper; modality chart (shown earlier) on chart paper or projected, and also as a handout.

Activities

- Show the students the following sentences (or choose similar ones related to the topic you are teaching):

  1. This book is worth reading.
  2. This book is not worth reading.
  3. This book should be read.
  4. This book may be worth reading.
  5. This book might be worth reading.
  6. This book could be worth reading.

- Discuss with the students how different are the opinions expressed in these sentences. The sentences 1 and 2 are statements without modality, so they close the door to other opinions. Sentence 3 denotes obligation. Other modals expressing obligation are *must* and *have to*. Sentences 4–6 open the door to other opinions to different degrees.
- Discuss with students why an author would choose one or the other. Say, if you are writing a letter to the principal asking for a pet for your room, would you write: *You must/should get us a pet for our room* or *You may consider getting a pet for our classroom*. Although *may* expresses less authority/strength than *must/should*, because the principal is someone with more authority than you, making a softer request is more effective.
- Have groups think of two or three examples of persuasive statements using modality given different writers and audiences, including the scenario for the argument they are working on for the class.
- Show students the modality chart, and have the groups think of sentences with language other than modal verbs, such as *definitely*, *probably*, *perhaps*, and so on. Have them share and comment on each other's examples. (Ideally have them work on an electronic document that can be projected, shared, and, if necessary, edited.)

Lesson 20. Learn How to Moderate the Argument by Using Concessive Clauses (Grades 6–8)

Goal: To teach students that concessive clauses allow them to introduce a different point of view while affirming their own.

Materials: Examples of sentences projected or written on an anchor chart.

Activities

- Show these sentences to the students:

  - *Although zoos protect animals from disease, animals are happiest in the wild.*
  - *Animals enjoy life in the wild. However, zoos are instrumental in protecting endangered species.*
  - *Modern zoos have better spaces imitating the wild, but they still do not compare to the expanse of the wild.*

- Ask students to discuss with their partners the position of the authors that wrote these sentences with respect to whether animals should be kept in zoos or not.
- Have them share and clarify if there is disagreement.
- Ask them how they know the author's position.
- Discuss what the authors did and why they did it.
- Have students identify the grammatical structures:

  - *Although* subordinate clause (counter position) + clause (favored position).
  - Clause (counter position) + *However* (favored position).
  - Clause (counter position) + *but* + Clause (favored position)

- Have students find examples in the mentor texts they have been using. For example, in the mentor text *Malaria* at the end of chapter:

  Some policy makers believe that treatment is the solution. However, a major program launched by the WHO failed.

  In spite of heroic efforts to cure malaria, preventing the disease is a much more affordable solution with general immediate benefits to the counties that apply the program.

- Have students work in groups and propose concessive sentences to add to their argument drafts.
- Have a group share theirs and discuss with the class.
- Have everyone insert their sentences in their essays.

Lesson 21. Teach Students to Quote Evidence and Use Verbs to Introduce the Quoted or Reported Evidence (Grades 6–8)

See Chapter 4, Lesson 17.

Lesson 22. Text Connectives

Goal: To teach students the function of text connectives and teach them to use them occasionally.

Materials: Copies of mentor texts with and without text connectives, anchor chart with text connectives table (see Table 8.10).

Activities

- Present the table with text connectives, point at the examples, and ask the students if they have ever seen or heard these words used.
- Go over the table. Explain to the students that the function of these words is to connect chunks of text and that they have different meanings.

- Give groups of students a copy of a mentor text with text connectives and one without them.
- Ask them to circle any that they find, and discuss the purpose of the connection, for example, sequencing, addition, contrast, and so on. Tell them that authors do not always use them.
- Apply the use later to the whole class project and their projects, if appropriate. Do not encourage their use.

Lesson 23. Write Planned Thesis, Reasons, and Evidence for the Whole Class Project and Review Language Features Learned in Previous Lessons

Goal: To produce the class project in the chosen medium as a model for the students to later produce their group/individual essays.

Materials: Samples of the medium they will write. Anchor charts with Background and Thesis and Reasons and Evidence. Chart paper or computer and projector. Checklist with language features studied so far.

Activities

- Give groups of students samples of the medium they will use, and ask them to notice the format so that they can create something comparable.
- Have them share their ideas with the whole class as you point it out in one sample that you are projecting for the whole class to share. For example,
  - Print ads: include phrases and whole sentences stating the thesis, reasons and evidence, and images reinforcing them.
  - Video ads: actors saying the script and captions stating the thesis, reasons and evidence, and images of product.
  - Brochures: several folded pages with phrases, sentences and short paragraphs stating the thesis, reasons and evidence, and images reinforcing them.
  - Essays: paragraphs for (a) background, thesis, and sometimes preview of reasons; (b) each reason supported with evidence; and (c) reinforcement of thesis and sometimes call to action. Each paragraph has a topic sentence stating the reason followed by several sentences expressing the evidence (the length will depend on the grade level). The evidence may include quotes from experts or from data sources, graphics, tables, or others. On rare occasions, authors start the paragraph with a text connective or transition word or phrase, such as *furthermore, finally, in conclusion,* and so on.
- Jointly decide on the medium and the features that the class project will have.
- Jointly construct each section with students and negotiate what will be included based on the notes in the anchor charts created in the planning process and the features you determined the medium has.
- As you create the phrases, sentences, or paragraphs, depending on the medium, remind students to use the language features that you have covered so far (refer to the checklist).
- For essays, depending on the grade level, you may jointly construct the introductory paragraph with background, thesis, and preview of reasons and the first paragraph with reasons and evidence, and then have groups of students create one of the other paragraphs. Then put the essay together, and read it with the whole class (see Chapter 4, Lesson 15 if you need to teach how to transform notes to paragraphs).

- Add images such as pictures or cartoon-like ones, depending on the medium. Essays do not include images.
- Read a section of the final product with the whole class to check if there is need for any revision. Make changes as needed.
- Have students in groups review other sections and propose and add any additional revisions.
- Have students do their own version of the class argument in their notebooks.

Lesson 24. Review Paragraphs With the Theme/New Information Tool (Grades 6–8 Essays)

Goal: To use the Theme/New Information principle to revise paragraphs to help the information flow.

Materials: A table to be projected or on chart paper with two columns, one with the themes from a paragraph of a published persuasive text that the students have not seen (left column), and the other with the themes of a paragraph from a student uncoached writing essay (right column).

Long before television was invented people	I think we
Books	So they
Many people	So when
Books	and so we
(from Humphrey et al., 2012, p. 191)	

Full samples of the mentor text and student work. Large Theme/New Information Worksheet (as shown) on Chart paper or the Smart Board; individual worksheets for the groups.

	Theme	New Information
1		
2		
3		
Etc.		

Activities

- Show the table with the two sets of themes without telling them which is the mentor text and which is the student work, and ask the students to identify what each paragraph is about. Ask, "What are the authors arguing about?"
- Discuss what from the columns helped to answer this question, and what made it difficult.
- Do the Theme/New Information analysis of one paragraph of the mentor text that you are using, inserting each sentence analyzed in one line:

	Theme	New Information
1		
2		
3		
Etc.		

- Discuss with the students what they see in the theme position. Does it help them to understand what the paragraph is about? How does the new information in one clause connect with the theme in the next?
- Take one paragraph of the class essay, and do a Theme/New Information analysis with the whole class.
- Cover the new information and ask the students whether they can tell what the paragraph is about from the themes. Ask them if they should make any adjustments.
- Look at both the theme and the new information. Do the themes connect with each other or with the new information (depending on the style used)? Do they want to make any adjustments?
- Using their individual Theme/New Information Worksheets, have each group look at one paragraph of the class essay and do the analysis. Conference with individuals or groups while they work.
- Have groups share with the class and make final edits to the class essay.
- Have them write the whole essay in their notebooks.

Lesson 25. Reinforcement of the Position

Goal: To teach students to create a conclusion that connects, but does not repeat, the thesis statement.

Materials: Class graphic organizer and group/individual graphic organizers that have been developed in previous lessons. Projector.

Activities

- Project the mentor text, and compare the conclusion with the thesis statement. While the thesis statement says, "Dogs . . . make good pets," the concluding statement reads, "To sum up, dogs are really friendly, civilized and loyal companions." Both sentences present the same idea, but they use different words. Moreover, the conclusion greatly reinforces the thesis statement. Repeat this activity with other mentor texts, including arguments to do something that include and do not include a call to action.
- Review the thesis statement or appeal in the class project, and brainstorm possible conclusions. Add it to the class chart sheet for reinforcement of statement.
- Discuss with the class which conclusion seems to be the strongest reinforcement of the position, always with the audience in mind, and include it in the final product.
- Have students add it to their notebooks.

Lesson 26. Produce Individual, Pair, or Group Argument

Goal: To have students produce an argument in the same medium as the class project.

Materials: Checklist with all the steps taken to produce the class project and the language aspects that were covered. Pages in the notebook to organize the stages of the argument: background and thesis, reasons and evidence, reinforcement of thesis. Anchor charts used to produce the class project. Research resources and mentor texts.

Activities

- Brainstorm topic of their argument.
- Identify research resources.
- Review steps in the checklist and in the anchor charts.

Structure of Argument	Aspects of Language
√ Introduction with background, thesis statement, and option of previewing reasons √ Reasons supported by evidence √ Reinforcement of thesis statement. Call to action if argument to do something. √ Layout given the medium	*List here aspects reviewed and taught. Point to anchor charts that further develop the aspects of language.*

- Have students start the process while you go around checking and reminding them what to do. Make sure that they take their time planning to produce a good project.
- Conference with students, especially in connection to aspects of language taught during the unit.

Lesson 27. Joint Revision of Aspects of Language

Goal To teach students how to revise their products.
Materials: Sections of a couple of students' products.

Activities

- With the author's permission, project a section of their final draft. Choose work from students who need extra help.
- Have the author read it aloud.
- Ask questions to get students to focus on specific issues related to things that you have taught. Remember to always talk about the impact on audience of their language choices. For example, in this paragraph from Isabella's essay, all three persons are used:

Why we should have zoos? Zoos are abusive to animals. When a animal dose a confusing trick wrong, the cruel trainer will hit, kicked or shocked the animal very baddly and possably kill the harm less animal. It's horrible what these repulsive trainers are doing—would you like if you were abused? Anmals belong in the wild not in zoo.

- Ask students to work in pairs and note the person used for each sentence. Then focus on the first sentences that uses first person and make the observation that she actually does not need that question because she is repeating the thesis. Discuss how it is not necessary to repeat the thesis with each reason and evidence paragraph (very common habit of students). Discuss the question with "you." What is the impact of that kind of question (e.g., it builds solidarity with the audience, but it also makes the essay less authoritative and interrupts the flow of the evidence)? What would the author like to do?
- Have students help each other revise their essays for person and make decisions about what they have used and whether it is their intended voice.
- Work with one or two other paragraphs from other students that raise other issues related to what you taught, and carry out the same process.
- With middle school students, revise one paragraph using the Theme/New Information tool.
- While groups are working, conference with individual students who need extra help.

Lesson 28. Images That Accompany Arguments

Posters, PowerPoints, brochures, and any type of advertisement require images. Scientific and math arguments may require images, graphs, or figures. Using sample mentor texts in the medium, follow the steps described in Chapter 2, Lesson 17.

ANALYSIS OF STUDENT WORK: PURPOSE, STAGES, AND LANGUAGE

Argument—Analysis of Student Work: Purpose, Stages, and Language

Key: 1. Needs substantial support; 2. Needs instruction; 3. Needs Revision; 4. Meets Standard; NA: Not applicable

	1	2	3	4	Comments
Purpose To persuade to do something or about something					
Stages follow the organization of an argument and the content relates to the thesis or appeal					
Introduction Background Information Thesis Statement or Appeal Preview of Reasons (optional)					
Reasons Evaluate for both structure and meaning					
Evidence Content supports corresponding reason Types of evidence appeal to the audience					
Reinforcement of Statement of Position Reinforces, does not repeat Includes a call to action in "to do" arguments					

	1	2	3	4	Uncoached piece
Generalized Participants (dogs, zoos, animals)					
Language That Reflects Expertise on the Topic					
Evaluative Language					
Graduation • Turns up or down the intensity • Narrows or widens the focus					
Types of Sentences					
Use of Person					
Modality					
Opening or Closing Doors to Other Positions (middle school)					
Introducing Others' Points of View (middle school)					
Cohesive Paragraphs: Theme/New Information (based on the analysis done in the following form)					

Criteria

1. Needs substantial support: The student writer needs extensive help developing that aspect of the genre.
2. There are gaps in the writer's understanding of the specific aspect. The writer has insufficient control. S/he needs instruction and practice.

3. The paper needs revision on one or two instances of the feature. A conference would be sufficient to help the writer meet the standard.
4. The paper reflects what the student should be able to accomplish and write independently given the instruction provided for this grade level.

(National Center on Education and the Economy, 2004)

Theme/New Information Analysis of the Second Paragraph
Insert paragraph here:

	THEME	NEW INFORMATION
1		
2		
3		
4		
5		

Graphic Organizers

One-sided Argument (with or without rebuttal)

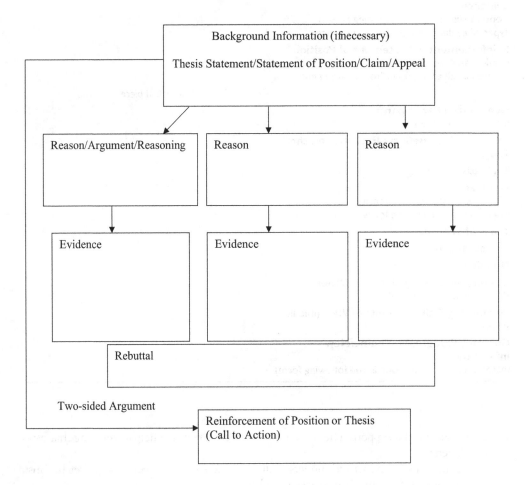

Two-sided Argument

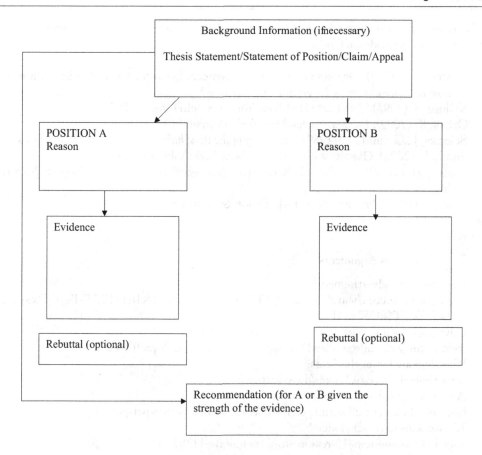

Mentor Texts That Illustrate the Genre; Two Full Mentor Texts

For Oral Activities

Steig, W. (2002). *Which Would You Rather Be?* New York: Harper Collins.

Written as Arguments

Leavitt, P. B. (2001). "The mosquito's song." In P. B. Janeczco (Ed.), *Dirty laundry pile: Poems in different voices.* New York: HarperCollins. (Persuasive poem)

Stead, T. (2000). *Should there be zoos? A persuasive text.* New York: Mondo Publishing. (Book written by students and their teacher)

Storybooks

(a) Books With Dilemmas

Cherry, L. (2000) The Great Kapok Tree. New York: Voyager Books, Harcourt. (translated to Spanish El Gran Capoquero).
YouTube read aloud in Spanish www.youtube.com/watch?v=RZtJqZBGPdE
Hoose, P. M. (1998), *Hey, little ant.* Tricycle Press. (*Oye, hormiguita*, Spanish version).

(b) Books Where the Characters Argue

There are a number of storybooks that illustrate the language of persuasion by showing characters trying to persuade each other.

Averbeck, J. (2015). *One word from Sophia*. Atheneum Books for Young Readers. (Illustrates how to change reasons depending on audience.)

Kellogg, S. (1992). *Can I keep him?* New York: Penguin Group (USA)

Orloof, K. (2009). *I wanna iguana*. New York: Putnam Juvenile.

Scieszka, J., & Smith, L. (1989). *True story of the three little pigs*. New York: Puffin Books.

Smith, L. (2006). *Glasses: Who needs 'em?* New York: Viking Juvenile.

Teague, M. (2002). *Dear Mrs. LaRue: Letters from obedience school*. New York: Scholastic, Inc.

Viorst, J. (1993). *Earrings!* New York: Simon & Schuster.

Internet Resources

- Texts Written as Arguments

  Anti-smoking advertisement:
  www.youtube.com/watch?v=xEDpJTTDZP8&index=2&list=PL5F-BsyODxxcU9c8fnTn2JlX-d050xztH
  Playing games is important for both children and adults:
  www.testmagic.com/test/ViewDtlEssay.asp?EssayID=29&TopicID=60
  Why dogs are better than cats:
  www.jamesabela.co.uk/exams/dogsvscats.pdf
  Adopting a pet from the pound:
  https://k12.thoughtfullearning.com/studentmodels/adopting-pet-pound
  10   Reasons to travel alone:
  www.fodors.com/news/10-reasons-to-travel-alone-11387

- Examples of How to Create Brochures

  www.stocklayouts.com/Downloads/PDF/Preview/TR0110101-Preview.pdf

- Resources to Teach About Evidence

  www.hhs.helena.k12.mt.us/Teacherlinks/Oconnorj/evidence.html (How to use evidence in persuasive communications.)
  www.toptenz.net/top-10-persuasive-tv-ads.php (Ten TV commercials with persuasive arguments for products.)
  www.toucaned.com/Products/PublicHealth/TeensAdultsPosterPamph.html   (Brochure about germs; how germs work and how to avoid them.)
  www.toucaned.com/Products/PublicHealth/ToolKitImages/adult/pamphlets/english/03.jpg
  www.youtube.com/watch?v=R9jaOROeYII&feature=PlayList&p=76F12E0A6994189E&index=4&playnext=2&playnext_from=PL (Toyota Tundra commercial.)

- Arguments With Both Sides

  Argumentative Book p. 5
  www.academic-englishuk.com/wp-content/uploads/2017/04/Argumentative-book-1.pdf

Full Mentor Text Examples

Mentor Text 1: Argument With a Rebuttal (Middle School Grades)

Malaria—One of The Oldest Diseases

Malaria is an infectious disease caused by parasites that are transmitted to people through female mosquitoes. Each year, over half a billion people will become infected with malaria, with roughly 80% of them living in Sub-Saharan Africa. Nearly half a million people die of malaria every year, most of them young children under the age of five. While there have been many programs designed to improve access to malaria treatment, the best way to reduce the impact of malaria in Sub-Saharan Africa is to focus on reducing the number of people who contract the disease in the first place, rather than waiting to treat the disease after the person is already infected.

Programs that focus on preventing infection from occurring are cheaper and more effective; reducing the number of people who contract malaria also reduces loss of work/school days which can further bring down the productivity of the region.

One of the cheapest and most effective ways of preventing malaria is to implement insecticide—treated bed nets (ITNs). These nets provide a protective barrier around the person or people using them. While untreated bed nets are still helpful, those treated with insecticides are much more useful because they stop mosquitoes from biting people and they help reduce mosquito populations in a community, thus helping people who don't even own bed nets. In fact, transmission of malaria can be reduced by as much as 90% in areas where the use of ITNs is widespread. Because money is so scarce in Sub-Saharan Africa, the low cost is a great benefit and a major reason why the program is so successful. Bed nets cost roughly 2 USD to make, last several years, and can protect two adults. Studies have shown that, for every 100–1000 more nets are being used, one less child dies of malaria. With an estimated 300 million people in Africa not being protected by mosquito nets, there's the potential to save three million lives by spending just a few dollars per person.

Reducing the number of people who contract malaria would also reduce poverty levels in Africa significantly, thus improving other aspects of society like education levels and the economy. When fewer people get sick, the working population is stronger as a whole because people are not put out of work from malaria, nor are they caring for sick relatives. Malaria—afflicted families can typically only harvest 40% of the crops that healthy families can harvest. Additionally, a family with members who have malaria spends roughly a quarter of its income on treatment, not including the loss of work they also must deal with due to the illness. It's estimated that malaria costs Africa 12 billion USD in lost income every year. A strong working population creates a stronger economy, which Sub-Saharan Africa is in desperate need of.

Some policy makers believe that treatment is the solution. However, a major program launched by the WHO failed. The number of people in Sub-Saharan Africa who contracted malaria as well as the number of malaria deaths actually increased over 10% during the time the program was active. The participating countries could not afford such an expensive program, and the widespread use of chloroquine created drug resistant parasites which are now plaguing Sub-Saharan Africa.

In spite of heroic efforts to cure malaria, preventing the disease is a much more affordable solution with general immediate benefits to the counties that apply the program.

Adapted from www.collegeessay.org/blog/argumentative-essay-examples

Mentor Text 2: Argument With Two Sides (Middle School Grades)

College Sports

As college sports continue to be hugely popular and the National Collegiate Athletic Association (NCAA) brings in large amounts of revenue, people have revived the debate on whether college athletes should get paid.

There are many ways payments could work. They could be in the form of a free-market approach, where athletes are able to earn whatever the market is willing to pay them, it could be a set amount of money per athlete, or student athletes could earn income from endorsements, autographs, and control of their likeness, similar to the way top Olympians earn money.

Proponents of the idea believe that, because college athletes are the ones who are training, participating in games, and bringing in audiences, they should receive some sort of compensation for their work. If there were no college athletes, the NCAA wouldn't exist, college coaches wouldn't receive there (sometimes very high) salaries, and brands like Nike couldn't profit from college sports. In fact, the NCAA brings in roughly $1 billion in revenue a year, but college athletes don't receive any of that money in the form of a paycheck. Additionally, people who believe college athletes should be paid state that paying college athletes will actually encourage them to remain in college longer and not turn pro as quickly, either by giving them a way to begin earning money in college or requiring them to sign a contract stating they'll stay at the university for a certain number of years while making an agreed-upon salary.

Supporters of this idea point to Zion Williamson, the Duke basketball superstar, who, during his freshman year, sustained a serious knee injury. Many argued that, even if he enjoyed playing for Duke, it wasn't worth risking another injury and ending his professional career before it even began for a program that wasn't paying him. Williamson seems to have agreed with them and declared his eligibility for the NCAA draft later that year. If he was being paid, he may have stayed at Duke longer. In fact, roughly a third of student athletes surveyed stated that receiving a salary while in college would make them "strongly consider" remaining collegiate athletes longer before turning pro.

Paying athletes could also stop the recruitment scandals that have plagued the NCAA. In 2018, the NCAA stripped the University of Louisville's men's basketball team of its 2013 national championship title because it was discovered coaches were using sex workers to entice recruits to join the team. There have been dozens of other recruitment scandals where college athletes and recruits have been bribed with anything from having their grades changed, to getting free cars, to being straight out bribed. By paying college athletes and putting their salaries out in the open, the NCAA could end the illegal and underhanded ways some schools and coaches try to entice athletes to join.

People who argue against the idea of paying college athletes believe the practice could be disastrous for college sports. By paying athletes, they argue, they'd turn college sports into a bidding war, where only the richest schools could afford top athletes, and the majority of schools would be shut out from developing a talented team (though some argue this already happens because the best players often go to the most established college sports programs, who typically pay their coaches millions of dollars per year). It could also ruin the tight camaraderie of many college teams if players become jealous that certain teammates are making more money than they are.

They also argue that paying college athletes actually means only a small fraction would make significant money. Out of the 350 Division I athletic departments, fewer than a dozen earn any money. Nearly all the money the NCAA makes comes from men's football and basketball, so paying college athletes would make a small group of men—who likely will be signed to pro teams and begin making millions immediately out of college—rich at the expense of other players.

Those against paying college athletes also believe that the athletes are receiving enough benefits already. The top athletes already receive scholarships that are worth tens of thousands per year, they receive free food/housing/textbooks, have access to top medical care if they are injured, receive top coaching, get travel perks and free gear, and can use their time in college as a way to capture the attention of professional recruiters. No other college students receive anywhere near as much from their schools.

People on this side also point out that, while the NCAA brings in a massive amount of money each year, it is still a non-profit organization. How? Because over 95% of those profits are redistributed to its members' institutions in the form of scholarships, grants, conferences, support for Division II and Division III teams, and educational programs. Taking away a significant part of that revenue would hurt smaller programs that rely on that money to keep running.

While both sides have good points, it's clear that the negatives of paying college athletes far outweigh the positives. College athletes spend a significant amount of time and energy playing for their school, but they are compensated for it by the scholarships and perks they receive. Adding a salary to that would result in a college athletic system where only a small handful of athletes (those likely to become millionaires in the professional leagues) are paid by a handful of schools who enter bidding wars to recruit them, while the majority of student athletics and college athletic programs suffer or even shut down for lack of money. Continuing to offer the current level of benefits to student athletes makes it possible for as many people to benefit from and enjoy college sports as possible.

Professional Articles That Describe Instruction of the Genre

Brisk, M. E., & Alvarado, J. (2020). Uncovering 'the story' behind meaningful texts: Bilingual students' intentions and linguistic choices. In M. Zappavigna & S. Dreyfus (Eds.), *Discourses of hope and reconciliation—On J. R. Martin's contribution to systemic functional linguistics* (pp. 167–183). London: Bloomsbury.

Khote, N. (2018). Translanguaging in systemic functional linguistics: A culturally sustaining pedagogy for writing in secondary schools. In R. Harmann (Ed.), *Bilingual learners and social equity: Critical approaches to systemic functional linguistics* (pp. 153–178). New York: Springer.

O'Hallaron, C. L. (2014). Supporting fifth-grade ELLs' argumentative writing development. *Written Communication, 31*(3), 304.

Shin, D. S. (2018). *Multimodal mediation and argumentative writing: A case study of a multilingual learner's metalanguage awareness development. Bilingual learners and social equity* (pp. 225–242). Cham: Springer.

Symons, C. (2017). Supporting emergent bilinguals' argumentation: Evaluating evidence in informational science texts. *Linguistics and Education, 38*, 79–91.

Zisselsberger, M. (2016). Toward a humanizing pedagogy: Leveling the cultural and linguistic capital in a fifth-grade writing classroom. *Bilingual Research Journal, 39*(2), 121–137.

References

Anderson, D. D. (2008). The elementary persuasive letter: Two cases of situated competence, strategy, and agency. *Research in the Teaching of English, 42*, 270–314.

Bermúdez, A. B., & Prater, D. L. (1994). Examining the effects of gender and second language proficiency on Hispanic writers' persuasive discourse. *Bilingual Research Journal, 18*(3 & 4), 47–62.

Brisk, M. E. (2021). *Language in writing instruction: Enhancing literacy in grades 3–8.* New York: Routledge.

Brisk, M. E., & Harrington, M. M. (2007). *Literacy and bilingualism: A handbook for all teachers* (2nd ed.). Mahwah, NJ: Lawrence Erlbaum Associates.

Bunch, G. C., Walqui, A., & Pearson, P. D. (2014). Complex text and new common standards in the United States: Pedagogical implications for English learners. *TESOL Quarterly, 48*, 533–559.

Butt, D., Fahey, R., Feez, S., & Spinks, S. (2012). *Using functional grammar: An explorer's guide* (3rd ed.). South Yarra, Victoria, Australia: Palgrave Macmillan.

Christie, F., & Derewianka, B. (2008). *School discourse: Learning to write across the years of schooling*. London: Continuum.

Coffin, C. (2006). *Historical discourse: The language of time, cause and evaluation*. New York: Continuum.

Common Core State Standards Initiative. (2010). *Preparing America's Students for College and Career*. Retrieved February 14, 2013, from http://www.corestandards.org

Derewianka, B. (2011). *A new grammar companion for teachers*. Marickville, NSW, Australia: Primary English Teaching Association.

Derewianka, B., & Jones, P. (2016). *Teaching language in context* (2nd ed.). Melbourne: Oxford University Press.

Droga, L. & Humphrey, S. (2003). *Grammar and meaning: An introduction for primary teachers*. Berry NSW, Australia: Target Texts.

Edelsky, C., & Smith, K. (1984). Is that writing—Or are those marks just a figment of the curriculum. *Language Arts, 61*, 24–32.

Fang, Z., & Schleppegrell, M. J. (2008). *Reading in secondary content areas: A language based pedagogy*. Ann Arbor: University of Michigan Press.

Ferretti, R. P., & Lewis, W. E. (2013). Best practices in teaching argumentative writing. In S. Graham, C. A. MacArthur, & J. Fitzgerald (Eds.), *Best practices in writing instruction* (2nd ed., pp. 113–140). New York: The Guilford Press.

Gebhard, M., Harman, R., & Seger, W. (2007). Reclaiming recess: Learning the language of persuasion. *Language Arts, 84*, 419–430.

Halliday, M. A. K., & Matthiessen, C. M. I. M. (2004). *An introduction to functional grammar* (3rd ed.). London: Hodder Arnold.

Harris, T. L., & Hodges, R. E. (Eds.). (1995). *The literacy dictionary: The vocabulary of reading and writing*. Newark, DE: International Reading Association.

Hinkel, E. (2002). *Second language writers' text*. Mahwah, NJ: Lawrence Erlbaum Associates.

Humphrey, S. (2017). *Academic literacies in the middle years: A framework for enhancing teacher knowledge and student achievement*. New York: Routledge.

Humphrey, S., Droga, L., & Feez, S. (2012). *Grammar and meaning*. Newtown, NSW, Australia: Primary English Teaching Association Australia.

Humphrey, S., & Vale, E. (2020). *Investigating model texts for learning*. Sydney: PETAA.

Kroll, B. M. (1984). Audience adaptation in children's persuasive letters. *Written Communication, 1*, 404–427.

Marks, G., & Mousley, J. (1990). Mathematics education and genre: Dare we make the process writing mistake again? *Language and Education, 4*(2), 117–130.

Martin, J. R., & White, P. R. R. (2005). *The language of evaluation: Appraisal in English*. New York: Palgrave MacMillan.

Martínez, R. A., Orellana, M. F., Pacheco, M., & Carbone, P. (2008). Found in translation: Connecting translating experiences to academic writing. *Language Arts, 85*, 421–441.

Massachusetts Comprehensive Assessment System. (2009). *2009 MCAS Grade 4 English Language Arts, Question 17*. Retrieved on 10/21/09 from www.doe.mass.edu/mcas/student/2009/question.asp?Grade4

McNeill, K. L., & Krajcik, J. (2012). *Supporting grade 5–8 students in constructing explanations in science: The claim, evidence, and reasoning framework for talk and writing*. Boston, MA: Pearson.

National Center on Education and the Economy. (2004). *Assessment for learning: Using rubrics to improve student writing*. Pittsburg, PA: The University of Pittsburg.

O'Hallaron, C. L., & Schleppegrell, M. J. (2016). "Voice" in children's science arguments: Aligning assessment criteria with genre and discipline. *Assessing Writing, 30*, 63–73.

Rog, L. J., & Kropp, P. (2004). *The write genre*. Ontario, Canada: Pembroke.

Rose, D., & Martin, J. R. (2012). *Learning to write, reading to learn: Genre, knowledge, and pedagogy in the Sydney School*. London: Equinox.

Sánchez Ares, R. (2012). SFL persuasive writing instruction: A case study for bilingual students' writing development & cultural identity formation. *Unpublished paper presented at the 2012 Genre conference*, June 28, Carleton University.

Stead, T. (2002). *Is that a fact?: Teaching nonfiction writing K-3*. Portland, ME: Stenhouse.

Wollman-Bonilla, J. (2004). Principled teaching to(wards) the test?: Persuasive writing in two classrooms. *Language Arts, 81*(6), 502–512.

Zembal-Saul, C., McNeill, K. L., & Hershberger, K. (2013). *What's your evidence? Engaging k-5 students in constructing explanations in science*. Pearson: Allyn & Bacon.

Chapter 9

Enhancing Writing Instruction for Bilingual Learners (Written in Collaboration With Mariam Gorbea Ramy)

Teachers using this book may find themselves in instructional contexts that (1) include speakers of a language other than English, often called English Language Learners, in their English-medium classrooms or (2) teach in English and another language to all students in the program or school, such as in Dual Language schools. The term *bilingual learners* is used in the context of this book to refer to students fluent in two or more languages, including English, or students in the process of acquiring a second language, whether English or the school's target language. Speakers of Black English (Baker-Bell, 2020) who speak or are learning the variety of English used in schools are also bilingual learners. To enhance teachers' understanding of bilingual learners and best school practices, this chapter covers an overview of children's writing development followed by recommendations to enhance the teaching in educational contexts that include bilingual learners.

Children's Language and Literacy Development

As children grow up in a specific social context, they develop language, literacy, and knowledge of the world. This development is influenced by cognitive and linguistic maturity, as well as the context of language use. Given their experiences, students come to school with knowledge of one or more written and/or oral languages. These language and literacy skills develop in stages.

There are broadly four stages after infancy: early childhood, primary school years, middle childhood, and adolescence (Christie, 2012; Menyuk & Brisk, 2005). While students develop at different rates depending on personal and contextual influences (Schleppegrell & Christie, (2018), during early childhood, children typically learn to interact with others, begin to narrate, and demonstrate initial knowledge of literacy. In the course of the early school grades, they learn to interact with the oral and written discourses of school. As they advance in age and schooling, children construct more abstract concepts and encounter in earnest the subject-specific language of the disciplines.

In the case of monolingual and simultaneous bilinguals (children who acquire more than one language simultaneously), these stages are comparable regardless of the language(s) in which the children are raised, provided students attend school in that language (Menyuk & Brisk, 2005). For sequential bilinguals (students who acquire another language later), these stages follow a similar progression but vary for each language, depending on when they are introduced and whether children are exposed to literacy and/or schooled in those languages. The profile of multilingual learners changes constantly depending on age, use, and context (Baker & Wright, 2017; Menyuk & Brisk, 2005).

Within the typical developmental progression, writing progresses depending on children's literacy experiences. During the first years of schooling, children express their ideas through drawings often accompanied with pseudo writing. Letters or groups of letters emerge, but do not

DOI: 10.4324/9781003329275-9

always follow the accepted directionality and alignment. The written text usually starts by describing the drawing and later by telling the story of a personal experience illustrated in the drawing. As children grow, texts become longer and more complex. Language increasingly carries meaning, slowly replacing drawings as the vehicle for the message.

Parallel to the development of the message is the development of the writing system. Children experiment with words, writing approximations of the correct spelling, with a few exceptions where words have been memorized and spelled correctly. The writing grows more conventional with further development, mainly related to the ability to pack language into clear, but meaning-rich clauses and sentences.

Children move from writing about concrete ideas to include more abstraction (Christie, 2012; Kress, 1994). Studies comparing the spoken and written language of elementary age children show changes between 3rd and 6th grades. These changes indicate that these years are important for supporting written language development (Kroll & Lempers, 1981; Lull, 1929). Christie (2012) suggests that children's language in their late childhood and early adolescent stage (ages 9–13) begins "to change, facilitated by a gradual expansion of language resources, so that children can make meanings in new ways" (p. 28). These changes pave the way for the understanding of the grammar of written language.

As children make the transition from oral to written discourse, they achieve a growing control of the thematic patterns of their writing and show greater control of internal reference to build cohesion in their texts. Students learn to compress more information into different types of prepositional phrases and to use nominalizations and other strategies to expand noun groups and create denser texts (Hunt, 1965). They also learn to make meaning through other semiotic resources such as graphs, images, tables, diagrams, and so on.

Some of the developmental features in students' writing in English result from being raised in more than one language or having English as their second language. Bilingual students who are developing writing in their second language go through similar development as native speakers of that language (Fitzgerald, 2006). They also have challenges related to their knowledge of another language, and cross-linguistic and cross-cultural influences (Brisk, 2011). It is important not to stereotype cultural differences because the writing of L2 students is not only influenced by culture, but also by personal experiences and instruction (Matsuda, 1997).

Strong writing ability in the native language supports writing development in the second language (Barratt-Pugh & Rohl, 2001; Carlisle & Beeman, 2000). Many bilingual students develop biliteracy abilities when they attend schools that promote them (Gort, 2006; Homza, 1995; Lindholm-Leary, 2001) or because they immigrated when they were already literate in their native language. A correlation between native language writing ability and performance in English writing exists even when the languages have a different script (Cummins, 1991). Second language writers successfully tap their native language resources to solve the problem of composing in the second language.

The initial demands of writing are such that children are usually behind from their oral language development (Christie, 2012; Loban, 1976). Halliday (1993) claims that children are behind by up to three years in their ability to make meaning through writing. Further, as Heath (1983) illustrated in her research, ways of communicating differ among communities of different cultural and social backgrounds. Some of the oral language dialects are closer to the written version than others, making learning to write a different experience given children's background (Kress, 1994).

Genre and medium preferences as well as cultural background impact students' writing. When children write in their preferred genre or medium, their writing is much better than when they write in those that they dislike. Some children like personal recount, while others prefer fantasies and adventure stories. Often, but not always, these preferences run along gender lines (Franklin

& Thompson, 1994; McPhail, 2009). Differences across gender were apparent in the quality of persuasive writing samples of Hispanic 4th-grade students. Female writers' essays "show a greater degree of elaboration and a clearer attempt to express the writer's point of view than those written by male Hispanic students, regardless of proficiency level" (Bermúdez & Prater, 1994, p. 53).

Some genres evidence different characteristics across cultures (Connor, 2002; Hinkel, 2002; Matalene, 1985). For example, most children come to school familiar with narrative genres acquired in the context of the home where oral storytelling or book reading may be part of their daily practice. However, narratives vary in structure across cultures (McCabe & Bliss, 2003; Pérez, 2004). When children are asked to write personal recounts in school, they will use their own cultural patterns of telling stories. Sometimes, children may feel conflicted because it is not appropriate to share personal matters in school in some cultures (Dien, 2004).

In summary, the development of writing is a difficult and complex task. This section has provided an overview of the development of language and writing in monolingual and bilingual students, and the way students' different backgrounds impact writing development. Throughout the genre chapters, features of students' writing illustrate the success and challenges students encounter when writing.

Enhancing Practices to Educate Students of Multiple Language and Cultural Backgrounds

Bilingual schools may already practice the recommendations included in this section. English medium schools need to consider the education of bilingual students, especially those who are in the process of learning English (or the school's target language) or have not been taught to write in English (or the school's target language). Just as all students, emergent bilinguals need content- and language-rich education to learn and develop in an academic environment. However, this access to the curriculum will elude them if they cannot fully participate in the classroom context. Avoiding marginalization of emergent bilinguals can be achieved in any class, regardless of language of instruction, under contextual conditions that promote equality (de Jong, 2011). The practices promoted in this book have proven supportive of bilingual learners because the instruction is explicit, and there is great emphasis on functional language instruction (Santiago Schwarz & Hamman-Ortiz, 2020). The recommendations included in this section further strengthen the support of bilingual learners, either in bilingual or English-medium schools.

Curricular Topics

It is important to make connections between the grade level curricular content and the cultures, histories, and experiences of bilingual and minoritized students. However, teachers should not always focus on immigration or surface level aspects of culture (e.g., Food and music) in lessons addressing biculturalism and diversity. For the case of many bilingual students, immigration may not be an experience that immediately resonates with them because they are children of immigrants born in the United States. Therefore, while students may have a sense of national and cultural identity to the United States and another country, talking about immigration will not connect to them personally. Teachers must find connections to students' cultures, histories, and experiences through other means. For example, a 2nd-grade teacher working on a unit on Native Americans, which included all about corn, connected the use of corn as a diet staple in Central America, the place of origin of several of her students. A 4th-grade teacher compared the dilemma that colonials in the United States felt toward their sense of identity during the struggle for independence with her own students'—who were mostly from the Dominican Republic— sense of national identity.

In bilingual schools, the culture of students of the school's target language should be covered during instruction in both languages. The responsibility of fostering biculturalism and critical consciousness should not fall only on the teachers of the language other than English. For example, 6th-grade history in a Spanish bilingual program featured Latin American history, while the English class included units on Magical Realism short stories, a narrative literary subgenre typical of Latin America.

Teaching the Genres

Depending on the language, there may be differences in the stages and/or the language features of the genres. In the case of Spanish and English, most of the differences are present with the language rather than the stages of the genre. For example, in both these languages, procedures have the goals, materials or ingredients, and method or steps. However, the verb form differs. While in English only the imperative is used, in Spanish there is a choice of three different verb forms: imperative, infinitive, and *se + verb*. Thus, the step, *Cut the paper in half*, can be written in Spanish as: *Corte/Cortar/Se corta el papel por la mitad*. Other languages may have differences in the structural organization of the text. Teachers need to analyze mentor texts in the languages of instruction to identify such features.

In bilingual schools, teachers of both languages should explicitly point out to students the similarities and differences in the structure and language features of the genre in each language, regardless of the language of instruction of the unit. These explicit metalinguistic connections will help students appropriately transfer their writing skills from one language to another. Teachers in these schools also must make decisions as to which genres will be taught in each language. If the classes in each language are teaching the same genre, it is important that the topic is different to avoid loss of student interest. For example, students write consequential explanations on World War II in English and the Spanish conquest of the Americas in Spanish.

Language of Instruction

When the language of instruction is English, teachers should encourage students to use all their language resources when discussing, researching, planning, drafting, and sharing. Allowing students to use their native language when planning, writing, and interacting was found to be more helpful in improving students' attitudes toward school (Fitzgerald, 2006) and comprehension of concepts (Garrett et al., 1994; Huss, 1995), rather than directly in improving English writing. Even when the teacher does not know students' native languages, allowing students to use their stronger language facilitates engagement in the classroom activities. For example, a 3rd grader who recently arrived from Guatemala wrote her predictions and observations in science class in Spanish and then, with the teacher coaching, looked at the word walls in the classroom and translated the phrases to English:

> Yo creo que el agua ba asubir
> I think the water will expand.
> El proximo dia el agua subio
> The next day the water up it expand.

Another teacher, who did not speak Spanish either, received a new Spanish-speaking student, literate in his language, as she was introducing the Declaration of Human Rights to her class. She fully integrated the student to her class by handing the student an iPad with the Spanish version of the document, including him in groups with students fluent in Spanish and

English, and encouraging him to write in Spanish and share his work with the class when his turn came (Brisk & Ossa Parra, 2018). The teacher's policy allowed the student not only to learn English but also to participate at his cognitive level in his education. Letting students use their native language does not deter English development and use. Even when encouraged to write in their first language, students often switch to writing mostly in English within a year (Graves et al., 2000).

In bilingual schools, allowing use of the school's target language in the English classroom helps to elevate the value of the target language. Because in most cases in the United States English is in a position of power and the target language is in a minoritized position, students may struggle to see the importance or value of the target language. When the language of power gives space to the minoritized language, it sends students the message that the target language is just as important as English. However, due to the limited access to input of the target language outside of school, teachers of the target language should continue to leverage student's entire linguistic repertoires but be very intentional as to how English is used in the target language classroom so as to not minimize the value of the target language or of the expertise of native speakers of the target language, nor take away from target language input and output opportunities (Hamman, 2017).

When teachers are bilingual themselves or are in bilingual schools, it is helpful to make explicit metalinguistic connections between the two languages. For example, in the context of teaching English reading, Spanish/English bilingual students analyzed the use of derivations and word order in both Spanish and English. These activities enhanced the full participation of all students because each student was an expert in at least one of the languages (Ossa Parra & Proctor, 2021).

Pre-Assessment

In order to gauge the full extent of students' knowledge of a genre, when assigning an uncoached writing prompt in the language of the unit, teachers should allow students to use their other language(s) or a combination of both for ease of expression. A bilingual piece will still give the teacher an idea of what the student is ready to do and what are the challenges.

Mentor Texts

In English-medium classes, it is best to use texts that are examples of the genre in English to show students how authors create that particular genre in English. In bilingual programs, teachers use mentor texts in the language of instruction. It is important to identify whether such texts were originally written in the language or are translations of the English version. The quality of the translation may vary. In addition, translated texts will follow the structure of the genre in the language it was originally written in. In bilingual programs, students may have access to versions of the books written in each language. It can be helpful for students to read a book in both languages to support comprehension in the weaker language. However, students may lose interest in the book when having to read it twice.

Research Resources

Students can use resources in a language other than the one they will be writing to acquire the content knowledge. The technical language, however, needs to be developed in the language they will use for writing. For example, if students read about the water cycle in Spanish but they will write a cyclical explanation in English, the teacher will want to introduce in English—with the help of a diagram—the terms that describe the main processes: *collection, evaporation, condensation*, and *precipitation*.

Projects

Although the goal is for projects to be written in the language of instruction, students, especially those who are beginners in the language of instruction, should be allowed to write in the other language or combine both. For example, Jen, an ESL middle school teacher working with newcomers, had her classes write autobiographies. Although she used a mentor text written in English and modeled her autobiography in English, she gave instructions in both English and Spanish. The students had the ability to choose the language to plan and write their autobiographies. Some students wrote in Spanish, some in both, and the one Portuguese-speaking student in her class wrote in Portuguese and then translated to English with the help of Google translate and his teacher.

One way to encourage students to write in a language that they do not feel confident is to give them an authentic audience who will only understand the target language of the unit.

Medium

The specific medium can ease the challenge to write in a new language. Certain media, such as posters, images with captions, PowerPoints, and brochures, require less language than essays and narratives. For example, a 3rd-grade teacher switched to doing biographies as posters. Students drew the image of the person, created a timeline with the events, and wrote a paragraph about the significance of the person. All the posters looked the same, but different students wrote more in their timeline and paragraph, depending on their English proficiency.

Units That Reflect the Pillars of Bilingualism

To implement dual language programs, schools consider the four pillars of bilingualism (Brisk, 1998, 2006; Howard et al., 2018; Palmer et al., 2019):

1. Bilingualism and biliteracy
2. Grade level academic achievement
3. Cross-cultural competence
4. Critical consciousness

Bilingualism and biliteracy refers to educating students who can not only speak and understand two or more languages (bilingualism) but also read and write in each of those languages (biliteracy). *Grade level academic achievement* addresses the need to prepare students to meet grade level standards established by the school, district, and/or state. *Cross-cultural competence* entails providing students the resources to understand and navigate two or more cultures. *Critical consciousness* encourages teachers to have students look critically at the content and linguistic choices schools make for their curricular content. This pillar proposes the creation of units of study that allow students to (a) continuously interrogate power, (b) historicize schools, (c) listen critically, and (4) engage with discomfort (Palmer et al., 2019). SFL provides the tools and language to perform context analysis that achieves this last pillar of bilingualism (Brisk, 2023; Mizell, 2021).

While these pillars were created for Dual Language Schools, classrooms in monolingual English schools that instruct in English to multilingual students should also consider pillars 2, 3, and

4. Because there is no instruction in the other language, the first pillar cannot be accomplished, even when students are allowed to use all their language resources (Brisk & Ossa Parra, 2018; Khote, 2018). Incorporating pillars 2–4 in monolingual English classrooms creates an environment that promotes equity among racial, ethnic, and language communities, consistent with a *culturally sustaining pedagogy* (Ladson-Billings, 2014).

References

Baker, C., & Wright W. E. (2017). *Foundations of bilingual education and bilingualism* (6th ed.). Bristol: Multilingual Matters.

Baker-Bell, A. (2020). *Linguistic justice: Black language, literacy, identity, and pedagogy.* New York: Routledge.

Barratt-Pugh, C., & Rohl, M. (2001). Learning in two languages: A bilingual program in Western Australia. *The Reading Teacher, 54*(7), 664–676.

Bermúdez, A. B., & Prater, D. L. (1994). Examining the effects of gender and second language proficiency on Hispanic writers' persuasive discourse. *Bilingual Research Journal, 18*(3 & 4), 47–62.

Brisk, M. E. (1998). *Bilingual education: From compensatory to quality schooling.* Mahwah, NJ: Lawrence Erlbaum Associates.

Brisk, M. E. (2006). *Bilingual education: From compensatory to quality schooling* (2nd ed.). Mahwah, NJ: Lawrence Erlbaum Associates.

Brisk, M. E. (2011). Learning to write in the second language: K – 5. In E. Hinkel (Ed.), *Handbook of research in second language teaching and learning volume II* (pp. 40–56). New York: Routledge.

Brisk, M. E. (2023). Teaching L2 academic language in K-12: A contextual and developmental perspective. In E. Hinkel (Ed.), *Handbook of second language teaching and learning.* New York: Routledge.

Brisk, M. E., & Ossa Parra, M. (2018). Mainstream classroom as bilingual environments: How SFL training develops language responsive teachers. In R. Harman (Ed.), *Critical systemic functional linguistics: Promoting language awareness and social action among K-12 students and teachers* (pp. 127–151). New York: Springer.

Carlisle, J. F., & Beeman, M. M. (2000). The effects of language of instruction on the reading and writing achievement of first-grade Hispanic children. *Scientific Studies of Reading, 4,* 331–353.

Christie, F. (2012). *Language education throughout the school years: A functional perspective.* Chichester: Wiley-Blackwell.

Connor, U. (2002). New directions in contrastive rhetoric. *TESOL Quarterly, 36,* 493-510.

Cummins, J. (1991). Interdependence of first- and second-language proficiency in bilingual children. In E. Bialystok (Ed.), *Language processing in bilingual children* (pp. 70–89). New York: Cambridge University Press.

Dien, T. T. (2004). Language and literacy in Vietnamese American communities. In B. Pérez (Ed.), *Sociocultural context of language and literacy* (pp. 137–177, 2nd ed.). Mahwah, NJ: Lawrence Erlbaum.

de Jong, E. J. (2011). *Foundations of multilingualism in education: From principles to practice.* Philadelphia, PA: Caslon Publishing.

Fitzgerald, J. (2006). Multilingual writing in preschool through 12th grade: The last 15 years. In C. A. MacArthur, S. Graham, & J. Fitzgerald (Eds.), *Handbook of writing research* (pp. 337–354). New York: The Guilford Press.

Franklin, E., & Thompson, J. (1994). Describing students' collected works: Understanding American Indian children. *TESOL Quarterly, 28,* 489–506.

Garrett, P., Griffiths, Y., James, C., & Scholfield, P. (1994). Use of mother-tongue in second language classrooms: An experimental investigation of the effects on the attitudes and writing performance of bilingual UK school children. *Multilingual and Multicultural Development, 15,* 371–383.

Gort, M. (2006). Strategic codeswitching, interliteracy, and other phenomena of emergent bilingual writing: Lessons from first grade dual language classrooms. *Journal of Early Childhood Literacy, 6,* 323–354.

Graves, A. W., Valles, E. C., & Rueda, R. (2000). Variations in interactive writing instruction: A study in four bilingual special education settings. *Learning Disabilities Research & Practice, 15*(1), 1–9.

Halliday, M. A. K. (1993). Towards a language-based theory of learning. *Linguistics and Education, 5,* 93–116.

Hamman, L. (2017). Translanguaging and positioning in two-way dual language classrooms: A case for criticality. *Language and Education, 32*(1), 21–42. https://doi.org/10.1080/09500782.2017.1384006

Heath, S. B. (1983). *Way with words: Language, life and work in communities and classrooms*. Cambridge: Cambridge University Press.

Hinkel, E. (2002). *Second language writers' text*. Mahwah, NJ: Lawrence Erlbaum Associates.

Homza, A. (1995). Developing biliteracy in a bilingual first-grade writing workshop. *Dissertation Abstracts International*, 53(12), 2148 (UMI No. 95-33133).

Howard, E. R., Lindholm-Leary, K. J., Rogers, D., Olague, N., Medina, J., Kennedy, B., Sugarman, J., & Christian, D. (2018). *Guiding principles for dual language education* (3rd ed.). Washington, DC: Center for Applied Linguistics.

Hunt, K. W. (1965). *Grammatical structures written at three grade levels*. Champaign, IL: National Council of Teachers of English.

Huss, R. L. (1995). Young children becoming literate in English as a second language. *TESOL Quarterly*, 29, 767–774.

Khote, N. (2018). Translanguaging in systemic functional linguistics: A culturally sustaining pedagogy for writing in secondary schools. In R. Harman (Ed.), *Critical systemic functional linguistics: Promoting language awareness and social action among K-12 students and teachers* (pp. 153–178). New York: Springer.

Kress, G. (1994). *Learning to write* (2nd ed.). New York: Routledge.

Kroll, B. M., & Lempers, J. D. (1981). Effect of mode of communication on the informational adequacy of children's explanations. *Journal of Genetic Psychology*, 138, 27–35.

Ladson-Billings, G. (2014). Culturally relevant pedagogy 2.0: A.k.a. the remix. *Harvard Educational Review*, 84(1), 74–84, 135.

Lindholm-Leary, K. J. (2001). *Dual language education*. Clevendon: Multilingual Matters.

Loban, W. (1976). *Language development: Kindergarten through grade twelve*. Research report 18. Urbana, IL: National Council of Teachers of English.

Lull, H. G. (1929). The speaking and writing abilities of intermediate grade pupils. *Journal of Educational Research*, 20, 73–77.

Matalene, C. (1985). Contrastive rhetoric: An American writing teacher in China. *College English*, 47, 789–808.

Matsuda, P. K. (1997). Contrastive rhetoric in context: A dynamic model of L2 writing. *Journal of Second Language Writing*, 6(1), 45–60.

McCabe, A., & Bliss, L. S. (2003). *Patterns of narrative discourse: A multicultural, life span approach*. Boston, MA: Allyn and Bacon.

McPhail, G. (2009). The bad boy and the writing curriculum. In M. Cochran-Smith & S. Lytle (Eds.), *Inquiry as stance. Practitioner research for the next generation* (pp. 193–212). New York: Teachers College Press.

Menyuk, P., & Brisk, M. E. (2005). *Language development and education: Children with varying language experience*. Hampshire: Palgrave MacMillan.

Mizell, J. D. (2021). Apprenticeship of pre-service teachers through culturally sustaining systemic functional linguistics. *Language and Education*, 35(2), 123–139. https://doi.org/10.1080/09500782.2020.1797770

Ossa Parra, M., & Proctor, C. P. (2021). Translanguaging to understand language. *TESOL Quarterly*, 55(3), 766–794. https://doi.org/10.1002/tesq.3011

Palmer, D. K., Cervantes Soon, C., Dorner, L., & Heiman, D. (2019). Bilingualism, biliteracy, biculturalism, and critical consciousness for all: Proposing a fourth fundamental goal for two-way dual language education. *Theory Into Practice*, 58(2), 121–133. http://doi.org/10.1080/00405841.2019.1569376

Pérez, B. (2004). *Sociocultural context of language and literacy* (2nd ed.). Mahwah, NJ: Lawrence Erlbaum.

Santiago Schwarz, V., & Hamman-Ortiz, L. (2020). Systemic functional linguistics, teacher education, and writing outcomes for U.S. elementary English learners: A review of the literature. *Journal of Second Language Writing*, 49. https://doi.org/10.1016/j.jslw.2020.100727

Schleppegrell, M., & Christie, F. (2018). Linguistic features of writing development: A functional perspective. In C. Bazerman, A. Applebee, V. Berninger, D. Brandt, S. Graham, J. Jeffrey, P. K. Matsuda, S. Murphy, D. Rowe, M. Schleppegrell, & K. Wilcox (Eds.), *The lifespan development of writing* (pp. 111–150). Urbana, IL: NCTE (National Council of Teachers of English).

Appendix A

Unit Template Sample With Explanations of What to Include

Members of the group are:

1.
2.
3.
4.

UNIT at A GLANCE

    Grade Level:
    Genre:

Phase I

Pre-Assessment	What prompt will you use that leads the students to write in the genre of the unit? Important: 1. This is NOT a test on content knowledge but on knowledge of the genre. 2. This information is for you to plan given the students' needs. IT IS NOT to have students work on it. 3. Although the prompt will be in the language of the unit, students can use their other language for ease of expression.
Topic (connection with content area)	What will be content focus of the unit? To which content are you connecting this unit? (i.e., reading, math, science, social studies, and others) For example, within the unit on the Declaration of Human Rights, students wrote arguments supporting a human rights activist to choose as the *Time* magazine person of the year. Make connections between content standards and cultures, histories, and experiences of students' cultural background.
Language(s) of Instruction (For teachers in (a) bilingual schools or (b)with bilingual students)	(a) Explain how you are going to use Spanish and/or English for instruction in the unit. Plan with the teacher who is teaching the other language so that even if the genre is the same, the topic and even the medium is different. For example, do craft procedures in Spanish and English procedures in science or vice versa. (b) Encourage students to use all their language resources when discussing, researching, planning, drafting, and sharing. Help students make connections between their dominant language and English.

Language: Aspects of language to be developed	Specify here after going over the material for Module 3. In bilingual programs, language is where the genres differ most between the two languages. For example, while in English we use the imperative for procedures (*cut*), in Spanish there are three possible forms of the verb to use (*cortar, corte, se corta*).
Mentor Texts	Select a few texts that are good examples of the genre. They can be in any topic. When using texts in Spanish, please note if they are translations or original text. Authenticity is important for modeling language and structure.
Research Resources	Select texts, Internet resources, and others to develop the knowledge of the topic. Students can also create the information by surveys, interviews, etc., appropriate for the topic. Students can use resources in a language other than the one they will be writing. The technical language of the content will then need to be developed in the language they will use for writing.
Projects (whole class, group, and/or individual) At least two projects over the course of a unit.	**Project 1:** **Project 2:** Plan for at least a couple of writing projects with different demands. For example, the class could co-construct a text with the teacher and later write group/individual pieces. This approach is highly recommended. For young writers, the co-constructed projects may be sufficient. When doing projects in two languages, make sure that the topic is different.
Intended Audience	Try making it as authentic as possible.
Medium	Teach the feature of the structure of text specific to that medium. For example, if students are producing brochures, what's the layout, etc. **Choice of medium** is a way to control the difficulty of writing. Use media that requires less language for students who are young or beginners in the language. For example, a poster is easier than an essay.

Standards

Content Standards

Language and Literacy Standards

Phase 2

Please fill in **Lessons Numbers, Objectives, and Strategies** for lessons on purpose, stages, and language. Insert lessons to introduce and practice aspects of language where appropriate and connected with lessons on purpose and stages. Indicate where you would be teaching content.

The first two lessons have been filled as an example of what to do.

Lesson # and Title	Lesson 1: Purpose of the Genre
Lesson Objectives	Students will be able to (SWBT) state the purpose of the unit genre, which is (*specify purpose*)
Strategies to Teach	Exposure to the genre by reading texts in the genre and discussing the purpose of it. • The teacher will read aloud one text [name the text]. • The class in small groups will look at other texts from the mentor text list (or copies of texts). • Questions will be asked to see if students have figured out the purpose.

Lesson # and Title	Lesson 1: Purpose of the Genre

Lesson #and Title	Lesson 2. Language: Name Feature
Lesson Objectives	SWBT identify XX (one aspect of language to be developed in the unit)
Strategies to Teach	• Choose one or two paragraphs from the mentor text used in Lesson 1.
	• Isolate the aspect of language as a whole class.
	(Give actual example of the paragraph with the items highlighted or in bold.)
	• Document on chart paper that will stay visible for the whole unit.
	• Have students do the same in their small groups with other paragraphs.

Lesson # and Title
Lesson Objectives
Strategies to Teach

Lesson # and Title
Lesson Objectives
Strategies to Teach

Lesson # and Title
Lesson Objectives
Strategies to Teach

Lesson # and Title
Lesson Objectives
Strategies to Teach

Lesson # and Title
Lesson Objectives
Strategies to Teach

Lesson # and Title
Lesson Objectives
Strategies to Teach

Lesson # and Title
Lesson Objectives
Strategies to Teach

Lesson # and Title
Lesson Objectives
Strategies to Teach

Index

Note: Page numbers in *italic* indicate a figure; page numbers in **bold** indicate a table on the corresponding page.